Crossing America

Crossing America

A Reading and Writing Rhetoric

Deborah W. Hunt
Southwest Tennessee Community College

Linda D. Patterson
Southwest Tennessee Community College

Upper Saddle River, New Jersey 07458

Library of Congress Cataloging-in-Publication Data
Hunt, Deborah W.
Crossing America : a reading and writing rhetoric / Deborah W. Hunt, Linda D. Patterson.
p. cm.
ISBN 0-13-192873-2
1. College readers. 2. English language—Rhetoric—Problems, exercises, etc. 3. Report writing—Problems, exercises, etc. I. Patterson, Linda D. II. Title.
PE1417.H86 2008
808′.0427—dc22

2007043640

Editorial Director: Leah Jewell
Editor-in-Chief: Craig Campanella
Editorial Assistant: Deborah Doyle
Full Service Production Liaison: Joanne Hakim
Operations Specialist: Christina Amato
Marketing Manager: Lindsey Prudhomme
Assistant Marketing Manager: Jessica Muraviov
Creative Director: Jayne Conte
Cover Photo: Polly Calistro, "Around America," "Quilts and Quiltmaking in America, 1978–1996," American Folklife Center, Library of Congress, Courtesy of the Library of Congress
Permissions Specialist: Jane Scelta
Director, Image Resource Center: Melinda Patelli
Manager, Rights and Permissions: Zina Arabia
Manager, Visual Research: Beth Brenzel
Manager, Cover Visual Research & Permissions: Karen Sanatar
Image Permission Coordinator: Frances Toepfer
Full-Service Project Management: Karen Berry/Pine Tree Composition, Inc.
Composition: Laserwords Private Limited
Printer/Binder: RR Donnelley & Sons Company

Credits and acknowledgments borrowed from other sources and reproduced, with permission, in this textbook appear on pages 419–420.

Pearson Education LTD., London
Pearson Education Singapore, Pte. Ltd
Pearson Education Canada, Ltd.
Pearson Education—Japan
Pearson Education Australia PTY, Limited
Pearson Education North Asia Ltd
Pearson Educación de Mexico, S.A. de C. V.
Pearson Education Malaysia, Pte. Ltd
Pearson Education, Upper Saddle River, New Jersey

10 9 8 7 6 5 4 3 2 1
ISBN-13: 978-0-13-192873-2
ISBN-10: 0-13-192873-2

To our moms, Dorothy Ward and Virginia Dabney
and to Corbett and Jill, Courtney and Brian, Albane, Valérie, Doug (1950–1990),
Jim, Ginny and Will, Dabney, Chris and little Tatum, and Jay

To my friend Debbie

To my friend Linda

Contents

Unit 5 Landmarks—Process Analysis 224

Unit 6 American Music—Classification 267

Unit 7 American Lifestyle—Cause and Effect 312

Unit 8 New Frontiers—Argumentation 363

Rhetorical Modes in *Crossing America*

Due to the nature of writing, many selections contain a combination of rhetorical modes. The Table of Contents by Rhetorical Modes provides a cross-reference based on the general writing patterns in the selections in *Crossing America.*

Narration

Description

Comparison and Contrast

Process Analysis

Classification

Cause and Effect

Argumentation

Alphabetical List of Readings

Preface

Overview

Crossing America is an interactive rhetoric with in-depth reading and writing exercises. Activities focus on competencies that skilled readers and writers must master. The text follows a thematic approach designed to provide cultural knowledge and awareness both to native speakers of English and to the limited–English-language population. Commonly-used rhetorical modes are covered in the book.

This book differs from other texts in that it combines the skills covered in traditional academic reading and writing courses into a single text. It can be used in courses that combine reading and writing, in courses that are taught separately, in English as a second language (ESL) courses, and in Web-based courses ranging from a beginning level through the freshman composition course. The text begins with an extensive introductory unit that presents an overview of methods used for strengthening reading and writing skills. At the same time, this textbook focuses on building an awareness of the diversity in American culture. It also introduces many writers' works from ethnic minorities in America. Additionally, each unit provides activities to supplement skills taught, rhetorical modes presented, and themes covered. Included in these modules are American idioms related to the theme, Web site visits with assigned activities and films to view.

Overall Goals of the Text

1. To teach students the basics of academic reading and writing through a thematic approach that expands their knowledge of American culture
2. To provide students with a variety of writing experiences that will enhance their ability to synthesize information
3. To provide experiences that enable students to recognize the strong, direct connections between the reading and writing process
4. To supplement reading and writing with the necessary grammar skills to enable the students' use of standard or formal English in all settings
5. To promote self-awareness of errors in writing through editing practice and charting

6. To teach the writing processes needed to organize and develop various types of paragraphs and essays and the steps involved in shifting between the two forms
7. To develop skills in recognizing main ideas, details, organizational patterns of reading passages, sequential order, cause and effect relationships, and conclusions drawn
8. To distinguish between fact and opinion
9. To build techniques for increasing vocabulary
10. To use a variety of sources to gather information

Unit Contents

To stimulate interest and discussion, each unit opens with a quotation that introduces the theme. A list of American idioms and an introduction to the rhetorical mode related to the unit's subject matter follow the quotation. Each unit contains at least one literary essay, a nonfiction article from a popular periodical, a work of fiction, and a poem. These selections support the theme of the unit and provide the framework for the unit's reading and writing activities. Included in the reading component are a glossary of vocabulary words and comprehension questions covering reading skills. Each reading was selected because of its high-interest content, its relationship to the mode covered, and its relevance to a diverse and rich American culture. Activities that facilitate vocabulary development and correct word usage are also included in each unit.

Within the writing component, students master the writing process as they learn to compose paragraphs and essays in a variety of rhetorical modes. Writing assignments include a summary that reinforces the comprehension of the readings, paragraph and essay assignments that focus on specific rhetorical modes, and reflective assignments that encourage critical thinking through further exploration of the unit's theme. Optional essay topics and exercises are listed within each unit. Multiple writing topics enable the professor to select those that interest the students and fulfill the goals of the course.

Internet research that combines reading and writing activities and encourages the exploration of the theme supplements the writing component. Follow-up activities vary from reading comprehension questions to summary writing to mapping activities to paragraphs and essays. These experiences are designed to motivate students to investigate topics of interest.

In addition, grammar pointers are given within each writing section of the units. They support the predictable errors commonly associated with the organizational patterns of writing.

Each unit concludes with a list of films related to the theme and activities that facilitate building background knowledge. Finally, a summary that incorporates student writing models with editing exercises ends each unit.

Here is an overall schematic of the structure of each unit:

- Introduction of the mode covered in the unit and idioms related to the theme
- Points to consider when writing and reading
- Purpose of the unit
- Organization and plan of a writing assignment using the rhetorical mode
- Points for writing paragraphs in the mode
- How to write essays in the mode
- Writing tools needed for developing the mode
- Paragraph format for writing
- Essay format for writing
- Writing worksheet used during the writing process
- Grammar and writing topics that include mistakes commonly made in writing in the specific mode
- Questions for review of writing
- Reading before writing section that presents the literature for students
- Reading comprehension questions following the selection
- Writing assignments for the selection
- Reflective writing assignments that encourage students to synthesize the theme
- Internet field trips with reading and writing assignments related to the theme
- Films to view with writing assignments
- Student writing sample
- Summary of the unit with editing exercises relating to the student model

ACKNOWLEDGMENTS

"Any man's life will be filled with constant and unexpected encouragement if he makes up his mind to do his level best each day."

Booker T. Washington

We never dreamed when we sat together in college English classes that we would be co-authoring an English textbook thirty-five years later. We work together, we celebrate life events together, and we enjoy the close friendship of one another. So once again we share another success!

We must thank our colleagues and students who make our lives interesting and fulfilling. They provide us with ample encouragement and abundant material. In addition, our families and friends deserve hearty thanks for tolerating our many hours of absence and inattention to normal duties. Special thanks go to Dr. Ada Shotwell, Dr. Cheryl Cleaves, and Mrs. Barbara Roseborough, our division and department leaders at Southwest Tennessee Community College. Additional thanks go to Dr. Nathan Essex, our college president, who encourages faculty creativity.

Special thanks to the following reviewers for their helpful suggestions: Sylviane S. Baumflek, Kingsborough Community College; Rosie Branciforte, International Academy of Design and Technology; Derek Bowe, Oakwood College; Don Brotherton, DeVry Chicago; Eric Cash, Abraham Baldwin College; Patsy J. Daniels, Jackson State University; Noelle Geiger, Valencia Community College; Karen Patty-Graham, Southern Illinois University; W. David Hall, Columbus State Community College; Douglas Hart, Cuyahoga Community College; Sarah Kirk, University of Alaska; Lee McKnight, Stillman College; Virginia Smith, Carteret Community College; Jeff Torricelli, St. Clair County Community College; Carla Witt, Cal Poly Pomona; Stephanie Woods, Hinds Community College; Lynn Wright, Pasadena City College; and April Van Camp, Indian River Community College.

We must acknowledge our children, who, as always, constantly remind us through their activity that the cycle of life continues. In addition to writing this book, we have jointly planned and held four weddings, and we have experienced the birth of a granddaughter. And our children continue to support us and uplift us through "little things."

We also appreciate our mothers, Virginia and Dorothy, whose pride and daily support and encouragement remind us that we can succeed. To Doug, whose love, creativity, and grit for eighteen years still serve as support today. To Jim, whose pride and enthusiasm never waivers.

And to those who have chosen to stay friends with us through this process—thanks! We especially recognize Teresa, Emily, Donna, and Margie for their help and support. And then there is Janice, who dared any friend to call, visit, or communicate in any way during these final days

From Debbie goes a special acknowledgment to French historian Éric Saugera, who generously shared not only the Lajonie letters but also much knowledge about the process of writing for publication. Those endless hours of work paid off in a finished product.

And warm thoughts go to special friends who often take care of the mundane routines of life while the writing process continues. For the rodents trapped, the trash cleared, the furniture moved—thanks!

We are also indebted to our Prentice Hall editor Craig Campanella and his staff for their support and patience.

—Debbie Hunt and Linda Patterson

Crossing America

Unit 1

Reading and Writing with Crossing America

A compass navigates travelers to a destination. What tools for navigation do readers and writers need?

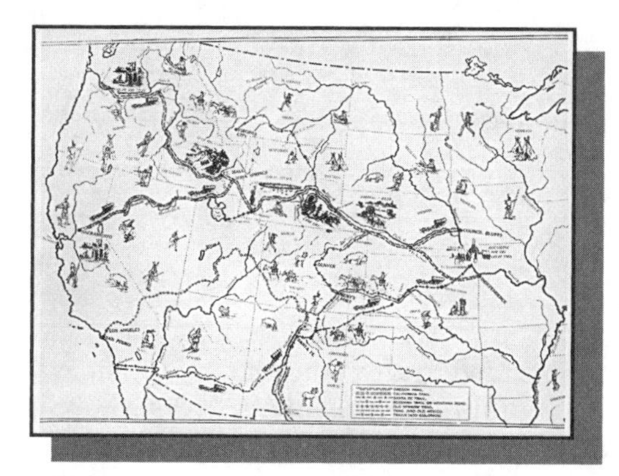

Maps direct users to places. How does a mind map enable a reader and writer to organize thoughts?

Welcome Message

The tips presented in this introductory material should help you navigate your way through the reading and writing activities in *Crossing America*. Good luck to each of you, and enjoy your journey toward understanding literature and the fiber that makes the American culture so rich.

Introduction to Reading Literature and Writing about Literature

Have you ever thought about a definition of the term *literature*? Because of past experiences with reading literature, many college students, not to mention many other people, react negatively to this word. Immediately, they recall boring high school English assignments in which they were required to read literature with little or no preparation. The language seemed awkward, and they knew little about the historical time period of the assigned reading selections. In general, many readers cannot appreciate literature because they do not know how to enjoy reading it. A general definition for *literature* should include the idea of a work that is written during a certain era in history and that often relates to the social and political mores and experiences of both the writer and the reader of that period. How can you enjoy a work of literature if you did not live in that era? The answer is simple! Many themes in literature, as in life, remain constant regardless of the century or the political climate. Can you name some universal *themes*, or messages?

Exercise: Name some universal themes in literature that cross the barriers of time.

____

____

____

Literature is intended to affect the reader in some way—emotionally, physically, mentally, or all three. Think of a speech you have heard or a film you have seen and the physical and emotional reactions you had to it. If you screamed, shouted, clapped, hid your eyes in your companion's shirt, or laughed, you reacted. Thus the literary work affected you with some physical or emotional sensation.

Exercise: Write your own definition of the term *literature*.

____

____

____

Literature can be divided into different *genres*, or categories. Included in this list are poetry, short stories, novels, plays, essays, speeches, and biographies and autobiographies. Even magazine and journal articles can be classified as literature and are often called popular literature or periodic literature.

Exercise: List the types of literature that you have read in the past. Name titles if possible.

____

____

____

Read the poem below by President Jimmy Carter and then read the student's analysis and reaction to the poem. What emotional and psychological effects does the poem have on the student writer Shamekia Merriweather?

I Wanted to Share My Father's World

Jimmy Carter, former President of the United States

This is a pain I mostly hide,
but ties of blood, or seed, endure
and even now I feel inside
the hunger for his outstretched hand,
a man's embrace to take me in, 5
the need for just a word of praise.
I despised the discipline
he used to shape what I should be,
not owning up that he might feel
his own pain when he punished me. 10
I didn't show my need to him,
since his response to an appeal
would not have meant as much to me,
or been as real.
From those rare times when we did cross 15
the bridge between us, the pure joy
survives.

I never put aside
the past resentments of the boy
until, with my own sons, I shared 20
his final hours, and came to see
what he'd become, or always was—
the father who will never cease to be
alive in me.

Exercise: Explain the feelings that President Carter expresses about his relationship with his father.

____

____

____

Student Essay Entitled "I Wanted to Share My Father's World"

The Love and Pain Felt Inside

Do you ever wish you could turn back the hands of time? I know I sometimes think back to past events or memories and wish that I would have done it differently. In Jimmy Carter's poem, "I Wanted to Share My Father's World," I believe that he regrets the type of relationship he had with his father. I can relate to this feeling because I also lost my father, and I am now left with some regrets.

My father died two years ago of cancer. We didn't have the closest relationship because he was in the military (which caused him to move around a lot) and he remarried. So because of that situation, I have a lot of pain because he wasn't there for me and I felt alone. However, I also had love for him at the same time since he was my father. Just like the feelings Carter describes, "this pain I mostly hide, but ties of blood, or seed, endure, and even now I feel inside the hunger for his outreached hand, a man's embrace to take me in, the need for just a word of praise" (5). He has some secret feelings towards his father that he is scared to express. He wants and needs his father, but there is something holding him back from having the relationship he wants.

Fathers are very essential and influential in a child's life. Children always want a person to look up to as their hero, and for most boys, it's their father. Maybe Carter wanted his father to be his hero, but he wasn't. He feels like something is missing in their relationship. So now he is scared that he will be the same way with his sons.

I believe that Carter sometimes holds something inside to avoid more hurt and pain. "I didn't show my need to him, since his response to an appeal would not have meant as much to me or been as real" (11–14). I never told anyone how much pain I was in by not having my father around. I didn't find out my dad had cancer until the week he died. He tried calling me because he said there was something he wanted to talk to me about. Even then I postponed talking to him. I had so much hurt and pain inside I just couldn't get past it. I couldn't see that that was the right thing to do. I now know that I should have called. That would have made things a whole lot clearer. The author is with his father during his last hours, and that's when he realizes the resentment he discusses causes us to hold on to hurt and pain. When that person is here, we are too angry to explain; and when they are gone, we hurt because it's too late. We sometimes turn into that person, and we are still left with that pain and hurt to be passed down to the next generation.

Shamekia Merriweather

This student essay typifies the reaction that a student might have as a personal reaction to a work of literature. In this particular essay, you can see how the reader's pain and grief relating to the relationship and death of her own father are illuminated as a response to Carter's poem about his own father.

Exercise: Explain the feelings that the student expresses about her relationship with her own father.

____

____

____

Explain how the student's essay demonstrates a reaction to Carter's poem.

____

____

____

When reading literature, allow yourself to react to the selection. Even a negative reaction demonstrates an effect that the literature has had on you. Ask yourself how the literature relates to your life or to the lives of those around you. If you do so, you will enjoy the reading much more. In *Crossing America,* you will be given the opportunity to write reactions to the selections in the text.

How to Read Any Passage Effectively

Stumbling Blocks to Successful Reading

Have you ever read a magazine article, a novel, a poem, or even a textbook chapter and then immediately afterward puzzled over what you read? You could not name the topic of the article or a character's name in the novel or a single term from the textbook chapter. This phenomenon is not unusual among adult readers. Many factors explain this lack of information retention.

The most obvious explanation is a lack of *concentration,* focusing for a sustained period of time on the material being read. Adults, in general, should be able to concentrate fully for about forty minutes without a break in thought. Concentration often diminishes as your life becomes more active. Whether you are involved in caring for children, working a full- or part-time job, or even going to college full time, the life you lead becomes more complicated as you mature. Thus your attention becomes divided. You might compare it to channel switching. You know what show or game is playing on a specific channel, but you do not retain the plot of the film or the events leading to the football score on the screen. Likewise, your brain may switch channels many times per hour.

Exercise: List several barriers to concentration in your life.

____

____

____

You may or may not be able to put aside temporarily these life events. Thus steps to improving concentration must be developed. You can set a timer and force yourself to focus for that length of time. After the alarm rings, try again and add a minute or two until you reach your maximum capacity. You might make yourself stand up every time you lose your concentration. Often sleepiness develops in overburdened students who try to attend classes, work full time, and raise children at the same time. Standing and/or movement can help you to retain the concentration and to overcome fatigue. Several well-known writers composed standing up. If English is not your first language, then fatigue may set in more rapidly as you try to master critical concepts that may be linguistically challenging or culturally based. For you, too, these steps may be taken to improve your concentration.

Motivation also plays a role in concentration. If you do not like to read, then the activity becomes a dreaded chore. You live in a visual culture; television and videos play a huge role in society. You write text messages rather than talking, send e-mails rather than letters, and now consult the Internet rather than encyclopedias for information. But reading can provide more information, can entertain, and can help to build verbal expression and vocabulary faster than any other form of communication. Perhaps an attitude change is necessary; for if you find a subject that you enjoy, then concentration and reading skills develop.

How to build concentration skills:

- Remove all distractions—radio, television, i-Pods, cell phones and text messaging, and conversation.
- Set an alarm and focus for a certain period of time. Increase the time as you can.
- Sit in a certain place that represents a study environment. Get off the bed and out of the bedroom if possible.
- Change your physical position when you discover the concentration waning. Move from sitting to standing or walking or pacing, for example. William Faulkner composed some of his best literature by writing on the wall. That scribble still exists today at Rowan Oak, his home in Oxford, Mississippi.
- Read aloud for a few seconds to regain your concentration. Then return to silent reading.

Exercise: What other helpful suggestions can you add to the list? Write them below.

____

____

____

Another probable cause of reading problems is the *method*, or style, of reading you do. You might read with your lips, with a vocal utterance—a whisper, for example—with a nonvocalized throat muscle movement, or with your finger. You might also read in a word-by-word method rather than in a phrasal clustering method. Practice reading this line to see what physical method of *subvocalization*, or discreet body movement, you do. Work to eliminate these physical actions as you read.

> She was young with a calm face whose lines bespoke repression and even a certain strength.
>
> *From* "The Story of an Hour" by Kate Chopin (The complete story is located at the beginning of the literary analysis information on pages 27–28. You will use this story in the writing section of this introduction.)

Exercise: What reading subvocalizations characterize your reading? Circle all that apply.

Lip Movement Vocal Utterance Muscle Movement Word-for-Word No Movement

Regardless of the method, comprehending and retaining the information depend on the smooth flow of words across the page. Practice the following lines without moving any part of the body. Also practice clustering the words into phrases rather than reading one word at a time. Scroll your eyes across the page by moving them to the three different points marked with italics on the line. Continue to practice this movement until you can read with more ease and comprehension.

Exercise: Focusing your eyes on the italicized words as you skim across the line, use your peripheral vision to read the entire statement with only three movements.

> She knew *that* she would weep again *when* she saw the kind, tender *hands* folded in death; . . .
>
> *From* "The Story of an Hour" by Kate Chopin

Were you able to focus only three times? Did you comprehend the line as you moved your eyes a limited number of times across the line? Continue to practice this reading skill.

Another reading problem that exists is a lack of any knowledge of the subject matter. *Prior,* or *background, knowledge* is a term used for this concept of knowing. If you have never seen the Eiffel Tower, can you still know much information about it—its history, its creator, its location? The answer is yes! You can gain background knowledge through books and textbooks, film, television, discussions, and life experiences. Before you could subtract, you had to learn to add. The process of doing addition became background knowledge for the subtraction. Before a doctor operates on a patient, he or she must learn anatomy. The information the doctor acquires in that course becomes prior knowledge for development of surgical skills. Similarly, acquiring a background in any subject aids readers in building comprehension skills. You also gain an interest in the subject matter and might even discover that you like the topic being read and want to know more about the subject explored in the passage. For example, as you read "The Story of an Hour," you might discover that you are interested in the plight of women in the mid-1800s. Or as you read about Chopin herself, you might discover that her works were banned, and you may want to know more about other books that were banned or why literary works were banned for decades. Think of the background knowledge you have just built with your new interest in reading!

Finally, failure to recognize the *strong words* in a passage can be another stumbling block to successful reading. Verbs and nouns contain the main message in any passage. Adjectives and adverbs add color and interest and additional detail, but they often represent ancillary, or secondary, details and information.

Have you ever learned that you can also skip over certain words when reading? Words that can be bypassed include *articles* (a, an, the) and sometimes other *connectors* and *prepositional phrases*. This fact is especially true for pleasure reading, reading done for enjoyment rather than for retention of facts. In an effort to build skill, speed, and comprehension, focus on the strong words, the nouns and verbs, in every sentence.

Exercise: Underline only the verbs and nouns/pronouns in the line below from "The Story of an Hour." Then read only the underlined words.

> She did not hear the story as many women have heard the same, with a paralyzed inability to accept its significance.

In your own words, explain the message you comprehended from the underlined words.

____

____

____

If you follow these suggestions, you should see improvements in your concentration and comprehension. Reading will become a pleasure rather than a dreaded task.

Student Commencement Address at Southwest Tennessee Community College

Andy Ling

Andy Ling is an international student at the college who, after completing his associate's degree, is currently pursuing a bachelor's degree in business and music. Recommended by two faculty members and based on his academic record and his involvement in campus activities, Andy was selected to deliver the student address at the spring 2006 commencement.

Dignified guests, faculty, staff, students, ladies and gentlemen, and most of all, the class of 2006:

The 31st of October, 2004, is still a vivid memory for me. At 10:30 P.M., I boarded my plane leaving my home country of Malaysia, headed for Memphis, TN. Leaving friends and loved ones, I was uncertain of my future. As I prepared to encounter this new experience, several questions nagged at my mind: What was life going to be like? What was the weather like? Was the Chinese food any good? What was education going to be like? But the question that lingered most on my mind was would I be able to fit in to this new culture? Coming from a different ethnicity, culture, and background, I wondered how different it would be to mingle with people not of the same culture. However, ladies and gentlemen, being a student at Southwest has answered that question. No longer will this student worry about whether he would fit in, no longer will this student care about the difference in culture because this student has finally seen that it does not matter from which part of the world you come from, we are all equal.

My experience at Southwest has indeed been a fulfilling one as I was meeting people from all over the world. I have come in contact with Whites, Blacks, Chinese, Vietnamese, Japanese, Taiwanese, Koreans, Australians, and with people all the way from Mongolia, Iran, Iraq, across the globe from Ethiopia, Uganda, Kenya, South Africa, from Turkey, Germany, Denmark, Russia, Ukraine, from Venezuela, Puerto Rico, and Mexico . . . all coming here to Southwest for one purpose: to achieve a higher education. Under one common goal, the differences in culture have vanished; under one common goal, we have studied together in harmony; under one common goal, we have enjoyed and experienced college life together . . . and friends, under one common goal, we have made it! Today, we receive that certificate which will push us further into the world, toward greater accomplishments, toward even bigger goals and higher ambitions. No longer can anyone tell us that we cannot achieve, for we have done just that. No longer will we sit and be envious of others who have completed their college education because today, we are those people!

My great and exciting experience at Southwest did not come just as it is; it is a combination of the various contributions that each and every one of you have put into it. Southwest could not exist without students, without faculty, and without the staff that builds it. I am thankful to the ever-toiling staff of the school, working so hard to make sure that the administration of the college is undertaken efficiently, for the great faculty that we have, who are constantly helping and guiding us students in an effort to broaden our perspectives and help us achieve greater heights; but most of all, I am thankful to you, the students, who have given me so much better an understanding of what American college life is like, who have attended classes with me, helping me in my learning process, having fun with me, because we all need a break once in a while, and also accepting me into your culture for who I am. You have shown to me, a person not from your culture, how to enjoy hush puppies with catfish and slaw, how to say "ya'll" without its sounding like "you all," how to enjoy listening to Blues music. I have learned what a touchdown is and what "three strikes, you're out" means in baseball. I have learned what "road kill" really means, and how to enjoy Memphis barbecue. No longer will I need to worry about whether I will fit into this new culture, for you have extended your friendship and care toward me just as if I were one of you. No more will I wonder whether cultural differences, ethnic differences, or religious differences are issues that I need to worry about because you have proven to me in your warm reception of this international student that we are all equal. And so I say to you, the class of 2006, go out into the world and get the best jobs, get into the best schools, get into the best graduate programs, go out and make a difference in your community, be a somebody, stand up for who you are, and do not just keep this to yourself, but share your enthusiasm, share your motivation, share your dreams and your ambitions with others, that they too may one day have the same opportunity that you have to march on forward in life.

Graduates, if you encounter setbacks one day, just remember, you have made a difference in your own life, you have made a difference in my life, and you can make a difference in every life with whom you come in contact. Carpe diem! Seize the day and the moment, for this moment is yours!

SQ9R—A Reading Strategy That Works

To build skill in reading a passage effectively, a system for attacking, or handling successfully, a reading selection can be used. This system is called **SQ9R—Survey, Question, Read, Recite, Record, Review, Recall, Reflect, React.** Practice the steps outlined below to build comprehension and concentration skills. This technique requires that you read with a pen or pencil in hand, a step often called *active reading*.

Step 1—SURVEY The first step to greater and easier comprehension is to survey a reading selection. Surveying, or looking over actively, a passage enables you to familiarize yourself with the general contents of the material you are about to read. Whether it is a textbook unit or a literary passage, follow the guidelines below.

- Read the title and author of the passage and any introductory notes that may be included.
- Read the first and last paragraph of the passage.
- Note and read chapter and/or unit organizers that aid in understanding the material: graphic organizers like boldfaced headings and italics, captions, charts and graphs, and photographs.
- Look for new words as you skim and review the glossary and other vocabulary-building aids.

This first step should take no more than five minutes. Most importantly, this process leads the reader into the initial meaning of the entire passage.

Exercise: Using Ling's work, answer the questions that follow.

What does the title of the speech mean?

____

____

What graphic organizers or transitional devices did you locate?

____

____

List some unfamiliar vocabulary words found in the selection.

____

Summarize in one or two sentences what you anticipate the passage to be about.

____

____

Step 2—QUESTION Questioning, step 2, requires two steps: assessing both the reader's prior knowledge and the concepts gained in the survey step. First, ask yourself what you already know about the subject; this is called *background knowledge* or *prior knowledge*. You might have gained this insight from past reading or previous course work, from television or film, or from daily life through conversations with others. Second, ask yourself what information you gained from the survey step. Before beginning the thorough reading, ask questions to guide yourself through the passage. Writing them in *telegraphic sentences*, short sentence forms similar to cell phone text messages with articles and other nonessential words omitted, will aid in comprehension. This step should take no more than five minutes.

Sample Questions

- What do I already know about author?
- What do I already know about topic, or subject, of the passage?
- What prior knowledge do I have about subject?
- What headings or sentences can be turned into comprehension questions?

Exercise: Using Andy Ling's commencement address, answer the sample questions.

____

____

____

Step 3—READ After ten minutes of previewing the reading selection, you are now ready to read. This step requires intense concentration. Reading one paragraph, stanza, or section at a time can enhance concentration. After each section, assess your comprehension by summarizing aloud what was read. Previously developed guide questions can be answered at the end of the section. The sole purpose of academic reading is to understand not only the words but also the deeper meaning of the selection. When reading literature, this third step is critical. Completing a section or a group of paragraphs at a time, proceed to read the selection until finished. Remaining mindful of the points where you should stop to verify comprehension will guarantee a thorough understanding of the entire passage.

Exercise: Read Ling's entire speech silently. Into what sizes of chunks did you break it down? Where did you stop to answer the guide questions created in step 2?

____

____

Step 4—RECITE Verbalizing, or reading aloud, the main points of the passage will enable you not only to comprehend a passage but also to remember the message, or theme, of the reading. Although you might find this step awkward, recitation is the best step to take when you are experiencing a loss of concentration. Recite a few lines each time you lose concentration. The sense of hearing is a powerful tool to concentration and comprehension. In addition, recite notes when you study.

Much literature is designed for oral reading. When you read poetry, for example, read the entire poem aloud. Read drama aloud, especially if several people can participate. How many times have you heard someone say, "Listen to this"? And then the person begins to read aloud a passage from the newspaper or a magazine. You might ask not to be read to, but recall that oral reading actually increases comprehension. It requires the use of two, or even three, senses: sight and sound and perhaps touch. Recall that learning is a sensory experience. Thus the more you read aloud, if only for a few moments, the better you will comprehend.

Exercise: Read Ling's commencement address aloud. What features of vocalization enhance the oral reading versus the silent reading?

____

____

____

____

Step 5—RECORD Take notes. Another step in comprehending is to record the important information gained from the reading step. After reading a section of the passage, perhaps from one boldface heading to the next boldface heading or from stanza of poetry or paragraph of an essay or short story to the next, write important points, concepts, definitions, and formulas. To complete this step successfully, use a systematic style of note taking. Many students like the T-note system because it is simple to complete and easy to review. See the format below. The end result of recording is increased comprehension and easier mastery of the concepts explained. In summary, always record or take notes on reading. But write them after each section, not during the initial reading.

CHAPTER NUMBER OR TITLE OF LITERARY WORK	
Concept, vocabulary word, point	**Explanation, definition, how expressed**

Exercise: Write study notes on Ling's commencement speech. Remember to include the topic, points made, examples used, and new vocabulary.

LING'S COMMENCEMENT SPEECH	

Step 6—REVIEW You have followed the previous steps. Now it is time to review, or study. Use the notes made in step 5, Record. The information that you wrote should now be mastered. By reciting aloud the information that you recorded, you can complete this step simply and thoroughly. Following this step seriously guarantees success in comprehension and prepares you for any examinations you might take on the material covered. The time required depends on the number of notes, your strength of concentration, and the purpose for the review. Immediate review of material read ensures the processing of the information into the mind. If you are reviewing for a test, then the amount of time spent should increase dramatically. Regardless of the purpose, reviewing immediately the material read will help in creating a firm comprehension of the material read.

Exercise: Review the notes made on Ling's commencement address. Without referring to your notes again, write three specific facts that you studied.

____

____

____

Step 7—RECALL The Recall step is often used when moving forward with the material that you are reading. If you are reading a textbook, then recalling the information that you have already mastered will enhance the linkage to the new concepts and readings that follow. Before moving forward with a passage, a new chapter, or a new literary work, think about the concepts, the material, and the definitions that you have learned previously. Link them to the new ideas to provide yourself with a smooth transition to the new material yet to be mastered. You are building a foundation, or base, on which new material will flow more smoothly.

Exercise: In a complete sentence, write the theme of Ling's commencement address.

____

Step 8—REFLECT Often you hear the word *reflection* in terms of thinking about philosophical concepts—love, hate, bigotry, joy. This comprehension step is similar in that you are applying the ideas discovered through reading to real life. Reflection is perhaps the most important step to provide you, the reader, with a firm idea of the concepts you have learned. Whether it be a unit on poetry or an essay about immigration rights, you will move forward smoothly to future information by reflecting on the world around you and applying the ideas and concepts that you have used in the material studied. This step requires *synthesizing*, the highest level of thinking for humans whereby you link what you have learned to events and situations. Connect what you have read with the events surrounding you in day-to-day life. In other words, reflections require that you think and apply the reading's theme to real life. This step cements the concepts learned. If you are reading a poem, then apply the message to your experience. How can you use the rhetorical mode of classification in your daily life? How does your existence improve through the exploration of outer space? Once you have read an essay, asking yourself what is important to you in the world of cooking or history or whatever the topic might be is an essential component in mastery. The end result of reflection is that the new concept provides you with a firm link to information yet to be mastered.

Exercise: Using Ling's speech, write what facts or emotions you have experienced when beginning a new school or moving to a new area. How did you feel when you began your college experience?

____

____

____

Step 9—REACT Have you ever been so excited or angry about an event that you had to go to the location of the event? Many young people felt compelled to visit the September 11 site in New York City to help with the cleanup or to rescue lost documents or other items missing from the blasts. Others traveled long distances to the Gulf of Mexico area to assist Hurricane Katrina victims with food and other necessary essentials lost in the hurricane. In fact, this travel to a place is an example of a physical reaction to an external event. Reacting to an event, to a piece of literature, or to material explaining a concept to learn, whether in English or chemistry class, provides a firm footing or, in other words, comprehension. Often the classroom sociology or English professor will ask you what you think about divorce or marriage or other life events. The reason for this questioning is to strengthen in your thinking processes the concepts the professor considers important in the course you are taking or in life. In other words, reacting to reading requires that you physically demonstrate an emotion or an action as a result of the reading material covered. To appreciate and enjoy literature, readers must react to it. Your reaction, either negative or positive, might be done with a pen in the form of an article for the campus newspaper or a letter to the editor or as a physical act like a community service project.

Exercise: If you have experienced or might experience a move to another part of the world, possibly through a study-abroad experience, what reactions did you have or would you have had? How do your reactions compare to Andy Ling's?

____

____

____

Vocabulary Building

Increasing your knowledge of word meaning is one key component to improving reading comprehension. Did you know that American English is comprised of more than 600,000 words? Furthermore, the language grows daily. Think of words that you use today that did not exist even five years ago. List three of them.

The average college student doubles his or her vocabulary while pursuing a degree. You likely can grow from the knowledge of 15,000 words to 30,000 words. Despite the many offerings of vocabulary-building books, the most effective means of building your vocabulary is through reading and observation of words. So to formalize building your vocabulary, follow the steps below. Using as many physical senses as possible is the key to vocabulary growth.

1. Buy some 3 × 5 note cards, lined or unlined, colored or white.
2. On the center front of the card, write every new word you encounter in reading.
3. Below the word, write the page number, the source, and a portion of the sentence where the word is located.
4. On the back, write the definition and the part/s of speech, either from your glossary or from a dictionary.
5. Below the definition, write a sentence that you create.

File the cards for review, study the definitions frequently, and repeat the meanings aloud. Test yourself on the meanings and, more importantly, on the use of the words.

Finally and most importantly, use the new words in your regular conversation. Remember this statement: "If you don't use it, you lose it!"

front of card

new word

"I noticed the (new word) as it . . ."

p. 63 "The String"

back of card

definition of new word

part of speech: noun/verb

Without any binoculars, he saw the (new word) disappear.

Three Ways to Determine the Definition of an Unknown Word Most students read with a dictionary in hand. Often the dictionary is the first step in determining the meaning of an unknown vocabulary word. However, constant use of a dictionary can distract you and impede comprehension. Focus on making the dictionary your last resort. Follow these steps in the order shown to determine the meaning of a word. Notice that the dictionary comes last in the list.

1. Context Clues. Determine the meaning of a word from the surrounding words in the sentence. This process is called context clues. The context is the wording that surrounds the unknown vocabulary. Using the following guide to clues, look for meanings of unknown words.

A. Synonyms and Antonyms. Often the meaning of a word surrounds the unknown word. Look for synonyms—what the word means—or antonyms—what the word does not mean.

Example:

> *Road kill,* the remains of an animal killed on a road or highway, is often the subject of many restaurant jokes.

B. Examples. A passage could reveal the meaning of a word from the examples near the targeted word, usually following it. From the list of examples, you may determine the meaning of the word in question.

Example:

> The hunting quota that the man brought home was really *road kill*—opossum, deer, raccoons, armadillos—that he found at the nearby highway cleanup dump.

C. Critical Reading for Word Meaning. You might determine the meaning of the word from the entire sentence. In other words, use your skills of inference to understand the ideas that the writer implies or suggests. How does the entire sentence relate to the meaning of the word?

Example:

In the South, people often say *ya'll* when addressing a group of people.

The word *ya'll* is not defined within the sentence, but from the thought presented, you can conclude that the word is a form of address used in the South. Furthermore, upon reviewing the word's form, you can identify it as a form of the word *you*, and in doing so, you are using critical thinking.

2. Word Parts. If you cannot determine the word by the context, then try to figure out the word's structure. A basic knowledge of word parts can help you to determine the meaning of thousands of words. Learning a short list of common *root* or *base words* (the part that tells the core meaning of the word), *prefixes* (syllables attached to the beginning of a word that alter the meaning of the base word), and *suffixes* (syllables attached to the end of a word that indicate a word's part of speech) will enable you to decipher the meaning of a word.

Latin Roots, Prefixes, and Suffixes. Latin was the language spoken by the ancient Romans. As the Romans conquered most of Europe, the Latin language spread throughout the region. Over time, the Latin spoken in different areas developed into separate languages, including Italian, French, Spanish, and Portuguese. These languages are considered "sisters," as they all descended from Latin, their "mother" language.

In 1066 England was conquered by William, duke of Normandy, which is in northern France. For several hundred years after the Norman invasion, French was the language of court and polite society in England. It was during this period that many French words were borrowed into English. Linguists estimate that some 60 percent of our common everyday vocabulary today comes from French. Thus many Latin words came into English indirectly through French.

Many Latin words came into English directly, though, too. Monks from Rome brought religious vocabulary as well as Christianity to England beginning in the sixth century. From the Middle Ages onward many scientific, scholarly, and legal terms were borrowed from Latin.

During the seventeenth and eighteenth centuries, dictionary writers and grammarians generally felt that English was an imperfect language whereas Latin was perfect. In order to improve the language, they deliberately made up a lot of English words from Latin words. For example, *fraternity*, from Latin *fraternitas*, was thought to be better than the native English word *brotherhood*.[1]

[1]Information Please ® Database, © 2006 Pearson Education, Inc. All rights reserved.

Because of the many battles for power that occurred in the early history of Europe, the American English language is a mixture of many languages, largely German and French (etymology or word derivation).

Many English words and word parts can be traced back to Latin and Greek. The following table lists some common Latin roots.

Latin Root	Basic Meaning	Example Words
-dict-	to say	contradict, dictate, diction, edict, predict
-duc-	to lead, bring, take	deduce, produce, reduce
-gress-	to walk	digress, progress, transgress
-ject-	to throw	eject, inject, interject, project, reject, subject
-pel-	to drive	compel, dispel, impel, repel
-pend-	to hang	append, depend, impend, pendant, pendulum
-port-	to carry	comport, deport, export, import, report, support
-scrib-, -script-	to write	describe, description, prescribe, prescription, subscribe, subscription, transcribe, transcription
-tract-	to pull, drag, draw	attract, contract, detract, extract, protract, retract, traction
-vert-	to turn	convert, divert, invert, revert

From the example words in the above table, it is easy to see how roots combine with prefixes to form new words. For example, the root *-tract-*, meaning "to pull," can combine with a number of prefixes, including *de-* and *re-*. *Detract* means literally "to pull away" (*de-*, "away, off") and *retract* means literally "to pull back" (*re-*, "again, back"). The following table gives a list of Latin prefixes and their basic meanings.

Latin Prefix	Basic Meaning	Example Words
co-	Together	coauthor, coedit, coheir
de-	away, off; generally indicates reversal or removal in English	deactivate, debone, defrost, decompress, deplane
dis-	not, not any	disbelief, discomfort, discredit, disrepair, disrespect
inter-	between, among	international, interfaith, intertwine, intercellular, interject
non-	Not	nonessential, nonmetallic, nonresident, nonviolence, nonskid, nonstop
post-	After	postdate, postwar, postnasal, postnatal
pre-	Before	preconceive, preexist, premeditate, predispose, prepossess, prepay
re-	again; back, backward	rearrange, rebuild, recall, remake, rerun, rewrite
sub-	Under	submarine, subsoil, subway, subhuman, substandard
trans-	across, beyond, through	transatlantic, transpolar

Words and word roots may also combine with suffixes. Here are examples of some important English suffixes that come from Latin:

Latin Suffix	Basic Meaning	Example Words
-able, -ible	forms adjectives and means "capable or worthy of"	likable, flexible
-ation	forms nouns from verbs	Creation, civilization, automation, speculation, information
-fy, -ify	forms verbs and means "to make or cause to become"	purify, acidify, humidify
-ment	forms nouns from verbs	entertainment, amazement, statement, banishment
-ty, -ity	forms nouns from adjectives	subtlety, certainty, cruelty, frailty, loyalty, royalty; eccentricity, electricity, peculiarity, similarity, technicality

3. Dictionary. If you cannot determine the meaning of a vocabulary word from its context or from the word's parts, then use the dictionary as your last resort. However, to avoid distractions, mark the word in the passage and then go back to it after reading a section. Or alternately, mark the words in your survey stage and review the meanings in the dictionary before reading the passage. Write the meaning on your cards and in the textbook margins. Some textbooks offer a glossary, a dictionary of words used in the textbook, inside a chapter or at the end of the textbook. If available, use it before opening the dictionary.

One type of dictionary that students often find helpful is a *thesaurus*, a dictionary of synonyms and antonyms. This resource provides a short list of one-word meanings of the targeted vocabulary. You might also use an online dictionary. One common site is **www.dictionary.com.** It offers the meanings of most words in the English language in both dictionary and thesaurus format. You can also find many other online dictionaries by searching for specific types of dictionaries—dictionaries of law, medicine, and so on.

Exercise: Look up the meaning and etymology of the term *carpe diem* either online or in a dictionary. Write the meaning below.

____

____

Surface Reading Versus Deep Reading

Reading can be done on two basic levels: the surface level and the deep level. *Surface reading*, sometimes called on-the-line reading, includes the obvious details that can be gleaned without much deep thinking. Details can be determined with surface reading. Sometimes the topic sentence can be found with surface reading. This level of reading is quite simple and is the first type of reading learned. Certain questions can be answered with surface reading: Who? What? Where? When? How?

Included often in the level of surface reading are the minor, or ancillary and interesting but unimportant or irrelevant, details. If the major details, those required for the meaning of the selection, are expressed explicitly, they can be considered a component of major details. Minor details add color and interest, but they are not required for the literature to be understood. In general, points that are stated directly are considered on-the-line reading. They are the fluff! Most readers have little difficulty with surface reading. If your professor asks students what color a character's dress is, that question demands surface reading.

Exercise: Read the paragraph below from "The Story of an Hour" and answer the questions that follow.

> . . . She [Mrs. Mallard] could see in the open square before her house the tops of trees that were all aquiver with the new spring life. The delicious breath of rain was in the air. In the street below a peddler was crying his wares. The notes of a distant song which some one was singing reached her faintly, and countless sparrows were twittering in the eaves . . .

What could the character see from her window?

____

During what season does the story take place?

____

What sounds does Mrs. Mallard hear?

____

The answers to these questions require surface, or on-the-line, reading.

Deep reading, often called *critical reading*, requires stronger, more insightful reading. This type of reading is called *critical reading*. Critical reading requires deep thinking or *synthesizing*, gleaning deeper meaning from stated ideas in the reading. In other words, a reader must determine the between-the-lines meaning by using the surface points—stated main ideas, major details, and certain minor details. Determining how a writer created a certain character or expressed a certain point requires critical reading. One major question asked and answered in deep reading is "why." Often reasons are not stated explicitly but rather implicitly. Determining what a writer implies overall is called *inference*. A writer implies; a reader infers. If your professor asks you why the character is wearing a red silk dress, the skill required to respond to the question is the critical reading skill of inference. Making inferences and judgments and drawing conclusions all require critical reading. Have you ever heard a joke and you did not get the punch line? Perhaps twenty minutes later, you start laughing. You got it! That ah-hah moment means you understood the between-the-lines meaning. Background knowledge is often needed for understanding critical reading. If you have never eaten sushi or seen sushi and you read a story in which sushi is used symbolically, will you get the deeper point? Not at all! Thus reading and understanding the deeper meanings require much thought and insightfulness.

Exercise: Read the paragraph below and answer the questions that follow from "The Story of an Hour." Use your critical reading skills.

> . . . When she abandoned herself a little whispered word escaped her slightly parted lips. She said it over and over under her breath: "free, free, free!" The vacant stare and the look of terror that had followed it went from her eyes. They stayed keen and bright. Her pulses beat fast, and the coursing blood warmed and relaxed every inch of her body . . .

Why would Mrs. Mallard, who has just learned about the death of her husband, shout that she is free?

____

____

Why does Chopin say that Mrs. Mallard's eyes stayed "keen and bright"?

____

____

Why does Mrs. Mallard whisper rather than shout the three words quoted?

____

____

Based on the paragraph above, what is the underlying message, or theme, of this short story?

____

____

____

Responding to questions like the ones above requires critical reading skills and concentration on the subject. Use the SQ7R format to build deep reading skills that will enable you to develop these skills. You will also learn to understand, enjoy, and appreciate the literature that you read in *Crossing America*.

How to Read Different Genres of Literature

Each genre of literature requires a slightly different style of reading and searching for meaning. Read below to determine some simple steps to follow to read each type of literature covered in *Crossing America*. Always blend the points below into the SQ9R format for reading.

The Essay The *essay* is a work on nonfiction written in *prose*, or sentence, form. In general, the author presents one subject, or a *theme*, and then explains it with examples from real life. To read this type of literature effectively, follow the steps below.

1. Determine the subject of the essay.
2. Look for at least three points made about the theme.
3. Determine the author's overall attitude toward the subject—positive, negative.
4. Determine the author's specific tone—serious, humorous, satirical, factual, persuasive.
5. Locate the concluding remarks for summary points.

Use these steps as you read the essays in the textbook.

Poetry The shortest way of expressing a thought, *poetry* is often a challenge to understand because it is not written in prose, or full sentences. Poetry often rhymes and has a metric pattern, or beat. Thus often the reader might miss the meaning because of the missing words, the lack of some end punctuation, and often transposed wording like verbs located at the end of the line. Poems are often written in *stanzas*, the main divisions of this genre.

1. Read the entire poem aloud.
2. Read each stanza alone sentence by sentence, moving from period to period.
3. Put the stanza into normal sentence order.
4. Ask yourself what the poet is saying in each stanza.
5. Repeat these steps with each stanza.
6. After reading the entire poem, summarize in prose form the meaning of the poem.
7. List the figurative language and any other stylistic features of the poem.

Short Story Because short stories generally contain one main *plot*, or plan of action plan, they are considered easy to read. For this reason, they are a reader's favorite genre. The most effective way to read a short story is to apply the pyramid of the story as you read. In general, to read the short story with understanding, follow these steps:

1. Read the first and last lines five to ten sentences of the story.
2. Determine the characters' names and relationships to one another.
3. Read the entire story.
4. Determine the *plot*, or plan of action, of the story.
5. Ask yourself what the *theme*, or subject, of the story is.
6. Determine the highest point, or *climax*, of the story.
7. Decide how the story ends.
8. Locate any figurative language in the story—symbolism, personification, metaphors.
9. Summarize the point and the plot steps of the story.

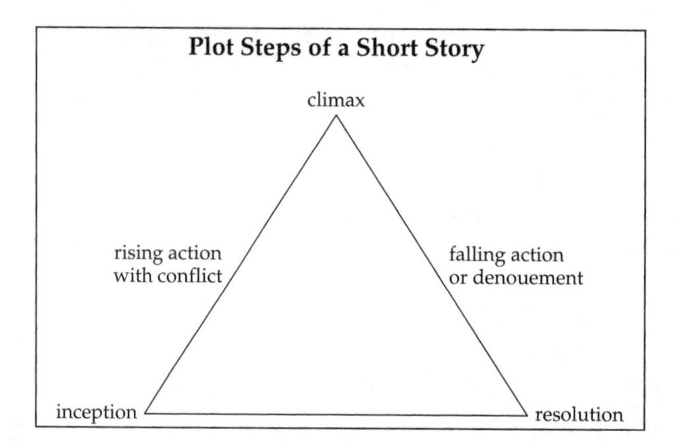

Exercise: Using Kate Chopin's "The Story of an Hour," plot the steps that occur in the short story. You may write on the inside of the pyramid above.

Article Most articles come from popular literature or professional journals. Being nonfiction, these works are sometimes difficult to read because they contain factual information and professional vocabulary, or jargon.

1. Determine the source, the title, the date, and the author of the article.
2. Find the topic sentence of the article.
3. Use the journalistic questions to identify the main points of the article: who, what, when, where, how, why.
4. Find details the author uses to expand the topic.
5. Determine the opinion the writer expresses or implies about his or her subject.
6. Find a summary statement or an implied summary.

You have read the information on reading comprehension. You have practiced with much of it. Now that you have mastered the material in this section, you are ready to move on to the next section, which covers the introductory notes on the writing process.

If you combine the reading skills developed with the writing process, you will be destined for success and appreciation of literature. At the same time, you will understand more about the many cultural influences that make up the fabric of America.

Literary Analysis

Just as a microbiologist breaks down a DNA sample to analyze its components, a student of literature analyzes a short story, a novel, a play, a poem, or any other piece of literature part by part to understand and appreciate the entire work. In this textbook, you are often asked to analyze the parts of a short story or poem in order to gain a better understanding of the whole. Before writing about literature, review these terms and strategies.

The Story of an Hour

Kate Chopin

Knowing that Mrs. Mallard was afflicted with a heart trouble, great care was taken to break to her as gently as possible the news of her husband's death.

It was her sister Josephine who told her, in broken sentences; veiled hints that revealed in half concealing. Her husband's friend Richards was there, too, near her. It was he who had been in the newspaper office when intelligence of the railroad disaster was received, with Brently Mallard's name leading the list of "killed." He had only taken the time to assure himself of its truth by a second telegram, and had hastened to forestall any less careful, less tender friend in bearing the sad message.

She did not hear the story as many women have heard the same, with a paralyzed inability to accept its significance. She wept at once, with sudden, wild abandonment, in her sister's arms. When the storm of grief had spent itself she went away to her room alone. She would have no one follow her.

There stood, facing the open window, a comfortable, roomy armchair. Into this she sank, pressed down by a physical exhaustion that haunted her body and seemed to reach into her soul.

She could see in the open square before her house the tops of trees that were all aquiver with the new spring life. The delicious breath of rain was in the air. In the street below a peddler was crying his wares. The notes of a distant song which some one was singing reached her faintly, and countless sparrows were twittering in the eaves.

There were patches of blue sky showing here and there through the clouds that had met and piled one above the other in the west facing her window.

She sat with her head thrown back upon the cushion of the chair, quite motionless, except when a sob came up into her throat and shook her, as a child who has cried itself to sleep continues to sob in its dreams.

She was young, with a fair, calm face, whose lines bespoke repression and even a certain strength. But now there was a dull stare in her eyes, whose gaze was fixed away off yonder on one of those patches of blue sky. It was not a glance of reflection, but rather indicated a suspension of intelligent thought.

There was something coming to her and she was waiting for it, fearfully. What was it? She did not know; it was too subtle and elusive to name. But she felt it, creeping out of the sky, reaching toward her through the sounds, the scents, the color that filled the air.

Now her bosom rose and fell tumultuously. She was beginning to recognize this thing that was approaching to possess her, and she was striving to beat it back with her will—as powerless as her two white slender hands would have been.

When she abandoned herself a little whispered word escaped her slightly parted lips. She said it over and over under her breath: "free, free, free!" The vacant stare and the look of terror that had followed it went from her eyes. They stayed keen and bright. Her pulses beat fast, and the coursing blood warmed and relaxed every inch of her body.

She did not stop to ask if it were or were not a monstrous joy that held her. A clear and exalted perception enabled her to dismiss the suggestion as trivial.

She knew that she would weep again when she saw the kind, tender hands folded in death; the face that had never looked save with love upon her, fixed and gray and dead. But she saw beyond that bitter moment a long procession of years to come that would belong to her absolutely. And she opened and spread her arms out to them in welcome.

There would be no one to live for during those coming years; she would live for herself. There would be no powerful will bending hers in that blind persistence with which men and women believe they have a right to impose a private will upon a fellow-creature. A kind intention or a cruel intention made the act seem no less a crime as she looked upon it in that brief moment of illumination.

And yet she had loved him—sometimes. Often she had not. What did it matter! What could love, the unsolved mystery, count for in face of this possession of self-assertion which she suddenly recognized as the strongest impulse of her being!

"Free! Body and soul free!" she kept whispering.

Josephine was kneeling before the closed door with her lips to the keyhole, imploring for admission. "Louise, open the door! I beg, open the door—you will make yourself ill. What are you doing Louise? For heaven's sake open the door."

"Go away. I am not making myself ill." No; she was drinking in a very elixir of life through that open window.

Her fancy was running riot along those days ahead of her. Spring days, and summer days, and all sorts of days that would be her own. She breathed a quick prayer that life might be long. It was only yesterday she had thought with a shudder that life might be long.

She arose at length and opened the door to her sister's importunities. There was a feverish triumph in her eyes, and she carried herself unwittingly like a goddess of Victory. She clasped her sister's waist, and together they descended the stairs. Richards stood waiting for them at the bottom.

Someone was opening the front door with a latchkey. It was Brently Mallard who entered, a little travel-stained, composedly carrying his gripsack and umbrella. He had been far from the scene of accident, and did not even know there had been one. He stood amazed at Josephine's piercing cry; at Richards' quick motion to screen him from the view of his wife.

But Richards was too late.

When the doctors came they said she had died of heart disease—of joy that kills.

Devices for Writing a Literary Analysis

1. The term **elements of the short story** usually refers to the plot, the characters, the theme, the setting, and the point of view. However, to understand the story, also consider the author's use of literary devices.
2. The **plot** is the action occurring in the story. The plot consists of the **inception** of the story, followed by the **rising action** with the introduction of the **conflict,** the **climax,** or highest point of interest, and the unraveling, or **denouement,** of the story. **Foreshadowing,** which generally occurs at the inception of the story, can be defined as the clues that the author gives the reader about what will happen in the story. Have you ever watched a movie and at the end said, "I should have known that was going to happen. There were clues at the beginning of the movie"? The rising action occurs at the conflict and can be defined as the tension or struggle that the characters face. The conflict can be classified as person against self, person against person, or person against nature. The highest point of interest, or climax, occurs at the peak of the action. The denouement, or the unraveling of events, refers to actions that lead to the solving or resolution of the problem. When analyzing the plot, do not summarize what happened; instead discuss foreshadowing, conflict, the highest point of action, and the resolution.
3. **Setting** of a short story or poem refers to the time, the place, and the atmosphere of the work. When analyzing the setting of the story, discuss the importance of the setting to the plot, the development of the characters, and the theme of the story. Ask yourself if the story would have a different meaning if the setting were different.
4. **Characters** are the people and sometimes animals in the literary work. Characters can be described as **round** characters, characters that make some sort of change in the story. Round characters are those you feel as though you know after finishing the story. You may like or dislike the characters, but you feel as if you know them. **Flat** characters are those that do not change throughout the story. These characters are not affected, as far as the reader can tell, by the action of the story. The **protagonist** in a short story is the hero or central character in the short story. The **antagonist** is the adversary, or enemy, in the short story. The reader gets to know the characters by what the characters say, by what others say about the characters, and by the actions of the characters.
5. **Theme** refers to an underlying idea that prevails throughout the story or poem. It can be compared to a thread that runs through the literary work. The author never says, "This is the theme of the work," but the reader can usually discern the theme. The theme is an abstract concept such as the effects of revenge, the power of love, or the realization of humankind's mortality. In short, theme refers to the message of the work, but do not confuse theme with the action of the story.
6. **Point of view** refers to the narrator of the story. Events may be told through the eyes of a character in the story, through the eyes of an objective narrator who can see into the hearts and minds of one or more of the

characters, or through an objective outside narrator who reports on what he or she sees and hears. When the story is told through the eyes of a character in the story and the reader only reads his or her version of the story, the point of view is **first person**. The character narrates the story by giving his version of the situation. The pronoun *I* is used. When the story is told through an all-knowing narrator, a narrator who knows what one or more of the characters are thinking, the point of view is referred to as **omniscient**. The **third-person objective** viewpoint refers to an outside narrator who can only report on what he sees and hears.

7. **Imagery** is language that paints a mental picture for the reader. The author uses language that helps the reader smell, taste, hear, see, and touch what is happening in the story. Imagery can often be detected through nouns, verbs, and adjectives.
8. **Figurative language** is wording that conveys an idea other than the literal meaning of the words. **Similes,** comparisons using *as* or *like,* and **metaphors,** comparisons that do not use *like* or *as,* are examples of figurative language. **Personification** is the use of words that give lifelike or human characteristics to inanimate objects or other living creatures. **Hyperbole** can be defined as an exaggeration used for effect.
9. **Symbolism** is the term used for one word or a group of words representing an idea or concept. For example, most sports teams have emblems, flags, or mascots that can be considered symbols for the teams. Religious symbols include the crescent and star for Islam, the cross for Christianity, and the Star of David for Judaism. Authors also use symbols to represent ideas or emotions.
10. **Alliteration** is the repetition of initial consonant sounds of words or the sounds within words. Alliteration can be used in poetry, fiction, and nonfiction to highlight important words and concepts or to create a melody of sound.
11. **Assonance** is the repetition of vowel sounds in poetry.
12. **Rhyme** refers to repetition of the sounds within a line of poetry or at the end of a line of poetry.
13. **Rhyme scheme** is the pattern of final rhyming sounds in a poem. Rhyme schemes are marked with alphabetical patterns. Not all poems rhyme.
14. **Irony** is the difference between what is expected to happen and what actually occurs. Sarcasm is a form of irony.

Points to Remember in Writing a Literary Analysis Assignment

- Mention the author or poet and the literary work in the introductory paragraph.
- The first time you refer to the author, use the first and last name. After that, refer to the author by the last name. Never call the author by only his or her first name. Recall that the author is different from the main character or the narrator.

- If you are writing an essay, include a thesis statement in the introductory paragraph and topic sentences in each body paragraph.
- If you are writing a one-paragraph literary analysis, mention the author or the poet, the title of the literature to be discussed, and the literary element to be analyzed in the topic sentence.
- Write in the present tense. The idea that literature lives forever requires the writer to use the literary present tense.
- Use quotation marks correctly when you quote direct wording from the short story or poem.
- Following the MLA format, add parenthetical citations to identify the quotations you use. Include the author's last name and the page number for prose or the line number for poetry. Your handbook explains the MLA style. *Example*: (Chopin 33).
- Analyze, rather than summarize, the literary work. (You may write a short summary statement in the introductory paragraph.)

Writer's Workshop Activities for Understanding Poetry and Writing a Literary Analysis of a Poem

This worksheet may be duplicated.

To analyze the poetry in *Crossing America*, use this worksheet. Practice with the Carter poem "I Wanted to Share My Father's World" that you read in the first section on reading.

1. What is the overall effect of the poem? After reading the poem aloud, are you sad, amused, confused, thoughtful? Explain your answer. Cite examples from the poem to support your answer.
2. Review the summary and the reaction you wrote of the poem in your textbook activities.
3. Cite examples of imagery in the poem.
   - Sense of smell
   - Sense of sound
   - Sense of touch
   - Sense of taste
   - Sense of sight
4. Cite examples of figurative language.
   - Similes
   - Metaphors
   - Personification
   - Hyperbole
5. Examine the use of language to create sound in poetry. Cite any examples of alliteration, assonance, and onomatopoeia.
6. Analyze the rhyme scheme of the poem.

7. What is the point of view of the poem? What overall effect does the point of view have on the poem?
8. Does the poem tell a story? If so, analyze the plot of the story.
9. Discuss any symbolism in the poem.
10. Examine the rhyme of the poem. What is the rhyme scheme or the pattern of rhythm and how does pattern affect your enjoyment of the poem?
11. How has your reaction of the poem changed since you have analyzed the poem?

Writer's Workshop Activities for Understanding the Elements of a Short Story

This worksheet may be duplicated.

To analyze the short stories in *Crossing America*, use this worksheet. Practice with "The Story of an Hour" that you read previously in this unit.

1. Plot

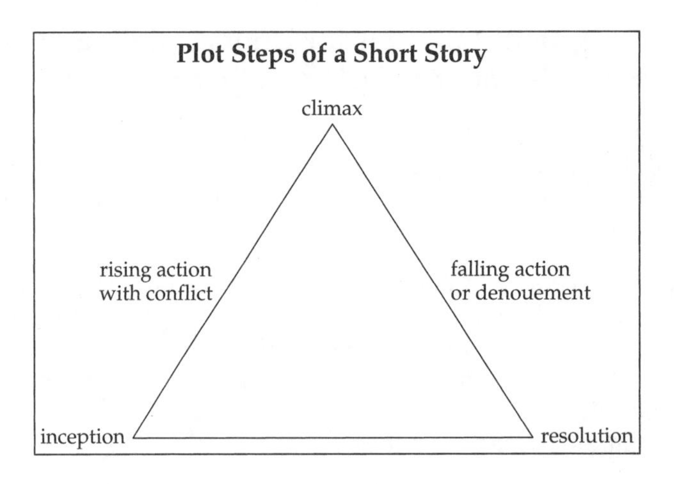

- What elements are present at the inception of the short story?
- Cite examples of foreshadowing.
- Discuss the rising action and conflict of the story.
- What is the highest point of interest or climax of the story?
- What are the events that lead to the resolution of the story?
- What is the resolution?
- List quotations from the story that support your evaluation of the plot.

2. Setting

- Where does the story take place?
- When does the story take place?
- What is the atmosphere of the setting?
- How important is the setting to the understanding of the plot, the characters, and the theme of the story?

- Would the outcome of the story be different if the setting were different?
- List quotations from the story that support your evaluation of the setting.

3. **Characters**
   - List each character in the short story.
   - Beside the character's name, tell if the character is round or flat, a protagonist or antagonist.
   - Write an adjective by the name of each major character.
   - Write quotations from the work to support your choice of adjectives.
4. **Theme**
   - What is the underlying theme of the short story? Explain your answer.
   - How does the author develop the theme?
   - Cite quotations from the short story to support your ideas.
5. **Point of View**
   - How is the story narrated?
   - What is the point of view?
   - How would the story be different if told through a different viewpoint?
6. **Imagery**
   - Write examples of images for the following:
     - Sense of smell
     - Sense of taste
     - Sense of sound
     - Sense sight
     - Sense of touch (texture)
   - How is imagery used to develop the plot, the characters, the setting, and the theme?
7. **Figurative Language**
   - Write examples of any similes used in the short story.
   - Write examples of any metaphors used in the short story.
   - Write examples of personification used in the short story.
   - Write examples of hyperbole.
   - Write examples of sound language.
8. **Symbolism**
   - List examples of symbolism used in the short story.
   - Explain the meaning of the symbols.
9. **Irony**
   - Discuss any examples of irony. Does the irony represent sarcasm?
10. **Reaction**
    - Discuss how your analysis of the parts of the short story has affected your original reaction to and understanding of the story.

SUMMARIZING

To summarize is to write or encapsulate the main ideas of a story or an essay. Another name for a summary is an abstract. When you are asked to do research in your college classes, you may first read abstracts on the articles from periodicals you are interested in reading. The abstract, or summary, of the article tells you the main ideas of the work. When you write summaries, you are writing an abstract. You are letting the reader know the most important ideas in the reading. Through summarizing, you are better able to distinguish between main ideas and subordinate ideas. Writing summaries is a good way to improve your writing abilities in general. Summaries are generally one-eighth the length of the original material, so you must use concise language and focus on the main ideas of the material.

HOW TO WRITE A SUMMARY

1. Read the material and take notes as you read. Ask yourself, "What is the focus of the reading?" Distinguish between the main ideas and the subordinating ideas.
2. The topic sentence of the summary should include the name of the author, the title of the selection you are summarizing, and the main idea. For example, if you are summarizing "The Story of an Hour" by Kate Chopin, your topic sentence may read: *In "The Story of an Hour," the author Kate Chopin explores the reaction of the main character, Mrs. Mallard, when she receives news about the death of her husband.*
3. Place quotation marks around the titles of short stories.
4. A summary should not be more the one-eighth the length of the material being summarized. Most of the summary activities in this text call for one-paragraph summaries.
5. When you are summarizing literature, write in present tense. Notice the topic sentence in tip number 2. What is the tense of the verbs?
6. Write in third person. Remember that you are retelling the main ideas of the reading.
7. A summary is objective, not subjective. Thus, you do not give your opinion of what you have read or explain what you would have done in a similar situation.
8. Use your own words when writing summaries. If you do quote even a few words from the passage, you must put quotation marks around the words.

Writing Activities for Summaries

For practice, choose one of the following summarizing activities.

1. Summarize the short story "The Story of an Hour" by Kate Chopin. You may use the sample topic sentence or you may write one of your own.

2. Summarize the commencement speech by Andy Ling.
3. Summarize the information on summaries in the introduction of this text.
4. Summarize the poem written by Jimmy Carter.

Paraphrasing

Webster's dictionary defines a paraphrase as *a restatement of a text, passage, or work giving the meaning in another form.* Paraphrasing is similar to summarizing, but a paraphrase is generally the same or close to the same length of the original material, especially in poetry. For example, if you summarized Carter's poem, your summary was probably one paragraph. However, if you paraphrased his poem, your paraphrase would be approximately the same length as the poem. Therefore, when paraphrasing, you should look for the most important material and only paraphrase those ideas. Just as required when summarizing, you *must* identify the source of the material. Many students make the mistake of believing that if they put the ideas in their own words, they do not need to cite the source of the material. This is not true. In fact, this is a form of plagiarism.

When should you paraphrase? Paraphrasing can be utilized when you think that the material is so vital to understanding the message of the author that the information must be restated to maintain the author's intent. Furthermore, paraphrasing is also an excellent tool to use when you have read a paragraph that you do not understand. Try paraphrasing the paragraph sentence by sentence, and you will be surprised at how much easier the literary work is to understand. This step is especially beneficial when trying to understand poetry.

How to Paraphrase

1. As you read, mark phrases that you consider vital to the understanding of the intent of the author.
2. Reread the material and mark phrases that support the points you are making in your writing assignment. For example, if you are writing a paper about the figurative language Chopin uses in "The Story of an Hour," you may underline or take notes on the description of the scene from the window in Mrs. Mallard's bedroom.
3. Turn your notes over and write the information in your words.
4. Paraphrase no more than a sentence or two unless asked to paraphrase an entire poem.
5. Keep the length the same as or shorter than the original.
6. Place the author's name in parentheses after the paraphrase.
7. Use your own words rather than those in a thesaurus to replace the author's words.

Writing Activities for Paraphrasing

1. Paraphrase the following lines from Kate Chopin's "Story of an Hour."

   She was young, with a fair, calm face, whose lines bespoke repression and even a certain strength.

   ____

   The notes of a distant song which some one was singing reached her faintly, and countless sparrows were twittering in the eaves.

   ____

   There were patches of blue sky showing here and there through the clouds that had met and piled one above the other in the west facing her window.

   ____

2. Paraphrase the following from Andy Ling's commencement speech found in the reading section of this introduction.

   No longer will I need to worry about whether I will fit into this new culture, for you have extended your friendship and care toward me just as if I were one of you.

   ____

   ____

   ____

3. Paraphrase the following lines from the poem "I Wanted to Share My Father's World" by Jimmy Carter.

   From those rare times when we did cross
   the bridge between us, the pure joy
   survives.

   ____

   ____

To review the concepts of paraphrasing and summary, read the first paragraph of Edgar Allen Poe's short story "The Cask of Amontillado."

THE CASK OF AMONTILLADO
Edgar Allan Poe (1846)

The thousand injuries of Fortunato I had borne as I best could, but when he ventured upon insult I vowed revenge. You, who so well know the nature of my soul, will not suppose, however, that I gave utterance to a threat. At length I would be avenged; this was a point definitely, settled—but the very definitiveness with which it was resolved precluded the idea of risk. I must not only punish, but punish with impunity. A wrong is unredressed when retribution overtakes its redresser. It is equally unredressed when the avenger fails to make himself felt as such to him who has done the wrong.

1. To understand better the first paragraph of Poe's short story, paraphrase the first line of the story.

 ____

 ____

 ____

2. Paraphrase another sentence of your choice.

 ____

 ____

 ____

3. Summarize the first paragraph of Poe's short story.

 ____

 ____

 ____

 ____

 ____

 ____

PLAGIARISM

Plagiarism is the illegal use of someone else's words and ideas. When students think of plagiarism, they often think of cases of the intentional stealing of another person's ideas or work. Certainly, most students know that copying another person's work, buying or copying a paper from the Internet, turning in a paper copied from a textbook, or cutting and pasting from the Internet is cheating and has serious consequences. However, there are other forms of plagiarism that can also have serious consequences. For example, taking a sentence from an outside source, rewording it, and not giving credit to the author or source of the information is also plagiarism. Choosing a few words from another source and not putting the words in quotation marks is also plagiarism. After all, you would not take a few dollars from a cash register at a department store and say you were not stealing just because you did not take all of the money!

Exercise: Understanding Plagiarism

1. Find the Academic Honesty policy for your college or class and summarize the statement.
2. Interview a college professor and summarize his or her policy on plagiarism.

SQ9R—A WRITING STRATEGY THAT WORKS

Step 1—SURVEY

As in reading, to be a successful writer, you must survey the assignment and your thoughts before writing. To survey the assignment, you first must make sure you understand all the vocabulary used in the assignment. Try paraphrasing the assignment. Ask questions so that you clearly understand the purpose of the assignment, the intended audience, and the details of the assignment. How long should the assignment be? When is the assignment due? In what person should the paper be written (the point of view)? Is there any material you need to read or reread? Will you need to do research in order to write the assignment? If so, what kind of research? Should you conduct interviews or do library research? Is Internet research appropriate? Should you reread your reading and reaction journals assigned in *Crossing America* for ideas?

During this stage of the writing process, choose your topic. If you are having trouble doing this, you can try several strategies to help you come to a decision about your topic.

- If your time frame and professor allow it, discuss your topic choices with classmates and your professor. Usually, discussing your ideas and concerns about an assignment is the best approach to understanding the requirements and deciding upon a topic.
- Try freewriting on the general assignment topic. If you have several topics to choose from and you cannot decide the direction of your topic, this is an excellent prewriting activity for you! In this process, write for five minutes without stopping. If, during this time, you do not like a topic you are pursuing, change topics, but do not stop writing! After five minutes, stop and read what you have written; highlight any ideas that you especially like. Continue this activity for twenty-five to thirty minutes. At the end of the activity, you will probably see that you have not only discovered your topic, but you have also begun to actually see a plan of development. In addition, you will probably find that you have several well-worded and interesting phrases that you will want to keep for your first draft. This type of prewriting is excellent for long-term assignments. If you do not have to decide upon a topic and write in a short time frame, such as in a one- or two-hour class period, try freewriting.
- Read through your reading and reaction journals. These journals will serve as excellent tools for discovering new ideas and recalling past experiences, all of which can be used to help you decide upon a topic. If you think you are not interested in any of your topics, your journals will serve as a springboard to new thoughts on the subjects presented.
- Keep a private journal on your reaction to daily news and happenings, not only in your life and your community but also in the world. Do not simply record what has happened, but also react to the situations. Your recordings will help you explore new interests and will build background knowledge for future assignments.

- Make a list of all the subjects you are interested in now and those that you think you will be interested in as you progress through life. Categorize those interests into topics such as science, sports, psychology, and religion. Under each topic, list questions and subtopics. This practice will help become aware of your interests and will remind you that learning is a life-long project. Keep your list active long after you have completed this course.

The Survey step may take only a few minutes, a class period, or even several weeks, depending on the type of assignment. This step is a vital part of the writing process; therefore, do not skip it in your haste to get the assignment started. You do not want to complete an entire assignment only to find out that your assignment will not be accepted because you did not follow the requirements of the assignment.

Exercise: Survey the textbook *Crossing America* for the following information.

1. What type of information is in the introduction to the textbook?
2. What questions do you have about the information in the Preface?
3. Where are the writing assignments in the units?
4. Choose one unit from the textbook. Survey the types of writing assignments given. What do all of the writing assignments have in common? How do you foresee using the information in the Survey step to approach the writing assignments?
5. Explain a situation where the Survey step could have helped you in a previous assignment.
6. Try one of the prewriting activities to answer this question. What are your interests? Discuss your results with your classmates.

Step 2—QUESTION

Questioning is also an important part of the prewriting/planning stage of writing. After you have chosen your topic, you will want to explore your knowledge of the topic and again question your understanding of the focus of the topic you have chosen. With pen in hand, consider these questions when entering this stage of the writing process.

- What background information do I have on the topics I am considering?
- Does my interest in the topic come from reading I have done, movies I have seen, and/or experiences my friends and I have had?
- Do I have extensive knowledge on my topic or am I writing on a topic in which I will explore my feelings and reactions to what I have read?

In this stage of writing, you should also use journalistic or reporter's questions (Who? What? Where? When? Why? How?) to help you develop and organize your ideas on your chosen your topic. List each question and answer the questions either in a few words or phrases or in a freewriting style. Find a method that best suits you and helps you develop needed ideas and examples.

Also, in this stage, you should organize and map your essay or paragraph. Ask yourself these questions.

- What will be my thesis statement or topic sentence?
- What pattern of development will I follow?
- What examples do I want to include?
- Where do I want to place my examples in my paragraph or paragraphs?
- How much information should I include?
- What will be my key words, the words that focus on the main idea of the assignment, in my paper?
- What types of transitional words should I use?

Besides using journalistic questions in this stage, you may also want to consider doing a visual diagram of your topic. Draw a circle in the center of your page with your topic written inside the circle. Extending from the circle, draw your main ideas and the details of your main ideas. See the example below of a clustering exercise used to develop and organize ideas on an essay exploring ways to pay for a college education.

Clustering Activity

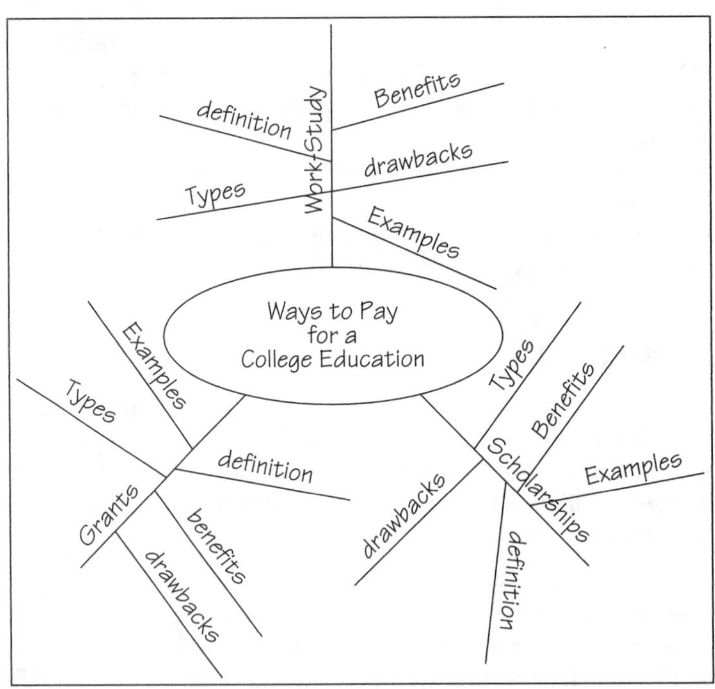

Exercise: Reread Ling's commencement speech as a springboard to thinking about the benefits of a college education. Then do reporter's questions and/or a clustering activity to begin a paragraph on the topic of the benefits of a college education.

Step 3—RELATE

In the Relate step, take the opportunity to "talk through" your paper. With your writing group, if your professor allows, discuss the organizational plan of your paper. During the discussion, listen for the purpose of the assignment and the organizational plans of your group members. The writing sections of the units have clear organizational plans for each assignment. If your assignment or professor does not call for collaboration, then learn to "talk yourself" through the organizational plan of your essay. You probably cannot host a Super Bowl party for fifty people or backpack across America or through Europe or Latin America without thinking through and planning your activities. Similarly, you should not write an academic paper simply by picking up a pen and writing or sitting at a computer and pounding words on the keyboard. You must think, plan, and organize before you write. Planning is the most important part of the writing process.

Step 4—RECORD

In this step, record, or write, your first draft. Follow your organizational plan. As you write, understand that this is your first draft and that you will want to revise and edit your paper. Some writers like to write their first draft without paying attention to grammar. Others like to do their very best on the first draft. Certainly, you want to become familiar enough with grammar rules that you do notice when you are making errors, but the purpose of the assignment is to write your ideas in an organized fashion.

Exercise: Skim through your textbook, paying attention to the types of writing patterns discussed. Decide which pattern of organization you would use for your paragraph on the benefits of a college education. Discuss with your writing group or your classmates why you chose the method you did. As you work through the book during the semester, you will better understand the type of organizational plan you would use for your approach to your topic. Write a paragraph on the benefits of a college education you discussed with your group members.

Step 5—READ and REVISE

Oh, how nice it would be to write down your thoughts, place the final period, write your name on the paper, turn it in, and walk away. Unfortunately, the writing process does not end with writing the first draft. Even if you are answering discussion questions for a timed test or writing a paragraph or essay under timed conditions, take the time to read and revise your paper! If you are working with an editing or writing group, read your paper aloud to your group members and allow them to listen and ask questions. This practice will help you organize and place details. If you are not working in a group, you can do this yourself. Take a break from your paper, even if only a few seconds, and then read your paper—aloud if possible. Ask questions! Does your paper make sense? Do you have the needed details? Simply because you know that your great aunt Sally is an octogenarian who teaches yoga three times a week does not mean that your reader does! As you read or listen to a paper, train yourself to ask journalistic questions. After reviewing your own comments and the comments of your peers, make revisions in the content of your paper. You may have sentences you need to delete, paragraphs you want to reorder, and details you need to add. Do not be afraid to make changes.

Exercise: Read the paragraph on the benefits of a college education to your editing group and have group members ask questions. Each group member should pose at least two questions. Likewise, as you listen to the papers of your peers, remember to ask journalistic questions. Ask questions about details. Ask group members to write their questions and give them to you for revision. Using the questions and comments of your group members, revise your paragraph.

Step 6—REVIEW

After you have revised the content of your paper, you now need to review, or edit, your paper for organization, content, logic, word choice, and overall effectiveness. Each unit in *Crossing America* contains questions for review. The questions pertain to the pattern of development used, unity, word choice, and logical thinking. These editing worksheets can be used for group or individual editing. The overall purpose is to help you edit your own papers. As you become a stronger and more confident writer, you may find that you can edit for content and details at the same time as you edit for patterns of development and word choice.

Exercise: Within your group, with a partner, or individually, answer the following questions about your paragraph:

1. What is title of the paragraph?
2. What is the topic sentence of the paragraph?
3. What examples are used to support the topic sentence?
4. What transitional words are used?
5. What key words are used to give the paragraph unity?
6. What is the concluding sentence of the paragraph?
7. What is the most effective part of the paragraph?
8. Do I accept the changes recommended in Spell check and Grammar check?

Step 7—REFLECT

Reflection is the step in which you consider or reflect upon the comments of your peers or your own observations. If your peer editors could not find a topic sentence in your paragraph, then you need to add one or discuss with them why they do not see what you are seeing! Look at the answers of your peers and make any needed changes. If you do not agree with their comments, discuss them. Review the questions and see what changes you need to make. Before making any changes, evaluate the comments of your peers and choose which suggestions you want to incorporate into your revised copy. You are the final editor. Thus, you are the one who must make the final decisions about your paper.

Exercise: Reflect upon the comments of your peers concerning your paragraph on the benefits of a college education. Make the necessary revisions.

Step 8—REREAD

Now that you have made changes in content, word choice, organization, or logic, you will need to reread your paper for grammatical and punctuation errors, often called mechanical errors. To do this step, read from the bottom of the paper to the top. This will remove your mind from the content and help you to focus on the structure of the sentences. You will be able to read what you actually wrote and not what you meant to write! As you check for grammatical errors, keep in mind the grammar pointers made in each chapter. Also, become aware of the types of errors you tend to make. If you make comma usage errors, review comma rules and then check your paper carefully for comma errors. Likewise, if you know you often make errors in sentence structure, review the rules for combining sentences, for coordination and subordination, and for correcting comma splices and fused sentences. Also, mark the subject and verb in each sentence. When you do that, you can check for verb usage errors, subject-verb agreement, and sentence structure errors.

Exercise: Read your paper paragraph on the benefits of a college education from bottom to top. Mark each subject and verb. Check carefully for sentence structure, subject-verb agreement, and verb usage errors. Make any necessary corrections.

Step 9—READ Your Paper Aloud!

Before turning in your paper, read it aloud! You are much more likely to catch errors, especially word omissions, when you read your paper orally. At the completion of this step, finally, you can turn your paper in and relax.

Exercise: Read your paper out loud and make any needed changes. Turn your paper in to your professor! Smile!

A Guide to Terminology Used in *Crossing America*

Argumentative/Persuasive Writing: A form of writing used to convince the reader to think as the writer does or to call the reader to action about a particular issue. Arguments should be supported with logical reasons and explanations. The principles of writing, reading, and analyzing arguments can be used not only in reading, composition, and literature classes but also in all college classes, the workplace, and the community.

Audience: The reader of the work of literature. Good writers know the audience for which they are writing. The audience determines the vocabulary, tone, references, and content. If asked to write an essay on the topic of how to cook spaghetti for two different audiences—college freshmen and master's-level nutritionists—the content will be very different.

Background Knowledge: Prior knowledge of a subject before reading or before researching a topic. This insight may have been gained from past reading or previous course work, from television or film, or from daily life through conversations with others.

Classification: A pattern of organization of dividing items or ideas into categories. The categories must have a unifying principle without overlapping. This mode is often called "types of" such as types of students found on a college campus, types of food in the cafeteria, or three styles of music that originated in America.

Concrete Language: Specific wording rather than vague and abstract wording. For example, the sentence *The man ran away* can be improved by clarifying which man and where he ran. *The frightened and confused witness quickly disappeared into the angry mob.*

Cause-Effect Analysis: A pattern of organization used to explain why an event or problem occurred and what the effects, or consequences, of this event are. A causal analysis, also referred to as cause and effect, may focus on the reasons, or causes, for a situation; the results, or effects, of the situation; or both the causes and the effects.

Comparison/Contrast: A pattern of organization in which two concepts, people, or things are analyzed through a discussion of similarities, differences, or both similarities and differences. Comparison means to look at similarities, and contrast means to look at differences. However, the term *comparison essay* often refers to both similarities and differences.

Concentration: Focusing for a sustained period of time on the material being read or the writing process. Generally, you should be able to concentrate fully for about forty minutes without a break in thought.

Connotation: Feelings that words evoke for the reader or listener. The dictionary meaning of *school* may be a place where instruction is given, but the word *school* may connote feelings of happiness and memories of childhood friends for some people and memories of strict instructors and embarrassment for others. However, some words have clearly positive or negative connotations, so writers must consider their words carefully. *Frugal*, *thrifty*, and *cheap* may have similar dictionary meanings, but the connotations differ greatly. For this reason, writers should avoid haphazardly selecting words from a thesaurus. Readers should be aware of the words chosen by the author.

Deep Reading: A method of reading requiring critical thinking, gleaning deeper meaning from stated ideas in the reading. In critical or deep reading, a reader must determine the between-the-lines meaning by using the surface points—stated main ideas, major details, and certain minor details. Critical, or deep, reading requires stronger, more insightful reading.

Definition: An organizational pattern of writing in which the author uses examples to define abstract terms such as *love, honor, greed, patriotism, bigotry*. This organizational plan is often developed through the use of other rhetorical modes of development such as classification and comparison and contrast or exemplification.

Denotation: The dictionary definition of *word*. For example, one of the definitions for *school* according to **www.dictionary.com** is "an institution where instruction is given, esp. to persons under college age: *The children are at school.*"

Descriptive Writing: The use of specific details, concrete nouns, and strong verbs to paint a picture of a situation, an object, a person, or an event. Descriptive writing, as an organizational pattern, should have a dominant impression and purpose. For instance, an author may describe the emergency room of a hospital in order to show the fear of the patients or the dedication of the employees. The dominant impression the author wants to portray will determine the words the author uses.

Dominant Impression: The overall idea that an author wants the reader to understand or see in descriptive writing. For example, if the writer is describing a college cafeteria at 6:00 A.M., the focus of the paper, or the dominant impression, may be the quietness of the cafeteria or the busyness of the workers while they prepare for an onslaught of hungry students.

Exemplification: A pattern of development in which the author analyzes the topic through the use of examples, details, and illustrations. This type of development can generally be used to enhance all patterns of writing.

Genre: Category or type of writing in literature. Literature can be divided into these categories: poetry, short stories, novels, plays, essays, speeches, and biographies and autobiographies, and journals. These are examples of genres of literature found in *Crossing America*.

Idioms: Unusual use of language in which words have figurative meaning instead of literal meaning. For example, the idiom *Face the music* does not literally mean to turn oneself toward the radio or the band, but figuratively, it means to face the consequences of one's actions. Idioms provide richness to a language and can be culture specific based on a country's natural resources and historical events.

Inference: Ideas the author suggests or implies in his or her writing, which can be considered deep, or critical, reading. Inferences are logical conclusions that the reader makes from the clues given in the selection. In "The Story of an Hour," the reader can surmise that Mrs. Mallard's sister and Richards do not think she is strong enough to hear the news of her husband's presumed death.

Journalistic Questions: Reporter's questions used to identify the main points of the article: who, what, when, where, how, why. Journalistic questions are useful in analyzing literary works.

Key Words: The words or phrases that focus on the main idea of a writing assignment. For example, if you are writing about the benefits of a college education, the key words should be *benefits* and *college education*.

Literary Analysis: A paper in which the writer discusses, critiques, interprets, or evaluates literature. A literary analysis allows the writer to look at specific parts of the written work so that the entire work can be better understood and appreciated. In this text, you will find questions to answer to help you analyze fiction, nonfiction, and poetry.

Literature: A work or piece of writing that is written during a certain era in history that often relates to the social and political mores and experiences of both the writer and the reader of that period.

Narrative Writing: The telling of a story, factual or fictional, about what happened to either the writer or to someone else. Essays can be purely narrative, in which the writers record significant events in their lives or in history. Narratives can also be used in introductory paragraphs and to develop body paragraphs.

Organizational Pattern of Writing: The form or method that writers use to develop an essay. Organizational patterns include argumentation, causal analysis, classification, comparison/contrast, definition, exemplification, description, narration, and process analysis. Many essays are combination of patterns.

Point of View: The author's choice of narration for a work of literature. The narrator of a short story or poem may use first-person pronouns, which include *I, we, me, us, my, mine, our, ours.* Sometime in an essay, the author will tell the story in first person; in other words, the narrator is recounting the story as he or she lived it or understood it. For example, in Unit Two, the student essay *The Time I Realized I Hated Fishing* is written in first person. Third-person objective refers to narrators who report the events as a newspaper writer would. The story or the essay is written without the author's having the ability to look into the minds of the characters. Third-person omniscient refers to a narrator in fiction who can look into the minds of the characters or some of the characters. Third-person pronouns include *he, she, it, they, him, her, them, his, her, hers, its, their, theirs.* The point of view determines how much information the reader learns about the characters.

Process Analysis: A pattern of development in which the author gives an explanation on either how something is made or how something occurred. A process paper is organized in chronological order and should include transitions that take the reader from one step to another.

Purpose: The author's rationale, or reason, for writing a piece of literature. All written material should have a purpose. A general purpose will be to entertain, persuade, or inform. The excerpts from the Jacques Lajonie correspondence in Unit Two are written to inform the reader of the writer's experiences. During the composing process, writers must determine the purpose of their assignments. This purpose is generally expressed in the thesis statement of the paper.

Reading Method: Style, or type, of reading that may include reading with a finger running across the line, lip movements, vocal utterances, and nonvocalized throat muscle movements (subvocalization). Some readers use a word-by-word method rather than a phrasal clustering method.

Sensory Detail: A reference to using descriptive language to convey what the author wants the reader to hear, taste, touch, feel, and smell. Sensory details add to the understanding and enjoyment of all forms of literature because the reader can identify with the experiences.

Subvocalization: Discreet body movement used when reading that may include lip movement, vocal utterance, muscle movement, or word for word.

Surface Reading: On-the-line reading that includes the obvious details. The reader can answer the questions who, what, when, and where, and how from surface reading.

Telegraphic Sentences: Short sentence forms. These sentence forms are similar to cell phone text messages, with articles and other nonessential words omitted.

Theme: The message or underlying idea that an author weaves throughout the piece of literature. Universal themes of literature include, but are not limited to, greed, love, abandonment, fulfillment, realization of goals and dreams, oppression, and regret.

Thesaurus: A book of synonyms, antonyms, and related words. A thesaurus is an excellent tool for writers. It can help the writer choose the correct word for a sentence and helps with the development of vocabulary. However, writers must be careful about the choices they make in substituting words and consider shades of meaning, or the connotation intended.

Tone: The feeling the author conveys about the subject and expresses through the denotation and connotation of words, the details chosen, the dialogue of the characters in the narrative, and sometimes, in fiction, through the names the author gives the characters. Tone can be considered the attitude of the writer toward the subject. The author's overall attitude toward the subject can be positive or negative. The specific tone of the work can be serious, humorous, informative, sarcastic, persuasive, or factual.

Transitional Devices: Expressions that take the reader from one part of the writing to another. Transitional expressions may be used to introduce time elements, to show comparison or contrast, to introduce new ideas or to add additional information, and to show direction. Transitional expressions used to indicate time include *after, after a while, afterward, as soon as, again, always, at first, at last, at that time, at the same time, before, during, earlier, finally, first, immediately, in the meantime, in the past, lately, later, meanwhile, now, presently, second, simultaneously, since, so far, soon, subsequently, then, until, when, while.* Transitional phrases that are used to show comparison and contrast include *on the contrary, contrastively, notwithstanding, but, however, nevertheless, in spite of, in contrast, yet, on one hand, on the other hand, rather, or, nor, conversely, at the same time, while* ________________, *despite*________________. Transitional phrases used to introduce new ideas or to offer explanation include *for example, to illustrate, such as, for instance, first, second, third.* Transitional devices used to show direction include phrases like *to the left, across the room, in front of, behind, north, south, east, west.*

Writing Process: The method of writing a paragraph or essay that includes planning, writing, revising, reviewing, and editing. Successful writers know how to generate ideas on a topic, plan their papers, write them, and revise them.

Unit 2

American Foundations

If you would not be forgotten as soon as you are dead and rotten, either write things worth reading, or do things worth the writing.

—BENJAMIN FRANKLIN

American settlers of all generations have a story to tell. What story is being told in this image? What image would you choose to narrate your story? Based on your selection, what story will you tell?

Certain icons become a part of the foundation of the country. The actress Marilyn Monroe and the artist Andy Warhol have gained their places in the fabric of America. What story does each one tell about America? How do icons become a part of a cultural foundation?

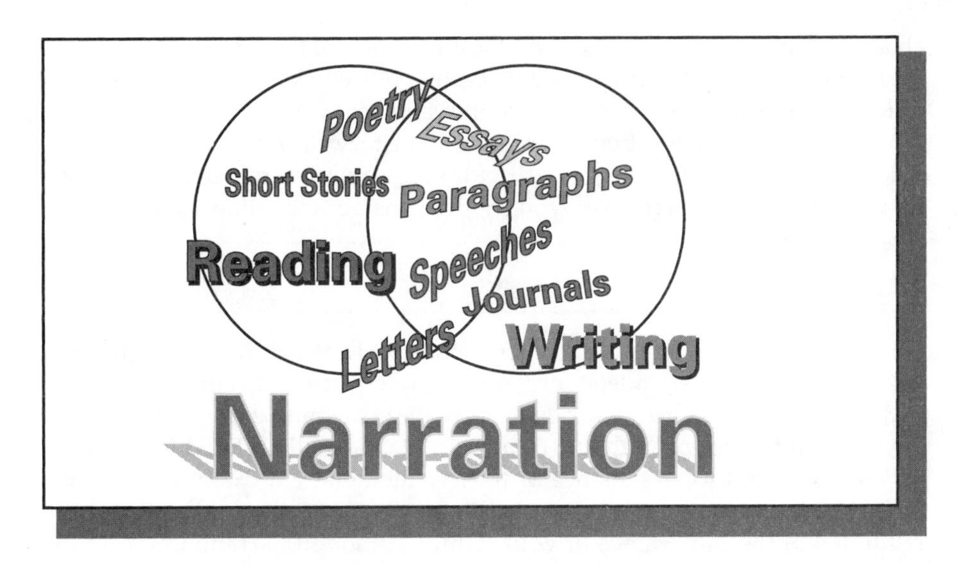

Purpose of Unit:

- *To understand the pattern of narration as it relates to reading comprehension and narrative writing*

Idioms for a New Nation

Review the American idioms below. Discuss their meaning. Apply these idioms to life in early America, to an event in your early childhood, or to life today.

Easier said than done.
If at first you don't succeed,
try, try again.
Many hands make light the work.
Nothing ventured, nothing gained.
When in Rome, do as the Romans do.
The streets are paved with gold.
Tall oaks grow from little acorns.
Where there's a will, there's a way.

Narration: Points to Consider

Narrative writing is telling a story, a story about what happened to either the writer or to someone else. Whenever the writer's purpose is to relate the order of events in a story, either as fact or fiction, the author is using the narrative pattern of writing. This method of writing may be recognized in essays, short stories, fables, reflective journal writing, travel journals, personal letters, poetry, speeches, and novels. Generally, the story is told in chronological order so that the audience will understand the order of events. Survivors of an earthquake tell what happened when, during, and after the quake. Friends tell each other about applying for a new job, taking their children to kindergarten for the first time, and resolving a conflict with a family member or a co-worker. A college student takes a trip to another country and e-mails her friends and family about the flight, the lost baggage, and the adventures of the first day. Maybe you are keeping a personal journal telling about your experiences your first year of college—your classes, your fellow students, and how you feel about these experiences. To answer a question on an exam in history class, you must relate the events that led to September 11. All of these examples are narratives. When reading and writing narratives, you should consider the following points.

Purpose

Narratives inform, entertain, and even persuade. Travel narratives, such as the Jacques Lajonie correspondence excerpts, are often written to inform the reader of the writer's experiences. Academic narrative essays and paragraphs are usually written to support a theme or a main idea, usually related in either an implied or stated topic sentence or thesis statement. For example, you may write about your experience of nearly drowning to show how you were reminded of the importance of your family. Although narration may be the main pattern in a piece of writing, it is also often used for support. In an argumentative essay, for instance, the author may use narration in the introduction to get the reader's attention or in the body to support the argument. To illustrate her argument that children need to learn American history, Lynne Cheney in the Constitution Day speech narrates the stories of three early Americans who fought for change.

Point of View

First person (*I, we, me, us, my, mine, our, ours*) is generally used in narration, but not always. If you are the writer and are writing about something that happened to you, then you will probably narrate your story in first person. However, if you are writing about something that happened to someone else, then you may choose to write in third person (*he, she, it, they, him, her, them, his, her, hers, its, their, theirs*).

In a poem or a short story, an author may tell his story in first person, third-person objective, or omniscient (all knowing). The point of view determines how much information the reader is given.

Read the first paragraph of the short story "The Tell-Tale Heart" by Edgar Allen Poe. In this story the narrator is a character who tries to convince his audience that he is not mad, only nervous. The reader immediately understands that even though the narrator claims to be only nervous and not mad, he is, indeed, insane and cannot be trusted to tell the "whole story."

> TRUE!—Nervous—very, very dreadfully nervous I had been and am; but why will you say that I am mad? The disease had sharpened my senses—not destroyed—not dulled them. Above all was the sense of hearing acute. I heard all things in the heaven and in the earth. I heard many things in hell. How, then, am I mad? Hearken! and observe how healthily—how calmly I can tell you the whole story.

TONE

The tone, how the author feels about the subject, is expressed through the denotation and connotation of words, the details the author chooses to include, the dialogue of the characters in the narrative, and sometimes, in fiction, through the names the author gives the characters. For example, notice the names of the characters in Peter Blue Cloud's short story "Waterbugs." How do the names contribute to the tone of the selection? The purpose of the narrative also determines the tone. In an academic narrative (for instance, a narrative reporting the founding a city), the tone is usually objective. However, a personal narrative is usually more subjective and may reflect how the author feels about the subject. The tone will show the author's anger, his or her sarcasm, support, and sense of humor. In other words, there are as many tones as there are attitudes.

INFERENCE

Often in narratives, the reader must use clues to determine an underlying theme or a deeper meaning of the writing. In other words, the reader must infer the author's meanings from hints and suggestions. As a reader, you must be alert to these clues the author gives, but as a writer of a narrative, you will need to plan these clues and place them strategically in your writing. Comedians often use inference in the punch lines of their jokes. Recall a time when you did not immediately get the meaning of a joke. Suddenly, the implication strikes your mind and you "get it." That is inference in practice.

ORDER OF SENTENCES

Although there may be flashbacks, narrative paragraphs and essays are usually written in chronological or time order. Often the order of sentences depends on the purpose of the writing. In fiction and in personal narratives, the author often uses flashbacks to get the reader's attention and help the reader understand the story. Historical accounts, on the other hand, are usually written in strict chronological order. Read the following account of the discovery of the Bay of San Francisco taken from *The Beginnings of San Francisco* (www.zpub.com/sf50/hbbeg1.htm) and notice how the events are chronologically placed.

> In the beginning of the year 1769, Don José de Galvez, visitador general of Spain and member of the council of the Indies, sent an expedition under command of Don Gaspar de Portolá to take possession of and fortify the ports of San Diego and Monterey in Alta California. The expedition consisted of two sea and two land divisions with the rendezvous at San Diego Bay. By the first of July 1769, the divisions were assembled at San Diego and on the 14th, the march to Monterey began. On the last day of September, the command reached Monterey Bay, but failing to recognize it from the description furnished them, passed on and discovered the bay of San Francisco. The expedition then returned

> to San Diego, and in the spring of 1770, another attempt was made and Monterey was reached on May 24th. This time they recognized the bay and on June 3, 1770, the presidio and mission of San Cárlos Borromeo de Monterey were founded with appropriate ceremonies.

The dates and events must be organized in this manner to maintain the logical organization of the thought.

Transitional Devices Used in Narrative Writing

Transitional devices are important in narration because they help the reader understand the order of events. As a reader, it is important to notice the transitional words and use them as a guide to understanding the order of events. Thus as a writer, you must use them correctly so that the reader easily understands what happened first, next, and last as well as the events that happened simultaneously.

Transitional expressions used to indicate time include *after, after a while, afterward, as soon as, again, always, at first, at last, at that time, at the same time, before, during, earlier, finally, first, immediately, in the meantime, in the past, lately, later, meanwhile, now, presently, second, simultaneously, since, so far, soon, subsequently, then, until, when, while.*

Verb Usage

A narrative tells of an event or events that happen in the past, so past tense is generally used for narrative writing. However, sometimes a tense change is necessary so that the reader understands that the author is adding a flashback or is reflecting on what he or she has learned from the experience. Thus, in reading and writing, paying attention to verb tense is important. Occasionally, a story that actually happened in the past is deliberately told in the present tense in order to add a sense of immediacy. Have you ever told a story and said, "So, here I am, minding my own business and suddenly . . . "? Your story happened in the past, but you unconsciously pull your listeners into the story by using present tense.

The following excerpt comes from Chapter One of the novel *The Secret Life of Bees* by Sue Monk Kidd. In this novel, Monk uses the main character Lily Owens to tell the story of what Lily remembers about her mother's death and how it affected her life. Notice how the narrator tells her story in past tense but then changes to present tense when telling how she feels about her experience she has narrated.

THE SECRET LIFE OF BEES—UNIT 1

> At night I would lie in bed and watch the show, how bees squeezed through the cracks of my bedroom wall and flew circles around the room, making that propeller sound, a high-pitched *zzzzzz* that hummed along my skin. I watched their wings shining like bits of chrome in the dark and felt the longing build in my chest. The way

those bees flew, not even looking for a flower, just flying for the feel of the wind, split my heart down its seam.

During the day I heard them tunneling through the walls of my bedroom, sounding like a radio tuned to static in the next room, and I imagined them in there turning the walls into honeycombs, with honey seeping out for me to taste.

The bees came the summer of 1964, the summer I turned fourteen and my life went spinning off into a whole new orbit, and I mean *whole new orbit.* Looking back on it now, I want to say the bees were sent to me. I want to say they showed up like the angel Gabriel appearing to the Virgin Mary, setting events in motion I could never have guessed. I know it's presumptuous to compare my small life to hers, but I have reason to believe she wouldn't mind: I will get to that. Right now, it's enough to say that despite everything that happened that summer, I remain tender toward the bees.

Organization

Narrative essays and paragraphs usually are like all academic writing in that there will be a definite introduction, body, and conclusion. A narrative paragraph will usually have the topic sentence at the beginning of the paragraph that tells the main idea of the narrative—the reason that the narrative is being told. The body of the paragraph will tell the story that supports the topic sentence. The last sentence will be a concluding sentence that reinforces the topic sentence. In a narrative essay, the introduction will usually give background information about the story that is being told and will contain the thesis or main idea of the essay. The body paragraphs will actually tell the story, the events that make up your story. Generally, you will need to start a new body paragraph when you introduce a change of setting or a new event in the series of events that make up your story. In the concluding paragraph of your essay, you can summarize the story and actually come to a conclusion about the story. For instance, you may want to tell what you learned from the event or why the event is significant to you.

Paragraph Format for Narration

Topic/Subject ______________________

Point of View ______________________

Audience ______________________

Purpose ______________________

Title ______________________
(capital letter on first and last word and all main words)

Topic Sentence (the point of the narrative) ______________

Sequence of Events

Time Frame of Narrative (Ex: 3 hours, 24 hours, 2 days) ________

The number of events depends on your story.

Event One	Details of Event One
______________	______________________________
	______________________________
Event Two	Details of Event Two
______________	______________________________
	______________________________
Final event in story	Details of Final Event
______________	______________________________
	______________________________

Concluding sentence (summary of points, lesson learned) ________

____

Essay Format for Narration

Topic/Subject ____________________

Point of View ____________________

Audience ____________________

Purpose/Focus ____________________

Title ____

Thesis Sentence (the point of the narrative) ____________________

Introductory Paragraph

Information Needed for Introductory Paragraph ______________

____

Body Paragraphs

(With a "time-when assignment," consider starting a new paragraph when the time or action changes. If you are telling more than one story in your essay, change paragraphs with each new story and include a clear topic sentence.)

Sequence of Events

Time Frame of Story ______________________________

The number of events depends on your story.

Event One	Details of Event One
______________	______________________
	______________________
	______________________
Event Two	Details of Event Two
______________	______________________
	______________________
	______________________
Event Three	Details of Event Three
______________	______________________
	______________________
	______________________
Final event in story	Details of Final Event
______________	______________________
	______________________
	______________________

Concluding Paragraph (summary of points, lesson learned) ____

____

Make copies of this map to chart your narrative reading and writing assignments.

Map for Narration

Introduction

Main Idea—Focus of Narrative:

Time Line of Story

When analyzing narration, put the main events above the line and the details of the story below the line.

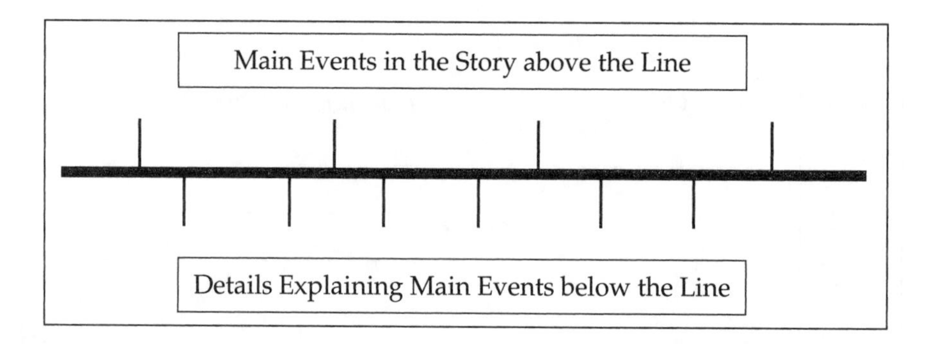

Conclusion

Lesson Learned—Concluding Statement

Key Words ____________________

Synonyms for Key Words ____________________

Transitional Words ____________________

Strong Verbs ____________________

Narrative Worksheet

1. Survey the assignment and choose your topic. Do one of the prewriting assignments discussed in the introduction of the text.
2. Question by answering the 5 W's + H about your narrative. Who? What? Where? When? Why? How?
3. Map your essay or paragraph. When you use the time line to chart your story, remember that in your "time-when" assignments the time frame should be a short period of time, not your entire lifetime! Put major events above the timeline. Put minor events and details below the time line.

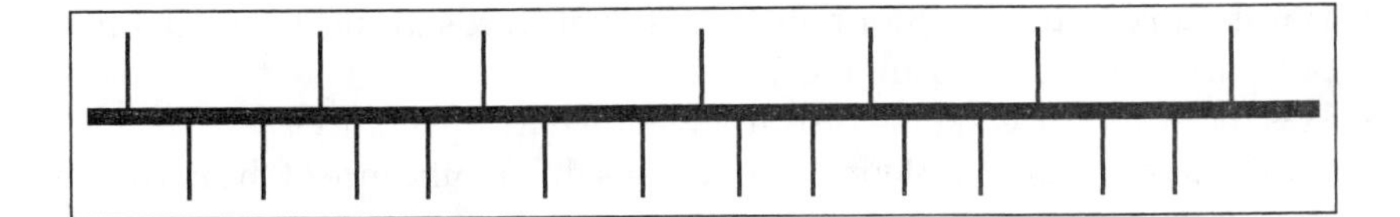

4. Relate or tell your narrative to your writing group. After you have finished, group members should ask you to clarify the parts of the story that are unclear, and they should use reporter's questions to pry you for more details.
5. Record (write) the first draft of your essay or paragraph.
6. Read your narrative aloud to a student partner. As you read, the partner should listen for understanding and jot down any questions. These questions may be about parts of your writing that are unclear. For example, if you are writing about your great uncle from Louisiana who founded a business in California, the reader may ask you how your uncle got from Louisiana to California. The questions may also relate to details of the story. For example, how old was your uncle when he founded the business? What kind of business was it? Make sure to answer reporter's questions.
7. Revise your essay, taking into account the questions that you and your peer editors asked about your paper. Add the needed details, but check to make sure you are staying on the subject.
8. Review your revised paper with your partner and answer Questions for Review.
9. Reflect upon the comments of your peers and make needed changes.
10. Reread your paper, checking for grammatical errors. Read your paper from top to bottom and from bottom to top. Reading your paper in reverse helps you to read what you wrote, not what you meant to write! As you read your paper, check carefully for consistent tense, correct sentence structure, and correct punctuation of dialogue.
11. Read your paper aloud.
12. Write your final draft!

Questions for Review

Paragraph Assignment

- What is the topic sentence?
- Does the topic sentence tell the main idea of the paragraph, the reason for telling the story?
- Is the story told in chronological order?
- Are there any parts of the story that are confusing?

- Has the author used appropriate transitional words to take the reader from one part of the story to another?
- Has the author used key words to give the narrative unity?
- Is there a concluding sentence that explains the significance of the narrative?

Essay Assignment

The Introductory Paragraph

- Does the introduction make you want to read the essay?
- What is the focus of the essay?

The Body Paragraphs

- Is the story told in chronological order?
- If there is a flashback, is it easy to understand?
- Are there any parts of the story that are confusing?
- Has the author used appropriate transitional words to take the reader from one part of the story to another?
- Has the author used key words to give the narrative unity?
- Has the author used strong verbs to tell the story?

The Conclusion

- Does the author come to a conclusion about his or her story? (Does the conclusion tell what was learned from the experience or how his or her life was affected by the experience?)

Sentence Structure Errors

When writing narratives, it is easy to let one sentence run into another, resulting in comma splices and fused sentences. Comma splices are two sentences joined only by a comma. Fused sentences are like comma splices except the two sentences are joined together (or run together) without any type of punctuation to separate the sentences.

Fused Sentence:

I pretended to have fun really I was miserable.

Comma Splice:

I pretended to have fun, really I was miserable.

These sentence structure errors can be corrected in six ways:

1. Two Sentences: I pretended to have fun. Really I was miserable.
2. Compound Sentence (Two independent clauses joined with a comma and a coordinating conjunction)—I pretended to have fun, but really I was miserable.
3. Compound Sentence (Two independent clauses joined with a semicolon)—I pretended to have fun; really I was miserable.

4. Compound Sentence (Two independent clauses joined with a semicolon, a transitional word, and a comma)—I pretended to have fun; however, really I was miserable.
5. Complex Sentence (Dependent Clause followed by an independent clause)—Even though I pretended to have fun, really I was miserable.
6. Complex Sentence: (Independent Clause followed by a dependent clause)—I was miserable even though I pretended to have fun.

Direct and Indirect Quotations

Dialogue can add an important dimension to narratives. Authors use dialogue to set the tone, develop the characters, and tell the story. In "Waterbugs," Peter Blue Cloud uses the conversation of Coyote and Fox Young Man to tell his story of "how stories are born." You may want to try using dialogue in some of your personal narrative assignments and in assignments that call for writing a short story or a fable. Although dialogue is effective in personal narration and in fiction and fables, it is usually not used when writing historical narratives.

When you do use conversation or dialogue, you want to punctuate the quotations correctly and discern between direct and indirect quotations. Direct quotations tell the exact words of a speaker. Place quotation marks around a direct quote. Indirect quotations tell what the speaker said, but the exact words are not used. Do not put quotation marks around indirect quotations.

Direct Quote:

Fox Young Man looked at Coyote. "Coyote, I think you are making it up," he said.

Indirect Quote:

Fox Young Man said that he thought Coyote was making it up.

(Notice how the pronouns change with an indirect quote.)

Verb Tense

When you are writing narratives, be careful to be consistent in tense when you are telling your story. Look at the following excerpt from a student essay. Can you find the tense error?

> After we ate our sandwiches, my dad says happily, "Are you ready for the second half of our adventure?"

Corrected Sentence:

After we ate out sandwiches, my dad **said** happily, "Are you ready for the second half of our adventure?"

READING BEFORE WRITING

Excerpt from "Constitution Day"—Fairfax County (VA) Public Library, Sept. 17, 2002

Lynne V. Cheney

Lynne Cheney is a historian and the wife of Vice-President Dick Cheney. She has spent her adult life encouraging the study of history. A noted speaker, she has made many presentations on the importance of knowing history, both American and family. Where does Cheney begin the narration in her speech? What is the purpose of using narration in this speech?

Being a grandmother has made me focus more **intensely** than ever on children and especially on their need for an education that provides them essential knowledge and skills. They need to know how to read and do math. They need the basic skills that will help them to pursue knowledge in many fields.

And there is one course of study that I particularly want to make the case for tonight: the study of history and American history in particular. If we want our children to become responsible adults who find meaning in their lives then we need to help them understand that they are operating in a stream of time, that the choices that they have before them are in large part the result of choices others made yesterday, and that the choices they make will help determine decisions still others will make tomorrow. "We are caught in an inescapable network of **mutuality,** tied in a single garment of destiny," Martin Luther King, Jr. once observed. Realizing that the network extends back in time as well as forward is part of leading a responsible life, part of understanding that deeds have consequences, some of them amazingly far-reaching.

Think how powerfully every one of us has been affected by the actions of a small, rather shy man named James Madison. Born 251 years ago into the energetic and horse-loving society of the Virginia **Piedmont,** he was not an athletic boy and probably spent a good deal of time in his younger years reading, first books at home and then in his schoolmaster's library. Early on, he learned the power of books to enlarge experience. He learned the power of the printed word to teach about times and places one could never otherwise know.

During his college years, spent at Princeton, Madison **encountered** more books than he had ever seen before and well-trained minds to test himself against. In a state of fine intellectual **frenzy,** he took a double class load and completed the required course of study in two years. After that he found an excuse to stay an extra six months, but finally, in 1772, at age twenty-one, he returned home.

Back in Virginia, he fell into deep depression. Some scholars speculate that it was brought on by a seizure, one that Madison thought was **epileptic.** Others suggest he was troubled by the death of a college friend. It may also have happened that he had trouble **decompressing** after Princeton. What use were his studies in history and philosophy, he may have asked himself as he considered his family's well-managed farm. What spur was there to probe deeper and learn more?

The American Revolution gave him in an **all-absorbing** purpose. He became a politician, though a more unlikely one is hard to imagine. He was small, no more than five and a half feet tall. He was shy and guarded around strangers. He was not a brilliant **orator.** But what he lacked in **charisma,** he made up for in brainpower—and in his willingness to study and prepare.

Once independence was won and the young country began to take stock of itself, many thoughtful people concluded that the **Articles of Confederation** did not provide a strong enough national government. As early as 1783, Madison began an intensive course of reading to assess the alternatives. He implored his friend Thomas Jefferson, then in Paris, to send him books. Jefferson responded by sending more than two hundred volumes across the Atlantic.

Madison read **Plutarch, Polybius,** and **Montesquieu.** He studied ancient governments and modern ones, and he pondered the lessons they taught: a republic was usually small, highly constricted in the area it covered. A republic was usually fragile, easy to tip over into **despotism.**

By the time of the Constitutional Convention in 1787, Madison had arrived at a plan for a republic that might both extend and endure. His theories took form in the Virginia Plan, the plan that would become the basis for the convention's deliberations. Madison thus shaped the agenda for the delegates and then went on to steer their debates, speaking more than 160 times, "always . . . the best informed man at any point," one of his fellow delegates wrote. Two hundred and fifteen years ago today, on September 17, 1787, the United States Constitution, a document that Madison, more than any other person, was responsible for, was signed in Philadelphia.

Douglass Adair, a scholar of the founding period, called the course of study that Madison undertook before the Constitutional Convention "probably the most fruitful piece of scholarly research ever carried out by an American." It is a fair assessment, a modest one even. The Constitution, bearing Madison's mark more than any other's, was crucial not just to this country, but to the history of the world. Nation after nation would use our Constitution as a model. Nation after nation would look to the freedom that our Constitution makes possible for inspiration in their own struggles for liberty.

The astonishing thing about Madison's influence is that he exercised it without ever traveling very far from where he was born. He never saw Europe.

He never saw most of this continent. If one were to draw a rectangle six or seven hundred miles long and four or five hundred miles wide, it would encompass entirely the area of which Madison had first-hand knowledge.

Within that rectangle, he was born, lived, and died. And from within it, using books as his lever, he managed to move the world.

Stories like Madison's—and our history has an abundance of them—should be familiar to our children. They should know about the founders and understand the ideas and ideals on which our country is built. And they should know about other men and women who have made our country what it is. They should know the story of a man who was born in 1818, shortly after James Madison's second term as president ended. Born into slavery, this man was separated from his mother while he was still an infant. She died when he was very young, but as an adult he remembered that a few times she had walked many miles from a distant farm to which she had been sent so that she could spend a few hours with him before he went to sleep. And then she would walk back the many miles so that she could be in the fields at sunrise. He had harsh masters, but also, when he was very young, a kind mistress who taught him his letters. When her husband discovered what she was doing he forbade her to continue on the grounds that education would "unfit" the little boy, whose name was Frederick Bailey, for life as a slave. But Frederick would not be stopped. He made friends with the white youngsters he encountered in the streets while he was running errands, and he converted them into teachers. He got hold of the *Columbian Orator,* a textbook of the time, and read it again and again. He practiced writing on fences and walls and on the pavement and in the spaces left in the copybook of a white child in the household.

By the time Frederick Bailey had reached young manhood and escaped to the North, he was capable of great **eloquence.** He took a new name—Frederick Douglass—and with powerful speeches setting forth the outrages that he and others he knew had suffered, he brought home the cruel truths of slavery. Frederick Douglass did what American heroes have often done. He pointed out that we had fallen short of our founding ideals and helped set us on a path toward being a better country.

Or consider a contemporary of Douglass's, a woman whose life was **animated** by the quest for justice. Born into a wealthy family in New York, she had five sisters and five brothers. But children often died young in the nineteenth century and only one of her brothers survived to adulthood. When he died at the age of twenty, the father of the family was **devastated,** and the girl, Elizabeth, remembered her whole life crawling onto his lap and trying to comfort him. "At length," she wrote years later, "he heaved a deep sigh and said, 'Oh, my daughter, I wish you were a boy!' " And to her grieving father she replied, "I will try to be all my brother was."

And she did exactly that. "She succeeded in what were then considered masculine fields," her biographer Elisabeth Griffith observes. "She won second place in the Johnstown Academy Greek competition, she learned to jump four-foot fences, and she became a skilled debater." But rather than being pleased, her father began to worry. In his eyes—and in the eyes of the world at the time—she was becoming entirely too good at undertakings that were suitable only for males.

And so Elizabeth Cady Stanton decided to change the world, and she had the intellect and **analytical** skills to do it. For fifty years she was the driving force behind the movement to improve the lot of American women. She argued, among other things, for property rights, the right to attend college, the right to participate in athletics, and the right to vote. She spoke and wrote and **agitated,** and, I should note, raised seven children. And although she died before all her ambitions for women were realized—American women's right to vote would not be recognized until nearly two decades after her death—Elizabeth Cady Stanton, like Frederick Douglass, moved the country along the path to justice.

Our country's history is full of stories of men and women working to make our country great and greater still. Our children should know these stories so that they can take up the task of making America a place where every person fully experiences his or her God-given rights to life, liberty, and the pursuit of happiness.

And notice the other lesson to be taken away from the lives of James Madison, Frederick Douglass, Elizabeth Cady Stanton, and so many other Americans, and that is the crucial role that knowledge plays in a life of leadership. People who have improved the world have generally used the tools that education provides in order to build a better society. If schools were forbidden or nonexistent or limited, these men and women took up their own education because they understood that knowledge is not only necessary for daily life, but crucial for those who would change minds and win hearts. This, surely, is an important lesson for our children. . . .

Glossary for "Constitution Day"

in·tense (ĭn-tĕns') *adj.* **in·tens·er, in·tens·est**

1. Possessing or displaying a distinctive feature to an extreme degree: *the intense sun of the tropics.*
2. Extreme in degree, strength, or size: *intense heat.*
3. Involving or showing strain or extreme effort: *intense concentration.*
4. a. Deeply felt; profound: *intense emotion.*
   b. Tending to feel deeply: *an intense writer.*

[Middle English, from Old French, from Latin intēnsus, *stretched, intent,* from past participle of intendere, *to stretch, intend.*]

in·tense'ly *adv.* **in·tense'ness** *n.*

Synonyms: *intense, fierce, vehement, violent*
These adjectives mean "of an extreme kind": *intense fear; fierce pride; vehement dislike; violent rage.*

mu·tu·al (myo͞o'cho͞o-əl) *adj.*

1. Having the same relationship each to the other: *mutual predators.*
2. Directed and received by each toward the other; reciprocal: *mutual respect.*
3. Possessed in common: *mutual interests.*
4. Of, relating to, or in the form of mutual insurance.

   n.

   A mutual fund.

[French mutuel, from Old French, from Latin mūtuus, *borrowed.*]

mu'tu·al'i·ty (-ăl'ĭ-tē) *n.* **mu'tu·al·ly** *adv.*

Pied·mont (pēd'mŏnt')

A historical region of northwest Italy bordering on France and Switzerland. Occupied by Rome in the first century B.C., it passed to Savoy in the eleventh century and was the center of the Italian Risorgimento after 1814.

1. A plateau region of the eastern United States extending from New York to Alabama between the Appalachian Mountains and the Atlantic coastal plain.

Pied'mon·tese' (-tēz', -tēs') *adj. & n.*

en·coun·ter (ĕn-koun'tər) *n.*

1. A meeting, especially one that is unplanned, unexpected, or brief: *a chance encounter in the park.*
2. a. A hostile or adversarial confrontation; a contest: *a tense naval encounter.*
   b. An often violent meeting; a clash.

v. **en·coun·tered, en·coun·ter·ing, en·coun·ters**
v. tr.

1. To meet, especially unexpectedly; come upon: *encountered an old friend on the street.*
2. To confront in battle or contention.
3. To come up against: *encounter numerous obstacles.*

v. intr.

To meet, especially unexpectedly.

[Middle English encountre, from Old French, from encontrer, *to meet*, from Late Latin incontrāre: Latin in-, *in*; see **en-** + Latin contrā, *against*; see kom in Indo-European Roots.]

fren·zy (frĕn'zē) *n. pl.* **fren·zies**

1. A state of violent mental agitation or wild excitement.
2. Temporary madness or delirium.
3. A mania; a craze.

   tr.v. **fren·zied, fren·zy·ing, fren·zies**

   To drive into a frenzy.

[Middle English frenesie, from Old French, from Medieval Latin phrenēsia, from Latin phrenēsis, back-formation from phrenēticus, *delirious.*]

ep·i·lep·sy (ĕp'ə-lĕp'sē) *n. pl.* **ep·i·lep·sies**

Any of various neurological disorders characterized by sudden recurring attacks of motor, sensory, or psychic malfunction with or without loss of consciousness or convulsive seizures.

[French épilepsie, from Latin epilēpsia, from Greek epilēpsis, from epilambanein, epilēp-, *to lay hold of*: epi-, *epi-* + lambanein, *to seize.*]

de·com·press (dē'kəm-prĕs') *v.* **de·com·pressed, de·com·press·ing, de·com·press·es** *v. tr.*

1. To relieve of pressure or compression.
2. To bring (a person exposed to conditions of increased pressure) gradually back to normal atmospheric pressure.

v. intr.

1. To adjust to normal atmospheric conditions after being exposed to increased pressure.
2. Informal. To relax: *decompressed after 12 hours of driving.*

ab·sorb (əb-sôrb', -zôrb') *tr. v.* **ab·sorbed, ab·sorb·ing, ab·sorbs**

1. To take (something) in through or as through pores or interstices.
2. To occupy the full attention, interest, or time of; engross.
3. To retain (radiation or sound, for example) wholly, without reflection or transmission.
4. To take in; assimilate: *immigrants who were absorbed into the social mainstream.*
5. To learn; acquire: "Matisse absorbed the lesson and added to it a new language of color" (Peter Plagen).
6. To receive (an impulse) without echo or recoil: *a fabric that absorbs sound; a bumper that absorbs impact.*
7. To assume or pay for (a cost or costs).
8. To endure; accommodate: *couldn't absorb the additional hardships.*
9. To use up; consume: *The project has absorbed all of our department's resources.*

[Middle English, *to swallow up*, from Old French absorber, from Latin absorbēre: ab-, *away*; see **ab-** + sorbēre, *to suck.*]

ab·sorb'a·bil'i·ty *n.*; **ab·sorb'a·ble** *adj.*; **ab·sorb'ed·ly** *adv.*; **ab·sorb'er** *n.*; **ab·sorb'ing·ly** *adv.*

Plu·tarch (plōō'tärk'), A.D. 46?–120?.
Greek biographer and Neo-Platonist philosopher. He wrote *Parallel Lives*, a collection of paired biographies of famous Greek and Roman figures that Shakespeare used as source material for his Roman plays.

Plu·tarch'an (-tär'kən) or **Plu·tarch'i·an** (-tär'kē-ən) *adj.*

Po·lyb·i·us (pə-lĭb'ē-əs), 200?–118? B.C.
Greek historian. Only five books of his forty-volume history of Rome are extant.

Mon·tes·quieu (mŏn'tə-skyōō', môN-tĕ-skyœ'), Baron de la Brede et de Montesquieu. Title of Charles de Secondat. 1689–1755.
French philosopher and jurist. An outstanding figure of the early French Enlightenment, he wrote the influential *Parisian Letters* (1721), a veiled attack on the monarchy and the *ancien régime*, and *The Spirit of the Laws* (1748), a discourse on government.

des·pot·ism (dĕs'pə-tĭz'əm) *n.*

1. Rule by or as if by a despot; absolute power or authority.
2. The actions of a despot; tyranny.

3. a. A government or political system in which the ruler exercises absolute power: "Kerensky has a place in history, of a brief interlude between despotisms" (William Safire).
   b. A state so ruled.

an·i·mat·ed (ăn'ə-mā'tĭd) *adj.*

1. Having life; alive.
2. Filled with activity, vigor, or spirit; lively.
3. Designed or constructed in the form of an animated cartoon.

an'i·mat'ed·ly *adv.*

dev·as·tate (dĕv'ə-stāt') *tr.v.* **dev·as·tat·ed, dev·as·tat·ing, dev·as·tates**

1. To lay waste; destroy.
2. To overwhelm; confound; stun: *was devastated by the rude remark.*

[Latin dēvāstāre, dēvāstāt-: dē-, *de-* + vāstāre, *to lay waste* (from vāstus, *empty, desolate.*).]

dev'as·tat'ing·ly *adv.;* **dev'as·ta'tion** *n.;* **dev'as·ta'tor** *n.*

an·a·lyt·ic (ăn'ə-lĭt'ĭk) or **an·a·lyt·i·cal** (-ĭ-kəl) *adj.*

1. Of or relating to analysis or analytics.
2. Dividing into elemental parts or basic principles.
3. Reasoning or acting from a perception of the parts and interrelations of a subject:
   "Many of the most serious pianists have turned toward more analytic playing, with a renewed focus on the architecture and ideas of music" (Annalyn Swan).
4. Expert in or using analysis, especially in thinking: *an analytic mind; an analytic approach.*
5. *Logic.* Following necessarily; tautologous: *an analytic truth.*
6. *Mathematics.*
   a. Using, subjected to, or capable of being subjected to a methodology involving algebra or other methods of mathematical analysis.
   b. Proving a known truth by reasoning from that which is to be proved.
7. *Linguistics.* Expressing a grammatical category by using two or more words instead of an inflected form.
8. Psychoanalytic.

[Medieval Latin analyticus, from Greek analutikos, from analûein, *to resolve.*]

an'a·lyt'i·cal·ly *adv.*

ag·i·tate (ăj'ĭ-tāt') *v.* **ag·i·tat·ed, ag·i·tat·ing, ag·i·tates**
v.tr.

1. To cause to move with violence or sudden force.
2. To upset; disturb: *was agitated by the alarming news.*
3. To arouse interest in (a cause, for example) by use of the written or spoken word; debate.

v. intr.

To stir up public interest in a cause: *agitate for a tax reduction.*

[Latin agitāre, agitāt- frequentative of agere, *to drive, do.*]
ag'i·tat'ed·ly (-tā'tĭd-lē) *adv.;* ag'i·ta'tive *adj.*

Reading Comprehension

Answer the following questions about Lynne Cheney's "Constitution Day" speech.

Word Meaning

Select the word from the glossary that best completes the sentences below.

1. The strong sense of __________ can be seen in the obvious behavioral links of identical twins.
2. The new students many new cultures __________ when they enrolled as freshmen in college.
3. The mother robin was in a state of __________ as humans viewed her newborn babies in their nest.
4. The citizens finally rebelled against the __________ exercised by the leader of their country.
5. The children suddenly demonstrated __________ behavior when the comedian entered their classroom.
6. The technician became so extremely __________ in the inner workings of his new computer that he worked until midnight.
7. After returning from a one-year tour of duty, the soldier had a problem with __________ to his old environment.

Literal Meaning

Mark the letter of the statement that best completes the meaning.

1. Lynne Cheney believes that children should learn more
   a. English.
   b. manners.
   c. history.
   d. writing.
2. James Madison's studies began with
   a. classroom lectures.
   b. books found at home.
   c. speeches.
   d. tutors.
3. Frederick Douglass learned his letters by
   a. studying with a lady of the house.
   b. befriending white children in the streets who became his tutors.
   c. writing on fences, walls, and the pavement.
   d. all of the above.
4. Elizabeth Cady Stanton argued for women's rights to
   a. wear high heels in public.
   b. write books.
   c. own property.
   d. learn to read.

5. Lynne Cheney states that leadership in every area of life requires above all
   a. knowledge.
   b. money.
   c. popularity.
   d. fame.
6. Place the following events in the life of Frederick Douglass in sequential order.
   _____ 1. Frederick Bailey changed his name to Frederick Douglass.
   _____ 2. Frederick Bailey was born into slavery in 1818.
   _____ 3. Frederick Bailey escaped to the North.
   _____ 4. When he was young, a kind mistress taught him his letters.
   _____ 5. With powerful speeches, he showed the cruel truths about slavery.
   _____ 6. Frederick Bailey was separated from his mother shortly after he was born.
   _____ 7. His speeches helped to set the country on a path toward justice.

Interpretive Meaning

Complete the questions with the response that best answers the statement.

1. Why does Lynne Cheney believe that children should learn American history?
   a. Because she is a grandmother.
   b. Because children need to understand that future decisions are based on past experiences.
   c. Because James Madison stated the importance of history in the Articles of Confederation.
   d. Because children spend too much time playing electronic games.
2. What does Cheney mean by the statement that students need to understand "that they are operating in the stream of time"?
   a. Students need to learn to read better.
   b. Students need to understand their place in history.
   c. Students need to memorize dates of important events.
   d. Students need to vote when old enough.
3. When Cheney says that "deeds have consequences, some of them amazingly far-reaching," she expresses the fact that
   a. James Madison knew that the airplane would be invented in the future.
   b. people need to travel overseas to learn.
   c. today's actions cause tomorrow's reactions.
   d. children should go to the library often.
4. The author narrates stories about the lives of three heroes from American history to show that
   a. she knows a lot about American history.
   b. people in history can teach important lessons, even after their deaths.
   c. students can become leaders.
   d. anyone can become rich.

5. James Madison became the fourth President of the United States because he
   a. was shy and lived on a farm.
   b. studied history and philosophy.
   c. possessed a knowledge of other governments that would help to shape the government of the young United States.
   d. thought that this job would cure his depression.
6. Douglas Adair called Madison's period of study before the Constitutional Convention "probably the most fruitful piece of scholarly research ever carried out by an American" because
   a. the information he gathered inspired other countries to search for liberty.
   b. he was proud of Madison's dedication to reading.
   c. Madison wanted to impress people so that they would elect him President.
   d. Madison wanted to consult with leaders of other countries to help them to write their constitutions.
7. Frederick Bailey probably changed his name to Frederick Douglass because
   a. he did not like the name Bailey.
   b. after his escape to the North, he wanted to develop a new identity.
   c. he was afraid of being discovered and murdered.
   d. he wanted to take his wife's last name.
8. Lynne Cheney thinks that if schools did not exist
   a. children would not be able to read.
   b. America would not exist today.
   c. people would search for other ways to learn.
   d. street violence would increase.
9. Elizabeth Cady Stanton decided to fight to change the world for women because
   a. her father wanted her to be a boy.
   b. she was a skilled debater.
   c. she believed that women could share in the operation of the country.
   d. she wanted to make her family proud of her.
10. What title would be most appropriate for this speech?
    a. "Yesterday, Today, Tomorrow"
    b. "A Grandmother's Passion"
    c. "A Fight for Freedom"
    d. "The Power of Knowledge"

Score: Number correct _____ out of _____

Writing Assignments

1. Journal Writing

Summary

Write a one-paragraph summary of the main ideas of Lynne Cheney's speech given on Constitution Day, September 17, 2002. Remember to start with a topic sentence that gives the main idea of her speech and tells the name of the speaker and the occasion. Follow with examples of how Cheney supported her main idea. You do not need to re-tell each narrative she tells. Instead summarize the main points. Write in third person. Do not tell your opinion of her speech.

Reaction

Write your opinion about the speech. Consider answering such questions as the following: Do you agree or disagree with Cheney? What did you think about the narratives that she used as examples? If you were giving the speech, what Americans would you include in your speech? Why do you think she chose the people she did? Are there lessons to be learned from your life or the lives of other family members that should be passed on to future generations?

2. ***Paragraph***
Write a narrative paragraph about a time when you, a member of your family, or a friend saw something that needed to be changed and changed it. Narrate the events that took place in order to implement the change.

3. ***Paragraph to Essay***
Use the narrative paragraph about change as the basis for your essay. Add an introduction that gets the reader's attention and gives the needed background information. Add a conclusion that tells how your life or the lives of others were affected by the change. You may need to expand your body paragraph into several paragraphs depending on the length of the story. Remember, the body paragraphs should tell your actual series of events. You may need to start a new paragraph when the action changes or when the setting changes.

4. ***Essay***
Write a narrative paragraph about three people in your family's history who should not be forgotten by future generations. For the controlling idea, make sure to have a single reason that these family members should not be forgotten. (Remember that in the "Constitution Day" speech, Cheney narrates stories of people who fought for positive change.) In the introduction, give the needed background information and end with a thesis statement. Write a body paragraph about each person. Write an interesting concluding paragraph that not only summarizes but also makes the reader consider the implications of your thesis.

Jacques Lajonie Lapeyre Correspondence . . . Excerpts

Jacques Lajonie (Lapeyre) lived with his wife Dorothée, his two children, and other family members, the Taupiers, in the Bordeaux, France, countryside at a chateau called Le Soulat until he was exiled from France in late 1816 as a result of his support of Napoleon. Before being injured and permanently discharged, he had been a Dragoon in Napoleon's army. A local law official falsely accused Lajonie of killing a gendarme, a policeman, because he did not like Lajonie's support of Napoleon. Most French Napoleonic exiles settled in other European countries, but Lajonie escaped from France on a ship bound for Philadelphia. He lived in the United States for twelve years before returning to France in March 1829. Over 200 original hand-written letters were recently found in the family archives of his descendants in Ste. Foy-La-Grande, France. Eric Saugera, a French historian, has written Arcola Road, *an historical account of this period based on these letters.* The Fighting Kentuckian *is a romanticized film version of this story starring John Wayne. As you read the letters, look for clues that present the tone of the author. What observations about early American life does Lajonie make that perhaps an American would overlook or that you might not have seen in a history book?*

Jacques Lajonie, *Philadelphia, Pennsylvania, early January, 1817*
To Pierre Taupier, *chateau of Le Soulac, Juillac, Gironde*

On January 3rd we entered Delaware Bay with the pilot we had with us since morning. On the 5th we entered the famous city of Philadelphia after a sea crossing of 55 days and 3 days spent leaving or entering a river.

. . . .

Philadelphia is a large beautiful city on the right bank of the Delaware about 30 leagues inland from the sea. It is one of the oldest cities of the United States, which have been independent for 42 years. It is laid out between two rivers that are perhaps one **league** apart at this place. It stretches along the Delaware and has a circumference of about five leagues. Its streets are very wide and very straight. They meet at right angles. They have names or numbers. Those parallel to the river are numbered and those perpendicular have names. The city itself is divided into two parts, North and South, which are added to the name or number of the streets so that one can find the location of the houses more easily. A large market divides Philadelphia in this way, perfectly well built along a very long and very wide street that goes through the center of the layout and divides it into two equal parts. The public buildings are very simple and do not come anywhere near European buildings, however they are quite elegant in their simplicity. All the houses are of red brick or painted wood. Almost all have marble foundations, doorjambs and window frames. And almost all have handsome steps with iron railings. There are different types according to people's taste. Both the exterior and the interior of the houses are kept extremely clean. The streets have the same merit: whatever the weather, one can walk without stepping into mud. The houses are no more than five stories tall and, in spite of the lightness of their construction, the red color of the bricks brings out their beauty at a certain distance. Seen close up, the white-painted mortar between the bricks gives the appearance of tiling and thus makes the architecture look quite good. Philadelphia's wharf is very convenient, sheltering ships from bad weather and ice and permitting them to unload without having to use boats. However, for all its advantages, Philadelphia loses quite a bit of its elegance for the following reason. Right near the various wharves that belong to different merchants, storehouses have been built that completely hide the facades of the houses which ornament the first street. Because of this disadvantage, the wharf is not at all pleasant to look at and is frequented only by merchants and **longshoremen.**

Order is kept in Philadelphia as it is in the entire United States of America: there are no policemen. Anyone has the right to arrest you if you are guilty, and in that case one rarely escapes! At night, in the cities of the United States, men are paid to see to public safety. They divide the city into sections to which are assigned as many watchman as are felt necessary to ensure the tranquility of each section. While they are looking out for criminals, they must also shout out, as they pass through the streets assigned to them: "It is such-and-such a time, the weather is good or bad, the night is dark or brightly moonlit." If they meet someone breaking the law of the land, they arrest him and bring him to the guardhouse where there is a head guard. The only arms they have are a stick and a large child's noisemaker that they whirl around rapidly when they need to call for reinforcements. Since all the streets are straight, one can often see some thirty of them appear within five minutes, arresting on their way any man who looks suspicious. Anyone who is arrested can get out of the guardhouse at once if he gives security or a certain sum of money. The next day he must appear before the mayor who is generally very honest and sensible.

. . .

Jacques Lajonie, *Philadelphia, January 17, 1817*
To Pierre Taupier-Letage, *chateau of Le Soulac, Juillac, Gironde*

The religions in the United States, as in Philadelphia which is their largest city, are all free and can also all furnish members for Congress. Now in this city there are ten or twelve of them. The Protestants who are the most numerous, the Catholics, the Jews, the Quakers, the Trembling Quakers, the Congregationalists, the Baptists, the Episcopalians, the Universalists, the Methodists, etc., etc. On Sundays, all the members of these sects are very religious. They abstain from all noisy pleasures. In some of these religions marriages are very mournful affairs and in others very joyous. Funerals are generally mournful. The closest relatives of the deceased are obliged to accompany him to his tomb;

all the other relatives and some family friends follow the procession on foot. The deceased, if he is of a good family, is in a black carriage hitched to two black horses. The carriages of the various persons who make up the procession follow that of the deceased in the strictest order.

The pleasures of the Americans are rather **monotonous.** However they do sometimes dance. Young men do not often attend social gatherings. They prefer to see beauties. In this way, they run no risk of losing public esteem, which could very well happen if they managed or simply tried to seduce a young lady, but even more a married woman. I cannot help laughing when I think of the diversity in the way of thinking of men on different continents.

Young ladies are extremely free in the entire United States of America and married women are generally model wives and mothers. On the other hand, I think that the husbands are most deserving.

•

Tables are rather nicely set in fine drawing rooms, but there are never any napkins, which are not used in the United States. The dishes are fairly good, but they must be eaten American style, that is, beginning with the best piece, as do priests. Woe to those who cling to their customs. I have been here only twelve days and I already know how to begin my meal by drinking beer at dinner, taking coffee with milk in the morning along with meat and doing without anything to drink at supper.

Jacques Lajonie, *Burlington, Delaware, January 20, 1817*
To Pierre Taupier, *Le Soulac Juillac*

This little town is very nice. It is beginning to grow and is situated on the Delaware five leagues from Philadelphia. It was pointed out to me by Monsieur Curcier as the most suitable place to give foreigners a taste for the English language. My meeting with two young Frenchmen who are in this town for the same reason as I will perhaps oblige me to change again. As for pleasures, I do not know any, unless they can be made to consist of staying nice and warm, for it is very cold in the winter. There are no gatherings like in Europe. In some cities in eastern America, people like dancing, however, and foreigners enjoy great esteem.

•

In taking up again the thread of my account, I am most anxious to explain to you how this lady happened to come into the very apartment where I was writing. I am lodged with two young Kuakers [sic] who, between the two of them are at the most 110 years old. In the same house we are blessed with a coquette of 70 and a doctor my age who never sleeps anywhere but on a chair in order to be ready to dash off and minister to his patients more quickly. The entire household gathers in a living room every day to enjoy the pleasures of the Kuaker life which consists in warming themselves only in one and the same room expressly reserved for this use and in taking their meals there. . . . These are the kind of people with whom I live from half past eight in the morning (breakfast time) until nine o'clock in the evening, a painful moment, not because I am leaving my pleasant company but because I go to freeze in my bed.

. . .

I must give you a bit of an idea of the American opinion concerning honors and fame. The laws of the United States give neither financial nor honorary rewards to the defenders of the fatherland, nor to anyone else. It therefore follows that there is no distinction between the citizens apart from the employment that they have, so that it is not rare to see generals and ship captains, often highly distinguished by their merit and their glorious actions, come home to their families bringing with them only the memory of the dangers to which they were exposed and the rank that they held. However, as a true patriot, one is pleased to give business to the engravers who honored them by capturing their resemblance perfectly and by selling their portrait. Detached from all service, they take up again absolutely the same habits that they had before being appointed to their posts, without aspiring to recognition or political consideration. In the United States, the love of liberty prevails over the love of fame, but especially over honors. The love of liberty produces soldiers and officers when necessary, without needing to offer titles and decorations. In the United States one can see true patriots and the honor of Liberty. They spurn all those qualities which are, they say, but children's toys.

•

The government of the United States is composed of representatives of the various governments that have associated to form a single body. Each government has its particular republican laws, which the head government has not the right to touch. This assembly of representatives is presided over by Madison who is not exempted from fulfilling the duties of a citizen and against whom the most humble man in the United States can say whatever he pleases, except that the former can bring suit against him for slander or calumny. Until now this republic has been advancing under favorable auspices and the best of guides, the equality of the rights of the citizens and the liberty of the human race. I do not know whether it is due to the happy results of wise laws that the inhabitants seem extremely peaceable, but it is certain that since I have been in this great republic I have not once heard an American become angry. Yet I have been in a few houses, if only inns and boarding houses. Dueling is, in the United States, punished by death and very few young men break this law. Their great art of fighting consists in boxing. The one who can give the best punches is renowned like Messrs Lambert, Hurion, etc., of Bordeaux. Sometimes, however, they fight with pistols.

•

I believe that I told you in my first letter that several important French émigrés were at the head of a French colony to which Congress was to make a concession of land payable at a rather distant time in the future. I am going to make inquiries concerning the things I do not know about this subject and, depending upon what I learn, it is very probable that I shall subscribe for my share as a colonist. I think that this will not exceed 150 francs, which I will give only when I have earnings.

. . .

Borlington [sic] [Delaware] is the hometown of Franklin, the inventor of the lightning rod and the Franklin stove. This man worked a great deal on the constitution of the Republic. Joseph Bonaparte lives two leagues from here; he has just had a house built, a rather ordinary one, for a king. Grouchy and Clauzel visit him often. He has few servants. His family is not in the United States.

•

. . .

Jacques Lajonie [*Pennsylvania, January, 1817*]
To Pierre Taupier, *Le Soulac, Juillac*

[. . .] . Now I shall tell you but one word about my plan for country life. I should like to buy land in a region where Blacks are slaves, where one could grow vines, which are very rare in the United States, and where the French language were on a par with English. I should like to be located at a very short distance from a small town situated on a river. I would choose a breezy place that is very fertile. All of that is as easy to find as bad land in France. Not even one tenth of the territory of the empire of the United States is cultivated. Its tilled land increases in proportion to the population, which doubles every twenty years.

[. . .] . What is more, I give you my word of honor that I have not found a single person who has not told me that planters were the most esteemed and the richest in honors and in possessions. An acre of land bought from the Congress costs one dollar or five francs, and Congress often extends credit for five or ten years if there are many people involved. An acre under cultivation costs from 25 to 1000 francs, but rarely more than 100 francs, and even then it must be near small towns or villages and of the highest quality. All domesticated animals reproduce easily here and are an investment. Wool is one of the most important products. Flour sells at a price of 70 francs for 180 pounds. But let us not expand upon this any further; it is good to keep in reserve a few surprises that are pleasant to look forward to.

. . .

Jacques Lajonie, *Philadelphia, January 31, 1817*
To Pierre Taupier, *Le Soulac, Juillac*

In Borlington I made the acquaintance of a French **ex-paymaster.** He planned to learn the English language perfectly when he was in this small town. His commercial plans seemed concentrated on Santo Domingo, but a letter from his brother who is here completely changed his mind. This letter told him of the real advantages that there were in subscribing for the colony of Proscriptpolis (or Demopolis), the name of the town of the colony which means, as you see: city of the proscripts. [. . .]But particular and certain interests for the first subscribers oblige me after this to be approximately the hundredth. The advantage given, that is, the advantage that the members of this great company possess consists in the company's sales of its own lands or goods, either to people who wish to settle there, or to strangers who wish to purchase products of the company, but I have not yet been able to see the secretary of the Society. I cannot say any more about this subject. It should suffice you to know that each member of the Society will have 1,100 acres of land and a plot of land in the town. There will be a drawing for the lots. It is said that the Society will not leave here until nearly the month of April. So I have definitely made up my mind. I have joined the Society.

. . .

Jacques Lajonie, *Baltimore, March 13, 1817*
Addressee unknown

Mr. Monerow [sic] has just replaced Mr. Madisson [sic]. The change took place so simply that it seems impossible that one should have to use any other means to manage it. Europe is far from being so wise.

The American is so **jealous** of his liberty that to defend it he needs to be stimulated neither by positions nor by decorations. All distinctions and honors are in the United States regarded as children's toys and consequently it is not rare to see a general or a commodore go back into the class of simple private citizens, having no other resource for subsistence but his industry or the possessions he had left to go to the defense of his fatherland. The French briefly had such love. . . .

Jacques Lajonie, *Baltimore, March, 1817*
to Marie Taupier Letage called Nauzille, and Dorothée Lajonie
chateau of Le Soulac, Juillac, Gironde

I have been in Baltimore for a month. I spent half the time in the capital where I had the honor of shaking Madisson's hand. His name is on C[illegible]'s mantelpiece. The Latour family, composed of husband and wife, four children two of whom are boys, and Monsieur Latour's mother, has received me better than you would do if I returned to Le Soulac. I have breakfast and supper with them constantly and have dined there several times. I could not do otherwise. Mademoiselle Eliza is a beautiful woman who plays the **pianoforte** and sings most pleasantly. I had the pleasure of accompanying these ladies on the journey to Washington. Despite all of the pleasures that I can enjoy in this city due to their warm welcome, I am only waiting for the deliberations of the Society that has formed a Committee in Philadelphia to leave for New Orleans. I expect to arrive there around April 15th or 30th.

Jacques Lajonie, *Baltimore, [after April 16], 1817*
To Pierre Taupier, *Le Soulac, Juillac*

According to the information that I have gathered on our Demopolian territory, I dare to assure you that we shall have the best soil of North America and the most pleasant climate. It is generally thought that the temperature is as unvarying as could be desired, in spite of the fact that it is situated between the 33rd and 34th degrees latitude. I no longer need tell you that it is on the Mobile, which flows from north to south and parallel and to the east of the Mississippi that our Society has decided to found the Republic. I have spoken to you so often of our **Tombecbian** society, of my plan to become a planter, of the departure of Fougnet and Audubert, of their arrival in New Orleans, of the people we must hire, that truly I do not know what to say on this subject. Upon my arrival in New Orleans, I shall give you more positive news of my future **lot.** I hope that it will be nothing less than pleasant if I can manage to reunite there my dear friends and my little family.

Jacques Lajonie, *New Orleans, July 20, 1817*
To Elisa Fougnet of *Saurel, Coubeyrac, Gironde*

All of Louisiana is a flat region that does not suit us. The Tombecby or Tombecbee area is better. The region is hilly. To give you briefly an idea of the environs of New Orleans, it is sufficient to know that when it rains, the water leaves the river and spreads into the woods or cypress swamps (low terrain, unfit for cultivation). Without the levees lining the Mississippi, this river would overflow constantly. In spite of all these drawbacks, the planters have discovered the secret of making up to 300,000 francs in revenue, either from sugar or from cotton and maize or Spanish wheat. The cultivated land is no more than 2,000 paces in depth. After that, the cypress swamps begin. For forty leagues the river banks are perfectly cultivated. There are landowners near this city who make up to 500 francs per day on vegetables, milk, and butter. The *savages* provide game. They are generally well built. They go naked, even on the street. However they have a little apron one foot wide and one and a half long. Sometimes they have a Roman-style blanket that serves as a bed when necessary. They do not wear hats. All of them are brown. Their skin is the color of an old sack. The women carry their burdens, but they also handle the money. They trade in furs. They change dwelling places like the French change styles. When the Mississippi is full, the streets of this city are two or three feet lower than the level of the river water. At first glance it looks as if the ships are on the levee.

Jacques Lajonie, *New Orleans, Louisiana, August 3, 1817*
To Pierre Taupier-Letage, *chateau of Le Soulac, Juillac, Gironde*

General considerations upon governments. A democratic government suits a people that is wise, valiant, educated and not very devout (philosophical). The government of the United States is democratic, and in a few years the Americans will have the qualities demanded by this kind of State.

A monarchical government suits a people that is fanatical, ignorant, superstitious, warlike and ambitious. France has sufficient men of merit to establish a democratic government, but the nation's masses oppose this by their ignorance and their fanaticism. Why do the United States, with fewer educated men, with fewer philosophers than France, keep their government? Why, although they are just as self-interested, just as religious and just as divided in their opinions as we, does their government remain intact and unshakeable? [. . .] Come, discontented Frenchmen, come and learn to do without superfluous things, colonial goods, come and learn to encourage the arts, do come, and you will see that the American, who is dominated by patriotism, finds good only what his compatriots harvest or manufacture. You have **disdained** using grape sugar, beet sugar, the finest that can be made; the American takes pride in consuming only the national sugar that everyone knows as brown sugar, raw sugar that cannot be refined; he has managed to give flavor to maize and to potatoes, his principal foods. He can do without your wine; he drinks water and sometimes whiskey, the spirituous liquor of the country. He can bring down your manufactures by putting high duty on your products and by paying his laborers well; no national product pays taxes or entry duty, and the government does more: it pays to encourage the exportation of salt meat and refined sugar from the country. With such principles, a nation is great and important and its citizens are admired by their neighbors . . . [Let us hope for] a man who is wise, virtuous, warlike when need be, who will establish in France "pure morality, man's true religion, in a word the religion of nature . . . , but what would a philosophical king not do for the happiness of his fellowmen; despotism has chased liberty from Europe, reason will bring it back within twenty years."

Jacques Lajonie, *Mobile, June 7, 1818* to Monsieur Gentillot, in *Veyres, near Pardon-sur-Dordogne*

The population of the United States is now eight million inhabitants. The ambitious views of its inhabitants draw its limits: first, from one ocean to the other from east to west, then from the Gulf of Mexico to the Saint Lawrence River and Lakes Erie, Ontario, Huron, etc., so that the circumference of this vast empire (Republic) is not less than 2,400 leagues. Twenty years ago the American eagle soared only above the northern states: Boston, New York, Philadelphia and Baltimore. Since the purchase of Louisiana, its powerful wing protects 40,000 people established on the right bank of the Mississippi and even accompanies some to the Pacific Ocean. All parts of the earth are contributing to this phenomenal progress. Since the **revolutions of 1813** it is estimated that the foreign population has increased by 100,000 souls.

•

I need to stride from one thing to another as far as style is concerned, in the same way in which the Americans cross their country, otherwise, you would still be in Mobile at the end of my letter . . . .

•

I am back to what I was saying. I could well imagine, if I were still in France, that a state or a rich company could create establishments and make them flourish, but I should never convince myself, especially if I had seen the country, that thousands of Americans go two, three, four and sometimes 500 hundred leagues from their usual dwelling to lay the foundations of a new establishment. Sometimes the head of the family has seen the region to which he is going, but often he knows it only very imperfectly. These families almost always leave separately, each one for itself. When roads go to their goal, they take them and leave them if they take them too far out of their way. Reeds, woods, thick [illegible word], streams, rivers, nothing stops our caravans, almost always composed of the head of a household with a troop of Negroes. The children and their wives follow the wagon or large cart resembling an ambulance. The men are on horseback, leading the cows and the pigs. If during the first year the land does not meet their expectations, they break camp and go farther. Ah! poor Frenchmen! If under a leader, however admirable he may be, you had to vanquish so many difficulties, you would a thousand times over curse the day on which you were born. It is with such people, my good friend, that a country prospers and becomes rich.

Jacques Lajonie, *Aigleville, "Nauzelbine," October 1, 1818 [Alabama]*
To Marie Taupier, *Le Soulac, Juillac*

People in Europe have a truly extravagant idea of the animals of the new world. You would not believe how ignorant we are in France concerning this country. When we hear about rattlesnakes it makes your blood curdle. Here they are fairly common, but they very seldom bite. I have killed three of them. The first was as thick as my thigh; it was the first that I had seen. Although it was nearly dead, when I approached it my heart beat faster. Now I kill them with a stick. The bears stay carefully out of sight. People go [illegible word] like they go **badger** or fox hunting in France. Panthers are seldom seen although they are rather common. Wolves are rather rare and smaller than ours. **Ocelots** are common, but they hide and cannot be killed without a dog. In short, no animal in the United States is dangerous except at times the rattlesnake and even it is less so than our vipers because it warns people with a noise as loud as that of a **cicada;** it is more or less the same sound, but it is not **cadenced** like the sound the cicada sometimes makes, but a continuous rattling.

•

Your newspapers have no doubt informed you that the United States had been at war with one or two Indian nations. The theater of war was some 80 leagues from here. The taking of Pensacola and the submission of the Indians were the result of this little campaign. It is not yet known whether the Americans will return Pensacola to the Spaniards. Everything seems to indicate that they will keep it in order to take control of the Floridas. It appears that there were several Englishmen and a few Spaniards among the Indians. In this war, large battles meant that there were fifty dead on both sides. Once again it was Jackson who pacified them. The government is about to negotiate to purchase the lands of the Choctaws. This nation has never been at war with foreigners; they like the French very much because formerly they were treated well by them. The Tombecby River separates us from them and they are here every day to sell us game or to buy rum.

Aigleville will prosper when we have these lands, that is when the American government has managed to purchase them. There may be some difficulties. The Choctaws are very attached to their lands, 100 square leagues, 30,000 inhabitants, 10,000 warriors. They detest the Americans. We are their brothers.

Jacques Lajonie, *Aigleville, "Nauzelbine," October 1, 1819*
To Pierre Taupier, *Le Soulac, Juilla*

Finally, dear friends, we have come to our family safe and sound. It was, my word, not without some difficulty. Never did a husband and wife, I think, have more trouble reuniting. Everything seemed to oppose our reunion, and, height of misfortune, the Orleans *fever* had to get involved. For two months I had been patiently waiting for Dorothée. I did not dare go to New Orleans for fear of missing her en route. Mobile's **diabolical** fever finally tired of protecting me; one day it decided to send me to bed and to make me wait for my wife in this pleasant position. It had undoubtedly foreseen my wife's arrival, for three days after my first attack Dorothée arrived toward eleven o'clock in the evening, just at the moment when the fever was entertaining me the most. I assure you that our embraces were hot. What a situation! What do you think of it, blessed inhabitants of Le Soulac? Lapeyre can do nothing but scold, he's an annoying individual who wanted us to leave between the month of August and February. Ah! I forgot that all is past and that in spite of the fact that my wife fell ill three times and that I had the most putrid fever, I should no longer grieve you. So, my friends, we are at Nauzelbine and happier [. . .]

•

Our dear colony has remained healthy whilst a great part of the United States has experienced this devastating fever; consequently we hope for a considerable increase in population. I have houses to rent for next summer.

Our harvest is excellent and abundant. The town of Aigleville is growing daily. There are often six carts busy bringing wood for construction. During my absence Fougnet put up a structure on our town lot. This year it will be used to store products for sale, as it will be nearer to the buyers.

•

Though we were convalescing, we made the journey from Mobile to here in seven days without any accidents. Dorothée confessed to me that you imagined, in France, that there were no well-laid-out roads. You will probably be quite astonished to hear that we came in a four-wheeled vehicle with a single horse and [. . .] goods in our phaeton which cost us 280 francs and will serve here for transporting our supplies.

My wife's illness and mine cost us a total of more than 400 francs. Mine alone cost 300 francs, 215 of which were for the doctor. We bought chickens for bouillon, 5 francs. The inhabitants of Mobile had never seen such an extraordinary year. When we left, consternation was general. People were dying like flies. Forty-eight hours after falling ill, they were dead.

Glossary for Jacques Lajonie Lapeyre Correspondence . . . Excerpts

league (lēg) *n. Abbr.* **lea.**

1. a. A unit of distance equal to 3.0 statute miles (4.8 kilometers).
   b. Any of various other units of about the same length.
2. A square league.

[Middle English lege, from Old French liue, leguee, from Latin leuga, *a easure of distance, of Gaulish origin.*]

mo·not·o·nous (mə-nŏt'n-əs) *adj.*

1. Sounded or spoken in an unvarying tone.
2. Tediously repetitious or lacking in variety.

[From Greek monotonos: mono-, *mono-* + tonos, *tone*; see **tone.**]

mo·not'o·nous·ly *adv.*; **mo·not'o·nous·ness** *n.*

pay·mas·ter (pā'măs'tər) *n.*
A person in charge of paying wages and salaries.

pro·scribe (prō-skrīb') *tr.v.* **pro·scribed, pro·scrib·ing, pro·scribes**

1. To denounce or condemn.
2. To prohibit; forbid.
3. a. To banish or outlaw (a person).
   b. To publish the name of (a person) as outlawed.

[Middle English proscriben, from Latin prōscrībere, *to put up someone's name as outlawed*: Prō-, *in front*; see **pro-** + scrībere, *to write*; see skrībh- in Indo-European Roots.]

pro·scrib'er *n.*

jeal·ous (jĕl'əs) *adj.*

1. Fearful or wary of being supplanted; apprehensive of losing affection or position.
2. a. Resentful or bitter in rivalry; envious: *jealous of the success of others.*
   b. Inclined to suspect rivalry.
3. Having to do with or arising from feelings of envy, apprehension, or bitterness: *jealous thoughts.*
4. Vigilant in guarding something: *We are jealous of our good name.*
5. Intolerant of disloyalty or infidelity; autocratic: *a jealous God.*

[Middle English jelous, from Old French gelos, *jealous, zealous,* from Vulgar Latin *zēlōsus, from Late Latin zēlus, *zeal.*]

jeal'ous·ly *adv.*; **jeal'ous·ness** *n.*

pi·an·o·for·te (pē-ăn'ō-fôr'tā, -fôr'tē, pē-ăn'ō-fôrt') *n.*
A piano.

[Italian, from (gravecembalo col) piano (e) forte, *(harpsichord with) soft (and) loud*: piano, *soft;* + forte, *loud;*.]

lot (lŏt) *n.*

1. An object used in making a determination or choice at random: *casting lots.*

2. a. The use of objects in making a determination or choice at random: *chosen by lot.*
   b. The determination or choice so made.
3. Something that befalls one because of or as if because of determination by lot.
4. One's fortune in life; fate.
5. A number of associated people or things: *placating an angry lot of tenants; kids who made a noisy lot.*
6. Kind; type: *That dog is a contented lot.*
7. Miscellaneous articles sold as one unit.
8. Informal.
   a. A large extent, amount, or number. Often used in the plural: *is in a lot of trouble; has lots of friends.*
   b. Used adverbially with *a* or in the plural to mean "to a great degree or extent" or "frequently": *felt a lot better; ran lots faster; doesn't go out a whole lot; has seen her lots lately.*
9. a. A piece of land having specific boundaries, especially one constituting a part of a city, town, or block.
   b. A piece of land used for a given purpose: *a parking lot.*
10. a. The complete grounds of a film studio.
    b. The outdoor area of a film studio.

tr. v. **lot·ted, lot·ting, lots**

1. To apportion by lots; allot.
2. To divide (land) into lots.

[Middle English, from Old English hlot.]

sav·age (săv'ĭj) *adj.*

1. Not domesticated or cultivated; wild: *savage beasts of the jungle.*
2. Not civilized; barbaric: *a savage people.*
3. Ferocious; fierce: *in a savage temper.*
4. Vicious or merciless; brutal: *a savage attack on a political rival.*
5. Lacking polish or manners; rude.

n.

1. A person regarded as primitive or uncivilized.
2. A person regarded as brutal, fierce, or vicious.
3. A rude person; a boor.

tr. v. **sav·aged, sav·ag·ing, sav·ag·es**

1. To assault ferociously.
2. To attack without restraint or pity: *The critics savaged the new play.*

[Middle English sauvage, from Old French, from Late Latin salvāticus, from Latin silvāticus, *of the woods, wild,* from silva, *forest.*]

sav'age·ly *adv.;* **sav'age·ness** *n.*

dis·dain (dĭs-dān') *tr.v.* **dis·dained, dis·dain·ing, dis·dains**

1. To regard or treat with haughty contempt; despise.
2. To consider or reject as beneath oneself.

n. A feeling or show of contempt and aloofness; scorn.

[Middle English disdeinen, from Old French desdeignier, from Vulgar Latin *disdignāre, from Latin dēdignārī: dē-, *de-* + dignārī, *to deem worthy* (from dignus, *worthy.*)]

badg·er (băj'ər) *n.*

1. Any of several carnivorous burrowing mammals of the family Mustelidae, such as *Meles meles* of Eurasia or *Taxidea taxus* of North America, having short legs, long claws on the front feet, and a heavy grizzled coat.
2. The fur or hair of this mammal.
3. Any of several similar mammals, such as the ratel.
   tr.v. **badg·ered, badg·er·ing, badg·ers**

   To harass or pester persistently.

[Perhaps from **badge.**]
Word History: Our name for the Eurasian species of this mammal, which is noted for defending its burrow like a knight of old, may come from the badger's knightly emblem. The creature's white head with a broad black stripe on each side of the snout may have brought to mind a badge, hence *badger.* Good evidence supporting this theory is that an earlier name for the animal was *bauson,* which comes from the Old French word *baucenc,* usually referring to a white patch on a horse and also meaning "badger." *Bauson* is first recorded by 1375, *badger* in 1523.

oc·e·lot (ŏs'ə-lŏt', ō'sə-) *n.*
A nocturnal wildcat *(Felis pardalis* or *Leopardus pardalis)* of the brush and forests of the southwest United States and Central and South America, having a grayish or yellow coat with black spots.

[French, from Nahuatl ocelotl.]

ci·ca·da (sĭ-kā'də, -kä'-) *n. pl.* **ci·ca·das** or **ci·ca·dae** (-dē')
Any of various insects of the family Cicadidae, having a broad head, membranous wings, and in the male a pair of resonating organs that produce a characteristic high-pitched, droning sound. Also called **cicala.**

[Middle English, from Latin cicāda.]

ca·dence (kād'ns) *n. pl.* **ca·denc·es**

1. Balanced, rhythmic flow, as of poetry or oratory.
2. The measure or beat of movement, as in dancing or marching.
3. a. A falling inflection of the voice, as at the end of a sentence.
   b. General inflection or modulation of the voice.
4. *Music.* A progression of chords moving to a harmonic close, point of rest, or sense of resolution.

[Middle English, from Old French *cadence, from Old Italian cadenza, from Vulgar Latin *cadentia, *a falling,* from Latin cadēns, cadent—present participle of cadere, *to fall.*]

ca'denced *adj.*

yellow fever *n.*
An infectious tropical disease caused by an arbovirus transmitted by mosquitoes of the genera *Aedes,* especially *A. aegypti,* and *Haemagogus* and characterized by high fever, jaundice, and often gastrointestinal hemorrhaging. Also called **yellow jack.**

di·a·bol·i·cal (dī'ə-bŏl'ĭ-kəl) also **di·a·bol·ic** (-ĭk) *adj.*

1. Of, concerning, or characteristic of the devil; satanic.
2. Appropriate to a devil, especially in degree of wickedness or cruelty.

[From Middle English deabolik, from Old French diabolique, from Late Latin diabolicus, from Latin diabolus, *devil*.]
di'a·bol'i·cal·ly *adv.*; **di'a·bol'i·cal·ness** *n.*

pu·trid (pyo͞o'trĭd) *adj.*

1. Decomposed and foul-smelling; rotten.
2. Proceeding from, relating to, or exhibiting putrefaction.
3. Morally rotten; corrupt: "and all the while scarlet thoughts, putrid fantasies, and no love" (Louis Auchincloss).
4. Extremely objectionable; vile.

[Middle English putred, from Old French putride, from Latin putridus, from putrēre, *to be rotten*, from puter, putr-, *rotten*.]
pu·trid'i·ty (-trĭd'ĭ-tē) or **pu'trid·ness** (-trĭd-nĭs) *n.*; **pu'trid·ly** *adv.*

Reading Comprehension

Answer the following questions about Jacques Lajonie's letters.

Word Meaning

Use the word from the glossary that best completes the sentences below.

1. His __________ in life as a descendant of the city's founder assured Jose of a successful career in public life.
2. The new cruise ship, the Queen Mary II, can travel one __________ in thirty seconds.
3. Such wild creatures as the __________ and the __________ roamed freely on the prairies of early America.
4. The evening song of the __________ marks the beginning of the summer season in the South.
5. The __________ __________ epidemic killed thousands of settlers before the medical community realized mosquitoes spread the disease.
6. Much to the __________ of the students, the chemistry professor announced a major examination for the next class meeting.
7. Such __________ behavior as killing pets and destroying property is a warning sign of a troubled youth who needs psychological counseling.
8. Salaam was so __________ of his newfound freedom that he refused to leave his property even to bring in supplies.
9. The interior designer painted the house an ugly __________ shade of yellow that made people ill when they saw it.
10. When the __________ went on strike, foreign cargo ships remained in the harbor just beyond the docks for over two weeks.

Literal Meaning

Mark the letter of the statement that best completes the meaning.

1. In the letters, descriptions are given of the
   a. American cities.
   b. American lifestyle.
   c. American government.
   d. all of the above.
2. Jacques Lajonie and the members of the new vine-growing Society finally settle in the Territory of
   a. Pennsylvania.
   b. California.
   c. Alabama.
   d. Louisiana.
3. According to the author, when American men fight, they most often participate in
   a. dueling.
   b. wrestling.
   c. knife throwing.
   d. boxing.
4. Jacques Lajonie proudly shakes the hand of which American leader?
   a. James Madison
   b. Ben Franklin
   c. James Monroe
   d. John Hancock
5. In his narration, Lajonie recounts his life and experiences in
   a. Philadelphia.
   b. Demopolis.
   c. New Orleans.
   d. all of the above.
6. Lajonie's letters largely reveal his thoughts about
   a. democracy.
   b. communism.
   c. socialism.
   d. racism.
7. The population of the United States in 1818 is
   a. 60 million inhabitants.
   b. 8 million inhabitants.
   c. 2 million inhabitants.
   d. 30 million inhabitants.
8. During the 1800s, Americans experience the deadly epidemic of
   a. the West Nile Virus.
   b. yellow fever.
   c. cholera.
   d. polio.
9. When the office of the Presidency changes, Lajonie explains that, unlike the changeovers in France, this transition occurrs
   a. simply and smoothly.
   b. violently.

c. controversially.
d. festively.

10. Mark with an **x** the statements that are major details in the Lajonie letters.
a. _____ On January 5, 1817, Lajonie enters Philadelphia from France.
b. _____ The crossing lasts 55 days on the ocean and 3 days leaving or entering a river.
c. _____ The only arms watchmen use are a stick and a child's noisemaker.
d. _____ "The religions in the United States are all free and can also furnish members for Congress."
e. _____ "Borlington is the hometown of Franklin, the inventor of the lightning rod and the Franklin stove."
f. _____ "The American is so jealous of his liberty that to defend it he needs to be stimulated neither by positions nor by decorations."

Interpretive Meaning

Complete the questions with the response that best answers the statement.

1. The main purpose of Lajonie's letters is to
a. explain life in the United States.
b. request money.
c. convey his homesickness.
d. all of the above.
2. The primary tone of Lajonie's letters is
a. hope for a successful life.
b. depression at being exiled from his country.
c. disdain for the American people.
d. humor at the wild behavior of the settlers.
3. Lajonie feels confident that the land grant in the Territory would succeed because
a. every settler had farming skills.
b. the topography of the land resembled that of his region in his native country.
c. the settlers had money to develop the land.
d. the settlers had seen the land in advance.
4. Mark each statement with either an **F** for Fact or an **O** for Opinion.
a. _____ "Europe is far from being so wise."
b. _____ "We shall have the best soils in North America and the best climate."
c. _____ "Borlington is the hometown of Franklin, the inventor of the lightning rod and the Franklin stove."
d. _____ "Joseph Bonaparte lives two leagues from here; . . . "
e. _____ " . . . he has just had a house built, a rather ordinary one, for a king."
f. _____ "This little town is very nice."
g. _____ "On Sundays, all of the members of these sects are very religious."
h. _____ "The pleasures of the American are rather monotonous."
5. Why does Lajonie describe the methods of maintaining civil order in the United States?
a. He is impressed that people obey the laws.
b. He approves of the tranquility of the cities.

c. He likes the system of maintaining order without weapons.
d. All of the above

6. The reader can conclude from the letters that in the early 1800s
   a. living conditions and lifestyle vary from region to region.
   b. the practice of religion is important during this period.
   c. Lajonie expects to be successful in his new settlement.
   d. all of the above.
7. Lajonie says that the ability to speak English is important in the U.S. because
   a. most immigrants speak English.
   b. most business is conducted in English.
   c. people will be arrested for speaking a foreign language.
   d. English is easy to learn.
8. Lajonie narrates the accounts of his life in America mostly in the present tense because
   a. he does not know how to use other tenses and cannot spell well in English.
   b. present tense gives the reader a feeling of being in the scene.
   c. something new happens every day.
   d. he is in a hurry to get the letters in the mail.
9. Why does Lajonie describe the love of liberty as a motivation for "producing soldiers and officers when necessary, even without the offer of titles and decorations?"
   a. He thinks this notion is silly.
   b. He believes that soldiers from his native country could learn from this concept.
   c. He wants to join the American military.
   d. He knows a war is being planned.
10. What factor does Lajonie believe most contributes to the success of a democracy (letter of August 3, 1817)?
   a. Fanaticism and ignorance.
   b. Education.
   c. People with a variety of opinions about government.
   d. Use of products manufactured by one's own countrymen.

Score: Number correct _____ out of ______

Writing Assignments

1. Journal Writing

Summary

Write a one-paragraph summary of the events in the Lajaonie correspondence or draw a time line and outline the letters.

Reaction

Write a one-paragraph reaction to the reading focusing on what surprised you about the correspondence. What did you find particularly interesting? What parts do you have questions about? If you were to meet the writer, what questions would you ask him?

2. ***Paragraph***

Pretend that you were an explorer on the trip with Lajonie. Choose one of the events described in the letters and write a narrative from your point of view about the event. Tell what happened in chronological order. Have a controlling idea for your paragraph.

3. ***Paragraph to Essay***

Expand the narrative paragraph to an essay by writing about three important events instead of just one. Narrate each event in a separate body paragraph. Add an introductory paragraph where you get the reader's attention and tell the main idea of your essay (the thesis statement). In the introduction, you will also need to add necessary background information and identify yourself as part of the expedition. Add a concluding paragraph where you tell what you learned from the experience and what you would like future generations to know about your adventures.

4. ***Essay***

Write a narrative about a trip you have taken. Focus your narrative on one controlling idea of the trip. For example, you may want to tell a story that tells you how the trip supports the saying "The unexpected always happens." Make sure your narrative has an introductory paragraph, body paragraphs that tell about your trip and support the controlling idea, and a concluding paragraph.

Follow the Drinking Gourd

Anonymous

"Follow the Drinking Gourd" is a coded escape poem that was used to teach slaves in the Deep South the route to freedom across the Ohio River. The gourd mentioned refers to the Big Dipper; the rivers mentioned are the Tombigbee, the Tennessee, and the Ohio Rivers. The only information known about Peg Leg Joe is that he helped slaves escape through the Underground Railroad system. Slave children learned this poem as a song in their early childhood. What benefit can you see of using natural phenomena in literature? Recall examples of coded language used today.

Follow the drinking **gourd!**
Follow the drinking gourd.
For the old man is **awaiting** for to carry you to freedom
If you follow the drinking gourd.

When the sun comes back and the first **quail** calls,
Follow the drinking gourd,
For the old man is awaiting for to carry you to freedom
If you follow the drinking gourd.

The riverbank makes a very good road,
The dead trees will show you the way,
Left foot, peg foot traveling on,
Following the drinking gourd.

The river ends between two hills,
Follow the drinking gourd,
There's another river on the other side,
Follow the drinking gourd.

Where the great big river meets the little river,
Follow the drinking gourd,
The old man is awaiting for to carry you to freedom
If you follow the drinking gourd.

The river ends between two hills,
Follow the drinking gourd,
There's another river on the other side,
Follow the drinking gourd.

Where the great big river meets the little river,
Follow the drinking gourd,
The old man is awaiting for to carry you to freedom
If you follow the drinking gourd.

Glossary for "Follow the Drinking Gourd"

gourd (gôrd, gōrd, go͝ord) *n.*

Any of several trailing or climbing plants related to the pumpkin, squash, and cucumber and bearing fruits with a hard rind.

1. a. The fruit of such a plant, often of irregular and unusual shape.
   b. The dried and hollowed-out shell of one of these fruits, often used as a drinking utensil.
   c. *Idiom:*
   off/out of (one's) gourd Slang

   Very foolish; crazy.

[Middle English gourde, from Anglo-Norman, ultimately from Latin cucurbita.]

a·wait (ə-wāt') *v.* **a·wait·ed, a·wait·ing, a·waits**

v. tr.

1. a. To wait for.
   b. To be in a state of abeyance until: *a contract awaiting signature.*
2. To be in store for: *Death awaits us all.*
3. Obsolete. To lie in ambush for.

v. intr.

1. To wait.
2. To be in store: *A busy day awaits.*

[Middle English awaiten, from Old North French awaitier: a-, *on* (from Latin ad-.) + waitier, *to watch*]

quail (kwāl) *n.pl.***quail** or **quails**

1. Any of various Old World chickenlike birds of the genus *Coturnix,* especially *C. coturnix,* small in size and having mottled brown plumage and a short tail.
2. Any of various similar or related New World birds, such as the bobwhite.

[Middle English quaille, from Old French, perhaps from Vulgar Latin *coacula, *of imitative origin.*]

Reading Comprehension

Answer the following questions about "Follow the Drinking Gourd."

Word Meaning

Use the word from the glossary that best completes the sentences below.

1. The countryside was covered with vines growing __________ that people used as bowls, drinking cups, and vases.
2. The sight of a mother __________ followed by her parade of babies signals the onset of spring.
3. Many pirates in the legends limp because they have a __________ leg from an injury often caused by dueling with another pirate.

Literal Meaning

Mark the letter of the statement that best completes the meaning.

1. The narrator in the poem says that people should follow the drinking gourd during the
   a. summer.
   b. winter.
   c. spring.
   d. autumn.
2. What path makes a successful route?
   a. The forest
   b. The riverbank
   c. The stream
   d. The asphalt
3. Signs of winter in the South include
   a. dead trees.
   b. quail.
   c. the position of the sun.
   d. all of the above.
4. Who will be waiting for the traveler?
   a. A train engineer
   b. A stagecoach driver
   c. An old man with a peg leg
   d. The immigration authorities
5. What body of water is mentioned in the poem?
   a. A lake
   b. A river
   c. An ocean
   d. A ditch
6. The narrator is
   a. the person who will lead the traveler to freedom.
   b. the person giving the travel directions
   c. a member of the police.
   d. a minister.

Sequential Order

By numbering from 1 to 7, place the steps below in the order of occurrence.

_____ An old man is waiting to meet at the big river.
_____ Travelers should start their journey when the sun comes and the quail calls.
_____ Always follow the drinking gourd.
_____ Follow the riverbank on the other side of the two hills.
_____ The dead trees show the way along the road.
_____ A great big river meets the little river.
_____ Freedom comes at the end of the journey.

Interpretive Meaning

Complete the questions with the response that best completes the statement.

1. The drinking gourd represents
   a. a pattern of stars.
   b. bowl for drinking.
   c. a piece of folk art.
   d. a ceramic bowl.
2. Why are the words *follow the drinking gourd* repeated in the poem?
   a. To give the poem a rhythmic pattern.
   b. To add unity to the poem.
   c. To emphasize the importance of the statement.
   d. All of the above.
3. In stanza 3, the statement "the dead trees will show you the way" is an example of
   a. onomatopoeia.
   b. personification.
   c. alliteration.
   d. symbolism.
4. The word *freedom* is repeated to emphasize
   a. the end of the Civil War.
   b. the feeling of a full stomach when hungry.
   c. the goal of the traveler.
   d. the sign carved on the trees.
5. This coded poem carries a message that
   a. the slave children learned young in life.
   b. only the master would understand.
   c. carried details of the escape route.
   d. both a and d.
6. Words that convey the meaning of escape and fleeing include
   a. *follow.*
   b. *carry you.*
   c. *good road.*
   d. all of the above.
7. The writer of the poem uses the gourd as a literary device because gourds
   a. were familiar vegetation to slaves in the South.
   b. symbolized freedom.
   c. were used by local Native American tribes as cooking and eating utensils.
   d. could be eaten on the journey.
8. Many lines in the poem end with the words *freedom* and *gourd* because
   a. they provide unity of thought in the poem.
   b. they emphasize the relationship between the goal of escaping and the means of accomplishing the escape.
   c. the repetition enables the escapee to memorize the message.
   d. all of the above.

9. Why does the author use appropriate natural signs of the season in the poem?
   a. To remind the slaves of the time to begin the escape
   b. To teach small slave children to look for signs in nature
   c. To provide a common framework for the hidden message
   d. All of the above
10. The author uses common objects in nature as directions because
   a. he was a nature lover.
   b. slaves were familiar with objects in local nature.
   c. he thought the words provided local color to his poem.
   d. he did not know much about the South.

Score: Number correct _____ out of _____

Writing Assignments

1. Journal Writing

Summary

Write a summary of the poem/song with the knowledge that it is a spiritual with hidden or coded meanings and open to interpretation.

Reaction

Write a one-paragraph reaction to the poem based on your understanding of the poem. Consider the following when reacting to the poem: What would you have done as slave to escape slavery or as a free person to help the slaves? Have you ever needed to write anything in code? Was it difficult? Was your code successful? What lessons can be learned from studying the Underground Railroad?

2. Paragraph

Using your understanding of the hidden meanings of the song, write a narrative paragraph explaining the route slaves would have to take to escape to the North if they followed the hidden directions in the song.

3. Paragraph to Essay

Using the narrative paragraph you wrote in assignment two as the body paragraph, expand the assignment to an essay by adding an introduction that gives needed background information and ends with a thesis. You may have to research history books or the Internet for more information or use the information gleaned from your classroom discussion. In the conclusion, summarize your main ideas and make a concluding statement.

4. Essay

Write a literary analysis of the song. In the first paragraph, consider narrating a brief history of the Underground Railroad and coded meanings. End with the main idea of your paragraph. In the body paragraphs, interpret the poem by discussing the language, the coded meanings, and the use of nature in the song. In the concluding paragraph, summarize your ideas.

Waterbugs

Peter Blue Cloud

Peter Blue Cloud is a noted Native American writer of Indian poetry and fiction. He is a member of the Turtle Clan of the Mohawk Nation at Caughnawaga. He writes the Coyote stories to entertain and amuse and says that Native Americans especially enjoy them. As you read this story, notice the names given to the characters. How do these names resemble those in fables that you may have read before? What other literary connections to fables do you see?

Fox Young Man was sitting by a mountain pool watching **waterbugs** circling one another, first one way, then another. He thought they resembled half-shells of small black nuts. They moved so swiftly that it was hard to keep focused on them. The edge of the pool was shallow and the shadows of the waterbugs went faster than their owners, having to climb stones and plants.

Coyote was passing by and came over to sit by Fox Young Man. He looked at the pool to see what was so interesting. All he could see were waterbugs and water. "Uh, what you looking at, Fox Young Man?"

"I'm watching those waterbugs. They sure move fast. I wonder how they do it! Do you suppose they paddle around with legs? If they do, their legs must really move. Or maybe they have underbelly fins and a tail so thin we can't see it, huh?"

Coyote sat awhile watching. The waterbugs really were kind of fascinating. He motioned across the pool to where a stream entered. "See that grass over there? Well, it's a kind of **salt grass** that's covered with tiny bugs that live on the salt warts which grow around the roots. That's all those little bugs eat, of course, and that's why they live underwater, 'cause if they ever surfaced they'd probably turn into salt crystals.

"If you went over there, you would see little bubbles always popping from those bugs burping. Yes, those, bugs are so small that we can't see them. They're called **Carbonated Buggers** 'cause there's so many of them.

"And those waterbugs, that's all they eat, those little Carbonated Buggers. So they're always full of gas. And that's how they swim so fast. They just fart themselves in circles all day long. You can actually hear them farting if you stick one ear underwater, plug the other and close your eyes."

Fox Young Man looked at Coyote. "Coyote, I think you're making it all up," he said.

"No, I wouldn't do that. It's an old, old story. Coyote Old Man himself told it to me. It was back when World-Maker was creating everything. He was working so fast one time, without resting, that he got what's called "**verbatim**" which is when you get suddenly real dizzy and start talking to yourself. He got spots in front of his eyes swimming around.

"Now, because he was the World-Maker, he figured that he'd created those spots for a reason. He was at a pool at the time, just making the first frog. So he took some of the spots swimming before his eyes and put them on Frog Person. But they weren't circling around on frog's skin, of course. They were just sitting there, but they looked okay so he left some on Frog Person.

"But he took the rest and turned them into waterbugs. And that's why so many pools of water look like eyeballs reflecting the sky and having waterbug spots swimming around in them. Yes, that's probably how it all happened."

Coyote got up then and walked away, saying over his shoulder, "Well, I gotta be going home for some **mush.** I guess I'll see you again if I ever run into you." So Coyote went over a hill, then circled back and looked at the pool from behind some brush. Sure enough, there was Fox Young Man with his head underwater, eyes closed and a paw covering one ear.

Coyote walked over the hill again and met Flicker. "You ever want to know about waterbugs," he told Flicker, "just go ask Fox Young Man. He'll tell you all about them."

"What?" said Flicker. "Coyote, what are you talking about?"

"Me?" answered Coyote, "Oh, I'm just letting you know how stories are born. That's all."

Glossary for "Waterbugs"

waterbug *n.*

1. Any of various aquatic insects, especially the water boatman and certain back-swimmers.
2. A large cockroach.

salt grass *n.*

Any of various grasses, especially North American perennial plants of the genus *Distichlis,* that grow in salt marshes and alkaline areas.

car·bon·ate (kär'bə-nāt') *tr.v.* **car·bon·at·ed, car·bon·at·ing, car·bon·ates**

1. To charge (a beverage, for example) with carbon dioxide gas.
2. To burn to carbon; carbonize.
3. To change into a carbonate.

n.

(-nāt', -nĭt) A salt or an ester of an carbonic acid.

car'bon·a'tion *n.;* **car'bon·a'tor** *n.*

bug·ger (bŭg'ər, bo͝og'-) *n.*

1. Vulgar Slang. A sodomite.
2. Slang. A contemptible or disreputable person.
3. Slang. A fellow; a chap: "He's a silly little bugger, then" (John le Carré).

[Middle English bougre, *heretic*, from Old French boulgre, from Medieval Latin Bulgarus.]

ver·ba·tim (vər-bā'tĭm) *adj.*

Using exactly the same words; corresponding word for word: *a verbatim report of the conversation.*

adv. In exactly the same words; word for word: *repeated their dialogue verbatim.*

[Middle English, from Medieval Latin verbātim, from Latin verbum, *word.*]

mush (mŭsh) *n.*

1. A thick porridge or pudding of cornmeal boiled in water or milk.
2. Something thick, soft, and pulpy.

Reading Comprehension

Answer the following questions about Peter Blue Cloud's "Waterbugs."

Word Meaning

Using the glossary, select the entry that best completes the sentences below.

1. The Asian chef used __________ to season his dishes and to enrich them with vitamins.
2. The frightened toddler screamed at the sight of thousands of __________ swimming around him in the lake.
3. The most fortifying food to eat in the forest is the __________ that comes from corn.
4. The victim of the robbery told the jury __________ what the thief said to her.
5. Too many __________ beverages can cause stomach problems.

Literal Meaning

Mark the letter of the option that best answers the statements.

1. The physical setting of the story is near
   a. a Native American tribal village
   b. mountain pool.
   c. the summit of a hill.
   d. a small town.
2. The waterbugs are called "Carbonated Buggers" to describe how they are full of
   a. light.
   b. water.
   c. gases.
   d. mud.
3. According to the short story, if the water bugs ever surface from their underwater environment, they would probably become
   a. ants.
   b. food for the other animals.
   c. salt crystals.
   d. mush.

4. Living creatures that are personified in the story include
   a. a coyote.
   b. a fox.
   c. a frog.
   d. all of the above.
5. According to the story, the universe was created by
   a. the Creator.
   b. the Universal One.
   c. the Great Inventor.
   d. the World-Maker.

Interpretive Meaning

Complete the questions with the response that best answers the statement.

1. The tone of "Waterbugs" is
   a. serious.
   b. humorous.
   c. sarcastic.
   d. argumentative.
2. The reader can conclude from the story that
   a. Fox Young Man was outsmarted by Coyote Old Man.
   b. Coyote Old Man did not have many friends.
   c. Frog Person likes water bugs.
   d. the Creator of the universe made a mistake.
3. As was mentioned in the resolution of the story, the purpose of "Waterbugs" is to explain how
   a. waterbugs were created.
   b. the short story was created.
   c. Frog Person got his warts.
   d. carbonation was discovered.
4. The author uses dialogue in his story to
   a. make his story more believable.
   b. emphasize the important parts of the story.
   c. humanize his characters.
   d. all of the above.
5. Coyote realizes he has convinced Fox Young Man of the truth of his tale about the waterbugs when
   a. Coyote leaves him.
   b. Coyote sees Frog Person.
   c. he sees Fox Young Man with his head underwater.
   d. he meets Flicker.
6. Why does the author give the characters animal names?
   a. To demonstrate the relationship between man and nature
   b. To pattern current movie themes so that his story can become a film
   c. To set a silly scene
   d. To prove he knows about animals in the region.

7. The reader can infer that Fox Young Man is
   a. sly.
   b. creative.
   c. clever.
   d. all of the above.
8. Native Americans often use an oral tradition, a story, to teach lessons. What lesson can be learned this story?
   a. Nature can be explained in story form.
   b. Humor exists in creation.
   c. One cannot believe everything one sees or hears.
   d. All of the above
9. This short story manifests many features of a fable, a tale that teaches a lesson through the actions and words of animal characters. What one feature does not represent the structure of a fable?
   a. Animal names and characters
   b. A setting in the past
   c. A moral as the purpose
   d. Dialogue within the framework of the story
10. Why does Coyote say he is going to eat some mush?
    a. His stomach can only tolerate mush.
    b. A typical Native American food, mush represents the Native American culture.
    c. Coyote likes the sound of the word.
    d. Coyote is trying to impress the other characters.

Score: Number correct _____ out of _____

Writing Assignments

1. *Journal Writing*

Summary

Write a one-paragraph summary of short story "Waterbugs" by Peter Blue Cloud.

Reaction

What is your reaction to the short story? When writing your reaction, consider what you liked or what you did not like about the short story. Include any questions you have about the short story. Considering that the author Peter Blue Cloud is well known for combining Native American myths with contemporary issues, you may want to discuss how he blends these two components. You may also want to discuss what makes this story humorous and the importance of dialogue in the short story.

2. *Paragraph*

Cloud ends his short story with "'Me?' answered Coyote, 'Oh, I'm just letting you know how stories are born. That's all.'" Think of a tradition in your family or with your friends and write a paragraph narrating the series of events that led to the birth of the tradition or family story.

3. ***Paragraph to Essay***
   Expand the paragraph assignment by adding an introductory paragraph and a concluding paragraph. Use the paragraph written for assignment two as the basis for the body paragraph or paragraphs. For the body paragraphs, you may want to add dialogue to enhance the action. Often in a narrative, a new paragraph is needed when the action or the setting changes. Therefore, you may have more than one body paragraph. Use strategies from Unit 1 to write your introductory and concluding paragraphs.

4. ***Essay***
   Think of an event in your life that taught you a lesson. Instead of writing about the event in first person, write in third person and change the characters from human to animals. Use dialogue to tell the story. Write the assignment as either a short story or as an essay with an introductory paragraph, body paragraphs, and a concluding paragraph.

REFLECTIVE ASSIGNMENTS

1. Reflect on the saying of Ben Franklin at the beginning of the chapter. Think of your own life, the life of a relative or friend you admire, or the life of someone you have studied. Narrate an experience in this person's life or in your own life that relates to this saying.
2. Narrate an event in your history that has contributed to your personal growth (for example, a time you were courageous, a time you learned from a mistake, a time when you gained new respect for yourself, a family member, or friends).
3. Choose a quality that is important to you such as honesty, perseverance, humility, courage, kindness. Narrate a personal experience or the experience of someone you know that illustrates the importance of that quality.
4. a. Relate a quotation from Benjamin Franklin to an experience in your life. Begin with an explanation of the meaning of the saying. Then describe a time when you found the proverb to be true or untrue. Consider one of the following quotations or find one of your own.
   b. Relate one of these sayings to the attitudes present during the start of the United States. Tie this thought into one of the readings.
   "Eat to live, and not live to eat."
   "He that lies down with dogs shall rise up with fleas."
   "The sleeping fox catches no poultry."
   "Diligence is the mother of good luck."
   "Half a truth is often a great lie."
   "When the well's dry, we know the worth of water."
   "No gains without pains."
   "He's a fool that cannot conceal his wisdom."

5. Choose a family member from the current time or from the history of your family. Tell what made (or makes) this person memorable by narrating this person's story. In the conclusion, summarize the ideas you have presented and/or make a forecast. (Predict what will happen to this person in the future or how he or she will be remembered or should be remembered by others.)
6. Explain to a friend or a group of students the benefits of knowing history. Use three figures from history to explain/amplify your points.

Internet Field Trips—Reading and Writing Assignments

1. Search the Internet for information about notable women such as Mercy Warren, Phillis Wheatley, and Catherine Ferguson in the American Revolution. Find out what contributions they made to the history of America. Choose one of the women and write a narrative about her contributions. These Web sites will be helpful:
   - http://www.earlyamerica.com/earlyamerica/notable/notable2.html
   - www.earlyamerica.com
   - http://womenshistory.about.com/od/slaveryto1863/
2. Search the Web for information about the origins of the Underground Railroad. Make a time line of its history and then write a historical narrative of the major events and people who contributed to its success. The following Web sites should help you get started in your search:
   - http://www.nationalgeographic.com/railroad/
   - http://www. pbs.org/wgbh/aia/part4/4p2944. html
   - http://www.nps.gov/undergroundrr/
3. Search the Internet for information about Douglass's escape from slavery. Draw a time line to of his first five days of freedom. These Web sites will be beneficial to you:
   - http://www.americaslibrary.gov/cgi-bin/page.cgi/aa/activists/douglass/escape_1
   - www. eyewitnesstohistory.com/ fdoug.htm
4. Search the Web for authentic slave narratives. Choose one to read. Then write a summary and a reaction to what you have read. Try these Web sites:
   - http://xroads.virginia.edu/~hyper/wpa/wpahome.html
   - http://xroads.virginia.edu/~HYPER/wpa/index.html

Films to View

The Patriot (directed by Roland Emmerich—2000)
Glory (directed by Edward Zwick—1989)
Abraham Lincoln (directed by D.W. Griffith—1930)
Cold Mountain (Directed by Anthony Minghella—2003)

Gods and Generals (directed by Ronald F. Maxwell—2003)
The Fighting Kentuckian (directed by George Waggner—1949—film about the founding of Demopolis, Alabama, and corresponding to the letters of Lajonie.)
The Scarlet Letter (directed by Robert G. Vignola—1934)

Writing assignments based on *Glory* directed by Edward Zwick

1. Write a paragraph discussing the importance of the letters of Robert Shaw to the development of the plot and theme of the movie.
2. Choose one of the scenes from the movie. Narrate the action of the scene through the eyes of either Trip, the character played by Denzel Washington, or Sgt. Maj. John Rawlins, the character played by Morgan Freeman.
3. Taglines are short summaries and statements about movies used for advertisement. Read the tagline for *Glory: Their innocence. Their heritage. Their lives. Nothing would be spared in the fight for their freedom.* Write a paragraph explaining how this tagline summarizes the plot of the movie.
4. Write a letter from Colonel Robert Shaw to the families of Major Cabot Forbes, Private Trip, or Major John Rawlins. In the letter, narrate an incident that illustrates the courage of the character.
5. Write several journal entries in the voice of Thomas Searles, the character played by Andre Braugher. Using the first person point of view in the journal, narrate a story and comment on the experiences of Searles as a member of the Fifty-fourth Massachusetts Volunteer Regiment.
6. Research the life of Colonel Robert Gould Shaw. Write a time-line showing events leading to his decision to lead the 54th Regiment of the Massachusetts Volunteer Infantry.

Summary of Unit 2—American Foundations—Narration

Read the student essay entitled "The Time I Realized I Hated Fishing" by Tabitha Wiley. Analyze it for its content, its organization, and its mechanics. Then, in the Summary of Unit 2 on page 102, complete the column to the right with your responses. Apply the information learned in Unit 2.

The Time I Realized I Hated Fishing

Have you ever done something you hated for someone you loved? I was nine years old and it was Father's Day. My father loved to fish; so, my mom, my four-year-old brother and I took my dad fishing. That was the day I realized I hated fishing.

The day before Father's Day, we drove to Arkansas to fish on the Little Red River. Before the sun came up on Father's Day morning, we were getting into the boat to start our day of fishing. I was trying to go back to sleep on the boat, but the dirty, fishy smell was keeping me up. After a couple of minutes, the sun was up. It was time to start fishing. My dad baited the hooks for everyone and showed us how to cast the line into the water. Little did I know, casting the line was going to be the highlight of my whole day. I discovered very quickly that we were not allowed to talk. Every time I would try to ask a question my mom would say, "SHHHHH!" Then I sat there watching the sun get brighter and feeling it get hotter.

About noon we stopped to eat some lunch. We put our fishing poles up and I was thinking to myself, "Yes, we are done!" After we ate our sandwiches, my dad says happily, "Are you all ready for the second half of our fishing adventure?" I looked at my mom and whispered, "Are we going to stay here all day?" She answered back quietly, "Yes, I think so." That was the worst news I had ever heard in my nine-year-old life. I literally thought I was not going to make it. I wanted to jump out of the boat and swim to shore; but I just sat in silence. Watching everyone catch fish after fish, it seemed as if the fish knew not to bite my line. With my pole in my hand, I stared at my line waiting for it to bobble. I pretended to have fun, but really I was miserable. After the sun went down, my dad finally allowed us to get off the river.

At the end of the day I was tired, sun burned, and bored stiff. I was so happy to be off the river. I was almost as happy as my dad was because he got to do what he loved with the people he loved. In his eyes our day of fishing was a wonderful family experience. Even though I have not been fishing since, that was a gift I do not regret giving. It made it all worthwhile when my dad looked at me and said, "That was the best Father's Day I have ever had."

Summary of Unit 2—Narration	
1. The thesis of the essay is	1.
2. The main tense in the narrative is	2.
3. Three transitions used include	3.
4. The tone of this essay is	4.
5. The purpose of this essay is to	5.
6. The writer concludes by	6.
7. The reader can infer that the writer	7.
8. Traits of narration present in the essay are	8.
9. Three mechanical errors include	9.

Unit 3

Traditions and Celebrations

The holiest of all holidays are those
Kept by ourselves in silence and apart;
The secret anniversaries of the heart.

—Henry Wadsworth Longfellow, *Holidays*

Americans love parades. Describe the festivity depicted in the picture.

In this image of a celebration, what is the dominant impression?

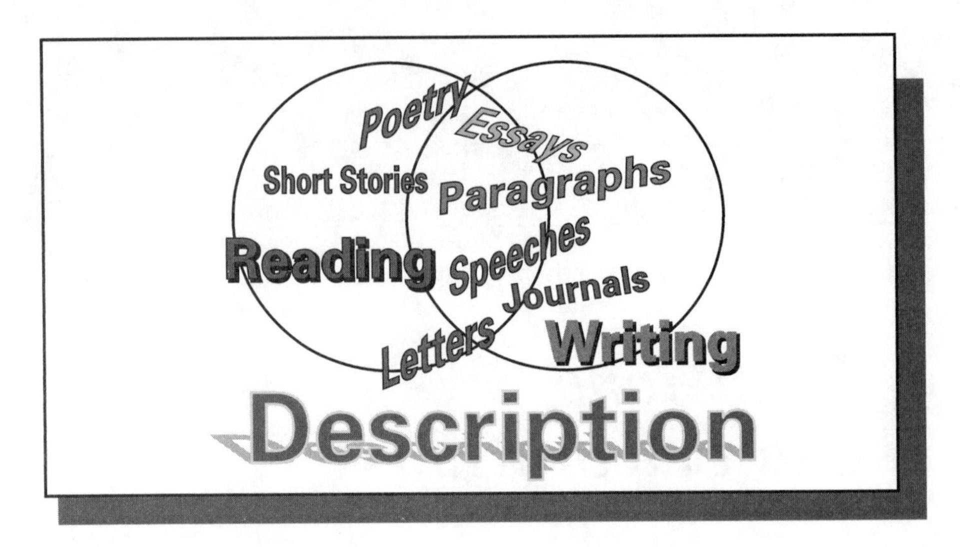

Purpose of Unit:

- *To understand the pattern of description as it relates to reading comprehension and writing*

Idioms for Holidays and Celebrations

Review the idioms below and discuss their meaning. Apply these idioms to a celebration in your life.

Don't look a gift horse in the mouth.
Gung ho
Heart-to-heart
Have one's heart set on
With all one's heart
Heart skips a beat
Labor of love
Let's talk turkey.
A busman's holiday
Paint the town red
Nutty as a fruitcake
Too many cooks spoil the broth.
The dog days of summer
Eat, drink, and be merry.

Description: Points to Consider

Have you ever read a restaurant review that made you think you could taste the barbecue or smell and hear the steak sizzling? Have you read an account of a baseball game and been able to see the dust fly as the player slid into home plate? Descriptive essays portray events, people, and things to make them become lifelike on paper. In Unit 1, "Narration," you learned to use descriptive writing techniques to help the reader taste, hear, smell, and feel the experience you were explaining. Descriptive writing is also used in other modes of writing such as argumentation, causal analysis, and process analysis. When reading and writing descriptive essays, consider the following points.

PURPOSE

The descriptive mode of writing depicts people, places, and things in such a way that readers hear, smell, feel, and taste what is being described. Unlike other modes of writing that use descriptive writing, the focus of a purely descriptive essay or paragraph will be the dominant impression of the event or person being described that the author wants to portray. For example, if you are describing a child's birthday party, the dominant impression may be the excitement of the children. The details you use—the cake, the games, the gifts, and the decorations—will be the ones that support that dominant impression.

TYPES OF DESCRIPTIVE WRITING

Types of descriptive writing include objective, subjective, and a combination of the two. Objective descriptive writing focuses on the details of the object being described rather than the feelings or emotions associated with the object. If you describe your pet rattlesnake in an objective way, you may explain the length, the weight, the width, and the coloring of the snake. Scientists and engineers often use the objective tone to describe technology. On the other hand, subjective descriptive writing focuses on feelings and emotions associated with the subject. If you describe your pet rattlesnake in a subjective way, you will include the information about the size, but you will also include details about your feelings for your pet and its activities. With an objective description, readers should not be able to interpret your feelings about your pet, but when they read the subjective description, they will understand those feelings. Some authors use a combination of objective and subjective viewpoints, especially in longer essays. For instance, in the essay about the pet snake, the first part of the essay could deal with the snake in an objective way, but other parts of the essay could be subjective.

ORGANIZATION

Descriptive writing can be organized in several ways, but the most common are spatial, chronological, size, and sensory.

Spatial—If you are describing an ocean view, you could use spatial order, going from one space to another, to depict the scene from east to west and north to south.

Size—If you are describing puppies in a picture or children at a park, try describing them according to size, from smallest to largest or largest to smallest.

Chronological—If you are describing the scenes as you walk along the beach, through a park, or through a city, chronological order will be the best form of organization. What do you see first, second, and last on your walk?

Sensory—Descriptive writing is often organized around sensory impressions or the five senses: the senses of sight, sound, taste, touch, and smell. If you are describing your neighborhood's annual fourth of July picnic, you could organize your paper according to sensory impressions, possibly starting with sights and ending with smells.

Combination—Authors often use a combination of patterns. In all forms of organization, use sensory details to convey the dominant impression.

Transitional Devices Used in Descriptive Writing

The transitional devices used in descriptive writing depend on the organization of the writing. For chronological order, use transitional phrases such as *next, after, later, afterward, in the morning, in the afternoon, in the evening*. For spatial order, use transitional phrases that give direction such as *above, below, adjacent to, to the right of, to the left of, nearby, next to, to the north, south, east, west.*

Read the following excerpts from "A City Surprises New Orleans," written by American Automobile Association (AAA) writer Sandy Klim, and answer the following questions on each passage:

1. Is the writing objective or subjective?
2. What type of organization is used?
3. What transitional devices are used in each passage?

EXCERPT 1

Overlooking Jackson Square is the St. Louis Cathedral. Dating back to 1794, it's the oldest in the country. It's open for tours, weddings and, of course, worship. Flanked on either side of the cathedral are the beautiful and ornate *Cabildo* and *Presbytere,* part of the Louisiana State Museum complex of national landmarks. The Cabildo houses thousands of artifacts and works of art reflecting Louisiana's legacy of historic events and cultural diversity. It was also the site of the signing of the Louisiana Purchase. The Presbytere is now a Mardi Gras museum.

A short stroll from Jackson Square is the French Market. Spanning over five blocks, the French Market features a Farmer's Market, flea market, gift shops, upscale restaurants and outdoor cafes with live jazz. Strolling visitors are treated to a dazzling array of unique and colorful merchandise from scented soaps to handmade jewelry, t-shirts, masks, dolls and more. The open-air stalls of the Farmer's Market are a delight for the senses with fresh fish, chocolates, scented teas, cheeses and aromatic spices.

Making your way over to the famous Bourbon Street, be prepared to meander and shop a bit. Throughout the French Quarter, quaint shops, antique stores, cafes and art galleries abound. Shop windows cleverly display the unique and wondrous array of offerings inside. It's virtually impossible not to duck in for "just a peek." Shops specialize in everything from handmade linens and lace to teas, upscale clothing, china and, of course, candy.

(*Going Places* July/August 2006)

EXCERPT 2

Gastronomical pleasures begin at breakfast or brunch with poached eggs resting on artichoke hearts smothered in rich hollandaise, or Tchoupitou-las omelets (stuffed with indocile sausage and shrimp) covered in a rich Cajun sauce. For lunch, po-boy sandwiches and gumbo soothe the soul.

Mother's Restaurant is a local and visitor favorite for both of these classic New Orleans dishes. The modest cafeteria-style eatery belies the culinary delights waiting inside. Mother's offers classic po-boys—battered oysters, shrimp or catfish in crusty French rolls topped with mayo, mustard, pickles and crispy cabbage.

As evening rolls around, decisions on dinner must be made. No easy feat in a city that's known for pleasing the palate with traditional dishes as well as an eclectic assortment of inspired cuisines from Asia, Spain and the Mediterranean.

Antoine's is one of the most famous restaurants in the city and has been operated by the same family for 165 years. It boasts one of the finest wine cellars in the city and the country. Another popular haunt for foodies is one of Emeril Lagasse's three restaurants in the city.

(*Going Places* July/August 2006)

Paragraph and Essay Formats for Writing Descriptions

Use the following planning guides for *descriptive* paragraphs.

Plan of Organization: Spatial

Subject ______________________________

Dominant Impression ______________________________

Topic Sentence ______________________________

List details in spatial order.

1.

2.

3.

4.

5.

Concluding Sentence ______________________________

Plan of Organization: Chronological

Subject ______________________________

Dominant Impression ______________________________

Topic Sentence ______________________________

List details in chronological order.

1.

2.

3.

4.

5.

Plan of Organization: Sensory

Dominant Impression ______________________________

Topic Sentence ______________________________

1. Sight
2. Sound
3. Touch
4. Smell
5. Taste

Use the following guides for *descriptive* essays.

Plan of Organization

This plan can be used with any of the organizational plans. Decide on your organizational plan and write a clear topic sentence for each body paragraph. Before you start, list all of the sensory details you want to include.

Subject ______________________________

Dominant Impression ______________________________

Thesis Statement ______________________________

Introductory paragraph

First body paragraph

Details

Second body paragraph

Details

Third body paragraph

Details

Concluding paragraph

Descriptive Writing Worksheet

1. Survey the assignment and choose your topic. Do one of the prewriting assignments discussed in Unit 1.
2. Question the assignment. What is the focus of the assignment? Is the focus of the assignment to write description based on a dominant impression? Is the focus to narrate an event using descriptive phrases? Is the focus to analyze descriptive writing used in a poem or essay? Does the assignment call for an objective or subjective tone?
3. Map your essay or paragraph. Decide if you are going to organize your paragraph according to spatial order or sensory details.
4. Relate or tell your plan of writing to your writing group. After you have finished, group members should ask you to clarify the parts of your plan that are unclear, and they should use reporter's questions to pry you for more details.
5. Record (write) the first draft of your essay or paragraph.
6. Read your paragraph or essay aloud to a student partner. As you read, the partner should listen for understanding and jot down any questions. These questions may be about parts of your writing that are unclear. The questions should also concern details.

7. Revise your essay, taking into account the questions that you and your peer editors asked about your paper. Add the needed details, but check to make sure you are staying on the subject.
8. Review your revised paper with your partner and answer Questions for Review.
9. Reflect upon the comments of your peers and make needed changes.
10. Reread your paper, checking for grammatical errors. Read your paper from top to bottom and from bottom to top. Reading your paper in reverse helps you to read what you wrote, not what you meant to write! As you read your paper, check carefully for consistent tense, correct sentence structure, and correct punctuation of dialogue.
11. Read your essay aloud.
12. Write your final draft!

Questions for Review

Paragraph Assignment

- What is the topic sentence?
- Does the topic sentence mention what is being described?
- What is the focus of the paper? Is the author following the guidelines of the assignment?
- If the author is writing a purely descriptive paragraph, what is the dominant impression that the author wants to achieve?
- What is the pattern of development for the paragraph?
- Are there any parts of the paragraph that are unclear? Is so, how can this problem be corrected?
- What transitional words has the author used to take the reader from one part of the description to another?
- What key words are used to give the paragraph unity?
- What is the concluding sentence and does it reinforce the dominant impression of what is being described?
- What is the most effective part of the paragraph?
- What suggestions do you have for improvement?

Essay Assignment

The Introductory Paragraph

- Does the introduction make you want to read the essay?
- What is the focus of the essay? What is being described and what is the dominant impression the author is trying to achieve?
- What is the thesis statement?

The Body Paragraphs

- What is the pattern of development for each body paragraph?
- Is the description objective or subjective? How do you know?
- Are there any parts of the paragraphs that are confusing? If so, how can this problem be corrected?
- What are the transitional words used within the body paragraphs to take the reader from one part of the description to another?

- What are the transitional words used to guide the reader from paragraph to paragraph?
- What key words have been used to give the essay unity?
- Evaluate the verbs in the essay. Has the author used strong verbs? Has the author used more active voice verbs than passive voice verbs?

The Conclusion

- Does the author come to a conclusion in the essay, or does he or she summarize his or her ideas?
- Does the author both conclude and summarize?

The Entire Essay

- What part of the essay is most effective?
- What parts should the author change? Give suggestions for the changes.

Concrete Language Versus Vague and Abstract Wording

Using concrete, expressive language instead of vague, nondescriptive words strengthens your writing. Look at the sentences below, and notice how using reporter's questions can make the sentences more effective.

Sentence 1

The boy hit the ball.

What boy? Small boy, with a toothless grin
How did he hit the ball? Slammed
What kind of ball? Rubber t-ball
When did he hit the ball? During the Fourth of July tournament
Where did he hit the ball? Into the parking lot

Rewritten sentence 1

During the Fourth of July tournament, the small boy with the toothless grin slammed the rubber t-ball into the parking lot.

Use the reporter's questions exercise to transform the following sentences.

Sentence 2

The children had refreshments at the party.

What children?
When did they have refreshments?
What kind of refreshments?
How did they have refreshments?
What party?
Where was the party?
Why did they have a party?

Rewritten sentence 2 ____________________

Sentence 3

We went to the parade.

Use reporter's questions to add details and replace vague words in this sentence.

Who? ____________________

What? ____________________

Where? ____________________

When? ____________________

Why? ____________________

How? ____________________

Rewritten sentence ____________________

____

Misplaced Modifiers and Dangling Participles

Avoid writing dangling and misplaced modifiers since they confuse the reader and distract the reader from the focus of your paper. Words that modify or describe phrases and words other than those they are intended to describe are called misplaced modifiers. Dangling modifiers do not modify any of the words or phrases in the sentence. The word or words they are intended to modify are missing from the sentence.

Misplaced Modifier

Cuddled under a stack of old papers, the elderly woman spotted the lost puppies.

Corrected Sentence

The elderly woman spotted the lost puppies cuddled under a stack of old papers.

Dangling Modifier

In order to listen carefully to the teacher's detailed instructions, the room grew quiet.

Corrected Sentence

In order to listen carefully to the teacher's detailed instructions, students in the room grew quiet.

READING BEFORE WRITING

El Olto Lado (The Other Side) from Caramelo

Sandra Cisneros

In this chapter from Cisneros's novel Caramelo, *a fine example of Latino American literature, the narrator relates the death of her grandfather and her grandmother's reaction to it. Look for family customs and relationships as you read this excerpt.*

The Little Grandfather died on a Tuesday in the time of rain. He had an attack of the heart while driving on the ***periferico*** and crashed into a truck filled with brooms. The Grandfather's face looked startled. This was not the death he had imagined for himself. An **avalanche** of plastic brooms of all colors spilling onto the windshield like crayons. The *thwack* of brooms under car wheels. The *thunk-thunk* of their tumbling on metal. Brooms twirling in the air and bouncing. The Grandfather, who never lifted a broom in his life, buried under a mountain of plastic brooms, the ones Mexican housekeepers use with a bucket of sudsy water to scrub the patio, to scrub the street and curb. As if Death came with her apron and broom and swept him away.

At first the family thinks they can outrun Death and arrive in time to say their good-byes. But the Little Grandfather dies in his automobile and not in a hospital room. The Grandfather, who paid so much attention to being ***feo, fuerte, y formal*** in his life, backed up traffic for **kilometers;** a *feo* diversion, a *fuerte* nuisance for the passing motorists, a sight as common as any yawning **Guanajuato** mummy, as *formal* as any portrait of Death on the frank covers of the *¡Alarma!* scandal magazine.

When they dug him out from under the brooms, they say he mumbled a woman's name before dying, but it was not the name "Soledad." A garbled swamp of syllables bubbled up from that hole in his chest from the war. That's what the *periferico* witnesses said. But who can say whether it was true or simply a story to weave themselves into that day's drama.

He had a bad heart, it will be explained when explanations can given.—It's that we have a history, we Reyes, of bad hearts. And I wonder if it means we love too much. Or too little.

The brothers Reyes hurry to make their reservations south. In our family it's Father and me who fly down for the funeral. Father insists I go with him even though it's almost the end of the school year and the week of my finals. Father talks to the school principal and arranges for me to make up my exams later, so I can be promoted to the eighth grade. I'll miss the end-of-the-year assembly where my class is to sing "Up, Up, Away."—I can't go without Lala, Father keeps saying. Father and me on an airplane again, just like in the stories he likes to tell me about when I was a baby.

The Grandmother is already beyond grief by the time we get there. She busies herself making great pots of food nobody can eat and talking nonstop like a parrot that has bit into a *chile.* When she's exhausted her stories with us, she talks on the telephone to strangers and friends, explaining again and again the details of her husband's death, as if it was just a story that happened to someone else's husband and not hers.

It only gets worse at the burial. When the time comes to pour dirt on top of the coffin, the Grandmother shrieks as if they'd put a pin through her heart. Then she does what is expected of every good Mexican widow since the time of the **Olmecs**. She tries to throw herself into the open grave.

—Narcisooooooo!!!

All three of her sons and several husky neighbors have to hold her back. How did the Grandmother become so strong? There's a commotion of huddled bodies, shouts, yelps, screeches, and muffled sobs, and then I can't see.

—Narcisooooooo!!!

Please. Too terrible. The Grandmother collapses into a trembling heap of black garments, and this bundle is tenderly lifted and loaded into a car.

—Narcisooooooo!!! the Grandmother hiccups as she is led away. The last syllable stretched out long and painful. Narcisooooooo, Narcisooooooo!!! The "o" of a train whistle. The longing in a coyote's howl.

Maybe she's seeing into the future. Maybe she can foresee selling the house on Destiny Street, packing up her life, and starting a new life up north *en el otro lado,* the other side.

To tell the truth, the Grandmother didn't realize how much she loved her husband until there was no husband left to love. The smell of Narciso haunts her, his strange tang of sweet tobacco and **iodine.** She opens all the windows, but can't get the smell out of the house.—Don't you smell it? You don't? A smell that makes you sad, like the ocean.

Days later, when everyone who has tried to help has gotten out of the way and events have settled to a startling **solitude,** the Grandmother decides.

—The house on Destiny Street must be sold, she says, surprising everyone, especially herself.—There is no changing my mind.

The Grandmother decides everything, same as always.

—And so that's how it is that Aunty Light-Skin is summoned back to Mexico City to help the Grandmother say good-bye to the past. And that's how it is we go back, after the Grandfather's burial, **recruited** as involuntary volunteers to help move the Grandmother up north. At least the half of the family still young enough to have to obey Father. The older ones have perfect excuses; summer jobs, graduate school, summer classes. Father, Mother, Toto, Lolo,

Memo, and me are stuck with her. And that's how it is we lose another summer vacation and head one last time to the house on Destiny Street.

By the time we arrive, the house has already been sold to the family who rents the downstairs portion, the apartments where Aunty and Antonieta Araceli once lived. The rooms closest to the street, where we always stayed, will be rented to strangers. All that's left is for the Grandmother is to pack up her things and come up north with us to Chicago. She plans to buy a house in the States with the money from the Destiny Street house and its furnishings.

The Grandmother insists on overseeing every little thing, and that's why everything takes twice as long. Father has to make sure she is given something to keep her busy, and now she is sorting through the walnut-wood armoire, the doors standing open exhaling a stale breath of soft apples. She pauses at her husband's favorite flannel robe, holds it up to her face, and inhales. The smell of Narciso, of tobacco and iodine, still in the cloth. She had avoided sorting through his clothes. And now here she is, holding her husband's ratty old robe to her nose and relishing the smell of Narciso. A pain squeezes her heart.

What does she miss most? She is ashamed to say—laundry. She misses his socks swirling in the wash, his darks mixed with her florals, his clean undershirts plucked stiff from the clothesline, folding his trousers, steam-ironing a shirt, the arrow of the iron moving across a seam, a dart, the firm pressure along the collar, and the tricky shoulder. Here, this is how. That silly girl! Leave my husband's things. Those I'll iron myself. Cursing all the while about how much work it was to iron undershirts and underpants, men's shirts with their troublesome darts and buttons and stitching, but she did them all the same. The complaining that was a kind of bragging. Scrub out the sweat stains—by hand!—with a bar of brown soap and the knuckles stropped raw, scrub with lots of suds, like this. Put the shirts to the nose before soaking them in the outdoor sink with the ridged bottom, the smell of you like no one else. The smell of you, your heat I roll toward in my sleep, your wide back, your downy bottom, the curled legs, the soft, fat feet I embrace with my feet. Your man shirts puffed with air, your trousers hooked on the doorknob, your balled socks shaken out of the sheets, a tie lying on the floor, a robe draped behind a door, a pajama top slouched on a chair. I'll be right back, they said. I'll be right back. I'll be . . . right . . . back.

And she misses sleeping with somebody. The falling asleep with and waking up next to a warm someone.

—*Abrázame,* he 'd demand when she came to bed. Hug me. When she did wrap her arms around her husband, his fleshy back, his tidy hipbones, the furry buttocks tucked against her belly, the bandaged chest, his wound with its smell of iodine and stale cookies, this is when he would sandwich her plump feet with his plump feet, warm and soft as *tamales.*

The talk in the night, that luxurious little talk about nothing, about everything before falling asleep: —And then what happened?

—And then I said to the butcher, this doesn't look like looks like dog cutlets if you ask me . . .

—You're kidding!

—No, that's what I said . . .

How sometimes he fell asleep with her talking. The heat of his body, furious little furnace. The softness of his belly, soft swirl of hair that began in the belly button and ended below in that **vortex** of his **sex.** All this was hard to put into language. It took a while for the mind to catch up with the body, which already and always remembered.

Everyone complains about marriage, but no one remembers to praise its wonderful **extravagances,** like sleeping next to a warm body, like sandwiching one's feet with somebody else's feet. To talk at night and share what has happened in a day. To put some order to one's thoughts. How could she not help but think—happiness.

—Father says I'm not to come and help you, I say, entering the room and startling the Grandmother from her thinking.

—What? No, I'll do it myself. You'll only make more work for me. Run along, I don't need you.

All over the floor and spilling out of the walnut-wood **armoire** is a tangled mess of junk impossible not to want to touch. The open doors let out the same smell I remember from when I was little. Old, sweet, and rotten like things you buy at Maxwell Street.

In a shoe box full of the Grandfather's things, a photograph of a young man. A brown **sepia**-colored photo pasted on thick cardboard. I recognize the dark eyes. It's the Grandfather when he was young! Grandfather handsome in a fancy striped suit, Grandfather sitting on a caned bentwood settee, his body leaning to the side like a clock at ten to six. Somebody's cut around him so that only the Little Grandfather exists. The person whose shoulder he's leaning on is gone.

—Grandmother, who was cut out of this picture?

The Grandmother snatches the photo from my hand. —Shut the door when you leave, Celaya. I won't be needing your help anymore today.

The key double-clicks behind me, and the springs from the bed let out a loud complaint.

Behind a drawer of stockings, rolled in a broomstick handle, wrapped in an old pillowcase with holes, the ***caramelo rebozo,*** the white no longer white but ivory from age, the unfinished *rapacejo* tangled and broken. The Grandmother snaps open the *caramelo rebozo.* It gives a soft flap like wings as it falls open. The candy-colored cloth unfurling like a flag—no, like a hypnotist's spiral. And if this were an old movie, it would be right to insert in this scene just such a hypnotist's spiral circling and circling to get across the idea of going into the past. The past, *el pasado. El porvenir,* the days to come. All swirling together like the stripes of a *chuchuluco* . . .

The Grandmother unfolds it to its full width across the bed. How nice it looks spread out, like a long mane of hair. She plays at braiding and unbraiding the unfinished strands, pulling them straight with her fingers and then smoothing them smooth. It calms her, especially when she's nervous, the way some people braid and unbraid their own hair without realizing they're doing it. With an old toothbrush, she brushes the fringe. The Grandmother hums bits of songs she doesn't know she is humming while she works, carefully unworking the kinks and knots, finally taking a comb and nail scissors to snip off the ragged ends, holding the swag of cloth in her arms and sniffing its scent. Good thing she thought to burn dried rosemary to keep it smelling sweet all these years.

When the Grandmother had slept in the pantry of Regina Reyes' kitchen, she'd tied her wages in a knot in one end of this *rebozo.* With it she had blown her nose, wiped the sleep from her face, muffled her sobs, and hiccupped hot, syrupy tears. And once with a certain shameless pharmacist named Jesus, she had even used it as a weapon. All this she remembers, and the cloth remembers as well.

The Grandmother forgets about all the work waiting but simply unfolds the *caramelo rebozo* and places it around her shoulders. The body remembers the silky weight. The diamond patterns, the figure eights, the tight basket weave of strands, the fine sheen to the cloth, the careful way the *caramelo rebozo* was dyed in candy stripes, all this she considers before rolling up the shawl again, wrapping it in the old pillowcase, and locking it back in the walnut-wood armoire, the very same armoire where Regina Reyes had hid Santos Piedrasanta's wooden button until her death, when someone tossed it out as easily as Santos had knocked out her tooth. As easily today as someone tossing out a mottled-brown picture of a young man in a striped suit leaning into a ghost.

Glossary for "El Olto Lado"

pe·riph·er·y perifico (Spanish) (pə-rĭf'ə-rē) ***n.pl.*****pe·riph·er·ies**

1. A line that forms the boundary of an area; a perimeter.
2. The surface of a solid.
3. a. The outermost part or region within a precise boundary.
   b. A zone constituting an imprecise boundary.

[Middle English periferie, from Medieval Latin periferia, from Late Latin periphería, from Greek periphereia, from peripherēs, *carrying around*: peri-, *peri-* + pherein, *to carry;* see bher-[1] in Indo-European Roots.]

av·a·lanche (ăv'ə-lănch') ***n.***

1. A fall or slide of a large mass, as of snow or rock, down a mountainside.
2. A massive or overwhelming amount; a flood: *received an avalanche of mail.*

v. **av·a·lanched, av·a·lanch·ing, av·a·lanch·es**
v. intr.
To fall or slide in a massive or overwhelming amount.
v. tr.
To overwhelm; inundate.
[French; akin to Provencal `lavanca`, *ravine*, perhaps ultimately from Latin lābī, *to slip*.]

fe·o–a (Spanish) ***adj.*** **(*que carece de belleza*)**

1. ugly, hideous
2. (*horroroso*) horrible, disgusting
3. (*muy serio*) serious, nasty
4. (*poco decoroso*) unbecoming, indecorous

Idioms:
dejar feo to slight, hurt

más feo que Picio or ***un feo que asusta*** as ugly as sin
quedar feo to be slighted *or* offended
tocarle a uno bailar con la más fea *figurative*, *colloquial* to get the short end of the stick *or* deal
adv. *America* nasty, awful
huele feo it smells awful*m.*

1. *colloquial* (*desaire*) insult, slight
2. (*fealdad*) ugliness, hideousness

Idiom:
hacer un feo a alguien to slight *or* offend someone

fuer·te (Spanish) ***adj.***

1. strong
   brazo fuerte strong arm
2. (*robusto*) vigorous, strong
3. strong
   tabaco fuerte strong tobacco
4. (*fortificado*) fortified
5. (*intenso*) powerful, forceful
   un argumento fuerte a forceful argument
6. (*resistente*) tough, sturdy
7. (*energético*) energetic
8. (*valiente*) courageous, strong
9. (*áspero*) harsh, severe
10. loud
    un grito fuerte a loud shout
11. (*considerable*) great, large
    una fuerte cantidad de dinero a great deal of money
12. heavy, rich
    un almuerzo fuerte a heavy lunch
13. *figurative* (*versado*) well-versed, proficient
    está fuerte en la historia he is well-versed in history
14. *grammar* strong (verb)

Idiom:
plato fuerte main dish, entrée

m.

1. (*fortaleza*) fort, fortress
2. *figurative* (*talento*) forte, strong point
3. *music* forte

adv.

1. (*fuertemente*) hard
   le pegó fuerte he hit it hard
2. (*mucho*) heavily, copiously
   bebieron fuerte they drank heavily
3. loudly
   hablaban fuerte they were talking loudly

   Idiom:
   imas fuerte! louder!, speak up!

y

conj. and

Idioms:

¿y bien? and then?, and what?
y eso que although, even though
¿y qué? so what?

for·mal

adj.

(*perteneciente a la forma*) formal

1. (*serio*) correct, proper
2. (*expreso*) strict, formal

instrucciones formales strict instructions

kil·o·me·ter (kĭlŏm'ĭ-tər, kĭl'ə-mē'tər) *n. Abbr.* **km**

A metric unit of length equal to 1,000 meters (0.62 mile).

kil'o·met'ric (kĭl'ə-mĕt'rĭk) *adj.*

Usage Note: Although the pronunciation of *kilometer* with stress on the second syllable, (kĭ-lŏm'ĭ-tər), is often censured because it does not conform to the stress pattern in *millimeter* and *centimeter* (it originally came about by false analogy with *barometer* and *thermometer*), it continues to thrive in American English.
pronunciation (kĭl'ə-mē'tər).

Guanajuato (gwänähwä' tō), state (1990 pop. 3,982,593), 11,805 sq mi (30,575 sq km), W central Mexico, on the central plateau. The city of Guanajuato is the capital. The state's high average elevation (6,000 ft/1,829 m) provides a moderately cool, healthful climate. Guanajuato is crossed in the north by transverse ranges of the Sierra Madre Occidental, some of which reach heights of 11,000 ft (3,353 m). In the south are fertile plains supporting stock raising and the cultivation of wheat, corn, other grain crops, and beans. The Lerma and its tributaries form the chief river system.

Ol·mec (ŏl'mĕk, ōl'-)

n. pl. **Olmec** or **Ol·mecs**

1. An early Mesoamerican Indian civilization centered in the Veracruz region of southeast Mexico that flourished between 1300 and 400 B.C., whose cultural influence was widespread throughout southern Mexico and Central America.
2. A member of any of various peoples sharing the Olmec culture.

i·o·dine (ī'ə-dīn', -dĭn, -dēn') ***n.***

1. *Symbol* **I**[2] A lustrous, grayish-black, corrosive, poisonous halogen element having radioactive isotopes, especially I 131, used as a medical tracer and in thyroid disease diagnosis and therapy. Iodine compounds are used as germicides, antiseptics, and dyes. Atomic number 53; atomic weight 126.9045; melting point 113.5°C; boiling point 184.35°C; specific gravity (solid, at 20°C) 4.93; valence 1, 3, 5, 7.
2. A liquid containing iodine dissolved in ethyl alcohol, used as an antiseptic for wounds.

[French iode, *iodine* (from Greek ioeidēs, *violet-colored*: ion, *violet* + -oeidēs, *-oid*) + **-ine**[2].]

sol·i·tude (sŏl'ĭ-to͞od, -tyo͞od) ***n.***

1. The state or quality of being alone or remote from others.
2. A lonely or secluded place.

[Middle English, from Old French, from Latin sōlitūdō, from sōlus, *alone*.]

vor·tex (vôr'tĕks') *n. pl.* **vor·tex·es or vor·ti·ces** (-tĭ-sēz')

1. A spiral motion of fluid within a limited area, especially a whirling mass of water or air that sucks everything near it toward its center.
2. A place or situation regarded as drawing into its center all that surrounds it: "As happened with so many theater actors, he was swept up in the vortex of Hollywood" (*New York Times*).

[Latin vortex, vortic-, variant of vertex, from vertere, *to turn*.]

sex (sĕks) ***n.***

1. a. The property or quality by which organisms are classified as female or male on the basis of their reproductive organs and functions.
   b. Either of the two divisions, designated female and male, of this classification.
2. Females or males considered as a group.
3. The condition or character of being female or male; the physiological, functional, and psychological differences that distinguish the female and the male.
4. The sexual urge or instinct as it manifests itself in behavior.
5. Sexual intercourse.
6. The genitals.

ex·trav·a·gance (ĭk-străv'ə-gəns) ***n.***

1. The quality of being extravagant.
2. Immoderate expense or display.
3. Something extravagant.

ar·moire (ärm-wär', ärm'wär)

n.

A large, often ornate cabinet or wardrobe.

[French armoire, from Old French armaire, from Latin armārium, *chest*, from arma, *tools*.]

se·pi·a (sē'pē-ə) ***n.***

1. a. A dark brown ink or pigment originally prepared from the secretion of the cuttlefish.
   b. A drawing or picture done in this pigment.
   c. A photograph in a brown tint.
2. A dark grayish yellow brown to dark or moderate olive brown.

adj.

1. Of the color sepia.
2. Done or made in sepia.

[Middle English, *cuttlefish,* from Latin sēpia, *cuttlefish, ink,* from Greek sēpia, *cuttlefish* perhaps akin to sēpein, *to make rotten.*]

ca·ra·me·lo *n. m.*

1. caramel
2. (*dulce*) candy, sweet

   Idiom:

   de caramelo colloquial excellent, fine

re·bo·zo *n. m.*

1. (*mantilla*) shawl, mantilla
2. *figurative* (*pretexto*) pretext, excuse

   Idioms:

   de rebozo underhandedly, secretly; ***sin rebozo*** openly, frankly

re·cruit (rĭ-kro͞ot') *v.* **re·cruit·ed, re·cruit·ing, re·cruits**

v. tr.

1. To engage (persons) for military service.
2. To strengthen or raise (an armed force) by enlistment.
3. To supply with new members or employees.
4. To enroll or seek to enroll: *colleges recruiting minority students.*
5. To replenish.
6. To renew or restore the health, vitality, or intensity of.

v. intr.

1. To raise a military force.
2. To obtain replacements for or new supplies of something lost, wasted, or needed.
3. To regain lost health or strength; recover.

n.

1. A newly engaged member of a military force, especially one of the lowest rank or grade.
2. A new member of an organization or body.

[French recruter, from obsolete recrute, *recruit,* variant of recrue, from feminine past participle of recroître, *to grow again,* from Old French recroistre: re-, *re-* + croistre, *to grow* (from Latin crēscere.)]

re·cruit'er *n.* **re·cruit'ment** *n*

Reading Comprehension

Answer the following questions about Sandra Cisneros's "El Olto Lado" from *Caramelo.*

Word Meaning

Using the glossary, select the entry that best completes the sentences below.

1. The auto accident that caused the death of Princess Diana occurred in a tunnel inside the __________ that encircles Paris, France.

2. The three virtues that the knight lived by included __________, __________, and __________, the rule of order for all honorable young men of that period.
3. The star high school soccer player has been __________ by all of the major universities in the United States, but she signed with a small private college.
4. The old man thought that __________ would cure any ailment that he experienced, and he drank a teaspoonful every morning.
5. Once the children had left to spend the weekend with their grandparents, the weary mother enjoyed the __________ of the quiet house.
6. Most of the treasures guarded by the family were stored in the antique __________.
7. The students __________ every moment of the fall break journey to the old town of the province by touring, dining, and spending time with local youth.
8. The old grandmother rested every afternoon in her __________, and after her death, her grandson inherited this family heirloom.
9. Most pictures taken in the Old West were taken in a __________-toned tinplate.
10. Many people consider car and home ownership __________ that they hope to own as they become financially stable.

Literal Meaning

Mark the letter of the option that best answers the statements below.

1. The physical setting of the story is
   a. Chicago.
   b. San Francisco.
   c. a section of Mexico City.
   d. a small town on the border of Texas.
2. The grandmother's name is
   a. Alarma.
   b. Caramelo.
   c. Olmec.
   d. Soledad.
3. In the story, the United States is referred to as
   a. the other side.
   b. the North.
   c. up there.
   d. all of the above.
4. The narrator of the selection is
   a. the granddaughter.
   b. the grandmother's neighbor.
   c. the son of the grandmother.
   d. a motorist.
5. How did the grandfather die?
   a. He had a heart attack.
   b. He had a fatal car accident.
   c. He took an overdose of iodine.
   d. He received a thwack of a broom.

Interpretive Meaning

Complete the questions with the response that best answers the statement.

1. One part of the double meaning of "El Olto Lado" refers to
   a. the move to a new home in town.
   b. the Christian concept of going to heaven.
   c. the two wings of the home.
   d. two sections of the city.
2. The reader can conclude from the story that
   a. the couple did not love each other.
   b. the wife was expected to behave in a certain way at a funeral.
   c. Celaya does not want her grandmother to move in with her.
   d. the grandmother is pleased to be moving to another home.
3. Death is personified in the selection as a
   a. woman who came to sweep the grandfather away with a broom.
   b. motorist who caused the accident.
   c. lady who rescued the grandmother from her grief.
   d. beautiful woman in an ivory veil who swirls around the grandfather.
4. The senses are used strongly in the selection as exemplified by the following forms except
   a. a heap of black garments.
   b. the "thunk-thunk" of the brooms.
   c. the sound of the water rippling in the backyard fountain.
   d. plump feet as warm as tamales.
5. Why does Cisneros name the grandmother's street Destiny Street?
   a. She wants to show that the grandmother will never be happy again.
   b. She uses the name to symbolize the fact that people have many changes within one life.
   c. She likes the sound of the word.
   d. She hopes the reader will think about moving to Mexico.
6. Why does the author use Spanish words in the selection?
   a. She wants to demonstrate the close relationship of people to their native language.
   b. She wants to teach the reader some Spanish.
   c. She does not know the words in English.
   d. She wants to show how smart she is that she knows two languages.
7. The fact that the other person is cut out of the sepia-toned photograph shows that
   a. the grandmother is jealous.
   b. the grandfather has a mistress.
   c. the grandfather had a child by another woman.
   d. the grandmother did not like the way she looked in the photo.
8. When the grandmother is holding the caramelo rebozo, Cisneros wants to reader to understand that
   a. The caramelo represents the memories of her life.
   b. The caramelo is personified as having a memory even before the owner remembers.

c. The caramelo represents all that is beautiful in life.
d. All of the above.

9. Why does Cisneros compare the movement of the *caramelo rebozo* to the spiral circling of a hypnotist?
   a. Because the grandmother is moving from the past to the future
   b. Because the grandmother frequently visits a hypnotist
   c. Because the grandmother is swirling in a daze
   d. Because the grandmother is losing her mind
10. Why is it ironic that the brooms are included in the description of the accident?
   a. Because the grandfather sold brooms
   b. Because the grandfather never used a broom
   c. Because brooms symbolize death
   d. Because brooms are colorful objects

Writing Assignments

1. Journal Writing

Summary

Before summarizing the story, analyze the elements of the short story, using the short story analysis exercise in Unit 1. Then, using the information you gleaned from the activity, write a one-paragraph summary of the story.

Reaction

Write a one-paragraph reaction to this story. Consider the following questions: What visual images of the story make you laugh or make you sad? Why do you think that this fictional excerpt is included in a unit on description? Why is a story about the death of a grandfather included with the theme of celebrations?

2. Paragraph

Write a paragraph analyzing Cisneros's use of sensory images (images of sight, sound, smell, touch, or taste) in the story. Start with a clear topic sentence and support the topic with examples and quotations from the story. Focus on one sense. When preparing to write, review the information in both your summary and reaction as well as the reading comprehension questions. You may use the following as a topic sentence or think of a topic sentence of your own:

Cisneros uses images of __________ to make the story come alive for the reader.

3. Paragraph to Essay

A literary analysis is a paper in which the writer discusses, critiques, interprets, or evaluates literature—a short story, a poem, an essay, journals, or any type of written work. Write an essay analyzing the descriptive writing in the short story. Instead of covering only one type of image Cisneros uses, as you did in assignment two, analyze two or three types of figurative language. In your introduction, state the name of the short story and of the author. You may also include a brief summary of the story. End this paragraph with the thesis of your essay. For one of your body paragraphs, consider using all or part of the paragraph written for assignment two. In the concluding paragraph, summarize the main points of the essay and arrive at a conclusion about the effectiveness of the descriptive writing in the story. Before writing, review "Points to Remember in Writing a Literary Analysis Assignment" in Unit One.

4. ***Essay***

Write an essay describing an activity at a home, church, hospital, or other place preceding or following a milestone event, such as a funeral, a wedding, or a birth. Decide if your description will be subjective or objective. Also decide on the dominant characteristic or mood you want to portray in your description. In the introductory paragraph, name the place of the event you are describing and give any background information needed to help the reader understand the setting and the significance of the event. In the thesis statement, mention what the dominant characteristic or mood of the setting is. In each body paragraph, describe a section or a part of the setting. Use sensory images and descriptive phases as Cisneros does in "El Otro Lado." Summarize and/or come to a conclusion about the event in the final paragraph.

Packing for America

Frank McCourt

What would you bring if you were coming to a new country? This reading gives a look inside the suitcases—and hearts—of the newest Americans.

. . . there are thirteen faces. There are no smiles. Why should there be? They haven't learned yet the value of the American smile. But there is the look. It's the look of people just arrived. It is **tentative,** hopeful, **yearning,** a look that says "We're here. It's America. We're safe. We don't have to check over our shoulders. We'll sleep well tonight. No one will crash through our door with gun or **machete.** Our children are safe." [Three families] arrived in the United States in August 2004: the Banguras from Sierra Leone; the Mostoslavskyys from Ukraine; the Jahanyars from Afghanistan. . . . Of the three families, the Mostoslavskyys are probably the most fortunate. They have relatives in the U.S., in New York, Los Angeles, and Boston. Oleksandr, 49, will join his 77-year-old father in Boston. Joining his father was a major reason for coming here. Oleksandr brings with him his wife, Yuliya, 46, and their son, Anatoliv, 13. He also has a cousin in Boston who will give him a job in his auto-repair shop. The cousin worked at the shop for a while and then managed to buy it out.

Look what they've packed: sheets, if you don't mind, sheets, pillows, blankets. Some know-it-all Ukrainian assured them these items were tremendously expensive in America and (here, Americans should stand and protest) of inferior quality. There are other precious items in the bags: bottles of vodka, ceramic mugs, photographs. What will Yuliya think when she sees her first white sale in Boston?

The Banguras of Sierra Leone traveled lightly, not by choice: They simply had nothing. They have scars. They have memories: In 1999, Mohammed, 35, was beaten so badly his hearing is damaged forever; his wife, Kadiatu Kamara, 32, was stabbed in the chest; their son, Ibrahim, 9, was stabbed in the groin. There are two other children: a girl, 11; a boy, 6. The family fled Sierra Leone to Liberia, then to Ghana. In their bags they carry a few items of clothing, Kadiatu's X-ray, Mohammed's medical evaluations. It will be a while before they realize, in Gretna, Louisiana, that they're not living on the edge of life and death anymore.

Centerpiece in any picture of the Jahanyars is the Koran, the book that has **sustained** Ahmad, 37, and his family since they first fled Kabul in 1993. He worked in Mazar-e Sharif till 1998, when the approach of the Taliban forced another move, this time to Moscow. He and his wife, Rona, 39, grabbed their children, the Koran, some jewelry and photos, and that is all they have left from their native land. They will live in San Diego, where, they hope, they can pray in peace.

The look. They will carry the look a long time, but in a few weeks if you stroll by certain schools in Boston, Gretna, San Diego, you'll see any or all of these seven children chattering away on playgrounds while their parents, at home or at work, banish horror with hope. They may still be tentative about their new lives, but these families consider themselves lucky.

We may not understand their feelings, or we may not try to. We haven't been hungry lately, or ever. No one has threatened to stab our wives and children. We notice these people, or we don't. Books are cheap here, but if you can't afford them the public library is down the road. Education is available here, and if you don't take advantage of it, well, your loss. What do we have to concern ourselves with? The expanding waistline, the shrinking imagination, our favorite program, the team we root for.

And so will they, someday.

If I were still teaching in the high schools of New York City I'd take my students to Kennedy Airport so they could observe the faces of people landing here, people fleeing **tyranny,** hunger, religious persecution, **despair.** I'd like my students to be able to recognize the look that passes over those faces, ranging from fear to ecstasy. My students might say "Oh, what's the big deal?," and if they did I'd have to be patient. They don't know any better, and that's strange because no generation has been **endowed** with so much information. They've seen the starving African babies, flies on eyes, bellies swollen, sucking at breasts dried forever. They may be aware of the horrors of Bosnia, Rwanda, Sudan, but, like, you know, that's television, man. The Mostoslavskyys, the Banguras, the Jahanyars are among us. Their brothers and sisters are sneaking across the border from Mexico. The snakes are packing the holds of ships with dreaming Chinese, Vietnamese, Cambodians.

They are among us. The adults are slow to adjust, but the children take up the bat and the baseball, the football, the basketball, and, watch out, the pen. There will be a poetry, a literature, we cannot even imagine. And there will be music. Jazz, rap, hip-hop will be old stuff. Make way for those American-Ukrainians, American-Sierra Leoneans, American-Afghans.

We may demand that "something has to be done about those people sneaking in here."

What?

This cry is now heard everywhere. Ireland, long-suffering Ireland, now prosperous Ireland, recently held a referendum on immigration. Ireland has been invaded (if you choose to call it that) by Romanians, Nigerians, Chinese. There was talk of the country being swamped, so, in the referendum, nearly 80 percent of the voting Irish said, "Close the borders. Just because you had a baby here doesn't mean you have a right to stay. Out!" You can hear the cry here, of course. And why? These people, these Romanians, Nigerians, Chinese, Vietnamese, Cambodians, Mexicans, Ukrainians—they flatter us. In this time of Paris hating Washington, of Abu Ghraib, and of all manner of America-bashing, they want to join us. They need it—they need America—like they need food, water, air. To them, America is still the light of the world. It is free. It is still the dream.

There is a lurking sadness in the 13 faces . . . , the faces of people jolted, pushed, threatened, bullied. The Mostoslavskyys, the Jahanyars, the Banguras. There are millions behind them, and they are dreaming, too, of the day they'll arrive at Kennedy Airport with light baggage and the look.

Glossary for "Packing for America"

ten·ta·tive (tĕn'tə-tĭv) *adj.*

1. Not fully worked out, concluded, or agreed on; provisional: *tentative plans.*
2. Uncertain; hesitant.

[Medieval Latin tentātīvus, from Latin tentātus, past participle of tentāre, *to try*, variant of temptāre.]

ten'ta·tive·ly *adv.* **ten'ta·tive·ness** *n.*

yearn (yûrn) *ntr. v.* **yearned, yearn·ing, yearns**

1. To have a strong, often melancholy desire.
2. To feel deep pity, sympathy, or tenderness: *yearned over the child's fate.*

[Middle English yernen, from Old English geornan, giernan.]

yearn'er *n.*

ma·chet·e (mə-shĕt'ē, -chĕt'ē) *n.*

A large heavy knife with a broad blade, used as a weapon and an implement for cutting vegetation.

[Spanish, diminutive of macho, *sledge hammer*, alteration of mazo, *club*, probably from maza, *mallet*, from Vulgar Latin *mattea, *mace.*]

sus·tain (sə-stān') *tr. v.* **sus·tained, sus·tain·ing, sus·tains**

1. To keep in existence; maintain.
2. To supply with necessities or nourishment; provide for.
3. To support from below; keep from falling or sinking; prop.
4. To support the spirits, vitality, or resolution of; encourage.
5. To bear up under; withstand: *can't sustain the blistering heat.*
6. To experience or suffer: *sustained a fatal injury.*
7. To affirm the validity of: *The judge has sustained the prosecutor's objection.*
8. To prove or corroborate; confirm.
9. To keep up (a joke or assumed role, for example) competently.

[Middle English sustenen, from Old French sustenir, from Latin sustinēre: sub-, *from below;* see **sub-** + tenēre, *to hold;* see ten- in Indo-European Roots.]

sus·tain'a·bil'i·ty *n.* **sus·tain'a·ble** *adj.* **sus·tain'er** *n.*

tyr·an·ny (tĭr'ə-nē) *n.pl.* **tyr·an·nies**

1. A government in which a single ruler is vested with absolute power.
2. The office, authority, or jurisdiction of an absolute ruler.
3. Absolute power, especially when exercised unjustly or cruelly: "I have sworn . . . eternal hostility against every form of tyranny over the mind of man" (Thomas Jefferson).

4. a. Use of absolute power.
   b. A tyrannical act.
5. Extreme harshness or severity; rigor.

[Middle English tyrannie, from Old French, from Late Latin tyrannia, from Greek turanniā, from turannos, *tyrant*.]

de·spair (dĭ-spâr') *intr. v.* **de·spaired, de·spair·ing, de·spairs**

1. To lose all hope: *despaired of reaching shore safely.*
2. To be overcome by a sense of futility or defeat.

n.

1. Complete loss of hope.
2. One despaired of or causing despair: *unmotivated students that are the despair of their teachers.*

[Middle English despeiren, from Old French desperer, from Latin dēspērāre: dē-, *de-* + spērāre, *to hope*; see spē- in Indo-European Roots. N., from Middle English despeir from Anglo-Norman, from Old French desperer, *to despair*.]

en·dow [(ēn-dou') *tr. v.* **en·dowed, en·dow·ing, en·dows**

1. To provide with property, income, or a source of income.
2. a. To equip or supply with a talent or quality: Nature endowed you with a beautiful singing voice.
   b. To imagine as having a usually favorable trait or quality: *endowed the family pet with human intelligence.*
3. *Obsolete.* To provide with a dower.

[Middle English endowen, from Anglo-Norman endouer: Old French en-, *intensive pref.*; see **en-**[1] + Old French douer, *to provide with a dowry* (from Latin dōtāre, from dōs, dōt-, *dowry*.)]

Reading Comprehension

Answer the following questions about the article by author Frank McCourt.

Word Meaning

Using the glossary, select the entry that best completes the sentences below.

1. In the jungles of the Amazon forest, much of the ecological balance has been disturbed by __________-toting woodsmen who sell their chopped pulp for money.
2. As a result of the great __________ caused by a lack of basic human needs—food, shelter, and clothing—citizens of many third-world countries try to escape their dire circumstances through immigration to the West.
3. The child wanted a new I-Pod so desperately for her birthday that one could see the __________ in her eyes and facial expressions.
4. The hope for a happy future has __________ many young married couples who have been separated by geography caused by job transfers and soldiering during wars.
5. Bill Gates, the founder of Microsoft and the wealthiest person in the United States, has given a large portion of his money to charity in the form of

_________ scholarships and training grants in the fields of engineering and computer technology.

6. Many government rulers throughout history have operated through a system of _________ that caused death and destruction to the citizenry and the country.

Literal Meaning

Mark the letter of the option that best answers the statements below.

1. From which country did the immigrants NOT originate?
   a. Sierra Leone
   b. Afghanistan
   c. Iraq
   d. Ukraine
2. When did these three immigrant families arrive in the United States?
   a. 2001
   b. 1999
   c. 2005
   d. 2003
3. Which immigrants are considered fortunate because they already have family members in the United States?
   a. The Mostoslavskyys
   b. The Banguras
   c. The Jahanyars
   d. All of the above
4. What is the surface meaning of the article by McCourt?
   a. The reason for immigrating to the United States is varied.
   b. The items people pack when they relocate to another country tells a story.
   c. Immigration to the United States is the dream of people around the world.
   d. The new immigrants regretted having to leave their countries.
5. What common worries would typify the American lifestyle?
   a. Expanding waistlines caused by abundance.
   b. The loss of imagination and television programs.
   c. Sporting events and favorite teams.
   d. All of the above.

Interpretive Meaning

Complete the questions with the response that best answers the statement.

1. Why does McCourt repeat the expression "the look" of the new immigrants?
   a. He is emphasizing that aspect of an immigrant's demeanor upon arrival.
   b. All immigrants share a similar regard when they first arrive in the United States.

c. He recalls that he had "the look" when he arrived from Ireland.
d. "The look" frightens Americans when they meet the new immigrants.

2. What is the tone of the essay?
a. Humorous
b. Informative
c. Argumentative
d. Objective

3. Why does McCourt focus on what possessions the new immigrants packed?
a. He knows Americans are curious about the contents of suitcases.
b. Many people pack illegal items that can be easily confiscated at the border.
c. The items packed represent the most important possessions the immigrants own.
d. The items brought to America tell a unique story in themselves about the family's history.

4. Why does McCourt say that the most informed generation in America, the youth, would not care about "the look" on the faces of the new immigrants?
a. All American youth are apathetic.
b. The young people are afraid of foreigners.
c. American youth have so many possessions that they do not care about others.
d. Even though the American youth might be informed, they still experience a disconnection between reality and media coverage.

5. Why does McCourt say that the immigrant children adapt to American life faster than their immigrant parents?
a. They learn the English language faster than their parents.
b. They mix and mingle faster than their parents as a result of going to school.
c. They learn customs through games that they play with American children.
d. All of the above

6. For the Jananyars, from Afghanistan, what does the packed Koran symbolize?
a. The only possession they still owned when leaving their country
b. The end of a journey
c. The freedom to worship in their way without fear of retribution
d. A cherished memory of their native country

7. What does McCourt mean when he says these immigrants take up the pen?
a. The immigrants learn to write English.
b. The children of the immigrants will express themselves with words as McCourt himself, an immigrant and writer, has done.
c. These children will tell the truth when asked questions.
d. All of the above

8. Why does McCourt say that "Ireland has been invaded"?
a. The English have been fighting in Ireland over the last twenty-five years.
b. Ireland has become weak as a result of its history of long-suffering due to famines.

c. Different invaders attack Ireland because it is an island, thus an easy target.
d. Many immigrants have relocated to Ireland because of its thriving economy.

9. How does McCourt feel about the new immigration laws that Ireland has passed?
   a. He is in favor of any law that will keep the Irish culture intact.
   b. He thinks only Irish people should live in Ireland.
   c. He favors immigration to Ireland once a person has learned Gallic.
   d. He is ashamed of the new immigration laws that Ireland has passed.
10. Explain what McCourt means by the following expression with which he begins his summary: "... they need America—like they need food, water, air. To them, America is still the light of the world. It is free. It is still the dream."

    ____

    ____

Score: Number correct ________ out of ________

Writing Assignments

1. *Journal Writing*

Summary

Write a one-paragraph summary of the article. State the title and the author and use the reporter's questions to summarize the information in the article.

Reaction

Write a reaction to the article. Consider the items that the families brought with them to America. What would you take with you if you were in similar circumstances?

2. *Paragraph*

Imagine having to leave your home with no idea if you will be able to return. You can only take a backpack with you. Write a paragraph describing the items in your imaginary backpack. Use spatial or size order to write your description.

3. *Paragraph to Essay*

Expand the paragraph from assignment two to an essay by writing a descriptive essay explaining the contents of the backpacks your family members would take. Each body paragraph should focus on a different family member's backpack.

4. *Essay*

Look through your family photos and choose one that was taken at a family celebration or life event. Write an essay describing the picture. Use spatial order to organize your essay. Each paragraph in the body should describe a different part of the photograph.

Slightly Damp, Paradegoers Still Dressed for the Occasion

Charles Cochran

In this descriptive essay, the author relates the sights and festivities at the annual St. Patrick's Day Parade in Savannah, Georgia.

Although it was raining cats and dogs, the animals themselves were relatively scarce.

Savannah News

Creative wearing of the green is a bit more challenging in a downpour.

So is dressing up your favorite household pet.

Although green ran **rampant,** the creative and **innovative** costumes one usually sees were scarce during Monday's rainy St. Patrick's Day parade. Fully-dressed leprechauns—hard to find even under the best of circumstances—didn't appear to be out. Most, if not all, chose to stay close to their warm, toasty **leprechaun** homes.

Thanks largely to the **ubiquitous** street-corner **vendors,** festive (even if somewhat damp) green hats, beads and T-shirts were the rule of the day.

Despite the occasional green-dyed Chihuahua, pets were relatively rare.

Even the huge Budweiser **Clydesdales** stayed inside, peering snug and dry from the open doors of an 18-wheel trailer instead of actually clopping along the route.

Luck of the Draw

Kerry Coursey was wearing green, but it wasn't quite the way she'd planned it.

Sitting pretty in the opened rear door of a van on Chippewa Square, she huddled under a green poncho, relying on it to ward off a steady pre-parade drizzle.

The emerald rain gear had nothing to do with St. Patrick's Day. "It's just what we had in the house," Coursey said.

Not to worry: She was ready in case the weather cleared. Under the poncho, she wore the **requisite** green-and-white St. Patrick's Day shirt, and a **full-fledged** set of beads.

"I did dress appropriately," she said.

Garbed in Tradition

Tammy Sabo's life is rooted in Savannah's St. Patrick's Day traditions.

She stood under a huge umbrella with Keely Passman, a niece from Atlanta, watching the parade pass on Bull Street near Broughton.

This year, just as she has for two decades, Sabo dug out the same green "St. Patrick's Day, Savannah, Ga." T-shirt, and donned a festive green **boa.**

Keely showed off a special pair of socks, white with green toes and heels and besprinkled with shamrocks. She bought them in Dublin, Ireland, two years ago.

In addition to a "Kiss Me, I'm Irish" T-shirt, Keely sported a pair of **predominantly** green "Lucky Charms"—and vibrantly green hair.

Pets on Parade

Sebastian, a pit bull–collie mix with black-and-white fur, looked pretty dog-gone cool in his green Savannah Harley-Davidson shirt.

Alex Glen, who was walking Sebastian past the Savannah-Chatham Public Schools office on Bull Street during Monday's parade, had big plans for his friend.

All of Sebastian's white fur would be dyed green before the day was out. And he'd be bedecked with beads.

"He's just representing the local dogs," Glen said of Sebastian.

Glen was sort of bedecked himself, with a snazzy green velvet hat he bought four St. Patrick's Days ago.

Sebastian gets to wear the hat sometimes. "He wears it pretty good, too," Glen said.

A Beautiful Joker

Adorned with a green bandana and beads, Joker enjoyed his first St. Patrick's Day parade. It's a huge step up for the elegant, purebred collie that Melynda Loomis adopted two years ago from the Second Chance pet adoption agency.

"We brought him today just for fun," said Loomis, who took in the parade on Chippewa Square with Joker and her daughter, 8-year-old Tyler. "And he's a good watchdog." Perhaps somewhat ironically, they left the family's Irish Setter at home.

"She gets a little hyper in the rain," Loomis said.

Glossary for "Slightly Damp, Paradegoers Still Dressed for the Occasion"

ram·pant (răm'pənt)
adj.

1. Extending unchecked; unrestrained: *a rampant growth of weeds in the neglected yard.*
2. Occurring without restraint and frequently, widely, or menacingly; rife: *a rampant epidemic; rampant corruption in city government.*
3. a. Rearing on the hind legs.
   b. Heraldry. Rearing on the left hind leg with the forelegs elevated, the right above the left, and usually with the head in profile.
4. Architecture. Springing from a support or an abutment that is higher at one side than at the other: *a rampant arch.*

[Middle English rampaunt, from Old French rampant, present participle of ramper, *to ramp.*]

ram'pan·cy *n.*

ram'pant·ly *adv.*

in·no·va·tive (ĭn'ə-vā'tĭv)
adj.

Marked by or given to innovations.

in'no·va'tive·ness *n.*

lep·re·chaun (lĕp'rĭ-kŏn', -kŏn')
n.

One of a race of elves in Irish folklore who can reveal hidden treasure to those who catch them.

[Irish Gaelic luprachán, alteration of Middle Irish luchrupán, from Old Irish luchorpán: luchorp(lú-, *small;* see legʷh- in Indo-European Roots + corp, *body* from Latin corpus.]

lep're·chaun'ish *adj.*

Word History: Nothing seems more Irish than the leprechaun; yet hiding within the word *leprechaun* is a word from another language entirely. If we look back beyond Modern Irish Gaelic *luprachán* and Middle Irish *luchrupán* to Old Irish *luchorpán,* we can see the connection. *Luchorpán* is a compound of Old Irish *lú,* meaning "small," and the Old Irish word *corp,* "body." *Corp* is borrowed from Latin *corpus* (which we know from *habeas corpus*). Here is a piece of evidence attesting to the deep influence of Church Latin on the Irish language. Although the word is old in Irish, it is fairly new in English, being first recorded in 1604.

u·biq·ui·tous (yo͞obĭk'wĭ-təs)
adj.

Being or seeming to be everywhere at the same time; omnipresent: "plodded through the shadows fruitlessly like an ubiquitous spook" (Joseph Heller).

u·biq'ui·tous·ly *adv.*

u·biq'ui·tous·ness *n.*

ven·dor also **vend·er** (vĕn'dər)
n.

1. One that sells or vends: *a street vendor; a vendor of software products on the Web.*
2. A vending machine.

Clydes·dale (klīdz'dāl')
n.

A large powerful draft horse of a breed developed in the Clyde valley of Scotland, having white feathered hair on its fetlocks.

req·ui·site (rĕk'wĭ-zĭt)
adj.

Required; essential.

n.

Something that is indispensable; a requirement.

[Middle English, from Latin requīsītus, past participle of requīrere, *to require.*]

req'ui·site·ly *adv.*

req'ui·site·ness *n.*

full-fledged (fo͞ol'flĕjd')
adj.

1. Having reached full development; mature.
2. Having full status or rank: *a full-fledged lawyer.*
3. Having fully developed adult plumage.

bo·a (bō'ə)
n.

1. Any of various large, nonvenomous, chiefly tropical snakes of the family Boidae, which includes the python, anaconda, boa constrictor, and other snakes that coil around and suffocate their prey.
2. A long fluffy scarf made of soft material, such as fur or feathers.

[Middle English, from Latin boa, *a large water snake.*]

pre·dom·i·nant (prĭ-dŏm'ə-nənt)
adj.

1. Having greatest ascendancy, importance, influence, authority, or force.
2. Most common or conspicuous; main or prevalent: *the predominant color in a design.*

[Medieval Latin praedomināns, praedominant- present participle of praedominārī, *to predominate.*]

pre·dom'i·nant·ly *adv.*

Reading Comprehension

Answer the following questions about "Slightly Damp, Paradegoers Still Dressed for the Occasion."

Word Meaning

Select the word from the glossary that best completes the sentences below.

1. The Summer Olympics in Atlanta was known as the most commercial games because of the multitude of __________ who sold their items all over the city.
2. My childhood favorite memory of the state fair was my annual pilgrimage to visit the __________ who always came to pull the Budweiser beer wagon through the grounds.
3. Many Mexican children celebrate their __________, the feast day of the holy person after whom they are named.
4. The city of __________ proudly boasts that its St. Patrick's Day celebration is the oldest one in the United States.
5. Finally after six months of probationary work, I became a __________ employee at the State Department.
6. In order to succeed in a course, college students must purchase the __________ textbooks and other supplies each semester.
7. As a response to the loss of homes caused by Hurricane Katrina, many __________ rebuilding programs like modular homes built in Rockefeller Plaza and shipped to the Gulf of Mexico region began.
8. At most holiday celebrations, colorful decorations that depict cultural meanings are __________ in all of the area neighborhoods.

9. The little boy _________ his favorite traditional costume as he prepared to participate in the Posada Festival.
10. The winning Rose Bowl float was _________ with roses, lilacs, daisies, and asters.

Literal Meaning

Mark the letter of the statement that best completes the meaning.

1. The St. Patrick's Day festival described in the article took place in
   a. New York City.
   b. Chippewa.
   c. Savannah.
   d. New Orleans.
2. Because of the rain, festival-goers did what?
   a. They stayed home.
   b. They stayed inside local buildings.
   c. They cancelled the events.
   d. They met the challenge and wore festive clothing under their ponchos.
3. A typical kind of costume of this celebration includes
   a. green beads and shirts.
   b. leprechaun hats.
   c. anything green.
   d. All of the above
4. Pets, who usually participate in the St. Patrick's Day festivities,
   a. were generally left at home because of the rain.
   b. wore special jewelry.
   c. danced in a line.
   d. participated in a costume contest.
5. This festival occurs how often?
   a. Every two years
   b. Once a year in March
   c. At the beginning of fall
   d. When organizers decide it will occur

Interpretive Meaning

Complete the questions with the response that best answers the statement.

1. Why does Cochran say that this holiday required the "creative wearing of green"?
   a. Because participants try to outdo one another
   b. Because certain items must be worn
   c. Because organizers have a costume contest
   d. Because the rain posed a challenge to the normal costuming
2. What is the tone of the article?
   a. Serious
   b. Informative

   c. Argumentative
   d. Humorous
3. Cochran uses the past tense because
   a. Journalistic writing is always written in the past tense.
   b. He cannot write in the present tense for the newspaper.
   c. The event will happen tomorrow.
   d. The events happened the day before the article was published.
4. Cochran says it is ironic that Melynda Loomis left the Irish Setter at home because
   a. the dogs always participate in the parade.
   b. Loomis could not handle another dog leash.
   c. the dog's costume no longer fit the dog.
   d. one would expect a dog of Irish ancestry to attend an Irish celebration.
5. Why does Cochran name the pets and the owners in his article?
   a. He wants to readers to know who attended.
   b. He wants to promote more local participation.
   c. He hopes people will enjoy his article.
   d. All of the above
6. Why does Cochran mention that the purebred collie came from a pet adoption agency?
   a. He wants to call attention to the fact that good animals can be found through pet adoption.
   b. He is being paid by the Second Chance agency to mention its name in the article.
   c. He also adopted an animal at the adoption agency.
   d. He wants to show what a survivor the collie is.
7. Why do people wear silly clothing the festival?
   a. They do not have anything else to wear.
   b. People are proud of the color green.
   c. People try to celebrate the folklore of the Irish holiday.
   d. People feel that they are making a political statement.
8. Why did the author say that the leprechauns stayed in their toasty leprechaun homes?
   a. He was creating humor.
   b. He wanted to state directly where the leprechauns were stationed.
   c. People needed to visit the leprechauns.
   d. The organizers asked him to include this news in his article.

Score: Number correct _______ out of _______

Writing Assignments

1. Journal

Summary

Utilizing the reporter's questions (who, what, where, when, why, how, how much), summarize the newspaper article.

Reaction

Write a one-paragraph reaction to the paragraph focusing on the author's use of adjectives, adverbs, and verbs.

2. *Paragraph*

Write a descriptive paragraph of a parade, a celebration, or a festival in your city or community. In your prewriting activities, decide on the event and the dominant impression you plan to create. Organize accordingly.

3. *Paragraph to Essay*

Expand your paragraph in assignment two to an essay by adding an introductory paragraph, at least one additional body paragraph, and a concluding paragraph. In the introductory paragraph, inform the reader of the place, the event, and the significance of the event. In the thesis statement, mention the dominant impression. Make sure that your body paragraphs have clear topic sentences focusing on the dominant impression. Finalize by drawing a conclusion about the significance of this event to the citizens of your community.

4. *Essay*

Write an essay describing patriotic, personal, and/or religious holidays that you and your family celebrate. Think of a dominant characteristic of the events you are describing and use that as the focus of the essay. For example, are these holidays hectic, quiet, chaotic, stressful, relaxing, or invigorating? Follow the steps for writing an essay.

Day of the Refugios

Alberto Rios

The author describes two celebrations from his childhood: dia de los Refugios and the Fourth of July. He explains the significance of celebrating these two events in Nogales, Arizona, which is on the border between Mexico and the United States.

I was born in **Nogales,** Arizona,
On the border between
Mexico and the United States.

The places in between places
They are like little countries
Themselves, with their own holidays

Taken a little from everywhere.
My Fourth of July is from childhood,
Childhood itself a kind of country, too.

It's a place that's far from me now,
A place I'd like to visit again.
The Fourth of July takes me there.

In that childhood place and border place
The Fourth of July, like everything else,
It meant more than just one thing.

In the United States the Fourth of July
It was the United States.
In Mexico it was the ***día de los Refugios,***

The **saint's day** of people named Refugio.
I come from a family of people with names,
Real names, not-afraid names, with colors

Like the fireworks: Refugio,
Margarito, Matilde, Alvaro, Consuelo,
Humberto, Olga, Celina, Gilberto.

Names that take a moment to say,
Names you have to practice.
These were the names of saints, serious ones,

And it was right to take a moment with them.
I guess that's what my family thought.
The connection to saints was strong:

My grandmother's name—here it comes—
Her name was Refugio,
And my great-grandmother's name was Refugio,

And my mother-in-law's name now,
It's another Refugio, Refugios everywhere,
Refugios and shrimp cocktails and sodas.

Fourth of July was a birthday party
For all the women in my family
Going way back, a party

For everything Mexico, where they came from,
For the other words and the green
Tinted glasses my great-grandmother wore.

These women were me,
What I was before me,
So that birthday fireworks in the evening,

All for them,
This seemed right.
In that way the fireworks were for me, too.

Still, we were in the United States now,
And the Fourth of July,
Well, it was the Fourth of July.

But just what that meant,
In this border place and time,
it was a matter of opinion in my family.

Glossary for "Day of the Refugios"

día (Spanish) day

los (Spanish) the

refugio (Spanish) ref·uge (rĕf'yo͞oj)
n.

1. Protection or shelter, as from danger or hardship.
2. A place providing protection or shelter.
3. A source of help, relief, or comfort in times of trouble.

v. *Archaic* **ref·uged, ref·ug·ing, ref·ug·es**
v. tr.
To give refuge to.
v. intr.
To take refuge.
[Middle English, from Old French, from Latin refugium, from refugere, *to run away* ; re-, *re-* + fugere, *to flee.*]

ref·u·gee (rĕf'yo͞o-jē')
n.
One who flees in search of refuge, as in times of war, political oppression, or religious persecution.
[French réfugié, from past participle of réfugier, *to take refuge*, from Old French, from refuge, *refuge.*]

No·gal·es (nō-găl'ĭs, -gä'lĭs)

A city of southern Arizona south of Tucson on the Mexican border adjacent to **Nogales,** Mexico. Both cities are ports of entry and tourist centers. Nogales, Arizona, has a population of 19,489; Nogales, Mexico, has 14,254 inhabitants.

saint's day (sānts)

n. pl. **saints' days**

A day in a liturgical calendar that is observed in honor of a saint.

saint (sānt)

n.

1. a. *Abbr.* **St.** or **S.** *Christianity.* A person officially recognized, especially by canonization, as being entitled to public veneration and capable of interceding for people on earth.
   b. A person who has died and gone to heaven.
   c. **Saint** A member of any of various religious groups, especially a Latter-Day Saint.
2. An extremely virtuous person.

tr. v. **saint·ed, saint·ing, saints**

To name, recognize, or venerate as a saint; canonize.

[Middle English seint, from Old French saint, from Late Latin sānctus, from Latin, *holy,* past participle of sancīre, *to consecrate.*]

Reading Comprehension

Answer the following questions about Albert Rios's "Day of the Refugios."

Word Meaning

Select the word from the glossary that best completes the sentences below.

1. Many Latin songs contain the word __________ to mean "day."
2. My sister moved to __________ from Arkansas because she could speak two languages in this city, English and Spanish.
3. Many Mexican children celebrate their __________, the feast day of the holy person after whom they are named.
4. Many people believe that Mother Teresa should be canonized a __________ for her good works with the people of India.
5. Most Americans know that the word to express "the" in Spanish is __________.
6. Many __________ settled in America from Mexico and other countries during the 1990s.

Literal Meaning

Mark the letter of the statement that best completes the meaning.

1. Nogales is a border town between
   a. Texas and Louisiana.
   b. Washington and California.
   c. Mexico and Arizona.
   d. Alabama and Mississippi.

2. Día de los Refugio (the Day of the Refugios) is the name the Mexicans use to celebrate
   a. one's saint's day.
   b. one's birthday.
   c. one's citizenship day.
   d. the Fourth of July.
3. At the time the poem was composed, the narrator of the poem lived in
   a. Mexico.
   b. Canada.
   c. the United States.
   d. a mountain home.
4. The holiday was celebrated with
   a. fireworks.
   b. special jewelry and clothing.
   c. dancing.
   d. all of the above.
5. The narrator refers to childhood as a kind of
   a. party.
   b. difficult period.
   c. gift.
   d. country.
6. The author says her family members were all named
   a. refugio.
   b. Juanita.
   c. saint.

Interpretive Meaning

Complete the questions with the response that best answers the statement.

1. Why does the narrator say that the places in between places are like little countries?
   a. Because these places are not located on a map
   b. Because they have unique characteristics of both areas that they border
   c. Because they have their own form of government
   d. Because they have special schools
2. What does Rios mean by the statement that "The Fourth of July, like everything else, / It meant more that just one thing"?
   a. The holiday was celebrated with both American food and Mexican food.
   b. The holiday includes both flag waving and fireworks.
   c. The meaning of the holiday depends on the immigration status of the person celebrating it.
   d. The holiday's meaning is derived from the native culture of the person celebrating.
3. Why were so many of the family members of the narrator named Refugio?
   a. The family liked the sound of the name.
   b. The family always gave the same name to members of the next generation.

   c. The members of the family were all immigrants to the United States.
   d. The name meant power in the community.
4. Why does the narrator include refugios, shrimp cocktails, and soda in the same list?
   a. These words convey how prevalent the refugios were in the city.
   b. These are items that cost a lot of money, which adds to the value of the refugios.
   c. The narrator likes to compare using food items.
   d. These are the narrator's favorite food items for the Fourth of July.
5. Fireworks are mentioned throughout the poem to
   a. give the poem unity.
   b. symbolize the move to the United States.
   c. represent the confused feelings of an immigrant family.
   d. all of the above.
6. The narrator refers to "birthday fireworks" as a means to
   a. call attention to the difference between a birthday and a saint's day in the Mexican culture.
   b. remind the reader that the Fourth of July is the birthday of the United States.
   c. show how Americans celebrate the holiday.
   d. celebrate "everything Mexico" that goes way back.
7. Why does the author say that the meaning of the Fourth of July was a matter of opinion in his family?
   a. Everyone in the family celebrated in a different way.
   b. The family members felt more American than Mexican.
   c. The family members felt more Mexican than American.
   d. The family members had different attitudes about living in a new country where they felt neither Mexican nor American.
8. What other title would be most appropriate for this poem?
   a. "The Fourth of July"
   b. "Living in a Border Town"
   c. "Ambivalence"
   d. "Nogales"

Score: Number correct _______ out of _______

Writing Assignments

1. Journal Writing

Summary

Summarize the poem in prose. Explain what the author saying in your own words. To do this exercise, concentrate on each line and notice the punctuation marks.

Reaction

What did you enjoy about the poem? What questions do you have about the poem? What do you think the main idea of the poem is? How can you relate the author's ideas of celebrating the Fourth of July to any of the holidays that you celebrate? Consider these questions when writing a reaction paragraph.

2. ***Paragraph***
   Write a paragraph describing a celebration enjoyed by your family or friends. In the paragraph, focus on a particular atmosphere or an overall feeling of the celebration. Include the sights, sounds, smells, tastes, and textures of the celebration. Use strong verbs as well as adjectives and adverbs to write the description. While planning the paragraph, keep in mind that you are writing a descriptive paragraph, not a narrative paragraph. Rather than becoming distracted and writing about what you did on the holiday or what you did to celebrate the event, focus on a description of the atmosphere or venue of the celebration.

3. ***Paragraph to Essay***
   Expand the paragraph in assignment two to an essay. Use the paragraph as a draft and rewrite the body paragraphs so that you are focusing on one of the senses in each body paragraph. Add an introductory paragraph explaining the event and its importance to you and your family and friends. In your thesis, mention the dominant feeling or impression associated with the event. In the concluding paragraph, restate your thesis. Do not use the same words.

4. ***Essay***
   Write an essay describing a celebration, a holiday, or a festival that is important to you. In the introductory paragraph, consider explaining why the holiday is important or, if you are focusing on one particular event, such as becoming thirteen, fifteen, eighteen, or twenty-one, give background information about that particular event. Focus on one part of the celebration in each body paragraph. If you are writing about a place, such as a favorite vacation destination, organize the essay by focusing on one image in each body paragraph. In the concluding paragraph, consider discussing your hopes or plans in the future for this holiday.

Reflective Assignments

1. Reflect on the Longfellow quote at the beginning of the chapter. Define "secret anniversaries of the heart." Write a paragraph or short essay describing a real or fictional secret anniversary of the heart. Use literal and figurative language to describe the event.
2. Consider this quotation by Fred Rogers about holidays: "I like to compare the holiday season with the way a child listens to a favorite story. The pleasure is in the familiar way the story begins, the anticipation of familiar turns it takes, the familiar moments of suspense, and the familiar climax and ending." [Fred Rogers, *Mister Rogers Talks with Parents*, Chapter 11 (1983)]

Write a narrative describing a celebration you remember as a child. Use descriptive writing techniques learned in this chapter to make the story come alive for your audience. Remember to focus on the senses and to create a verbal photograph.

3. Write a paragraph or an essay relating one of the idiomatic expressions from the beginning of the unit to a holiday celebration in which you have participated. In your writing, use the descriptive techniques you have learned.
4. Write a poem describing a holiday that is meaningful to you. Use figurative language to enhance your poem. As a follow-up assignment, write a literary analysis of the figurative language used in your poem.
5. Write a paragraph analyzing the figurative language used in "Day of the Refugios." Before writing your paragraph, review the techiques for literary analysis discussed in Unit 1.
6. Create a holiday that you think should be celebrated. Write several paragraphs describing this holiday. Include the reasons for the holiday as well as when the holiday should be celebrated. Describe the festivities that should be included in the celebration.

Internet Field Trips—Reading and Writing Assignments

1. Visit the Web site of the Balch Institute for Ethnic Studies—Something Old, Something New: Ethnic Weddings in America, http://www2.hsp.org/exhibits/Balch%20exhibits/wedding/wedding. html. Pay close attention to the wedding pictures at the beginning of the article. Read through the table of contents and skim the articles listed. Read the article "The Photographer's View" by Katrina Thomas. Click the wedding pictures at the beginning of the Web site again and examine them. Choose one picture and write a descriptive paragraph of the picture.
2. Research jazz funerals on the Internet, and then write a descriptive paragraph describing jazz funerals in general or a specific jazz funeral you read about. The following Web sites will be helpful:
   - http://www2.hsp.org/exhibits/Balch%20exhibits/rites/african.html "Case Study; Jazz Funerals African Funerals and Memorial Services in America" by Elizabeth M. Holland
   - http://www.neworleansonline.com/neworleans/history/jazzfuneral .html "The Jazz Funeral" (originally printed in *The Soul of New Orleans.*)
   - http://www.post-gazette.com/pg/05252/568683.stm "New Orleans Jazz Funerals Are a Causality of Katrina" by Steven Gray and Evan Perez.
   - http://www.houstonculture.org/cr/jazz.html Cultural Crossroads Regional and Historical Perspectives; Houston Institute of Culture; "Regional Traditions: Jazz Funerals."
3. Research unusual holidays or celebrations. Write a paragraph describing the celebration you find the most interesting. To get started, find information

about the following holidays: Umbrella Day, Bumbershoot, Festival of Sleep Day, Cuckoo Warning Day, National Dress Up Your Pet Day, Better Breakfast Month. The Web sites listed below may help you.

- http://www.groundhog.org
- http://www.bumbershoot.com/info.html
- http://library.thinkquest.org/2886/jan.htm
- http://www.holidayinsights.com/moreholidays

FILMS TO VIEW

Last Holiday (directed by Wayne Wang, 2006)
The Wedding Singer (directed by Frank Coraci, 1998)
Father's Day (directed by Ivan Reitman, 1997)
Ferris Bueller's Day Off (directed by John Hughes, 1986)
My Big Fat Greek Wedding (directed by Joel Aurick and written by Nia Vardalos, 2002)

Writing assignments are based on *My Big Fat Greek Wedding* (2002), directed by Joel Aurick and written by Nia Vardalos.

1. The tagline of the movie is "Love is here to stay—so is her family."
   a. Write a paragraph explaining how this tagline can be considered the theme of the movie. Give examples from the movie to support your premise.
   b. Think of your own tagline for the movie. Write a paragraph explaining how your original tagline summarizes the main ideas of the movie.
2. Write several paragraphs describing the main character of the movie, Toula Portokalos. Describe her appearance and physical demeanor before and after she decides to return to school.
3. Write an essay describing three of the main or supporting characters in the movie. Consider Toula Portokalos, Gus Portokalos, Ian Miller, Nikki, Toula's brothers.
4. Write a paragraph describing one of the following: Toula's bridesmaid dresses; Toula's wedding dress; Toula and Michael's wedding reception; the Portoklos home; Dancing Zorbas, the restaurant owned by Gus Portokalos.
5. If you were writing a screenplay about wedding traditions in your own culture or ethnic group, what traditions would you want to include? Write a paragraph describing one or more of those customs.
6. Write an essay describing how Toula changes from the beginning of the movie to the end of the movie. Consider how education, her father's expectations, and her mother's personality affect these changes.
7. Select a favorite scene from the movie and write a description of the scene. Include not only description of the setting and characters but also of the audio. Explain how the audio and visual effects contributed to the development of the action in the scene.

SUMMARY OF UNIT 3—TRADITIONS AND CELEBRATIONS—DESCRIPTION

Read the student paragraph entitled "The House on Rose Cove" by Stacey Williams.

Analyze its content, its organization, its figurative language, and its mechanics. Then, in the Summary of Unit 3 complete the column on the right with your responses. Apply the information learned in Unit 3.

The House on Rose Cove

When I was a child, my cousin and I would walk down this street called Rose Cove. From Sunday through Saturday, we would walk. Then on one particular Sunday, we were walking and heard a voice. The voice said, "Psst, psst." We just kept on walking, talked, and ignoring the voice. The psst's got louder. My cousin asked, "Did you hear that?" I said, "Yes, it's coming from that old house!" So we walked back toward the house. This gray stone house had been empty for years. The lady who lived there had died several years ago. As we approached the sagging porch on the house, we saw an elderly lady. She said, "Come here, Stacey and Teena." We looked at each other frightened and wondering if we should see what she wanted. We decided to go into the spooky front room. To our surprise, the Victorian-style furniture in the house was beautiful. I had never seen such pretty furniture. The house was so pretty that we forgot about being afraid. The lady never said a word. She was just watching us look around in amazement. I turned and looked at the lady, and suddenly noticed that her feet were not there. My eyes got bigger than fifty-cent pieces. The lady was floating on thin air. I tugged on my cousin's coat because I couldn't say a word. I was speechless. My cousin then looked and also saw the lady floating. We both screamed and ran out of the house and down the street. When we made it home, we were out of breath. Screaming my mother's name, she ran into the kitchen where we were shivering. "What's wrong with the two of you?" asked my mother. We just saw a ghost! "A ghost!" my mother replied. "Please tell me you didn't answer to the calls from the house on Rose Cove!" We were forbidden to walk on Rose Cove ever again.

Summary of Unit 3

1. The topic sentence is	1.
2. The main tense in the description is	2.
3. Three transitions used include	3.
4. The tone of this paragraph is	4.
5. The purpose of this paragraph is to	5.
6. The writer concludes by	6.
7. The reader can infer that the writer	7.
8. Traits of description present are	8.
9. Three mechanical errors include	9.
10. An example of figurative language	10.
11. Examples of sensory impressions	11.

Unit 4

American Folklore

Time is a good story teller.

—Irish Proverb

Folklore represents the early oral literature of a culture. What contrasts do you see between the traditional story depicted and the contemporary style of the artist's rendering of the folk tale?

Much American folklore expresses the work ethic of the people of a nation. How do the images in the picture compare and contrast with your mental images of the characters and action of the John Henry folk tale?

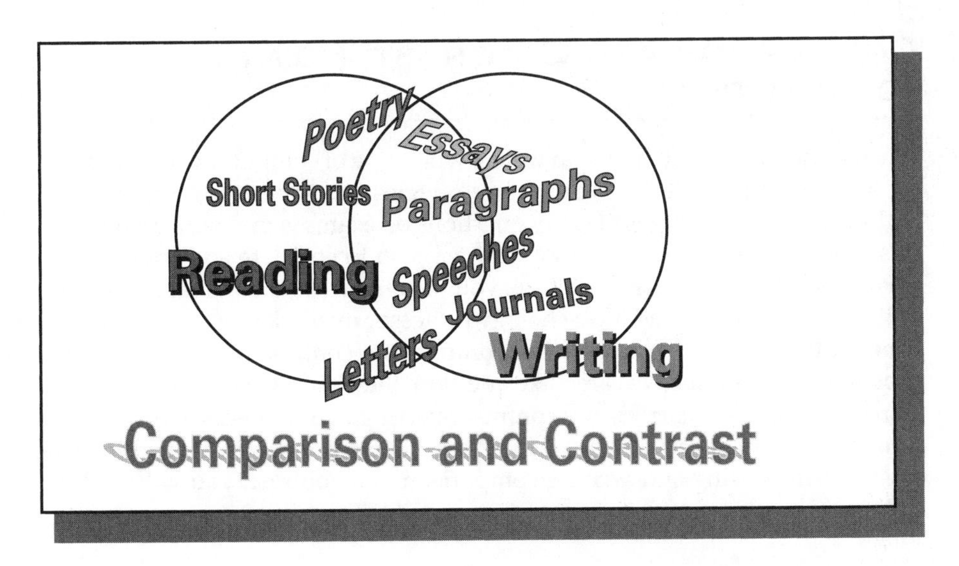

Purpose of Unit:

- *To understand the pattern of comparison and contrast as it relates to reading comprehension and writing*

Idioms for American Folklore

Review the idioms below and discuss their meaning. Apply these idioms to your understanding of American folklore, wisdom, and common sense.

The pen is mightier than the sword.
A penny saved is a penny earned.
Penny wise and pound-foolish
When pigs fly
Practice makes perfect.
Pride comes before a fall.
The proof of the pudding is in the eating.
A rolling stone gathers no moss.
Silence is golden.
Once upon a time
Evil eye
Opposites attract.
Birds of a feather flock together.
Elvis has left the building.
The road to hell is paved with good intentions.
People who live in glass houses should not throw stones.

Comparison and Contrast: Points to Consider

Whether deciding what movie to watch, what type of computer to buy, or what car gets better gas mileage, we use the strategies of comparison/contrast. One of the most common types of essay questions on exams is the comparison/contrast question. A history professor may ask you to compare and contrast two leaders, a biology professor may ask you to compare and contrast the growth pattern of two plants, and a psychology professor may ask you to compare and contrast two personality types. The comparison/contrast mode of writing is used to show how subjects are alike and how they are different, with comparison referring to similarities and contrast referring to differences. However, the term *compare* or *comparison paper* is often used to mean comparison and/or contrast. When reading and writing comparison and contrast, you will find the following points helpful.

Purpose

The purpose of a comparison/contrast essay is to analyze two subjects by exploring their similarities and differences. Comparison/contrast essays can be written with the purpose to present information to the reader, or comparison/contrast can be used to persuade or present an argument.

Tone

The tone, or the attitude of the writer, varies in comparison and contrast essays, just as it does in all essays. You will notice a playful and a sarcastic tone in David Sedaris's essay "Six to Eight Black Men." In the "What Is Folklife?" excerpts from "A Commonwealth of Cultures" by Mary Hufford and "Present at Creation: The Origin of John Henry" by Stephen Wade, the tone is academic.

Transitional Devices

Transitional words used for showing differences include *in contrast, however, although, in spite of, despite, even though, instead, nevertheless, on the other hand, conversely, but, yet.*

Transitional words used for showing similarities include *in comparison, in the same way, likewise, similarly, just as, also.*

ORGANIZATION

Because of the vast amount of information that may be required in a comparison/contrast essay, organization is important. Although, in general, assignments in this chapter require that you focus on either similarities or differences, comparison/contrast essays may focus on similarities, differences, or a combination of the two. The information presented within the writing should be in either **point-by-point** style or **subject-by-subject (block style).** In point-by-point style, the author will present each point at a time. For instance, if the author is comparing two types of weddings, a destination wedding and a hometown wedding, the three points might be the guests, the expenses, and the setting. In a **point-by-point** paragraph or essay, the author will write first about the guest list for a hometown wedding and a destination wedding. The next point would be about the expenses for both types of weddings; then the next point should focus on the setting for both the destination and hometown wedding. In subject-by-subject, the author will discuss the destination wedding and all of the information about it first and the hometown wedding next. The paragraph and essay formats will help you to organize effectively your assignments.

Paragraph Formats for Writing Comparison/Contrast

Topic ______________________________

Two subjects being compared ______________________________

Points being compared ______________________________

Subject-by-Subject Format

Topic Sentence ______________________________

(Mention both subjects in the topic sentence.)

Subject A (Points)

Subject B (Points)

Concluding Sentence ______________________________

Point-by-Point Format

Topic Sentence ______________________________

Point 1—Both subjects

Point 2—Both subjects

Point 3—Both subjects

Concluding Sentence ______________________________

Essay Formats for Writing Comparison/Contrast

Topic ____________________

Two subjects being compared or contrasted ____________________

Points being compared ____________________

Thesis statement: (In the essay, the thesis statement belongs in the introductory paragraph, usually the last sentence.) ____________

____

Subject-by-Subject Format

Introduction

Introduce the two subjects and end with a thesis statement.

____

Body Paragraph 1

Subject A

3 points of discussion

Body Paragraph 2

Subject B

3 points of discussion

Concluding Paragraph

Point-by-Point Format

Introduction

Introduce the two subjects and end with a thesis statement.

____

Body 1 Paragraph 1—Point 1

Subject A

Subject B

Body 2 Paragraph—Point 2

Subject A

Subject B

Body Paragraph 3—Point 3

Subject A

Subject B

Concluding Paragraph

Summary and/or conclusion

Combination Comparison/Contrast

Introductory Paragraph

Introduce the two subjects and end with a thesis statement.

____

Body Paragraph 1

Topic sentence

Focus on Similarities

Body Paragraph 2

Topic Sentence

Focus on Differences

Concluding Paragraph

Comparison and Contrast Writing Worksheet

1. Survey the assignment and choose your topic. Do one of the prewriting assignments discussed in the introduction of the text.
2. Question the assignment. What is the focus of the assignment? What are you comparing or contrasting? Ask the 5 W's + H about your writing. Who? What? Where? When? Why? How?
3. Map your essay or paragraph. Make sure you are "giving equal time" to both subjects you are comparing or contrasting.
4. Relate or tell your plan of writing to your writing group. After you have finished, group members should ask you to clarify the parts of your plan that are unclear, and they should use reporter's questions to pry you for more details.
5. Record (write) the first draft of your essay or paragraph.
6. Read your paragraph or essay aloud to a student partner. As you read, the partner should listen for understanding and jot down any questions. These questions may be about parts of your writing that are unclear. The questions should also concern details.
7. Revise your essay, taking into account the questions that your peer editors asked about your paper. Add the needed details, but check to make sure you are staying on the subject.
8. Review your revised paper with your partner and answer Questions for Review.
9. Reflect upon the comments of your peers and make needed changes.
10. Reread your paper, checking for grammatical errors. Read your paper from top to bottom and from bottom to top. Reading your paper in reverse helps

you to read what you wrote, not what you meant to write! As you read your paper, check carefully for consistent tense, correct sentence structure, and punctuation of complex sentences.

11. Read your paper aloud.
12. Write your final draft!

Questions for Review

Paragraph Assignment

- What is the topic sentence?
- Does the topic sentence mention both subjects that are being compared or contrasted?
- What is the pattern of development for the paragraph—block or point by point?
- Are there any parts of the paragraph that are unclear? If so, how should this problem be corrected?
- What transitional words are used to take the reader from one idea to another?
- What key words are used to give the paragraph unity?
- What is the concluding sentence?
- What part of the paragraph is most effective?
- What parts of the paragraph should the author change? Give suggestions for the changes.

Essay Assignments

The Introductory Paragraph

- Does the introduction make you want to read the essay?
- What is the focus of the essay? What is being compared or contrasted?
- What is the thesis statement?

The Body Paragraphs

- What is the pattern of development for each body paragraph?
- Is "equal time" given to both subjects?
- What is the topic sentence for each body paragraph? Does the topic sentence mention both subjects being compared?
- Are there any parts of the paragraphs that are confusing? If so, what are they and how can the problem be solved?
- What are the transitional words used to guide the reader from one body paragraph to the next?
- What are the transitional words used within the body paragraphs?
- What key words has the author used to give the essay unity?
- Write examples of strong verbs the author has used. Select several verbs that need to be stronger and make suggestions for change.

The Conclusion

- How does the author conclude the essay?

The Entire Essay

- What is the strongest part of the essay?
- What changes should the author make?

Topic Sentences and Thesis Statements

When writing comparison/contrast papers, be careful that both subjects being compared are stated in the topic sentences and in the thesis statement. The thesis statement and topic sentences are contracts with the reader, your promise that you will develop the ideas stated. If you are comparing urban myths to folktales in the body paragraph and your thesis statement only states urban myths, then your paragraph can only be about urban myths.

Correct Topic Sentence

> Both urban myths and folktales attempt to teach lessons and warn people of danger.

Incorrect Topic Sentence (for a Paragraph Discussing Both Folktales and Urban Myths)

> Folktales attempt to teach lessons and warn people of danger.

Punctuation of Conjunctive Adverbs and Subordinate Conjunctions

When editing, check carefully for correct use and punctuation of words that introduce subordinate clauses and conjunctive adverbs. *However, in spite of, despite* are conjunctive adverbs. *Although* is a subordinate conjunction and is punctuated differently.

Correct Form

> *Although* Cinderella stories from around the world have similar plots, older versions of the story seem to be more frightening.

Correct Form

> Cinderella stories from around the world have similar plots; however, older versions of the story seem to be more frightening.

Correct Form

> In spite of the similarities in plot, older versions of Cinderella stories seem to be more frightening.

Correct Form

> Despite differences in plot, older versions of Cinderella stories seem to be more frightening.

Punctuate the following sentences.

1. John Henry was a very strong man however he had a weakness for women.
2. Despite the green pastures of Bessie the Yellow Cow's native lands she loved Babe the Blue Ox strongly enough to relocate to his colder climate.

READING BEFORE WRITING

What Is Folklife? Excerpts from A Commonwealth of Cultures

Mary Hufford

In this essay, author Mary Hufford, a folklife specialist at the American Folklife Center and a member of the executive board of the American Folklore Society, defines folklife and discusses the importance of preserving cultural diversity.

What Is Folklife?

Like Edgar Allen Poe's **purloined** letter, folklife is often hidden in full view, lodged in the various ways we have of discovering and expressing who we are and how we fit into the world. Folklife is reflected in the names we bear from birth, invoking **affinities** with saints, ancestors, or cultural heroes. Folklife is your grandfather and great-uncles telling stories of your father when he was a boy. It is the secret languages of children, the codenames of CB operators, and the working slang of watermen and doctors. It is the sung **parodies** of the "Battle Hymn of the Republic," and the **parables** told in church or home to delight and instruct. It is African-American rhythms embedded in gospel hymns, bluegrass music, and hip hop, and it is the Lakota flutist rendering anew his people's ancient courtship songs.

Folklife is society welcoming new members at **bris** and christening, and keeping the dead incorporated on All Saints Day. It is the marking of the Jewish New Year at **Rosh Hashanah** and the Persian New Year at Noruz. It is New York City's streets enlivened by Lion Dancers in celebration of Chinese New Year and by Southern Italian immigrants dancing their towering giglios in honor of St. Paulinus each summer. It is the ubiquitous appearance of yellow ribbons to express a complicated sentiment about war, and displays of orange pumpkins on front porches at Halloween.

Folklife is the recycling of scraps of clothing and bits of experience into quilts that tell stories, and the stories told by those gathered around quilting frames. It is the evolution of **vaqueros** into buckaroos, and the variety of ways there are to skin a muskrat, preserve shuck beans, or join two pieces of wood. It is the oysterboat carved into the above-ground grave of the Louisiana fisherman, and the eighteen-wheeler on the trucker's tombstone in Illinois.

Folklife is the thundering of foxhunters across the rolling Rappahanock hunt country, and the listening of hilltoppers to hounds crying fox in the Tennessee mountains. It is the twirling of lariats at western rodeos, and the spinning of double-dutch jumpropes in West Philadelphia. It is scattered across the landscape in Finnish saunas and Italian vineyards; engraved in the split rail boundaries of Appalachian "hollers" and in the stone fences around Catskill "cloves"; scrawled on urban streetscapes by graffiti artists; and projected on skylines into which mosques, temples, steeples, and onion domes taper.

Folklife is community life and values, artfully expressed in myriad interactions. It is universal, diverse, and enduring. It enriches the nation and makes us a commonwealth of cultures.

Folklore, Folklife, and the American Folklife Preservation Act

The study of folklore and folklife stands at the **confluence** of several European academic traditions. The terms folklore and folklife were coined by nineteenth-century scholars who saw that the industrial and agricultural revolutions were outmoding the older ways of life, making many customs and technologies **paradoxically** more **conspicuous** as they disappeared. In 1846 Englishman William J. Thoms gathered up the **profusion** of "manners, customs, observances, superstitions, ballads, proverbs, etc., of the olden time" under the single term folk-lore. In so doing he provided his colleagues interested in "popular antiquities" with a framework for their endeavor and modern folklorists with a name for their profession.

As Thoms and his successors combed the British **hinterlands** for "stumps and stubs" of disappearing traditions, the folklife studies movement was germinating in continental Europe. There scholars began using the Swedish folkliv and the German Volksleben to designate vernacular (or folk) culture in its entirety, including customs and material culture (the ways in which people transform their surroundings into food, shelter, clothing, tools, and landscapes) as well as oral traditions. Today the study of folklife encompasses all of the traditional expressions that shape and are shaped by cultural groups. While folklore and folklife may be used to distinguish oral tradition from material culture, the terms often are used interchangeably as well.

Over the past century the study of folklore has developed beyond the romantic quest for remnants of bygone days to the study of how community life and values are expressed through a wide variety of living traditions. To most people, however, the term folklore continues to suggest aspects of culture that are out-of-date or on the fringe—the province of old people, ethnic groups, and the rural poor. The term may even be used to characterize something as **trivial** or untrue, as in "that's just folklore." Modern folklorists believe that no aspect of culture is trivial, and that the impulse to make culture, to traditionalize shared experiences, **imbuing** them with form and meaning, is universal among humans. Reflecting on their hardships and triumphs in song, story, ritual, and object, people everywhere shape cultural legacies meant to outlast each generation.

In 1976, as the United States celebrated its Bicentennial, the U.S. Congress passed the American Folklife Preservation Act (P.L. 94-201). In writing the legislation, Congress had to define folklife. Here is what the law says:

> "American folklife" means the traditional expressive culture shared within the various groups in the United States: familial, ethnic, occupational, religious, regional; expressive culture includes a wide range of creative and symbolic forms such as custom, belief, technical skill, language, literature, art, architecture, music, play, dance, drama, ritual, pageantry, handicraft; these expressions are mainly learned orally, by imitation, or in performance, and are generally maintained without benefit of formal instruction or institutional direction.

Created after more than a century of legislation designed to protect physical aspects of heritage—natural species, tracts of wilderness, landscapes, historic buildings, artifacts, and monuments—the law reflects a growing awareness among the American people that cultural diversity, which distinguishes and strengthens us as a nation, is also a resource worthy of protection. In the United States, awareness of folklife has been heightened both by the presence of many cultural groups from all over the world and by the accelerated pace of change in the latter half of the twentieth century. However, the effort to conserve folklife should not be seen simply as an attempt to preserve vanishing ways of life. Rather, the American Folklife Preservation Act recognizes the vitality of folklife today. As a measure for safeguarding cultural diversity, the law signals an important departure from the once widely-held notion of the United States as a melting pot, which assumed that members of ethnic groups would become homogenized as "Americans." We no longer view cultural difference as a problem to be solved, but as a tremendous opportunity. In the diversity of American folklife we find a marketplace teeming with the exchange of traditional forms and cultural ideas, a rich resource for Americans who constantly shape and transform their cultures.

Sharing with others the experience of family life, ethnic origin, occupation, religious beliefs, stage of life, recreation, and geographic proximity, most individuals belong to more than one cultural group. Some groups have existed for thousands of years, while others come together temporarily around a variety of shared concerns—particularly in America, where democratic principles have long sustained what Alexis de Tocqueville called the distinctly American "art of associating together."

Taken as a whole, the thousands of grassroots associations in the United States form a fairly comprehensive index to our nation's cultural affairs. Some, like ethnic organizations and churches, have explicitly cultural aims, while others spring up around common environmental, recreational, or occupational concerns. Some cultural groups may be less official: family members at a reunion, coworkers in a factory, or friends gathered to make back-porch (or kitchen, or garage) music. Other cultural groups may be more official: San Sostine Societies, chapters of Ducks Unlimited, the Mount Pleasant Basketmakers Association, volunteer fire companies, and senior citizens clubs. Sorting and re-sorting themselves into a vast array of cultural groups, Americans continually create culture out of their shared experiences.

The traditional knowledge and skills required to make a pie crust, plant a garden, arrange a birthday party, or turn a lathe are exchanged in the course of daily living and learned by imitation. It is not simply skills that are transferred in such interactions, but notions about the proper ways to be human at a particular time and place. Whether sung or told, enacted or crafted, traditions are the outcroppings of deep **lodes** of worldview, knowledge, and wisdom, navigational aids in an ever-fluctuating social world. Conferring on community members a vital sense of identity, belonging, and purpose, folklife defends against social disorders like delinquency, **indigence,** and drug abuse, which are themselves symptoms of deep cultural crises.

As cultural groups invest their surroundings with memory and meaning, they provide, in effect, blueprints for living. For American Indian people, the landscape is **redolent** of origin myths and cautionary tales, which come alive as grandmothers decipher ancient place names to their descendants. Similarly, though far from their native countries, immigrant groups may keep alive mythologies and histories tied to landscapes in the old country, evoking them through architecture, music, dance, ritual, and craft. Thus Russian immigrants flank their homes with birch trees reminiscent of Eastern Europe. The call-and-response pattern of West African music is preserved in the gospel music of African Americans. Puerto Rican women dancing La Plena mime their Jibaro forebears who washed their clothes in the island's mountain streams. The passion of Christ is annually mapped onto urban landscapes in the Good Friday processions of Hispanic Americans, and Ukrainian-Americans, inscribing Easter eggs, overlay pre-Christian emblems of life and fertility with Christian significance.

Traditional ways of doing things are often deemed unremarkable by their practitioners, until cast into relief by abrupt change, confrontation with alternative ways of doing things, or the fresh perspective of an outsider (such as a folklorist). The diversity of American cultures has been **catalytic** in this regard, prompting people to recognize and reflect upon their own cultural distinctiveness. Once grasped as distinctive, ways of doing things may become emblems of participation. Ways of greeting one another, of seasoning foods, of ornamenting homes and landscapes may be deliberately used to hold together people, past, and place. Ways to wrap proteins in starches come to distinguish those who make pierogis, dumplings, pupusas, or dim sum. The weave of a blanket or basket can bespeak African American, Native American, or Middle Eastern identity and values. Distinctive rhythms, whether danced, strummed, sung, or drummed, may synchronize Americans born in the same decade, or who share common ancestry or beliefs.

Traditions do not simply pass along unchanged. In the hands of those who practice them they may be vigorously remodeled, woven into the present, and laden with new meanings. Folklife, often seen as a casualty of change, may actually survive because it is reformulated to solve cultural, social, and biological crises. Older traditions may be pressed into service for mending the ruptures between past and present, and between old and new worlds. Thus Hmong immigrants use the textile tradition of **paj ntaub** to record the violent events that hurled them from their traditional world in Vietnam into a profoundly different life in the United States. South Carolina sweetgrass basketmakers carry on a two-centuries-old tradition that reaches back to Africa. And a Puerto Rican street theater troupe dramatizes culture conflict on the mainland in a bilingual **farce** about foodways.

Retirement or the onset of old age can occasion a return to traditional crafts learned early in life. For the woman making a memory quilt or the machinist making models of tools no longer in use, traditional forms become a way of reconstituting the past in the present. The craft, the recipe, the photo album, or the ceremony serve as thresholds to a vanishing world in which an elderly person's values and identity are rooted. This is especially significant to younger witnesses for whom the past is thus made tangible and animated through stories inspired by the forms.

Cultural lineages do not always follow genealogical ones. Often a tradition's "rightful" heirs are not very interested in inheriting it. Facing indifference among the young from their own cultural groups, and pained by the possibility that their traditions might die out, masters of traditional arts and skills may deliberately rewrite the cultural will, taking on students from many different backgrounds in order to bequeath their traditions. Modern life has broadened the pool of potential heirs, making it possible for a basketmaker from New England to turn to the craft revival for apprentices, or a master of the Chinese Opera in New York to find eager students among European Americans.

The United States is not a melting pot, but neither is it a fixed **mosaic** of ethnic enclaves. From the beginning, our nation has been a meeting ground of many cultures, whose interactions have produced a unique array of cultural groups and forms. Responding to the challenges of life in the same locale, different ethnic groups may cast their lot together under regional identities as "buckaroos," "Pineys," "watermen," or "Hoosiers," without surrendering ethnicity in other settings. Distinctive ways of speaking, fiddling, dancing, making chili, and designing boats can evolve into resources for expressing and celebrating regional identity. Thus ways of shucking oysters or lassoing cattle can become touchstones of identity for **itinerant** workers, distinguishing Virginians from Marylanders or Texans from Californians. And in a Washington,

D.C., neighborhood, Hispanic-Americans from various South and Central American countries explore an emerging Latino identity, which they express through an annual festival and parade that would not occur in their countries of origin.

Over the past two centuries, the intercultural transactions that are so distinctly American have produced uniquely New World blends whose origins we no longer recognize. When one tradition is spotlighted, others fade into the background. We tend to forget that the banjo, now played almost exclusively by white musicians, was a cultural idea introduced here by African-Americans, and that the tradition of lining out hymns that today flourishes mainly in African-American churches is a legacy from England. Without this early nineteenth-century interchange, perhaps these distinct traditions would have disappeared. And out of the same cultural encounters in the upper South that produced these transfers, there grew distinctly American styles of music **suffused** with African-American ideas of **syncopation.**

Other forgotten legacies of early cultural encounters spangle the landscape. Early American watermen freely combined ideas from English punts, Swedish flatboats, and French bateaus to create small wooden boats that now register subtleties of wind, tide, temperature, and contours of earth beneath far-flung waters of the United States. Thus have Jersey garveys, Ozark john boats, and Mackenzie River skiffs become vessels conveying regional identity. The martin birdhouse complexes commonly found in yards east of the Mississippi River hail from gourd dwellings that American Indians devised centuries ago to entice the insect-eating birds into cohabitation. Descendants of those American Indians now live beyond the territory of martins, while the descendants of seventeenth-century martins live in houses modeled on Euro-American architectural forms.

The early colonists' adoption of an ingenious form of mosquito control exemplifies a strong pattern throughout our history, the pattern of one group freely borrowing and transforming the cultural ideas of another. We witness the continuance of this pattern in the appropriation of the Greek **bouzouki** by Irish-American musicians, in the influence of Cajun, Yiddish, and African styles on popular music, in the co-opting of Cornish pasties by Finnish Minnesotans, and in the embracing of ancient Japanese techniques of joinery by American woodworkers.

American folklife stoutly resists the effects of a melting pot. If it simmers at all it is in many pots of gumbo, burgoo, chili, goulash, and booya. And the American people are the chefs, concocting culture from the resources and ideas in the American folklife repertory. Folklife flourishes when children gather to play, when artisans attract students and clientele, when parents and grandparents pass along their traditions and values to the younger generations, whether in the kitchen or in an ethnic or parochial school. Defining and celebrating themselves in a constantly changing world, Americans enliven the landscape with parades, **sukkos,** and powwows, seasonally inscribing their worldviews on doorways and graveyards, valiantly keeping **indeterminacy** at bay. Our common wealth circulates in a free flowing exchange of cultural ideas, which on reflection appear to merge and diverge, surface and submerge throughout our history like contra dancers advancing and retiring, like stitches dropped and retrieved in the hands of a lacemaker, like strands of bread ritually braided, like the reciprocating bow of a master fiddler.

Glossary for "What Is Folklife?" Excerpts from "A Commonwealth of Cultures"

pur·loin (pər-loin', pûr'loin') *v.* **pur·loined, pur·loin·ing, pur·loins**

v. tr.

To steal, often in a violation of trust.

v. intr.

To commit theft.

[Middle English purloinen, *to remove*, from Anglo-Norman purloigner: pur-, *away* (from Latin prō-.[1]) + loign, *far* (from Latin longē, from longus, *long*.]

pur·loin'er *n.*

af·fin·i·ty (ə-fĭn'ĭ-tē) *n. pl.* **af·fin·i·ties**

1. A natural attraction, liking, or feeling of kinship.
2. Relationship by marriage.
3. An inherent similarity between persons or things.
4. *Biology.* A relationship or resemblance in structure between species that suggests a common origin.
5. *Immunology.* The attraction between an antigen and an antibody.
6. *Chemistry.* An attraction or force between particles that causes them to combine.

[Middle English affinite, from Old French afinite, from Latin affīnitās, from affīnis, *related by marriage*.]

par·o·dy (păr'ə-dē) *n. pl.* **par·o·dies**

1. a. A literary or artistic work that imitates the characteristic style of an author or a work for comic effect or ridicule.
   b. The genre of literature comprising such works.
2. Something so bad as to be equivalent to intentional mockery; a travesty: *The trial was a parody of justice.*
3. *Music.* The practice of reworking an already established composition, especially the incorporation into the Mass of material borrowed from other works, such as motets or madrigals.

tr. v. **par·o·died, par·o·dy·ing, par·o·dies**

To make a parody of.

[Latin parōdia, from Greek parōidiā: para-, *subsidiary to*; see **para-**[1] + aoidē, ōidē, *song*; see wed-[2] in Indo-European Roots.]

pa·rod'ic (pə-rŏd'ĭk) or **pa·rod'i·cal** (-ĭ-kəl) *adj.* **par'o·dist** *n.* **par' o·dis'tic** *adj.*

par·a·ble (păr'ə-bəl)
n.

A simple story illustrating a moral or religious lesson.
[Middle English, from Old French, from Late Latin parabola, from Greek parabolē, from paraballein, *to compare*: para-, *beside*; see **para-**[1] + ballein, *to throw*; see gʷelə- in Indo-European Roots.]

bris (brĭs)
n. Judaism pl. **bris·es**

The rite or ceremony of male circumcision, usually performed on the eighth day of life.
[Ashkenazi Hebrew brīs, from Hebrew bərit (mīlâ), *covenant (of circumcision).*]

Rosh Ha·sha·nah also **Rosh Ha·sha·na** or **Rosh Ha·sho·na** or **Rosh Ha·sho·nah** (rôsh' hə-shô'nə, -shä'-, hä-, hä-shä-nä')
n.

The Jewish New Year, observed on the first day or the first and second days of Tishri and marked by solemnity as well as festivity.
[Hebrew rō'šhaš-šānâ: rō's̆, *head, beginning*; see r's̆ in Semitic Roots + ha-, *the* + šānâ, *year*; see šn in Semitic Roots.]

va·que·ro (vä-kâr'ō)
n. *Chiefly Texas pl.* **va·que·ros**

[Spanish, from vaca, *cow*, from Latin vacca.]
Regional Note: Used chiefly in southwest and central Texas to mean a ranch hand or cowboy, the word *vaquero* is a direct loan from Spanish; that is, it is spelled and pronounced, even by English speakers, much as it would be in Spanish. In California, however, the same word was Anglicized to *buckaroo.* Craig M. Carver, author of *American Regional Dialects,* points out that the two words also reflect cultural differences between cattlemen in Texas and California. The Texas vaquero was typically a bachelor who hired on with different outfits, while the California buckaroo usually stayed on the same ranch where he was born or had grown up and raised his own family there.

con·flu·ence (kŏn'flo͞o-əns) *n.*

1. a. A flowing together of two or more streams.
   b. The point of juncture of such streams.
   c. The combined stream formed by this juncture.
2. A gathering, flowing, or meeting together at one juncture or point: "A confluence of negative events conspired to bring down bond prices" (Michael Gonzalez).

par·a·dox (păr'ə-dŏks') *n.*

1. A seemingly contradictory statement that may nonetheless be true: *the paradox that standing is more tiring than walking.*
2. One exhibiting inexplicable or contradictory aspects: "The silence of midnight, to speak truly, though apparently a paradox, rung in my ears" (Mary Shelley).
3. An assertion that is essentially self-contradictory, though based on a valid deduction from acceptable premises.

4. A statement contrary to received opinion.

[Latin paradoxum, from Greek paradoxon, from neuter sing. of paradoxos, *conflicting with expectation*: para-, *beyond*; see **para-**[1] + doxa, *opinion* (from dokein, *to think*. See dek- in Indo-European Roots).]

par'a·dox'i·cal *adj.* **par'a·dox'i·cal·ly** *adv.* **par'a·dox'i·cal·ness** *n.*

con·spic·u·ous (kən-spĭk'yo͞o-əs) *adj.*

1. Easy to notice; obvious.
2. Attracting attention, as by being unusual or remarkable; noticeable.

[From Latin cōnspicuus, from cōnspicere, *to observe*: com-, *intensive pref.*; see **com-** + specere, *to look*; see spek- in Indo-European Roots.]

con·spic'u·ous·ly *adv.* **con·spic'u·ous·ness** *n.*

pro·fu·sion (prə-fyo͞o'zhən, prō-) *n.*

1. The state of being profuse; abundance.
2. Lavish or unrestrained expense; extravagance.
3. A profuse outpouring or quantity: "A profusion of chiles—mild Anaheim to hot jalapeño—perks up everything" (Gene Bourg).

hin·ter·land (hĭn'tər-lănd') *n.*

1. The land directly adjacent to and inland from a coast.
2. a. A region remote from urban areas; backcountry.
   b. A region situated beyond metropolitan centers of culture.

[German: hinter, *behind* (from Middle High German, from Old High German hintar.]

triv·i·al (trĭv'ē-əl) *adj.*

1. Of little significance or value.
2. Ordinary; commonplace.
3. Concerned with or involving trivia.
4. *Biology.* Relating to or designating a species; specific.
5. *Mathematics.*
   a. Of, relating to, or being the solution of an equation in which every variable is equal to zero.
   b. Of, relating to, or being the simplest possible case; self-evident.

[Middle English trivialle, *of the trivium* (from Medieval Latin triviālis, from trivium, *trivium*.), Latin triviālis, *ordinary* (from trivium, *crossroads*).]

triv'i·al·ly *adv.*

im·bue (ĭm-byo͞o') *tr.v.* **im·bued, im·bu·ing, im·bues**

1. To inspire or influence thoroughly; pervade: *work imbued with the revolutionary spirit.*
2. To permeate or saturate.
3. To stain or dye deeply.

[Middle English enbuen, imbeuen, from Latin imbuere, *to moisten, stain.*]

lode (lōd) *n.*

1. a. The metalliferous ore that fills a fissure in a rock formation.
   b. A vein of mineral ore deposited between clearly demarcated layers of rock. Also called **lead.**
2. A rich source or supply.

[Middle English, *way, load*, from Old English lād, *way]*

in·di·gence (ĭn'dĭ-jəns) *n.*
Poverty; neediness.

red·o·lent (rĕd'l-ənt) *adj.*
1. Having or emitting fragrance; aromatic.
2. Suggestive; reminiscent: *a campaign redolent of machine politics.*

[Middle English, from Old French, from Latin redolēns, redolent—present participle of redolēre, *to smell* : re-, red-, *re-* + olēre, *to smell.*]
red'o·lent·ly *adv.*

cat·a·lyt·ic (kăt'l-ĭt'ĭk) *adj.*
Of, involving, or acting as a catalyst: "Deregulation's catalytic power . . . is still reshaping the banking, communications, and transportation industries" (Ellyn E. Spragins).

[Greek katalutikos, *able to dissolve*, from katalusis, *dissolution.*]
cat'a·lyt'i·cal·ly *adv.*

Paj Ntaub Textile tradition of the Hmong culture of Laos, Vietnam, and Thailand, embroidered story cloth, also known as Flower Cloth, Pa Ndau.

farce (färs) *n.*
1. a. A light dramatic work in which highly improbable plot situations, exaggerated characters, and often slapstick elements are used for humorous effect.
   b. The branch of literature constituting such works.
   c. The broad or spirited humor characteristic of such works.
2. A ludicrous, empty show; a mockery: *The fixed election was a farce.*
3. A seasoned stuffing, as for roasted turkey.

tr. v. **farced, farc·ing, farc·es**
1. To pad (a speech, for example) with jokes or witticisms.
2. To stuff, as for roasting.

[Middle English farse, *stuffing*, from Old French farce, *stuffing, interpolation, interlude*, from Vulgar Latin *farsa, from feminine of farsus, variant of fartus, past participle of farcīre, *to stuff.*]

mo·sa·ic (mō-zā'ĭk) *n.*
1. a. A picture or decorative design made by setting small colored pieces, as of stone or tile, into a surface.
   b. The process or art of making such pictures or designs.
2. A composite picture made of overlapping, usually aerial, photographs.
3. Something that resembles a mosaic: *a mosaic of testimony from various witnesses.*
4. Botany. A viral disease of plants, resulting in light and dark areas in the leaves, which often become shriveled and dwarfed.
5. A photosensitive surface, as in the iconoscope of a television camera.
6. Biology. An individual exhibiting mosaicism.

tr. v. **mo·sa·icked, mo·sa·ick·ing, mo·sa·ics**
1. To make by mosaic: *mosaic a design on a rosewood box.*
2. To adorn with or as if with mosaic: *mosaic a sidewalk.*

[Middle English musycke, from Old French mosaique, from Old Italian mosaico, from Medieval Latin mūsāicum, neuter of mūsāicus, *of the Muses*, from Latin Mūsa, *Muse*, from Greek Mousa.]
mo·sa'i·cist (mō-za'ĭ-sĭst) *n.*

i·tin·er·ant (ī-tĭn'ər-ənt, ĭ-tĭn'-) *adj.*

Traveling from place to place, especially to perform work or a duty: *an itinerant judge; itinerant labor.*

n.

One who travels from place to place.

[Late Latin, itinerāns, itinerant—present participle of itinerārī, *to travel,* from Latin iter, itiner-, *journey.*]

i·tin'er·ant·ly *adv.*

suf·fuse (sə-fyo͞oz') *tr. v.* **suf·fused, suf·fus·ing, suf·fus·es**

To spread through or over, as with liquid, color, or light: "The sky above the roof is suffused with deep colors" (Eugene O'Neill).

[Latin suffundere, suffūs-: sub-, *sub-* + fundere, *to pour;* see gheu- in Indo-European Roots.]

suf·fu'sion *n.* **suf·fu'sive** (-fyo͞o'sĭv, -zĭv) *adj.*

syn·co·pa·tion (sĭng'kə-pā'shən, sĭn'-) *n.*

1. Music. A shift of accent in a passage or composition that occurs when a normally weak beat is stressed.
2. Something, such as rhythm, that is syncopated.
3. Grammar. Syncope.

bou·zou·ki (bo͝o-zo͞o'kē, bə-) *n. pl.* **bou·zou·kis**

A Greek stringed instrument having a long fretted neck and usually pear-shaped body.

[Modern Greek mpouzouki, *probably of Turkish origin.*]

Sukkos Sukkos is a seven-day holiday followed immediately by a one day holiday called Shmini Atzeres. The first day of Sukkos is a full-fledged Yom Tov when most forms of work are prohibited, similar to Shabbos but to a lesser degree. The following six days are called Chol HaMo'ed. During Chol HaMo'ed many forms of work are permitted, provided that certain conditions are met. The eighth day, Shmini Atzeres, is also a full-fledged Yom Tov. Outside of Israel the days of Yom Tov are doubled. Therefore we have two days of Yom Tov followed by five days of Chol HaMo'ed and another two days of Yom Tov, making for a total of nine days all together.

in·de·ter·mi·na·cy (ĭn'dĭ-tûr' mə-nə-sē) *n.*

The state or quality of being indeterminate.

Reading Comprehension

Answer the following questions about Mary Hufford's "What Is Folklife?

Word Meaning

Using the glossary, select the entry that best completes the sentences below.

1. Juan's father created a wonderful __________ to teach his son the meaning of honesty in everyday life.

2. At the invitation of the imam, the English professor visited the Friday service at the Islamic __________ to explain the benefits of taking English as a second language courses.
3. The alcoholic was quite embarrassed at the __________ appearance of his large red bulbous nose, a visible sign of years of drinking too much.
4. While the seeds of peace were __________ in the neighborhood formerly filled with violence, the Neighborhood Watch group kept a keen and protective eye on the young people of the area.
5. The young lovers attempted to __________ their relationship with proof of their commitment to each other: cards exchanged regularly, telephone calls made hourly, e-mail messages sent at late hours of the night.
6. Although the clues to the robbery were quite __________, the experienced detective was able to unearth the evidence and catch the criminal.
7. Covered in banners, posters, colorful balloons, confetti, and sports fans dressed in school colors, the football stadium was __________ with proof of the university's school spirit.
8. Before, during, and after Hurricane Katrina virtually destroyed the city of New Orleans and claimed thousands of lives, many journalists __________ themselves in the streets of New Orleans to report the catastrophe.
9. As the young students tried to regain their footing in the new country, the landscape around them was __________ of their homeland in the smells of the local vegetation, the lights illuminating the buildings, and the language heard in the new neighborhood.
10. Many of today's popular forms of music—rock and roll, jazz, and country—are __________ with the rhythms and themes of Blues and Gospel songs.
11. The law provides that the children of __________ workers laboring in the United States must be educated in American schools, even if only for the months the parents are employed.
12. The beautiful Mexican tile __________ presented a most impressive history of the experiences of the people of Guanajuato during the colonial era.
13. Normally, parents state __________, though often to deaf ears, the directions and expectations they maintain for their children's public and private behavior.

Literal Meaning

Mark the letter of the option that best answers the statements below.

1. The purpose of Hufford's essay is to
   a. explain the meaning of folk life and its relationship to the development of culture in America.
   b. demonstrate her knowledge of foreign cultures.
   c. show the reader how many cultures are present in the United States.
   d. cite examples of what icons are located in the National Archives in Washington.
2. In her explanation of folk life, Hufford mentions all but the following:
   a. All Saint's Day.
   b. Christenings.

c. Juneteenth.
d. Yellow ribbons to express one's feelings about a war.

3. In the selection, the current-day United States is called a/an
   a. cultural melting pot.
   b. country at battle with itself over its identity.
   c. country enriched by a variety of traditions and cultural practices.
   d. place where cultural identity is immediately lost.
4. As examples of how cultures blend in the United States, Hufford mentions
   a. the banjo as a formerly African-American instrument now identified as used predominantly by Caucasian musicians.
   b. hymns used today in African-American churches that came originally from England.
   c. different styles of boats used in different regions of the country.
   d. all of the above.
5. How does Hufford define tradition?
   a. Skills transferred in a chance meeting of cultures
   b. Notions about how to be human in a particular time and place
   c. Loss of cultural identity
   d. Remarkable ways of doing particular things
6. What obstacles to preserving culture does Hufford mention?
   a. Freeways that divide neighborhoods
   b. Condominiums that replace traditional hunting grounds
   c. Regulations that discourage the use of the mother language of residents
   d. All of the above

Interpretive Meaning

Complete the questions with the response that best answers the statement.

1. Why does Hufford say that folk life is often hidden in full view?
   a. She means that people do not realize their daily behaviors are by-products of culture.
   b. She means that people are blind to the life around them.
   c. The Library of Congress has done its best to hide culture in the United States.
   d. None of the above
2. The reader can conclude from the essay that
   a. the life of a typical American is full of cultural identity.
   b. the way of doing certain activities is a sign of culture.
   c. folk life and culture in the United States are similar in definition.
   d. all of the above.
3. Why does Hufford say that America is a "commonwealth of cultures"?
   a. Because the country began under British rule, the term *commonwealth* is appropriate.
   b. Because she uses the term *commonwealth* as a synonym for the American government.

c. Because by its nature, folklife is both universal and communal.
d. Because all American ethnic groups belong to the same clubs and organizations.

4. By using cooking terms, Hufford is implying that
   a. all American people are the chefs of culture.
   b. Americans can create a great pot of chili or stew.
   c. the stories told in the kitchens of households are poisonous to the minds of children.
   d. cooking is a favorite activity of Americans, thus causing the problem with obesity.
5. Hufford uses the term *commonwealth,* but she also uses the term *common wealth* to mean what?
   a. She actually misspelled the word.
   b. She is expressing the vast wealth of a country when it recognizes the richness in the identity of many cultures.
   c. She likes the use of double meanings.
   d. She is saying that all American people are wealthy.
6. In the essay, Hufford expresses the free flowing exchange of culture in America in the phrases "like stitches dropped and retrieved in the hands of a lacemaker," "like strands richly braided," "like the bow of a master fiddler." These expressions are examples of what literary device?
   a. Personification
   b. Alliteration
   c. Simile
   d. Hyperbole
7. Rhetorical modes used in the essay include the following:
   a. definition.
   b. exemplification.
   d. comparison/contrast.
   d. all of the above.
8. What could be another title for this selection?
   a. "The Melting Pot"
   b. "Unity in Diversity"
   c. "The American Kitchen"
   d. "Harmony"
9. Why does Hufford use examples in the essay?
   a. She is demonstrating how much research she has done.
   b. She wants the reader to understand clearly the points that she is making.
   c. She knows a lot about culture and folklife because she works in the Library of Congress.
   d. She loves words.
10. Why does Hufford trace the historical development of folklore as a serious study of culture?
    a. She is setting the theme for her essay.
    b. She is providing background to the development of her thesis.

c. She conveys the idea that research in the area of folk life is a legitimate study.
d. All of the above

Score: Number correct _____ out of_____

Writing Assignments

1. Journal Writing

Summary

Write a one- or two-paragraph summary of the essay. As you organize the summary, pay attention to the title of the essay and the subtitles.

Reaction

Write a one-paragraph reaction to this essay. Consider the following questions: What did you learn about folklore in the essay? What information in the essay surprised you? What is the difference between a commonwealth of cultures theory and the melting pot theory? What questions do you have about the essay?

2. Paragraph

Reflect upon this quotation from the essay: "Traditions do not simply pass along unchanged. In the hands of those who practice them they may be vigorously remodeled, woven into the present, and laden with new meanings." Write a paragraph comparing or contrasting the way a tradition was honored in the past to the way the tradition is kept or honored in the present. For example, perhaps in your family when you were a child, birthdays were always celebrated with all your family members at your grandmother's house the Sunday before the birthday. You opened presents, ate cupcakes, and played tag and other outdoor games with your cousins. Conceivably, you have kept the tradition intact through the years or perhaps it has changed to accommodate new family members and changes in lifestyle. Your paragraph then would compare or contrast the tradition of your childhood to the current tradition. Remember to start your paragraph with a clear topic sentence that mentions the key words in your assignment.

Example A: *The birthday parties of the children in my family today are very different from (or similar to) the parties my sisters and I had when we were children.* Develop this paragraph by discussing the similarities or differences between birthday parties when you were a child to parties of children in your family today.

Example B: *The annual Fourth of July parade in my neighborhood has (or has not) changed dramatically in the past thirty years.* Develop this paragraph by comparing or contrasting the parade held thirty years ago to the parade of today. For example, perhaps only a few neighborhood children participated in the parade thirty years ago, but now the parade has almost 100 participants with children, grandchildren, and former neighbors participating.

3. ***Paragraph to Essay***

   Expand the paragraph written for assignment two to an essay by focusing on three ways the tradition in your family, community, or organization has or has not changed through the years. Use one of the preceding essay outlines to organize your paper.

4. ***Essay***

   Hufford states, "Distinctive ways of speaking, fiddling, dancing, making chili, and designing boats can evolve into resources for expressing and celebrating regional identity." With this statement in mind, write a comparison/contrast essay on one of the topics listed below.

   Two types of dance

   Two ways of making chili (or fried chicken, stew, barbeque—any regional favorite)

   Two types of music

   Two handicrafts

   Two musicians

   Two cultures

   Two buildings in your community or city

   Two politicians in your area

Tam and Cam (A Cinderella Tale from Vietnam)

Anonymous

This Cinderella story explores the theme of good vs. evil. In this Vietnamese version, the familiar evil stepmother adores her daughter Cam and mistreats her stepdaughter Tam.

There were once two stepsisters named Tam and Cam. Tam was the daughter of their father's first wife. She died when the child was young so her father took a second wife. Some years later the father died and left Tam to live with her stepmother and stepsister.

Her stepmother was most severe and treated the girl harshly. Tam had to labor all day and long into the night. When there was any daylight she had to care for the buffalo, carry water for the cooking, do the washing and pick vegetables and water-fern for the pigs to eat. At night she had to spend a lot of time husking the rice. While Tam worked hard her sister did nothing but play games. She was given pretty clothes to wear and always got the best food.

Early one morning the second-mother gave two creels to Tam and Cam and told them to go to the paddy fields to catch tiny shrimp and crab. "I will give a *yêm* of red cloth to the one who brings home a full creel," she promised.

Tam was very familiar with the task of finding shrimp and crab in the paddy fields, and by lunchtime she had filled her creel. Cam walked and waded from field to field but she could not catch anything. She looked at Tam's full creel and said to her, "Oh, my dear sister Tam, your hair is covered in mud. Get into the pond to wash it, or you will be scolded by mother when you return home."

Believing what her sister told her, Tam hurried to the pond to wash herself. As soon as her stepsister entered the water, Cam emptied the shrimp and crab into her own creel, and hurried home to claim the *yêm* of red cloth.

When she had finished washing and saw her empty creel Tam burst into tears.

A Buddha who was sitting on a lotus in the sky heard her sobs and came down beside her. "Why are you crying?" asked the Buddha.

Tam told him all that had happened and the Buddha comforted her. "Do not be tearful. Look into your creel and see if anything is left."

Tam looked into the creel and said to the Buddha, "There is only one tiny *bông* fish."

"Take the fish and put it in the pond near your home. At every meal you must save a bowl of rice with which to feed it. When you want the fish to rise to the surface to eat the rice you must call like this:

Dear *bông*, dear *bông*,
Rise only to eat my golden rice,
For that of others will not taste nice.

Goodbye child, I wish you well." After saying this the Buddha disappeared.

Tam put the fish in the pond as she had been bidden, and every day, after lunch and the evening meal, she took some rice to feed it. Day by day the *bông* fish grew, and the girl became great friends with it.

Seeing Tam take rice to the pond after each meal the second-mother became suspicious, and bade Cam go to spy on her stepsister. Cam hid in a bush near the pond. When Tam called the *bông* fish the hidden girl listened to the words and rushed to her mother to tell her of the secret.

That evening, the second-mother instructed Tam that on the following day she must take the buffalo to the far field.

"It is now the season for vegetables. Buffalo cannot graze in the village. Tomorrow you have to take the buffalo to the far field. If you graze in the village it will be taken by the notables."

Tam set off very early the next morning to ride the buffalo to the far field. When she was gone, Cam and her mother took rice to the pond and called the *bông* fish. It rose to the surface and the woman caught it. She then took it to the kitchen where she cooked and ate it.

Tam returned in the evening, and after eating her meal took rice to the pond to feed her friend. She called and called, again and again, but she saw only a drop of blood on the surface of the water. Tam knew that something terrible had happened to the *bông* fish and began to weep.

The Buddha appeared by her side again. "Why do you weep this time, my child?"

Tam sobbed out her story and the Buddha spoke. "Your fish has been caught and eaten. Now, stop crying. You must find the bones of the fish and put them in four jars. After doing this you must bury the jars. Put one under each of the legs of your bed."

Tam searched and searched for the bones of her beloved friend but could not find them anywhere. As she looked even further a rooster came and called to her.

Cock-a-doodle-do, cock-a-doodle-do,
A handful of rice,
And I'll find the bones for you.

Tam gave rice to the rooster, and when it had eaten it strutted into the kitchen. In no time at all the elegant fowl returned with the bones and laid them at Tam's feet. The girl placed the bones into four jars and buried one under each of the legs of her bed.

Some months later the king proclaimed that there would be a great festival. All the people of Tam's village were going to attend, and the road was thronged with well dressed people making their way to the capital. Cam and her mother put on their finest clothes in readiness to join them. When the woman saw that Tam also wanted to attend the gala day she winked at Cam. Then she mixed a basketful of unhusked rice with the basket of clean rice Tam had prepared the previous evening. "You may go to the festival when you have separated this grain. If there isn't any rice to cook when we return home you will be beaten."

With that, she and her daughter joined the happy people on their way to the festival, and left Tam to her lonely task. She started to separate the rice, but she could see that it was hopeless and she began to weep.

Once again the Buddha appeared by her side. "Why are there tears in your eyes?" he asked.

Tam explained about the rice grains that had to be separated, and how the festival would be over by the time she had finished.

"Bring your baskets to the yard," said the Buddha. "I will call the birds to help you."

The birds came and pecked and fluttered until, in no time at all, they had divided the rice into two baskets. Not one single grain did they eat, but when they flew away Tam began to weep again.

"Now why are you crying?" asked the Buddha.

"My clothes are too poor," sobbed Tam. "I thank you for your help, but I cannot go dressed like this."

"Go and dig up the four jars," ordered the Buddha. "Then you will have all you need."

Tam obeyed and opened the jars. In the first she found a beautiful silk dress, a silk *yêm* and a scarf of the same material. In the second jar she found a pair of embroidered shoes of a cunning design which fitted her perfectly. When she opened the third jar great was her surprise when she saw a miniature horse. It neighed once, and grew to become a noble steed. In the fourth jar there was a richly ornamented saddle and bridle which grew to fit the horse. She washed herself and brushed her hair until it shone. Then she put on her wonderful new clothes and rode off to the festival.

On the way she had to ride through a stream flowing over the road. As she did so, one of her embroidered shoes fell into the water and sank beneath the surface. She was in such a hurry that she could not stop to search for it, so she wrapped the other shoe in her scarf and rode on.

Shortly afterwards, the king and his entourage, led by two elephants, arrived at the same spot. The elephants refused to enter the water and lowered their tusks, bellowing and trumpeting. When no amount of goading would force them on, the king ordered his followers to search the water. One of them found the embroidered shoe and brought it to the king, who inspected it closely.

Finally he said, "The girl who wore a shoe as beautiful as this must herself be very beautiful. Let us go on to the festival and find her. Whoever it fits will be my wife."

There was great excitement when all the women learned of the king's decision, and they eagerly waited for their turn to try on the shoe.

Cam and her mother struggled to make it fit, but to no avail, and when they saw Tam waiting patiently nearby the woman sneered at her. "How can someone as common as you be the owner of such a shoe? And where did you steal those fine clothes? Wait till we get home. If there isn't any rice to cook I am going to beat you severely."

Tam said nothing, but when it came her turn to try on the shoe it fitted perfectly. Then she showed the other one that was wrapped in the scarf, and everyone knew that she was the future queen.

The king ordered his servants to take Tam to the palace in a palanquin, and she rode off happily under the furious and jealous gazes of her stepsister and stepmother.

Tam was very happy living in the citadel with the king, but she never forgot her father. As the anniversary of his death came nearer she asked the king if she could return to her village to prepare the offering.

When Cam and her mother saw that Tam had returned, their jealous minds formed a wicked plan. "You must make an offering of betel to your father," said the stepmother. "That areca tree over there has the best nuts. You are a good climber, so you must go to the top of the tree and get some."

Tam climbed the tree and when she was at the top her stepmother took an axe and began to chop at the trunk. The tree shivered and shook and Tam cried out in alarm. "What is happening? Why is the tree shaking so?"

"There are a lot of ants here," called her stepmother. "I am chasing them away."

She continued to chop until the tree fell. Its crown, with Tam in it, toppled into a deep pond and the beautiful young woman was drowned. The wicked murderer gathered Tam's clothes, gave them to Cam, and led her to the citadel. She explained about the terrible "accident" to the king and offered Cam as a replacement wife. The king was very unhappy, but he said nothing.

When Tam died she was transformed into a *vang anh* bird. The bird flew back to the palace gardens and there she saw Cam washing the king's clothes near the well. She called out to her. "Those are my husband's clothes. Dry the clothes on the pole, not on the fence, lest they be torn."

Then she flew to the window of the king's room, singing as she went. The bird followed the king everywhere and he, who was missing Tam greatly, spoke to it, "Dear bird, dear bird, if you are my wife, please come to my sleeve."

The bird sat on the king's hand and then hopped onto his sleeve. The king loved the bird so much that he often forgot to eat or sleep, and he had a golden cage made for it. He attended to it day and night and completely ignored Cam.

Cam went to her mother and told her about the bird. The woman advised that she must kill it and eat it, and make up a story to tell the king. Cam waited until the king was absent then she did, as her mother had instructed. She threw the feathers into the garden afterwards.

When the king returned he asked about the bird and Cam answered, "I had a great craving for bird meat so I had it for a meal." The king said nothing.

The feathers grew into a tree. Whenever the king sat beneath it the branches bent down and made a parasol to shade him. He ordered a hammock to be placed under the tree and every day he rested there.

Cam was not happy about this, and once again she sought her mother's counsel.

"You must cut down the tree in secret. Use the wood to make a loom and tell the king you will weave some cloth for him."

On a stormy day Cam had the tree felled and made into a loom. When the king asked her about it she said that the wind had blown it over, and that now she would weave cloth for him on the loom made from its timber. When she sat down at the loom it spoke to her, "Klick klack, klick klack, you took my husband. I will take your eyes."

The terrified Cam went to her mother and told her of the loom's words. "Burn the loom and take the ashes far away from the palace," she told her daughter.

Cam did as she was bidden and threw the ashes at the side of the road a great distance from the king's home. The ashes grew into a green *thi* tree, and when the season came it bore one piece of fruit, with a wonderful fragrance that could be smelled from far away.

An old woman, who sold drinking water at a nearby stall, was attracted by the scent and she stood beneath the tree. She looked at the fruit, opened her pocket and called longingly, "Dear *thi*, drop into my pocket. I will only smell you, never eat you."

The fruit fell into her pocket, and she loved and treasured it, keeping it in her room to look at and to smell its fragrance.

Each day, when the old woman went to her stall, a small figure stepped from the *thi* fruit and grew into the form of Tam. She cleaned the house, put things in order, cooked the rice and made soup out of vegetables from the garden. Then she became tiny again and went back inside the *thi* fruit.

The old woman was curious and decided to find out who was helping her. One morning she pretended to go to her stall and hid behind a tree near the back door. She watched through a crack and saw Tam emerge from the *thi* fruit and grow into a beautiful girl. The old woman was very happy and rushed into the house and embraced her. She tore apart the skin of the fruit and threw it away.

Tam lived happily with the old woman and helped her with the housework every day. She also made cakes and prepared betel to sell on the stall.

One day the king left his citadel and rode through the countryside. When he came to the old woman's stall he saw that it was neat and clean, so he stopped. The old woman offered him water and betel, and when he accepted it he saw that the betel had been prepared to look like the wings of an eagle. He remembered that his wife had prepared betel exactly in this fashion.

"Who prepared this betel?" he asked.

"It was done by my daughter," replied the old woman.

"Where is your daughter? Let me see her."

The old woman called Tam. When she came the king recognized his beloved wife, looking even younger and more beautiful. The king was very happy, and as the old woman told him the story he sent his servants to bring a rich palanquin to carry his wife back to the citadel.

When Cam saw that Tam had returned she was most fearful. She did her best to ingratiate herself and asked her stepsister the secret of her great beauty.

"Do you wish to be very beautiful?" asked Tam. "Come, I will show you how." Tam had her servants dig a hole and prepare a large jar of boiling water. "If you want to be beautiful you must get into this hole," Tam told her wicked stepsister.

When Cam was in the hole Tam ordered the servants to pour in the boiling water, and so her stepsister met her death. Tam had the body made into *mam*, a rich sauce, and sent it to her stepmother, saying that it was a present from her daughter.

Each day the woman ate some of the *mam* with her meals, always commenting how delicious it was. A crow came to her house, perched on the roof ridge and cawed, "Delicious! The mother is eating her own daughter's flesh. Is there any left? Give me some."

The stepmother was very angry and chased the bird away, but, on the day when the jar of *mam* was nearly empty, she saw her daughter's skull and fell down dead.

Writing Assignments

1. Journal Writing

Summary

Write a summary of "Tam and Cam." In the topic sentence include the name of the folktale, its origin, and the main idea of the folktale.

Reaction

Write a three-paragraph reaction. In the first paragraph, focus on the theme of good and evil in the folktale. In the second paragraph, discuss the similarities and differences in the Tam and Cam story to the Cinderella story you know best. In the third paragraph, focus on the story's appeal.

2. ***Paragraph***
   Write a paragraph comparing or contrasting the characters Tam and Cam. Observe their attitudes, their words and actions, and what others say about them.

3. ***Paragraph to Essay***
   Expand the paragraph about Tam and Cam to an essay. In each body paragraph, discuss one similarity or difference, depending on the focus of your paper. Support the topic sentence of the paragraph with examples from the folktale. Add introductory and concluding paragraphs.

4. ***Essay***
   Write an essay comparing or contrasting two siblings, two friends, or two co-workers. Follow all of the steps for writing comparison/contrast that you have learned.

"The Invisible One" (A Cinderella-style Micmac Native legend) from Algonquin Legends of New England

Charles Godfrey Leland

This Native-American version of the Cinderella story depicts the cruelty that sometimes accompanies village life.

There was once a large Indian village situated on the border of a lake,—_Nameskeek' oodun Kuspemku_ (M.). At the end of the place was a lodge, in which dwelt a being who was always invisible, "the moose," whence he took his name. In the Passamaquoddy version nothing is said about a moose. He had a sister who attended to his wants, and it was known that any girl who could see him might marry him. Therefore there were indeed few who did not make the trial, but it was long ere one succeeded:

And it passed in this wise. Towards evening, when the Invisible One was supposed to be returning home, his sister would walk with any girls who came down to the shore of the lake. She indeed could see her brother, since to her he was always visible, and beholding him she would say to her companions, "Do you see my brother?" And then they would mostly answer, "Yes," though some said, "Nay,"—_alt telovejich, aa alttelooejik_. And then the sister would say, "_Cogoowa' wiskobooksich_?" "Of what is his shoulder-strap made?" But as some tell the tale, she would, inquire other things, such as, "What is his moose-runner's haul?" or, "With what does he draw his sled?" And they would reply, "A strip of rawhide," or "A green withe," or something of the kind. And then she, knowing they had not told the truth, would reply quietly, "Very well, let us return to the wigwam!"

And when they entered the place she would bid them not to take a certain seat, for it was his. And after they had helped to cook the supper they would wait with great curiosity to see Him eat. Truly he gave proof that he was a real person, for as he took off his moccasins they became visible, and his sister hung them up; but beyond this they beheld nothing not even when they remained all night, as many did.

There dwelt in the village an old man, a widower, with three daughters. The youngest of these was very small, weak, and often ill, which did not prevent her sisters, especially the eldest, from treating her with great cruelty. The second daughter was kinder, and sometimes took the part of the poor abused little girl, but the other would burn her hands and face with hot coals; yes, her whole body was scarred with the marks made by torture, so that people called her _Oochigeaskw_ (the rough-faced girl). And when her father, coming home, asked what it meant that the child was so disfigured, her sister would promptly say that it was the fault of the girl, herself, for that, having been forbidden to go near the fire, she had disobeyed and fallen in.

Now it came to pass that it entered the heads of the two elder sisters of this poor girl that they would go and try their fortune at seeing the Invisible One. So they clad themselves in their finest and strove to look their fairest; and finding his sister at home went with her to take the wonted walk down to the water. Then when He came, being asked if they saw him, they said, "Certainly," and also replied to the question of the shoulder-strap or sled cord, "A piece of rawhide." In saying which, they lied, like the rest, for they had seen nothing, and got nothing for their pains.

When their father returned home the next evening, he brought with him many of the pretty little shells from which _weiopeskool_ (M.), or wampum, was made and they were soon engaged _napawejik_ (in stringing them). That day poor little Oochigeaskw', the burnt-faced girl, who had always run barefoot, got a pair of her father's old moccasins, and put them into water that they might become flexible to wear. And begging her sisters for a few wampum shells, the eldest did but call her "a lying little pest," but the other gave her a few. And having no clothes beyond a few paltry rags, the poor creature went forth and got herself from the woods a few sheets of birch bark, of which she made a dress, putting some figures on the bark. And this dress she shaped like those worn of old. So she made a petticoat and a loose gown, a cap, leggins, and handkerchief, and, having put on her father's great old moccasins,—which came nearly up to her knees,—she went forth to try her luck. For even this little thing would see the Invisible One in the great wigwam at the end of the village.

Truly her luck had a most inauspicious beginning, for there was one long storm of ridicule and hisses, yells and hoots, from her own door to that which she went to seek. Her sisters tried to shame her, and bade her stay at home, but she would not obey; and all the idlers, seeing this strange little creature in her odd array, cried "Shame!" But she went on, for she was greatly resolved; it may be that some spirit had inspired her.

Now this poor small wretch in her mad attire, with her hair singed off and her little face as full of burns and scars as there are holes in a sieve, was, for all this, most kindly received by the sister of the Invisible One; for this noble girl knew more than the mere outside of things as the world knows them. And as the brown of the evening sky became black, she took her down to the lake. And erelong the girls knew that He had come. Then the sister said, "Do you see him?" And the other replied with awe, "Truly I do,—and he is wonderful." "And what is his sled-string?" "It is," she replied, "the Rainbow." And great fear was on her. "But, my sister," said the other, "what is his bow-string?" "His bow-string is _Ketaksoowowcht_" (the Spirits' Road, the Milky Way).

"Thou hast seen him," said the sister. And, taking the girl home, she bathed her, and as she washed all the scars disappeared from face and body. Her hair grew again; it was very long, and like a blackbird's wing. Her eyes were like stars. In all the world was no such beauty. Then from her treasures she gave her a wedding garment, and adorned her. Under the comb, as she combed her, her hair grew. It was a great marvel to behold.

Then, having done this, she bade her take the _wife's seat_ in the wigwam—that by which her brother sat, the seat next the door. And when He entered, terrible and beautiful, he smiled and said, "_Wajoolkoos_!" "So we are found out!" "_Alajulaa_." "Yes," was her reply. So she became his wife.

"Mi'kmaq Indian Cinderella vs. Perrault's Cinderella" Unsigned Web Site

kstrom.net

This essay explains how the Cinderella story is so universal that it has entered the Native American culture.

An Indian Cinderella? It seems faintly ludicrous—the idea of a Native-told tale like that—what? cruel stepmother and envious step-sisters? The Fairy Godmother with fashion-sense, access to pumpkin-model 12-mousepower Mercedes coach? Prince Charming? The elaborate, expensive, magically-provided ball gown and jewels? The glass slipper? The whole thing seems to have nothing to do with any uncorrupted Native culture. Nevertheless, there are several versions of *Cinderella* retold in the mid-19th century by Mi'kmaq storytellers of Hantsport, Nova Scotia, and others told by Maine Passamaquoddies. These were peoples who were acculturated for more than 200 years, but are among the poorest and most "Native"—often described by the tale collectors as requiring interpreters. There were also some educated, literate tribespeople who wanted to preserve these surviving bits of knowledge. So, before the end of the 19th century, many of these stories were collected.

Contrasting what Native storytellers did creatively with the European Cinderella myth—and looking more closely than kids do at the values underlying that durable myth—will provide insights about Native cultural survivals, showing what values may still survive. It helps to show how those values survive, too, by adaptations, by creative modifications.

A whole literature of Native storytellers' creative interactions with European folk-tales is mostly ignored, excluded, by anthros and ethnologists, hell-bent on collecting "myths and legends" of what they want to believe are uncontaminated pre-contact indigenous cultural expressions. They exclude or comment extensively on the effects Christianity has had on the "pure" religion, its mythic expressions. It usually *is* Chrisitianity—for instance, ministers and preachers vigorously pushed the "Great Spirit" as the Christian God—because hardly anybody else was socializing with Indian people telling them their stories, other than preachers.

There's only one area where a lot of European folk-tales, fairy tales, ghost stories, were even *heard* by Natives. That is the Woodland peoples north of the St. Lawrence, in Canada, and west to the Canadian Plains, and southerly of the Great Lakes in Michigan, Wisconsin, and Minnesota. Anishinaabeg peoples, and relatives: Mi'kmaq, Penobscot (and other New England so-called Algonquians), Potawotami, Menomini, Cree.

These people mixed closely with the Frenchmen of the fur trade period. The Frenchmen—voyageurs, coureurs du bois, loggers, farmers in the Atlantic colonies—liked to party hearty. They were singers, fiddlers, dancers, storytellers—not preachers. They intermarried with local Natives to form two unique cultures: the Acadians (who were forced out of Canada, mostly to Louisiana—Cajuns) and in the west, the Métis. Among the Frenchmen who liked and lived with Indian people of the 17th through 19th centuries were those who told stories to their Indian friends and families. They were not hell-bent on "civilizing" them. Unlike the English, they got along well, they intermarried often.

Mi'kmaq people had an unusually close and good social relationship to an early French Canadian Atlantic seaboard colony—Acadia. Thousands of whose members were forcibly expelled by the English resulting in tragic family separations and deaths of at least 1/3 of the people, in 1755. The unique good relations, for more than 100 years, between the French Acadians and the Mi'kmaq and Maliseet peoples resulted in cultural exchanges without the usual robberies, deaths, devastations.

Charles Leland, a journalist and folklorist, in 1882 amassed a large collection of surviving myths and tales among the Passamaquoddy of Maine, and received manuscript copies of tales collected by others (including some written down by various educated Indians of the time). Leland said he had "enough of these French Indian stories to form what would make one of the most interesting volumes of the series *Contes Populaires*," but he never got around to it. In the collection he did publish, *Algonquin Legends*, there is just the one tale that he thinks might be "an old solar myth worked up with the story of Cinderella, derived from a Canadian-French source."

In a curious (but very typical of his misreadings) non-review, Canadian children's lit prof (and "Indian lit expert") Jon Stott chastises the 1992 children's book *The Rough-Face Girl* (by Rafe Martin, gorgeous illustrations, David Shannon):

"Picture books must be culturally accurate. *The Rough-Face Girl*, a beautiful picture book written by Rafe Martin . . . is, as the Author's Note states, about an Algonquin Indian Cinderella. Yet the opening sentence sets the story 'by the shores of Lake Ontario', even though the shores of that lake were peopled by tribes speaking Iroquoian, not Algonquian, languages. In addition, the term 'Cinderella' implicitly brings with it the European cultural values associated with the French and German versions of a story familiar to most young readers." Of course, that's exactly what the Mi'kmaq storyteller wanted—to play off against the well-known Cinderella.

Throughout his recent book, *Native Americans in Children's Literature*, Stott shows almost total blindness to Native cultural values, as well as inability to read plain text (or anyway to report accurately what is said) and inability to see what a picture plainly shows. Stott is either unaware or considers it unimportant that the European Cinderella tale was raw material for the Mi'kmaq storyteller, he probably isn't aware of the actual source. (He pays attention to actual

Native sources only if it fits his model of (Joseph) Campbell canned chicken soup myth-analysis.) Too, it doesn't matter where non-existent Algonquians (this is a pejorative term—"bark eaters"—applied by Mohawks to some enemy tribe or other) lived.

The Native storyteller might just be doing a "far away" conventional placement of the story's locale. Since the Mi'kmaq opening phrase about the locale is actually given parenthetically (in the original source) we'll see there's more to the question of where this story takes place. That it's not part of some traditional old myth, but a 19th-century revisioning of *Cinderella* is not only indicated by Leland's remarks, but also by the fact that in other actually traditional tales, Mi'kmaq storytellers begin with a conventional phrase, "*N'karnayoo*—of the old times" which isn't done with the Cinderella re-fit.

Writing Assignments

1. *Journal Writing*

Summary

Write a one-paragraph summary of the essay. Remember that you are summarizing the *essay* about the two Cinderella stories, not the actual stories.

Reaction

When writing your reaction to this essay, consider the content as well as the structure of the essay in relationship to what you have learned about comparison/contrast writing.

2. *Paragraph*

Write a paragraph comparing or contrasting the Cinderella story you are familiar with and the Mi'kmaq story or another version of Cinderella. Focus on several differences or several similarities. Add examples to support your claim.

3. *Paragraph to Essay*

Using your paragraph assignment as your starting point, expand your paragraph to an essay. Decide which points you want to focus on, and write a body paragraph for each point. Add introductory and concluding paragraphs.

4. *Essay*

Compare and contrast two versions of a family story or an event in your personal history. For example, one version may be the way the event actually occurred and another may be the way that some members of your family remember it or tell it. Use the guidelines to write a compare/contrast essay and follow the three-point discussion method. Use the thesis as the guide to the essay and conclude with a summary or other finalizing device you have studied.

Cinderella

Anne Sexton

In this satirical poetry version of the Cinderella story, Anne Sexton explains the ways of cruel stepmothers in today's world. The poem parodies the ancient version.

You always read about it:
the plumber with the twelve children
who wins the Irish Sweepstakes.
From toilets to riches.
That story.
Or the nursemaid,
some **luscious** sweet from Denmark
who captures the oldest son's heart.
from diapers to Dior.
That story.
Or a milkman who serves the wealthy,
eggs, cream, butter, yogurt, milk,
the white truck like an ambulance
who goes into real estate
and makes a **pile.**
From **homogenized** to martinis at lunch.
Or the charwoman
who is on the bus when it cracks up
and collects enough from the insurance.
From mops to Bonwit Teller.
That story.
Once
the wife of a rich man was on her deathbed
and she said to her daughter Cinderella:
Be devout. Be good. Then I will smile
down from heaven in the seam of a cloud.
The man took another wife who had
two daughters, pretty enough
but with hearts like blackjacks.
Cinderella was their maid.
She slept on the sooty hearth each night
and walked around looking like Al Jolson.
Her father brought presents home from town,
jewels and gowns for the other women
but the twig of a tree for Cinderella.
She planted that twig on her mother's grave
and it grew to a tree where a white dove sat.
Whenever she wished for anything the dove

would drop it like an egg upon the ground.
The bird is important, my dears, so heed him.
Next came the ball, as you all know.
It was a marriage market.
The prince was looking for a wife.
All but Cinderella were preparing
and **gussying up** for the event.
Cinderella begged to go too.
Her stepmother threw a dish of **lentils**
into the cinders and said: Pick them
up in an hour and you shall go.
The white dove brought all his friends;
all the warm wings of the fatherland came,
and picked up the lentils in a jiffy.
No, Cinderella, said the stepmother,
you have no clothes and cannot dance.
That's the way with stepmothers.
Cinderella went to the tree at the grave
and cried forth like a gospel singer:
Mama! Mama! My turtledove,
send me to the prince's ball!
The bird dropped down a golden dress
and delicate little slippers.
Rather a large package for a simple bird.
So she went. Which is no surprise.
Her stepmother and sisters didn't
recognize her without her cinder face
and the prince took her hand on the spot
and danced with no other the whole day.
As nightfall came she thought she'd better
get home. The prince walked her home
and she disappeared into the pigeon house
and although the prince took an axe and broke
it open she was gone. Back to her cinders.
These events repeated themselves for three days.
However on the third day the prince
covered the palace steps with cobbler's wax
and Cinderella's gold shoe stuck upon it.
Now he would find whom the shoe fit
and find his strange dancing girl for keeps.
He went to their house and the two sisters
were delighted because they had lovely feet.
The eldest went into a room to try the slipper on
but her big toe got in the way so she simply
sliced it off and put on the slipper.
The prince rode away with her until the white dove

told him to look at the blood pouring forth.
That is the way with amputations.
They just don't heal up like a wish.
The other sister cut off her heel
but the blood told as blood will.
The prince was getting tired.
He began to feel like a shoe salesman.
But he gave it one last try.
This time Cinderella fit into the shoe
like a love letter into its envelope.
At the wedding ceremony
the two sisters came to curry favor
and the white dove pecked their eyes out.
Two hollow spots were left
like soup spoons.
Cinderella and the prince
lived, they say, happily ever after,
like two dolls in a museum case
never bothered by diapers or dust,
never arguing over the timing of an egg,
never telling the same story twice,
never getting a middle-aged spread,
their darling smiles pasted on for eternity.
Regular **Bobbsey Twins.**
That story.

Glossary for "The Invisible One" from Charles Godfrey Leland's *Algonquin Legends of New England,* "Mi'kmaq Indian Cinderella vs. Perrault's "Durable Myth," and "Cinderella" by Anne Sexton

lus·cious (lŭsh'əs) *adj.*

1. Sweet and pleasant to taste or smell: *a luscious melon.*
2. Having strong sensual or sexual appeal; seductive.
3. Richly appealing to the senses or the mind: *a luscious, vivid description.*
4. Archaic. Excessively sweet; cloying.

[Middle English lucius, alteration of licious, perhaps short for delicious, *delicious.*]

lus'cious·ly *adv.* **lus'cious·ness** *n.*

pile (pīl) *n.*

1. A quantity of objects stacked or thrown together in a heap.
2. Informal. A large accumulation or quantity: *a pile of trouble.*
3. Slang. A large sum of money; a fortune: *made their pile in the commodities market.*
4. A funeral pyre.
5. A very large building or complex of buildings.
6. A nuclear reactor.
7. A voltaic pile.

v. **piled, pil·ing, piles**

v. tr.

1. a. To place or lay in or as if in a pile or heap: *piled books onto the table.*
   b. To load (something) with a heap or pile: *piled the table with books.*
2. To heap (something) in abundance: *piled potato salad onto the plate.*

v. intr.

1. To form a heap or pile.
2. To move in, out, or forward in a disorderly mass or group: *pile into a bus; pile out of a car.*

Phrasal Verb: pile up

1. To accumulate.
2. <u>*Informal*</u> To undergo a serious vehicular collision.

[Middle English, from Old French, from Latin pīla, *pillar*.]

ho·mog·e·nize (hə-mŏj'ə-nīz', hō-) *v.* **ho·mog·e·nized, ho·mog·e·niz·ing, ho·mog·e·niz·es**

v. tr.

1. To make homogeneous.
2. a. To reduce to particles and disperse throughout a fluid.
   b. To make uniform in consistency, especially to render (milk) uniform in consistency by emulsifying the fat content.
   v. intr.
   To become homogenized.

[From **homogeneous.**] **ho·mog'e·ni·za'tion** (-nĭ-zā'shən) *n.* **ho·mog'e·niz'er** *n.*

gussy up

v.: put on special clothes to appear particularly appealing and attractive; "She never dresses up, even when she goes to the opera"; "The young girls were all fancied up for the party" [syn: dress up, fig out, fig up, deck up, fancy up, trick up, deck out, trick out, prink, attire, get up, rig out, tog up, tog out, overdress] [ant: dress down]

len·til (lĕn'təl) *n.*

1. A leguminous plant *(Lens culinaris)* native to southwest Asia, having flat pods containing lens-shaped, edible seeds.
2. The round, flattened seed of this plant.

[Middle English, from Old French lentille, from Vulgar Latin *lentīcula, from Latin lenticula, diminutive of lēns, lent-, *lentil.*]

Idiom: curry favor

To seek or gain favor by fawning or flattery.

[Middle English curreien, from Anglo-Norman curreier, *to arrange, curry,* from Vulgar Latin *conrēdāre: Latin com-, *com-* + Vulgar Latin *-rēdāre, *to make ready* (*of Germanic origin.* See reidh- in Indo-European Roots). *Curry favor,* by folk etymology from Middle English currayen favel from Old French correier fauvel, *to curry a fallow-colored horse, be hypocritical (from the fallow horse as a medieval symbol of deceit).*]

Bobbsey twins *noun*

a facetious name for two people who are often seen together and look or act alike. from the trademarked characters of a series of children's books.

du·ra·ble (do͝or'ə-bəl, dyo͝or'-) *adj.*

1. Capable of withstanding wear and tear or decay: *a durable fabric.*
2. Able to perform or compete over a long period, as by avoiding or overcoming injuries: *a durable fullback.*
3. Lasting; stable: *a durable friendship.*
4. Economics. Not depleted or consumed by use: *durable goods.*
   n. Economics

   A manufactured product, such as an automobile or a household appliance, that can be used over a relatively long period without being depleted or consumed. Often used in the plural.

[Middle English, from Old French, from Latin dūrābilis, from dūrāre, *to last.*]

du'ra·bil'i·ty or **du'ra·ble·ness** *n.* **du'ra·bly** *adv.*

doc·ile (dŏs'əl, -īl') *adj.*

1. Ready and willing to be taught; teachable.
2. Yielding to supervision, direction, or management; tractable.

[Latin docilis, from docēre, *to teach.*]

doc'ile·ly *adv.* **do·cil'i·ty** (dŏ-sĭl'ĭ-tē, dō-) *n.*

pan·nier or **pan·ier** (păn'yər, -ē-ər) *n.*

1. A large wicker basket, especially:
   a. One of a pair of baskets carried on the shoulders of a person or on either side of a pack animal.
   b. A basket carried on a person's back.
2. A basket or pack, usually one of a pair, that fastens to the rack of a bicycle and hangs over the side of one of the wheels.
3. a. A framework of wire, bone, or other material formerly used to expand a woman's skirt at the hips.
   b. A skirt or an overskirt puffed out at the hips.

[Middle English panier, from Old French, from Latin pānārium, *breadbasket*, from pānis, *bread.*]

gaunt·let also **gant·let** (gônt'lĭt, gänt'-) *n.*

1. a. A form of punishment or torture in which people armed with sticks or other weapons arrange themselves in two lines facing each other and beat the person forced to run between them.
   b. The lines of people so arranged.
2. An onslaught or attack from all sides: "The hostages . . . ran the gauntlet of insult on their way to the airport" (*Harper's magazine*).
3. A severe trial; an ordeal.

[Alteration (influenced by **gauntlet**[1]), of gantlope from Swedish gatlopp: gata, *lane* (from Old Norse.) + lopp, *course, running* (from Middle Low German lōp).]

rep·li·cate (rĕp'lĭ-kāt') *v.* **rep·li·cat·ed, rep·li·cat·ing, rep·li·cates**

v. tr.

1. To duplicate, copy, reproduce, or repeat.
2. Biology. To reproduce or make an exact copy or copies of (genetic material, a cell, or an organism).
3. To fold over or bend back.
   v. intr.

To become replicated; undergo replication.

n. (-kĭt)

A repetition of an experiment or procedure.

adj. **replicate** (-kĭt) also **rep·li·cat·ed** (-kā'tĭd)

Folded over or bent back upon itself: *a replicate leaf.*

[Middle English replicaten, from Late Latin replicāre, replicāt- *to repeat*, from Latin, *to fold back*: re-, *re-* + plicāre, *to fold*; see plek- in Indo-European Roots.]

im·pro·vise (ĭm'prə-vīz') *v.* **im·pro·vised, im·pro·vis·ing, im·pro·vis·es**

v. tr.

1. To invent, compose, or perform with little or no preparation.
2. To play or sing (music) extemporaneously, especially by inventing variations on a melody or creating new melodies in accordance with a set progression of chords.
3. To make or provide from available materials: *improvised a dinner from what I found in the refrigerator.*

   v. intr.

1. To invent, compose, or perform something extemporaneously.
2. To improvise music.
3. To make do with whatever materials are at hand.

[French improviser, from Italian improvvisare, from improvviso, *unforeseen*, from Latin imprōvīsus: in-, *not*; see **in-**[1] + prōvīsus, past participle of prōvidēre, *to foresee*; see **provide.**]

im'pro·vis'er or **im'pro·vi'sor** *n.*

tac·i·turn (tăs'ĭ-tûrn') *adj.*

Habitually untalkative.

[French taciturne, from Old French, from Latin taciturnus, from tacitus, *silent.*]

tac'i·tur'ni·ty (-tûr'nĭ-tē) *n.* **tac'i·turn·ly** *adv.*

squal·id (skwŏl'ĭd) *adj.*

1. Dirty and wretched, as from poverty or lack of care.
2. Morally repulsive; sordid: "the squalid atmosphere of intrigue, betrayal, and counterbetrayal" (W. Bruce Lincoln).

[Latin squālidus, from squālēre, *to be filthy*, from squālus, *filthy.*]

squal'id·ly *adv.* **squal'id·ness** or **squa·lid'i·ty** (skwŏ-lĭd'ĭ-tē) *n.*

la·con·ic (lə-kŏn'ĭk) *adj.*

Using or marked by the use of few words; terse or concise.

[Latin Lacōnicus, *Spartan*, from Greek Lakōnikos, from Lakōn, *a Spartan (from the reputation of the Spartans for brevity of speech).*]

la·con'i·cal·ly *adv.*

dys·func·tion also **dis·func·tion** (dĭs-fŭngk'shən) *n.*

Abnormal or impaired functioning, especially of a bodily system or social group.

dys·func'tion·al *adj.*

im·pu·ni·ty (ĭm-pyo͞o'nĭ-tē) *n. pl.* **im·pu·ni·ties**

Exemption from punishment, penalty, or harm.

[Latin impūnitās, from impūne, *without punishment*: in-, *not*; see **in-**[1] + poena, *penalty* (from Greek poinē. See kʷei-[1] in Indo-European Roots).]

triv·i·al (trĭv'ē-əl) *adj.*

1. Of little significance or value.
2. Ordinary; commonplace.
3. Concerned with or involving trivia.
4. Biology. Relating to or designating a species; specific.
5. *Mathematics.*
   a. Of, relating to, or being the solution of an equation in which every variable is equal to zero.
   b. Of, relating to, or being the simplest possible case; self-evident.

[Middle English trivialle, *of the trivium* (from Medieval Latin triviālis, from trivium, *trivium.*), Latin triviālis, *ordinary* (from trivium, *crossroads*).]

triv'i·al·ly *adv.*

pal·try (pôl'trē)

adj. **pal·tri·er, pal·tri·est**

1. Lacking in importance or worth.
2. Wretched or contemptible.

[Probably from obsolete and dialectal paltry, *trash*, perhaps from Low German paltrig, *ragged*, from palte, *rag*.]

pal'tri·ly *adv.* **pal'tri·ness** *n.*

in·aus·pi·cious (ĭn'ô-spĭsh'əs) *adj.*

Not favorable; not auspicious.

in'aus·pi'cious·ly *adv.* **in'aus·pi'cious·ness** *n.*

Reading Comprehension

Answer the questions about the following selections: "Cinderella" by Anne Sexton, "The Invisible One" from Charles Godfrey Leland's *Algonquin Legends of New England*, and "Mi'kmaq Indian Cinderella vs. Perrault's Durable Myth."

Word Meaning

Select the words from the glossaries of these selections that best complete the sentences below.

1. The fresh chocolate-covered strawberries served at the reception were so sweet and __________ that they were eaten in only ten minutes.
2. Because the chef shared his recipe for the delicious chorizos that we ate at the local restaurant, we tried unsuccessfully to __________ them at home.
3. Often pets that would normally behave wildly can be trained carefully to make them more __________ and manageable in a family's household.
4. Some of the most original television shows are those in which the host offers a prize to a member of the audience to __________ a situation from real life.
5. The new American diet recommended by the health services suggests that people eat more __________ and other types of vegetable proteins.
6. Many soldiers who served in Iraq suffered __________ of legs and arms as a result of car bombings.

7. Because it was unlike the Mexican classmate to be so __________, the students wondered what event had caused her sudden shyness within their comfortable group.
8. Such unimportant events as the celebration of the flower planting and of the rain showers forced the tourists to recognize the __________ events celebrated in the village.
9. The old man living on the street wore such __________ rags that even the other street people offered to buy him some new clothing.
10. My brother __________ his eyebrows when he stepped too close to the flame when he ignited the fire in the grill.

Literal Meaning

Mark the letter of the statement that best completes the meaning.

1. In Anne Sexton's "Cinderella," the reader can see references to life in
   a. modern times only.
   b. olden times only.
   c. foreign countries only.
   d. all countries and both modern and olden times.
2. In "The Invisible One," the Cinderella character works
   a. for a merchant in the local village.
   b. in the home occupied by her father and step sisters.
   c. at the dwelling of the Invisible One.
   d. as a designer of wampum.
3. In the Native story, the young Cinderella character was nicknamed the
   a. burnt-face girl.
   b. barefoot girl.
   c. dancing girl.
   d. birchbark girl.
4. In both the poem and the Mi'kmaq story, the cruel stepsisters
   a. lived happily with the Cinderella character.
   b. supported their stepfather until his death.
   c. suffered a painful demise.
   d. became respectable citizens in the community.
5. In all of the accounts, the Cinderella character
   a. never finds her prince.
   b. wears a beautiful party dress designed by the fairy god-mother.
   c. is the most beautiful girl in the village.
   d. is a victim of abuse.

Interpretive Meaning

Complete the questions with the response that best answers the statement.

1. Why does the narrator say that the little burned girl is stronger than the traditional Cinderella?
   a. Because she has built strong muscles while working
   b. Because she is experiencing daily pain from her burns

c. Because she acts without the aid of a fairy godmother when she sets out to find the Invisible One
d. Because her father loves her and takes good care of her

2. Statements like "hair like a blackbird's wing" and "eyes were like stars" are examples of what figurative language?
a. Metaphor
b. Personification
c. Onomatopoeia
d. Simile

3. Why does the author of the essay comparing the Mi'kmaq version to the Perrault version of Cinderella use words like *Cindi, Limo, Pops, bro* in his passage?
a. He wants the reader to think he is modern because he knows dialectical language.
b. He is creating a tone of humorous satire.
c. He likes to use abbreviations in his language to save space.
d. He uses contrasting language to create an effect of seriousness.

4. The narrator of Anne Sexton's Cinderella poem refers to the Irish Sweepstakes, the Bonwit Teller, Al Jolson, and the Bobbsey Twins because
a. she wants the reader to learn history through her references.
b. she is making a point about modern life.
c. by using familiar references, she can demonstrate more clearly the points about the relevance of an old story in today's world.
d. she is trying to stimulate the reader to do research.

5. In every version of the traditional story, evil people are represented by characters to
a. demonstrate the fact that good prevails over evil.
b. provide an example of the cruel side of life.
c. represent a contrast to the goodness represented in the main character.
d. all of the above.

6. This version of the "Invisible One" clearly represents a later version of the original Mi'kmaq story because
a. this early tribe did not use birch bark and did not have birch trees.
b. wampum was a form of money used later in the history of the Mi'kmaq tribe.
c. the early tribal members did not wear moccasins.
d. the use of the word "Alajulaa" indicates the influence of Christianity on the tribe.

7. Why does Anne Sexton say "That's the way with stepmothers"?
a. In the traditional blended family, stepmothers are always cruel.
b. The stepmother becomes a symbol of evil in the society of the family.
c. Stepmothers are always on the hunt for the father's money.
d. Stepmothers are always given a bad image in literature.

8. What rhetorical mode is represented in the essay about Cinderella?
a. Illustration
b. Narration

c. Process Analysis
d. Comparison/contrast

Score: Number correct _____ out of _____

Writing Assignments

1. Journal Writing

Summary

Utilizing the reporter's questions (who, what, where, when, why, how, how much), write a one-paragraph summary of Anne Sexton's "Cinderella" and a one-paragraph summary of "The Invisible One."

Reaction

Write a reaction to both the poem and the folktale. In your reaction, mention the differences between the two versions of Cinderella as well as any differences in the versions with which you are familiar.

2. Paragraph

Compare or contrast the two versions of Cinderella. Focus on one difference or one similarity. Mention both titles in your topic sentence as well as the focus of your paper.

3. Paragraph to Essay

Expand your paragraph to an essay, by writing three body paragraphs on the differences and or similarities in the poem and in the folktale. Use the paragraph you wrote in the previous exercise as one of your body paragraphs. Consider the characters, the plot, and the theme (the underlying idea or lesson that the story teaches), or the setting when prewriting. Add an introductory and concluding paragraph to the essay.

4. Essay

Think of someone you consider to be a modern-day Cinderella. Compare and contrast that person's story to one of the Cinderella stories you have studied.

Present at Creation: The Origins of the Legend of John Henry

Stephen Wade (National Public Radio [NPR] report)

Wade explains the origins of the legend of the character John Henry, who was larger than life.

Sept. 2, 2002—In the late 1800s, as the country recovered from the Civil War, railroad tracks began to stitch the nation together. This made it possible to go from ocean to ocean in under a week, where it might have earlier taken up to six months. Among the men that built the railroads, John Henry stands tall, broad shoulders above the rest.

Little can be said for certain about the facts of John Henry's life, but his tale has become the stuff of myth. He has embodied the spirit of growth in America for over a century. But his legacy cannot be solely summed up in the image of a man with a hammer, a former slave representing the strength and drive of a country in the process of building itself. Something within his story established John Henry as a fixture of the popular imagination. He has been the subject of novels, a postage stamp and even animated films. Above all, "John Henry" is the single most well known and often recorded American folk song.

For NPR's ongoing series *Present at the Creation,* musician and researcher Stephen Wade explores John Henry's legacy and the long life of the **ballad** that it inspired. Wade reports that the abundance of music related to John Henry—and more specifically, his famous contest with a steam drill—provides a way of connecting the man himself with the citizens of the country that his work and his legend helped to build.

Though the story of John Henry sounds like the **quintessential** tall tale, it is certainly based, at least in part, on historical circumstance. There are disputes as to where the **legend** originates. Some place John Henry in West Virginia, while recent research suggests Alabama. Still, all share a similar back-story.

In order to construct the railroads, companies hired thousands of men to smooth out terrain and cut through obstacles that stood in the way of the proposed tracks. One such chore that figures heavily into some of the earliest John Henry ballads is the blasting of the Big Bend Tunnel—more than a mile straight through a mountain in West Virginia. Steel-drivin' men like John Henry used large hammers and stakes to pound holes into the rock, which were then filled with explosives that would blast a cavity deeper and deeper into the mountain. In the folk ballads, the central event took place under such conditions. Eager to reduce costs and speed up progress, some tunnel engineers were using steam drills to power their way into the rock. According to some accounts, on hearing of the machine, John Henry challenged the steam drill to a contest. He won, but died of exhaustion, his life cut short by his own superhuman effort.

Wade says that the song was born from the work of driving steel. "In the years before the song became known to the greater American public, it remained in folk possession," he explains. "Black songsters and white hillbilly musicians approached 'John Henry' equipped with a wealth of regional and personal styles."

Not surprisingly, the songs caught on and spread to a wider audience. Country music legend Merle Travis heard one version at an early age.

"Ever since I been big enough to remember hearing anybody sing anything at all, I believe I've heard that old song about the strong man that hammered hisself to death on the railroad," Travis said. "There's been dozens and dozens of different tales about where John Henry comes from."

The story of John Henry seems to have spoken to just about everyone who heard it, which probably accounts for why the ballad became so popular. And as the songs started to become more popular, the legend of the man grew to even larger proportions. But whatever exaggeration of deed may have **ensued,** an element of truth rings through. John Cephas is a blues musician from Virginia. "It was a story that was close to being true," he says. "It's like the underdog overcoming this powerful force. I mean even into today when you hear it, (it) makes you take pride. I know especially for black people, and for other people from other ethnic groups, that a lot of people are for the underdog." Today, John Henry's legend has grown beyond the songs that helped make him famous. "Though John Henry most often appears in song," notes Wade, "he has been depicted in numerous graphic mediums ranging from folk sculpture to fine art lithography, book illustration to outdoor sculpture." This art approaches the man himself in several different ways, sometimes placing him in a historically realistic perspective and focusing on his work and life, sometimes **deifying** him. One 1945 illustration by James Daugherty shows John Henry as a defense worker, supported by other famous black Americans such as Joe Louis and George Washington Carver.

"Over the years," Wade continues, "labor lore scholar Archie Green has researched what he calls 'the visual John Henry.' It's from his work that these illustrations come, touching, variously, the realms of fine, popular and folk art."

Thanks to these works of art, the story of John Henry reaches a new audience that, today, may not be familiar with the songs that gave rise to the legend. Wherever people discover John Henry, his influence promises to hold strong.

John Henry

Zora Neale Hurston, from *Mules and Men*

The poem demonstrates the popularity of John Henry and gives detail about his human side.

John Henry driving on the right hand side,
Steam drill driving on the left,
Says, 'fore I'll let your steam drill beat me down I'll hammer my fool self to death,
Hammer my fool self to death.
John Henry told his Captain, When you go to town Please bring me back a nine pound hammer And I'll drive your steel on down, And I'll drive your steel on down.
John Henry told his Captain,
Man ain't nothing but a man,
And 'fore I'll let that steam drill beat me down
I'll die with this hammer in my hand,
Die with this hammer in my hand.
Captain ast John Henry,
What is that storm I hear?
He says Cap'n that ain't no storm,
'Tain't nothing but my hammer in the air,
Nothing but my hammer in the air.
John Henry told his Captain,
Bury me under the sills of the floor,
So when they get to playing good old Georgy skin,
Bet 'em fifty to a dollar more,
Fifty to a dollar more.
John Henry had a little woman,
The dress she wore was red,
Says I'm going down the track,
And she never looked back.
I'm going where John Henry fell dead,
Going where John Henry fell dead.
Who's going to shoe your pretty lil feet?
And who's going to glove your hand?
Who's going to kiss your dimpled cheek?
And who's going to be your man?
Who's going to be your man?
My father's going to shoe my pretty lil feet;
My brother's going to glove my hand;
My sister's going to kiss my dimpled cheek;
John Henry's going to be my man,
John Henry's going to be my man.
Where did you get your pretty lil dress?
The shoes you wear so fine?
I got my shoes from a railroad man,
My dress from a man in the mine,
My dress from a man in the mine.

John Henry Blues

Fiddlin' Joe Carson

This song version of the John Henry legend develops the strong connection between the hammer and John Henry's women.

John Henry was a very small boy,
Fell on his mammy's knee;
Picked up a hammer and a little piece of steel,
"Lord, a hammer'll be the death of me,
Lord, a hammer'll be the death of me."
John Henry went upon the mountain,
Come down on the side;
The mountain so tall, John Henry was so small,
Lord, he lay down his hammer and he cried, "Oh, Lord,"
He lay down his hammer and he cried.
John Henry was on the right hand,
But that steam drill was on the left;
"Before your steam drill beats me down,
Hammer my fool self to death,
Lord, I'll hammer my fool self to death."
The captain says to John Henry,
"Believe my tunnel's fallin' in."
"Captain, you needn't not to worry,
Just my hammer hawsing in the wind,
Just my hammer hawsing in the wind."
"Look away over yonder, captain,
You can't see like me."
He hollered out in a low, lonesome cry,
"This hammer'll be the death of me,
Lord, this hammer'll be the death of me."
John Henry told his captain,
"Captain, you go to town,
Bring John back a twelve-pound hammer,
And he'll whup your steam drill down,
[And] he'll whup your steam drill down."
For the man that invented that steam drill
Thought he was mighty fine;
John Henry sunk a fo'teen foot,
The steam drill only made nine,
The steam drill only made nine.
John Henry told his **shaker,**
"Shaker, you better pray;
For if I miss this six-foot steel,
Tomorrow'll be your buryin' day,
An' tomorrow'll be your buryin' day."
John Henry told his lovin' little woman,
"Sick and I want to go to bed;

Fix me a place to lay down, child,
Got a rollin' in my head,
Got a rollin' in my head."
John Henry had a lovely little woman,
Called her Polly Ann;
John Henry got sick and he had to go home,
But Polly broke steel like a man,
Polly broke steel like a man.
John Henry had another little woman,
The dress she wore was blue;
She went down the track and she never looked back,
"John Henry, I've been true to you."

"John Henry Blues," performed by Fiddlin' John Carson
Transcribed by Norm Cohen in Long Steel Rail: The Railroad in American Folksong *(Urbana: University of Illinois Press, 2000)*

Writing Assignments

1. *Journal Writing*

Summary

Write a short summary for each selection. Include the theme and the main points used to develop that theme.

Reaction

In your reaction, discuss the similarities and differences between the two sets of lyrics, one a poem and the other a song, as well as your reaction to the essay.

2. *Paragraph*

Choice A: Using the information gleaned from the essay and song lyrics on John Henry, write a paragraph comparing or contrasting John Henry to a famous person (or a legendary person) in your family, community, region, or country.

Choice B: Write a paragraph comparing two famous or infamous people in your family, community, region, or country. Use the organizational format for the comparison/contrast mode.

3. *Paragraph to Essay*

Expand the paragraph you wrote to a comparison or contrast essay focusing on three similarities or three differences. Use a plan sheet to organize the essay.

4. *Essay*

Write a comparison/contrast essay on one of the topics listed below.

a. Two fictional characters in literature
b. The lyrics of two songs based on the same subject
c. Two versions to the same story
d. Two movies based on the same story or character

Babe the Blue Ox

retold by S. E. Schlosser

This American Paul Bunyan folk tall tale introduces Babe the Blue Ox and his spouse Bessie the Yeller Cow as a couple. Enjoy the delightful language and the exaggeration typical of a tall tale.

Well now, one winter it was so cold that all the geese flew backward and all the fish moved south and even the snow turned blue. Late at night, it got so **frigid** that all spoken words froze solid afore they could be heard. People had to wait until sunup to find out what folks were talking about the night before.

Paul Bunyan went out walking in the woods one day during that Winter of the Blue Snow. He was knee-deep in blue snow when he heard a funny sound between a bleat and a snort. Looking down, he saw a teeny-tiny baby blue ox jest a hopping about in the snow and snorting with rage on account of he was too short to see over the drifts. Paul Bunyan laughed when he saw the spunky little critter and took the little blue **mite** home with him. He warmed the little ox up by the fire and the little fellow fluffed up and dried out, but he remained as blue as the snow that had stained him in the first place. So Paul named him Babe the Blue Ox.

Well, any creature raised in Paul Bunyan's camp tended to grow to massive proportions, and Babe was no exception. Folks that stared at him for five minutes could see him growing right before their eyes. He grew so big that 42 axe handles plus a plug of tobacco could fit between his eyes and it took a murder of crows a whole day to fly from one horn to the other. The laundryman used his horns to hang up all the camp laundry, which would dry **lickety-split** because of all the wind blowing around at that height. Whenever he got an itch, Babe the Blue Ox had to find a cliff to rub against, 'cause whenever he tried to rub against a tree it fell over and begged for mercy. To **whet** his appetite, Babe would chew up thirty bales of hay, wire and all. It took six men with **picaroons** to get all the wire out of Babe's teeth after his morning snack. Right after that he'd eat a ton of grain for lunch and then come pestering around the cook—Sourdough Sam—begging for another snack.

Babe the Blue Ox was a great help around Paul Bunyan's logging camp. He could pull anything that had two ends, so Paul often used him to straighten out the pesky, twisted logging roads. By the time Babe had pulled the twists and kinks out of all the roads leading to the lumber camp, there was twenty miles of extra road left flopping about with nowhere to go. So Paul rolled them up and used them to lay a new road into new timberland.

Paul also used Babe the Blue Ox to pull the heavy tank wagon which was used to coat the newly-straightened lumber roads with ice in the winter, until one day the tank sprang a leak that trickled south and became the Mississippi

River. After that, Babe stuck to hauling logs. Only he hated working in the summertime, so Paul had to paint the logging roads white after the spring thaw so that Babe would keep working through the summer. One summer, as Babe the Blue Ox was hauling a load of logs down the white-washed road and dreaming of the days when the winter would feel cold again and the logs would slide easier on the "ice", he glanced over the top of the mountain and caught a glimpse of a pretty yeller calf grazing in a field. Well, he twisted out of his harness lickety-split and stepped over the mountain to introduce himself. It was love at first sight, and Paul had to abandon his load and buy Bessie the Yeller Cow from the farmer before Babe would do any more hauling.

Bessie the Yeller Cow grew to the massive, yet dainty proportions that were suitable for the mate of Babe the Blue Ox. She had long yellow eyelashes that tickled the lumberjacks standing on the other end of camp each time she blinked. She produced all the dairy products for the lumber camp. Each day, Sourdough Sam made enough butter from her cream to grease the giant pancake griddle and sometimes there was enough left over to butter the toast!

The only bone of contention between Bessie and Babe was the weather. Babe loved the ice and snow and Bessie loved warm summer days. One winter, Bessie grew so thin and pale that Paul Bunyan asked his clerk Johnny Inkslinger to make her a pair of green goggles so she would think it was summer. After that, Bessie grew happy and fat again, and produced so much butter that Paul Bunyan used the leftovers to grease the whitewashed lumber roads in summer. With the roads so slick all year round, hauling logs became much easier for Babe the Blue Ox, and so Babe eventually came to like summer almost as much as Bessie.

Writing Assignments

1. *Journal Writing*

Summary

Summarize the plot of "Babe the Blue Ox" in 150 words or less. To do this, start with a topic sentence that states the title of the story, the author, and the main idea. Use chronological order to summarize the story.

Reaction

In your reaction, discuss the similarities and differences between Babe and Bessie.

2. *Paragraph*

Discuss the idioms "Opposites attract" and "Birds of a feather flock together." Write a paragraph comparing or contrasting two friends or two people in a romantic or a platonic relationship.

3. *Paragraph to Essay*

Expand the ideas from the paragraph in assignment two to an essay comparing or contrasting the two people. In the introductory paragraph, give any needed background information. End with a clear thesis statement. Add a concluding paragraph that both summarizes and draws a conclusion. Try using the idiomatic expression that best describes the couple in the concluding paragraph.

4. *Essay*
   Write a humorous essay comparing a real-life couple to the fictional Babe and Bessie in "Babe the Blue Ox." Recall the details of Babe and Bessie's relationship and compare or contrast them to the couple you choose as your subject.

Glossary for "Present at Creation," "John Henry," "John Henry Blues," and "Babe the Blue Ox"

bal·lad (băl'əd) *n.*

1. a. A narrative poem, often of folk origin and intended to be sung, consisting of simple stanzas and usually having a refrain.
   b. The music for such a poem.
2. A popular song especially of a romantic or sentimental nature.

[Middle English balade, *poem or song in stanza form*, from Old French ballade, from Old Provençal balada, *song sung while dancing*, from balar, *to dance*, from Late Latin ballāre, *to dance*.]

bal·lad'ic (bə-lăd'ĭk, bă-) *adj.*

leg·end (lĕj'ənd) *n.*

1. a. An unverified story handed down from earlier times, especially one popularly believed to be historical.
   b. A body or collection of such stories.
   c. A romanticized or popularized myth of modern times.
2. One that inspires legends or achieves legendary fame.
3. a. An inscription or a title on an object, such as a coin.
   b. An explanatory caption accompanying an illustration.
   c. An explanatory table or list of the symbols appearing on a map or chart.

[Middle English, from Old French legende, from Medieval Latin (lēctiō) legenda, *(lesson) to be read*, from Latin, feminine gerundive of legere, *to read*.]

en·sue (ĕn-so͞o')

intr.v. **en·sued, en·su·ing, en·sues**

1. To follow as a consequence or result.
2. To take place subsequently.

[Middle English ensuen, from Old French ensuivre, ensu-, from Vulgar Latin *īnsequere, from Latin īnsequī, *to follow closely*: in-, *intensive pref.*; see **en-**[1] + sequī, *to follow*; see sek^{w}-[1] in Indo-European Roots.]

shak·er (shā'kər) *n.*

1. a. One that shakes: *a shaker of long-held beliefs and traditions.*
   b. One that impels, encourages, or supervises action.

2. a. A container used for shaking: *salt and pepper shakers.*
   b. A container used to mix or blend by shaking: *a cocktail shaker.*
3. **Shaker** A member of a Christian sect originating in England in 1747, practicing communal living and observing celibacy.
   adj. also **Shaker**

   Relating to or constituting a style produced by Shakers that is distinctively simple, unornamented, functional, and finely crafted: *Shaker furniture.*

quin·tes·sen·tial (kwĭn'tə-sĕn'shəl)
adj.

Of, relating to, or having the nature of a quintessence; being the most typical: "Liszt was the quintessential romantic" (Musical Heritage Review).

quin'tes·sen'tial·ly *adv.*

de·i·fy (dē'ə-fī', dā'-) *tr. v.* **dei·fied, dei·fy·ing, dei·fies**

1. To make a god of; raise to the condition of a god.
2. To worship or revere as a god: *deify a leader.*
3. To idealize; exalt: *deifying success.*
4. [Middle English `deifien`, from Old French `deifier`, from Late Latin `deificāre`, from `deificus`, *deific.*]

de'i·fi'er *n.*

frig·id (frĭj'ĭd) *adj.*

1. Extremely cold.
2. Lacking warmth of feeling.
3. Stiff and formal in manner: *a frigid refusal to a request.*
4. Persistently averse to sexual intercourse.

[Latin frĭgidus, *cold*, from frĭgus, *the cold.*]

fri·gid'i·ty (frĭ-jĭd'ĭ-tē) or **frig'id·ness** *n.* **frig'id·ly** *adv.*

mite (mīt) *n.*

1. a. A very small contribution or amount of money.
   b. A widow's mite.
2. A very small object, creature, or particle.
3. A coin of very small value, especially an obsolete British coin worth half a farthing.
   Idiom: a mite

   To a small degree; somewhat: *That remark was a mite unfair.*

[Middle English, from Middle Dutch, and Middle Low German mīte, *a small Flemish coin, tiny animal.*]

lick·e·ty-split (lĭk'ĭ-tē-splĭt')
adv. Informal

With great speed.

[lickety, *very fast* alteration of **lick,** *fast (dialectal)* + **split.**]

whet (hwĕt, wĕt) *tr.v.* **whet·ted,whet·ting,whets**

1. To sharpen (a knife, for example); hone.
2. To make more keen; stimulate: *The frying bacon whetted my appetite.*
   n.

1. The act of whetting.

2. Something that whets.
3. *Informal.* An appetizer.

[Middle English whetten, from Old English hwettan.]

pic·a·roon (pĭk'ə-ro͞on') *n.*

1. a. A pirate.
   b. A pirate ship.

intr.v. **pic·a·rooned, pic·a·roon·ing, pic·a·roons**
To act as a pirate.

[Spanish picarón, augmentative of pícaro, *picaro.*]

Reading Comprehension

***John Henry* by Zora Neal Hurston**
***John Henry Blues* recorded by Fiddlin' John Carson (original recorded version)**
***Present at Creation* by Stephen Wade (NPR)**
***Babe the Blue Ox* retold by S. E. Schlosser**

Answer the following questions about the above selections of folk literature.

Word Meaning

Using the glossaries from the selections, choose the entry that best completes the sentences below.

1. The history professor explained how the tall tale __________ the ideas of many different immigrant cultures and blended them into a new American mentality.
2. After the speaker made his controversial presentation, the class met in the auditorium, where a number of interesting discussions __________ on the ideas made in the talk.
3. After her Grammy award, the hip hop artist was so revered by the young teens that they began __________ her as if she were an idol to be worshipped.
4. The temperatures dropped so dramatically that the hub workers hands felt __________ after only ten minutes of loading packages on the plane.
5. In an attempt to __________ the appetites for learning the parts of the body, the professor took the students on a midnight field trip to the emergency room.
6. Jacques Cousteau's son explained the many __________ that he experienced when he sailed the seven seas with his father to uncover the mysteries of the ocean.
7. Many of the American __________ of the olden days arose from the cowboys who sat around the campfire telling stories of their adventures on the range.

8. The athletic __________ of the high school basketball player was so well known that he signed a ten-year contract with the NBA soon after his graduation.
9. The principal of the high school explained the __________ of working with the immigrant students' language skills without a course in English as a second language.
10. Many singers in the 1960s sang __________ that resulted from the events of the Civil Rights Movement and the war in Vietnam.

Literal Meaning

Mark the letter of the option that best answers the statements below.

1. In both versions of the John Henry legend, the hero was
   a. larger than life.
   b. stronger than any human.
   c. determined to beat the steam driver.
   d. all of the above.
2. According to Stephen Wade in "Present at Creation," the folk legend "John Henry"
   a. is the most recorded folk ballad in America.
   b. provides an American hero whose race is unimportant.
   c. represents a hero with whom all Americans can identify.
   d. all of the above.
3. The characters of John Henry and Paul Bunyan both represent
   a. the strength and work ethic of a young America.
   b. fictitious heroes who were developed by commercial enterprises.
   c. different styles of advertising.
   d. modern man against machine.
4. Babe the Blue Ox was a character who
   a. received his name as a result of the blue skies of Minnesota.
   b. magnified and emphasized the size of his master Paul Bunyan.
   c. was a fictitious animal created from the imagination of Paul Bunyan.
   d. was a pastry design made by Sourdough Sam.

Interpretive Meaning

Complete the questions with the response that best answers the statement.

1. Why does John Henry say that "the hammer will be the death of me?"
   a. He thinks someone will kill him with a hammer.
   b. He knows at an early age how determined he is to build the right hammer.
   c. He knows his stubborn determination to outlast the steam drill will cause his death.
   d. He grows up playing with dangerous hammers.

2. The reader can conclude from the essays that folk heroes
   a. have developed for commercial reasons only.
   b. identify and unite a particular culture.
   c. present a fictitious image of a culture.
   d. can only be claimed by a certain portion of a culture.
3. What tone is present in the two essays on folk heroes?
   a. Argumentative
   b. Mildly humorous
   c. Sarcastic
   d. Informative
4. The use of dialectical English in the two poems and in the quotes from Wade's essay about John Henry does what?
   a. It establishes the regional identity of the speakers.
   b. It creates a character who represents the ordinary man.
   c. It creates a feeling of local color.
   d. All of the above
5. Why do the different versions of the John Henry legend treat the character's relationship with women differently?
   a. Because the real John Henry had many wives
   b. Because the story changes to fit the product being sold
   c. Because John Henry was a womanizer
   d. Because folk literature changes to parallel the lives and needs of the local community

Score: Number correct _____ out of _____

Writing Assignments

1. *Journal Writing*

Summary

Summarize the article in one or two paragraphs, focusing first on Paul Bunyan and then on John Henry.

Reaction

In your reaction paragraph, discuss what you learned in the essay compared to what you already knew about Paul Bunyan and John Henry. Discuss the parts of the essay that surprised you the most. What larger-than-life characters like these two exist today?

2. *Paragraph*

Write a paragraph comparing or contrasting a cartoon or other fictional character to someone you know or someone who is famous.

3. *Paragraph to Essay*

Expand the paragraph in assignment two to a comparison or contrast essay. To add interest to the essay, try focusing on the similarities rather than on the differences between the person and fictional character. Write a controlling thesis and a memorable conclusion. You may use humor in your essay.

4. *Essay*

   Using your knowledge gained from the unit, write a comparison/contrast essay on Paul Bunyan and John Henry. Focus on the personality traits of the characters and the historical framework of the two stories. Be careful that you use only your own words.

"Six to Eight Black Men"

David Sedaris

Currently living in Paris, essayist David Sedaris, who is a frequent guest on NPR, is well known for his humorous vignettes of contemporary American life. This reading is a heartwarming tale of Christmas in a foreign land where, if you've been naughty, Saint Nick and his friends give you an ass-whuppin'.

I've never been much for guidebooks, so when trying to get my bearings in a strange American city, I normally start by asking the cabdriver or hotel clerk some silly question regarding the latest census figures. I say silly because I don't really care how many people live in Olympia, Washington, or Columbus, Ohio. They're nice enough places, but the numbers mean nothing to me. My second question might have to do with average annual rainfall, which, again, doesn't tell me anything about the people who have chosen to call this place home.

What really interests me are the local gun laws. Can I carry a concealed weapon, and if so, under what circumstances? What's the waiting period for a **tommy gun?** Could I buy a Glock 17 if I were recently divorced or fired from my job? I've learned from experience that it's best to lead into this subject as delicately as possible, especially if you and the local citizen are alone and enclosed in a relatively small space. **Bide** your time, though, and you can walk away with some excellent stories. I've heard, for example, that the blind can legally hunt in both Texas and Michigan. They must be accompanied by a sighted companion, but still, it seems a bit risky. You wouldn't want a blind person driving a car or piloting a plane, so why hand him a rifle? What sense does that make? I ask about guns not because I want one of my own but because the answers vary so widely from state to state. In a country that's become so **homogenous,** I'm reassured by these last touches of regionalism.

Guns aren't really an issue in Europe, so when I'm traveling abroad, my first question usually relates to barnyard animals. "What do your roosters say?" is a good icebreaker, as every country has its own unique interpretation. In Germany, where dogs bark "vow vow" and both the frog and the duck say "quack," the rooster greets the dawn with a hearty "kik-a-ricki." Greek roosters crow "kiri-a-kee," and in France they scream "coco-rico," which sounds like one of those horrible premixed cocktails with a pirate on the label. When told that an American rooster says "cock-a-doodle-doo," my hosts look at me with disbelief and pity.

"When do you open your Christmas presents?" is another good conversation starter as it explains a lot about national character. People who traditionally open gifts on Christmas Eve seem a bit more **pious** and family oriented than those who wait until Christmas morning. They go to mass, open presents, eat a late meal, return to church the following morning, and devote the rest of the day to eating another big meal. Gifts are generally reserved for children, and the parents tend not to go overboard. It's nothing I'd want for myself, but I suppose it's fine for those who prefer food and family to things of real value.

In France and Germany, gifts are exchanged on Christmas Eve, while in Holland the children receive presents on December 5, in celebration of Saint Nicholas Day. It sounded sort of quaint until I spoke to a man named Oscar, who filled me in on a few of the details as we walked from my hotel to the Amsterdam train station.

Unlike the jolly, obese American Santa, Saint Nicholas is painfully thin and dresses not unlike the pope, topping his robes with a tall hat resembling an embroidered **tea cozy.** The outfit, I was told, is a carryover from his former career, when he served as a bishop in Turkey.

One doesn't want to be too much of a cultural **chauvinist,** but this seemed completely wrong to me. For starters, Santa didn't use to do anything. He's not retired, and, more important, he has nothing to do with Turkey. The climate's all wrong, and people wouldn't appreciate him. When asked how he got from Turkey to the North Pole, Oscar told me with complete conviction that Saint Nicholas currently resides in Spain, which again is simply not true. While he could probably live wherever he wanted, Santa chose the North Pole specifically because it is harsh and isolated. No one can spy on him, and he doesn't have to worry about people coming to the door. Anyone can come to the door in Spain, and in that outfit, he'd most certainly be recognized. On top of that, aside from a few pleasantries, Santa doesn't speak Spanish. He knows enough to get by, but he's not fluent, and he certainly doesn't eat **tapas.**

While our Santa flies on a sled, Saint Nicholas arrives by boat and then transfers to a white horse. The event is televised, and great crowds gather at the waterfront to greet him. I'm not sure if there's a set date, but he generally docks in late November and spends a few weeks hanging out and asking people what they want. "Is it just him alone?" I asked. "Or does he come with backup?"

Oscar's English was close to perfect, but he seemed thrown by a term normally reserved for police reinforcement. "Helpers," I said. "Does he have any elves?"

Maybe I'm just overly sensitive, but I couldn't help but feel personally insulted when Oscar denounced the very idea as **grotesque** and unrealistic. "Elves," he said. "They're just so silly."

The words *silly* and *unrealistic* were redefined when I learned that Saint Nicholas travels with what was consistently described as "six to eight black men." I asked several Dutch people to narrow it down, but none of them could give me an exact number. It was always "six to eight," which seems strange, seeing as they've had hundreds of years to get a decent count.

The six to eight black men were characterized as personal slaves until the mid-fifties, when the political climate changed and it was decided that instead of being slaves they were just good friends. I think history has proven that something usually comes between slavery and friendship, a period of time marked not by cookies and quiet times beside the fire but by bloodshed and mutual hostility. They have such violence in Holland, but rather than duking it out among themselves, Santa and his former slaves decided to take it out on the public. In the early years, if a child was naughty, Saint Nicholas and the six to eight black men would beat him with what Oscar described as "the small branch of a tree."

"A switch?"

"Yes," he said. "That's it. They'd kick him and beat him with a switch. Then, if the youngster was really bad, they'd put him in a sack and take him back to Spain."

"Saint Nicholas would kick you?"

"Well, not anymore," Oscar said. "Now he just pretends to kick you."

"And the six to eight black men?"

"Them, too."

He considered this to be progressive, but in a way I think it's almost more perverse than the original punishment. "I'm going to hurt you, but not really." How many times have we fallen for that line? The fake slap invariably makes contact, adding the elements of shock and betrayal to what had previously been plain, old-fashioned fear. What kind of Santa spends his time pretending to kick people before stuffing them into a canvas sack? Then, of course, you've got the six to eight former slaves who could potentially go off at any moment. This, I think, is the greatest difference between us and the Dutch. While a certain segment of our population might be perfectly happy with the arrangement, if you told the average white American that six to eight nameless black men would be sneaking into his house in the middle of the night, he would barricade the doors and arm himself with whatever he could get his hands on.

"Six to eight, did you say?"

In the years before central heating, Dutch children would leave their shoes by the fireplace, the promise being that unless they planned to beat you, kick you, or stuff you into a sack, Saint Nicholas and the six to eight black men would fill your **clogs** with presents. Aside from the threats of violence and kidnapping, it's not much different from hanging your stockings from the mantel. Now that so few people have a working fireplace, Dutch children are instructed to leave their shoes beside the radiator, furnace, or space heater. Saint Nicholas and the six to eight black men arrive on horses, which jump from the yard onto the roof. At this point, I guess, they either jump back down and use the door, or they stay put and **vaporize** through the pipes and electrical wires. Oscar wasn't to clear about the particulars, but, really, who can blame him? We have the same problem with our Santa. He's supposed to use the chimney, but if you don't have one, he still manages to come through. It's best not to think about it too hard.

While eight flying reindeer are a hard pill to swallow, our Christmas story remains relatively simple. Santa lives with his wife in a remote polar village and spends one night a year traveling around the world. If you're bad, he leaves you coal. If you're good and live in America, he'll give you just about anything you want.

We tell our children to be good and send them off to bed, where they lie awake, anticipating their great bounty. A Dutch parent has a decidedly **hairier** story to relate, telling his children, "Listen, you might want to pack a few of your things together before you go to bed. The former bishop from Turkey will be coming along with six to eight black men. They might put some candy in your shoes, they might stuff you in a sack and take you to Spain, or they might just pretend to kick you. We don't know for sure, but we want you to be prepared."

This is the reward for living in Holland. As a child you get to hear this story, and as an adult you get to turn around and repeat it. As an added bonus, the government has thrown in legalized drugs and prostitution—so what's not to love about being Dutch?

Oscar finished his story just as we arrived at the station. He was a polite and interesting guy—very good company—but when he offered to wait until my train arrived, I begged off, saying I had some calls to make. Sitting alone in the vast terminal, surrounded by other polite, seemingly interesting Dutch people, I couldn't help but feel second-rate. Yes, it was a small country, but it had six to eight black men and a really good bedtime story. Being a fairly competitive person, I felt jealous, then bitter, and was edging toward hostile when I remembered the blind hunter tramping off into the Michigan forest. He might bag a deer, or he might happily shoot his sighted companion in the stomach. He may find his way back to the car, or he may wander around for a week or two before stumbling through your front door. We don't know for sure, but in pinning that license to his chest, he inspires the sort of narrative that ultimately makes me proud to be an American.

Glossary for "Six to Eight Black Men"

Tommy gun *n. Informal*
A Thompson submachine gun.

bide (bīd) *v.* **bid·ed,** or **bode** (bōd) **bid·ed, bid·ing, bides**
v. intr.
To remain in a condition or state.

1. a. To wait; tarry.
   b. To stay: *bide at home.*
   c. To be left; remain.

v. tr.

past tense **bided** To await; wait for.

Idiom: bide (one's) time

To wait for further developments.

[Middle English biden, from Old English bīdan.]

ho·mo·ge·ne·ous (hō'mə-jē'nē-əs, -jēn'yəs) *adj.*

Of the same or similar nature or kind: "a tight-knit, homogeneous society" (James Fallows).

1. Uniform in structure or composition throughout.
2. Mathematics. Consisting of terms of the same degree or elements of the same dimension.

[from Medieval Latin homogeneus, from Greek homogenēs: homo-, *homo-* + genos, *kind.*]

ho'mo·ge'ne·ous·ly *adv.* **ho'mo·ge'ne·ous·ness** *n*

pi·ous (pī'əs) *adj.*

1. Having or exhibiting religious reverence; earnestly compliant in the observance of religion; devout.
   a. Marked by conspicuous devoutness: *a pious and holy observation.*
   b. Marked by false devoutness; solemnly hypocritical: *a pious fraud.*
2. Devotional: *pious readings.*
3. Professing or exhibiting a strict, traditional sense of virtue and morality; high-minded.
4. Commendable; worthy: *a pious effort.*

[From Latin pius, *dutiful.*]

pi'ous·ly *adv.* **pi'ous·ness** *n.*

tea cozy

n.: a padded cloth covering to keep a teapot warm [syn: cosy, tea cosy, cosey, tea cosey, cozy, cozey, tea cozey, cozie, tea cozie]

chau·vin·ism (shō'və-nĭz'əm) *n.*

1. Militant devotion to and glorification of one's country; fanatical patriotism.
2. Prejudiced belief in the superiority of one's own gender, group, or kind: "the chauvinism . . . of making extraterrestrial life in our own image" (Henry S.F. Cooper, Jr.).

[French chauvinisme, after Nicolas Chauvin, a legendary French soldier famous for his devotion to Napoleon.]

chau'vin·ist *n.* **chau'vin·is'tic** *adj.* **chau'vin·is'ti·cal·ly** *adv.*

ta·pa (tä'pä) *n. pl.* **ta·pas** (-päs, -päz)

Any of various small, savory Spanish dishes, often served as a snack or with other tapas as a meal.

[Spanish, *lid, appetizer, of Germanic origin.*]

gro·tesque (grō-tĕsk') *adj.*

1. Characterized by ludicrous or incongruous distortion, as of appearance or manner.
2. Outlandish or bizarre, as in character or appearance.
3. Of, relating to, or being the grotesque style in art or a work executed in this style.

n.

1. One that is grotesque.

2. a. A style of painting, sculpture, and ornamentation in which natural forms and monstrous figures are intertwined in bizarre or fanciful combinations.
   b. A work of art executed in this style.

[From French, *a fanciful style of decorative art*, from Italian grottesca, from feminine of grottesco, *of a grotto*, from grotta, *grotto*.]

gro·tesque'ly *adv.* **gro·tesque'ness** *n.*

clog (klôg, klŏg) *n.*

1. An obstruction or hindrance.
2. A weight, such as a block, attached to the leg of an animal to hinder movement.
3. A heavy, usually wooden-soled shoe.

v. **clogged, clog·ging, clogs**

v. tr.

1. To obstruct movement on or in; block up: *Heavy traffic clogged the freeways.*
2. To hamper the function or activity of; impede: "attorneys clogging our courts with actions designed to harass state and local governments" (Roslyn L. Anderson and Patricia L. Irvin).

   v. intr.

1. To become obstructed or choked up: *The pipes had clogged with rust.*
2. To thicken or stick together; clot.
3. To do a clog dance.

[Middle English, *block attached to an animal's leg*.]

va·por·ize (vā'pə-rīz') *tr. & intr. v.* **va·por·ized, va·por·iz·ing, va·por·iz·es**
To convert or be converted into vapor.

va'por·iz'a·ble *adj.*

va'por·i·za'tion (-ĭ-zā'shən) *n.*

hair·y (hâr'ē) *adj.* **hair·i·er, hair·i·est**

1. Covered with hair or hairlike projections: *a hairy caterpillar.*
2. Consisting of or resembling hair: *a hairy overcoat.*
3. Slang. Fraught with difficulties; hazardous: *a hairy escape; hairy problems.*

   hair'i·ness *n.*

Reading Comprehension

Answer the following questions about the essay by David Sedaris.

Word Meaning

Using the glossary, select the entry that best completes the sentences below.

1. We __________ our time in the cockpit while flying on automatic pilot by playing Sudoku and completing crossword puzzles.
2. An essential component of gang membership in Southeast Asia is the ownership of a __________ for protection against rival gangs.
3. While in Barcelona, we participated in the dining pleasures of eating afternoon __________ in the town square.

4. The word used for a carbonated beverage—Coke, soda pop, soda, pop, soft drink—is a clear example of the _________ differences in English in the United States.
5. The _________ lyrics of some rap music indicate the macho attitudes that some men still have toward women.
6. At the moment the young men entered the mosque, they immediately became very _________ and thus showed respect to their wise elders.
7. Some studies prove that a/an _________ educational classroom setting is better for teaching both young boys and girls.
8. The _________ character in the *Phantom of the Opera* represents a true story of a fire victim in the old Paris opera house.

Literal Meaning

Mark the letter of the option that best answers the statements below.

1. In the essay, Sedaris speaks from what point of view?
   a. First person
   b. Second person
   c. Third-person objective
   d. Third-person omniscient
2. What is the subject matter discussed in the Sedaris essay?
   a. The differences among the six to eight Black men in the essay
   b. The differences between the American Santa Claus and the Dutch St. Nicholas
   c. The reason Dutch children are frequently kidnapped at Christmas time
   d. The reason Sedaris was visiting the Netherlands
3. Instead of stockings, what do Dutch children put out for St. Nick to fill at Christmas?
   a. Boots
   b. Fabric tulips
   c. Clogs
   d. Knit caps
4. On what day do the Dutch children celebrate St. Nicholas's bringing gifts?
   a. December 25
   b. January 6
   c. December 24
   d. December 5
5. How does Sedaris learn the story of the tradition of the Dutch St. Nicholas?
   a. He reads the story in a book on Christmas customs.
   b. He meets a man named Oscar on a sidewalk in Amsterdam.
   c. He visits a Dutch family during the Christmas season.
   d. He attends a lecture on culture and customs around the world.
6. Place a "D" for Dutch and an "A" for American to the following points that contrast the Christmas stories of the two countries.
   a. _____ Six to eight black men
   b. _____ A lump of coal

c. _____A slender man as St. Nicholas
d. _____North Pole
e. _____A sled
f. _____A tall hat resembling a tea cozy
g. _____A former bishop

Interpretive Meaning

Complete the questions with the response that best answers the statement.

1. Why does Sedaris begin and end his essay with the story of a blind man's hunting?
   a. This vignette creates unity in the essay.
   b. The fact that a blind man can hunt in America makes him proud to be American.
   c. He thinks all countries should allow blind men to hunt, fly planes, and drive.
   d. He believes the subject is important enough to be repeated.
2. What is the tone of the essay? (Mark all that apply.)
   a. Outrageously humorous
   b. Informative
   c. Argumentative
   d. Mildly satirical
3. According to Sedaris, what is the effect of the Dutch St. Nicholas story on children?
   a. The children are afraid to go to sleep on Christmas Eve.
   b. The children are afraid to misbehave.
   c. Dutch children like to be kidnapped and taken to Spain for vacation.
   d. The six to eight Black men support St. Nicholas in his work.
4. Based on the context of the sentences, which statement from the essay can be categorized as sarcasm?
   a. " . . . ultimately makes me proud to be an American."
   b. "Could I buy a Glock 17 . . . "?
   c. " . . . these last touches of regionalism."
   d. " . . . six to eight black men . . . "
5. Why does Sedaris say that he does not want to be a "cultural chauvinist" about the differences between the two countries' stories ?
   a. He prefers the American Santa story because it is not cruel toward children.
   b. He wants to become friends with Oscar and does not want to offend his culture.
   c. He lives in Amsterdam and must be careful.
   d. He wants to sell more books.
6. Why did the Dutch story about the six to eight black men change in the 1950s?
   a. The men did not like their former role as slaves to St. Nick.
   b. They took on a more significant job as the ones who would beat the children.
   c. The change reflected the political climate of the era where the term *slave* became taboo.
   d. St. Nick gave the six to eight black men their freedom.

7. Why does Sedaris not ask Europeans about their gun laws?
   a. People are not allowed to discuss gun ownership in Europe.
   b. Gun ownership is outlawed in Europe.
   c. Sedaris is more interested in the sounds that European animals make.
   d. Gun ownership is not a really big issue in Europe.
8. Whether in America or in Europe, when Sedaris asks questions of the local people, what is he really trying to learn?
   a. What accents people use
   b. What regional differences he can uncover in the conversation
   c. The intelligence levels of the different cultures
   d. The degree to which people accept strangers
9. Summarize the theme of the essay. Is this essay really about the St. Nick story, or is there a deeper point that can be detected? If so, what is it?

   ____

   ____
10. List all of the words that indicate contrast that can be found in the essay.

   ____

   ____

Score: Number correct _____ out of _____

Writing Assignments

1. Journal Writing

Summary

Write a one- or two-paragraph summary of the essay.

Reaction

When reacting to the essay, consider the tone of the essay as well as the content. What parts of the essay do you consider humorous? What parts of the essay do you consider serious? How does the combination of humor and seriousness affect your reaction as a reader?

2. Paragraph

In the essay, Sedaris compares traditions associated with St. Nicholas of Holland and Santa Claus of America. For this assignment, write a paragraph comparing or contrasting traditions associated with cultural holidays and events in families, communities, or regions of the country. When selecting a topic, consider not only traditions related to religious and secular holidays but also traditions associated with weddings, funerals, graduations, or any other family event.

3. Paragraph to Essay

Using the paragraph written for assignment two, expand the paragraph to an essay comparing or contrasting a tradition or traditions in two families or two geographical locations. Follow the format for the comparison/contrast mode of writing essays.

4. *Essay*
   Write a comparison or contrast essay on one of the following topics.
   a. Two folktales
   b. Two pets
   c. Two jobs
   d. Two neighborhoods
   e. Two schools
   f. Two methods of _________ (raising children, training pets, learning to drive, learning to swim)
   g. Two languages
   h. Two personality types

Reflective Assignments

1. Reflect on the quotation at the beginning of the chapter, "Time is a good story teller." Write a paragraph giving examples of why you think this statement is true or false.
2. Choose one of the idioms from Idioms for American Folk Life and explain how it relates to traditions in your family or in your region of the country.
3. Write a ballad similar to the John Henry ballads about someone who has become a legend in your community, city, state, or country.
4. Write a folktale explaining an answer to a scientific question.

Internet Field Trips—Reading and Writing Assignments

1. Follow the link http://www.americanfolklore.net/index.html to find examples of myths and legends from your state or region. Read at least three of the stories. While reading the folktales, underline any words you are unsure of and try to figure out the meaning through context clues. After reading the folktale, use reporter's questions to summarize each folktale.
2. Research information about urban legends. Try the following Web sites:
   - http://www.americanfolklore.net/urban-legends. html
   - http://urbanlegends.about.com
   - http://www.warphead.com/urbanlegends
3. Find a definition for an urban legend in the Web site. Search for examples of urban legends in the Web site. Write an essay about your research. In the introductory paragraph, explain urban legends. In the body paragraphs, discuss several urban legends. In the concluding paragraph, summarize the information and come to some type of conclusion about urban legends.

a. After reading about urban legends, choose one urban legend and write a paper comparing or contrasting the legend to reality. Try these Web sites for information:
http://www.snopes.com and http://www.urbanlegends.about.com.
b. Using the information you have learned about folklore and urban legends, write a paragraph or essay comparing or contrasting urban legends and folklore. Remember to correctly punctuate and cite the source for any information used from the Web sites. Additional Web sites you may want to explore include
- www.Snopes.com
- www.urbanlegendsonline.com
- http://hoaxbusters.ciac.org
- http://www.pantheon.org/areas/
- http://www.pitt.edu/~dash/folktexts.html

c. Read about folklore in the movies. Go to this Web site and read one of the articles listed: http://www.indiana.edu/~urbanflk/folklore_in_movies/index6.html. Summarize and react to the article.

FILMS TO VIEW

Urban Legend (directed by Jamie Blanks, 1988)
Cinderella Man (directed by Ron Howard, 2005)
Rodgers & Hammerstein's Cinderella (directed by Robert Iscove, 1997)
Napoleon (written and directed by David Grubin, 2000)
Fairy Tale: A True Story (directed by Charles Sturridge, 2003)
Ever After (directed by Andy Tennant, 1998)

Writing assignments are based on *Ever After: A Cinderella Story* written by Andy Tennant and Susannah Grant and directed by Andy Tennant

1. Write a comparison or contrast essay on the movie *Ever After* and the version of Cinderella with which you are familiar. In the essay, focus on characters, plot, and theme.
2. Write a paragraph explaining the literary references made in the movie. (You may need to watch the movie more than once to catch all of them.)
3. The tagline for *Ever After* is "Desire. Defy. Escape." Write a new tagline for the movie and write a paragraph explaining the relevance of the tagline.
4. Watch another movie based on the Cinderella story such as *The Slipper and the Rose* starring Richard Chamberlain and directed by Bryan Forbes, *Cinderella Man* staring Russell Crowe and directed by Ron Howard, or Rodgers & Hammerstein's *Cinderella* starring Whitney Houston and directed by Robert Iscove. Write an essay comparing *Ever After* to the movie of your choice. Do not summarize the movies. Instead choose two or three differences or similarities and focus on those points.
5. Write a paragraph analyzing the message *Ever After: A Cinderella Story* sends to young women in comparison to the message of the traditional stories.

SUMMARY OF UNIT 4—AMERICAN FOLKLORE—COMPARISON AND CONTRAST

Read the student essay entitled "Everyone Loves Hot Women" by Eric Carruth. Analyze it for its content, its organization, and its mechanics. Then, in the Summary of Unit 4 on page 223 complete the column on the right with your responses. Apply the information learned in Unit 3.

Everyone Likes Hot Women

Greek mythology has fascinated people since its conception. Countless movies and books have been based on these myths. Art is also very prevalent in many literary works and movies. It should not come as a surprise that many authors have used these myths in their stories to grab the reader's attention. Updike uses both art and Greek mythology to enhance the reader's understanding of his main characters in "A & P" and "Pygmalion."

Updike's "A & P" is a short story with a very artistic underlying theme. According to Saldívar this story has close ties to Botticelli's, "The Birth of Venus." This beautiful painting depicts Venus (the Greek goddess of love) standing in a scallop's shell. She is being blown ashore by the wind (a male figure) into the arms of a female figure onshore. There is also another female figure in the arms of the wind (the male figure). In Updike's "A & P," Sammy describes Queenie's body in a way that creates an image of a goddess-like beauty. It is easy to see that the image Updike is describing is parallel to, if not based on, the image of Venus in the painting. However, Sammy does not describe Queenie to the reader in the way that one would expect from a nineteen year old boy. He does not focus on the breasts or the buttocks. He focuses on her shoulder and neckline, and thus, shows the reader that Queenie is a classic beauty. He describes her as having "long white prima-donna legs." (285). Sammy depicts Queenie walking through the store "putting down her heals and then letting the weight move along to her toes" (285). He describes her legs and manner of walking to the reader in a way that gives her an aura of royalty. Just as her gate gives her a sense of superiority, her beauty closely mimics the classic beauty of Venus. In Botticelli's painting, Venus is pictured in the nude. The nudity is not meant to be erotic, it is meant to show that the human form is beautiful in a classic way. Updike's use of art helps to develop the reader's understanding of Sammy's feelings towards Queenie.

Updike uses the painting to give the reader an accurate image of how beautiful Queenie is, however, this is not the only area that the story and the painting have in common. In Saldívar's opinion, this painting is very ironic. He describes it as "gorgeous and sad." (2). Updike uses this same sense of irony in his story. At the end of "A & P" Sammy quits his job. He tells the manager that he is quitting while the young girls are still in the store. Updike explains to the reader that Sammy says, "I quit" loud enough for the girls to hear him (289). Sammy hopes that they will stop and watch him show his discontentment with how they were treated but they keep walking. The dialogue between Sammy and the manager lead the reader to believe that this is not merely a summertime job but this is actually Sammy's career. In the last paragraph of the story, we read about Sammy walking out of the store and hoping (but not expecting) the girls to be there waiting on their "unsuspected hero." (289). The irony in this story becomes apparent when Sammy has an epiphany in the last paragraph. He suddenly realizes that he has given up everything and received nothing in return. Sammy tells us, "my stomach kind of fell as I felt how hard the world was going to be for me hereafter." (290). Sammy is like the male figure in Botticelli's painting. By nature, the wind pushes away whatever it approaches, and thus, can never attain Venus (Queenie). The Greek mythology and art help the reader to appreciate Sammy's feelings after losing everything.

Just as Updike uses "The Birth of Venus" in "A & P," he also uses Greek mythology and irony in "Pygmalion." The Greek myth of Pygmalion is about a sculptor who created a statue of a beautiful woman. He then prayed to Venus to bring him a wife like the statue. His wish was granted and he was happy for the rest of his life. Updike chose the name "Pygmalion" for his short story because the main character had similar ideals to Pygmalion, and the use of mythology would help the reader understand Pygmalion's feelings. It is about a man who has an idea of the perfect wife. He divorces and remarries, attempting to obtain his ideal wife. At the end of the story his second wife has become remarkably similar to his first wife. In the Greek myth the sculptor used stone for his creations. Statues made of stone are virtually unaffected by time. In this same sense the main character of Updike's story wanted a beautiful wife that would not change. Much like in "A & P," Updike decided to use some ironic elements to this story. The main character's first wife would "ask to have her back rubbed and then, under his laboring hands, night after night, fall asleep." (291). Updike then introduced the irony by telling the reader that he wanted his second wife to keep her "liveliness in bed," (291) but he began to ask her, "Want a back rub?" (293). The fact that he is doing exactly what made him lose interest in his first wife is quite ironic. It is almost as if Updike is asking the reader, "Do we want everything in life to be perfect, or do we unconsciously push things out of equilibrium to keep our lives interesting?" Assuming that the reader is willing to think in such a way, Updike uses Greek mythology and art to help the reader to understand what the main character is doing, even if the main character is not aware of it.

If Updike had not used specific elements to allow the reader to identify with his character, his stories would be much blander. However, since he did use these elements, his stories are interesting and attractive to the reader. Updike's uses of Greek mythology and art in "A & P" and "Pygmalion" allow the reader to interact with, and feel as his character must have felt, thus, creating a much more powerful and memorable reading experience.

Works Cited

Saldívar, Toni. "The Art of John Updike's 'A & P'." Studies in Short Fiction Spring 1997: 215–25. EBSCOhost. University of Tennessee Library. 21 June 2006 http://web105.epnet.com.proxy.lib.utk.edu.

Updike, John. "A & P." Literature For Composition, 7th ed. Ed. Sylvan Barnet, et. al. New York: Pearson Longman, 2005. 285–90.

Updike, John. "Pygmalion." Literature For Composition, 7th ed. Ed. Sylvan Barnet, et. al. New York: Pearson Longman, 2005. 291–93.

SUMMARY OF UNIT 4	
1. The thesis of the essay is	1.
2. The main tense in the essay is	2.
3. Three transitions used include	3.
4. Three points of comparison	4.
5. The purpose of this essay is to	5.
6. The writer concludes by	6.
7. The reader can infer that the writer	7.
8. Three mechanical errors include	8.

Unit 5

Landmarks

To travel is to live.

—H. C. Andersen

Setting is an important element in fiction. Explain how landmarks represent a sense of belonging in the literature of America.

This traditional school building has been stylized with Asian architecture. How does the new architecture reflect the constantly changing demographics of America?

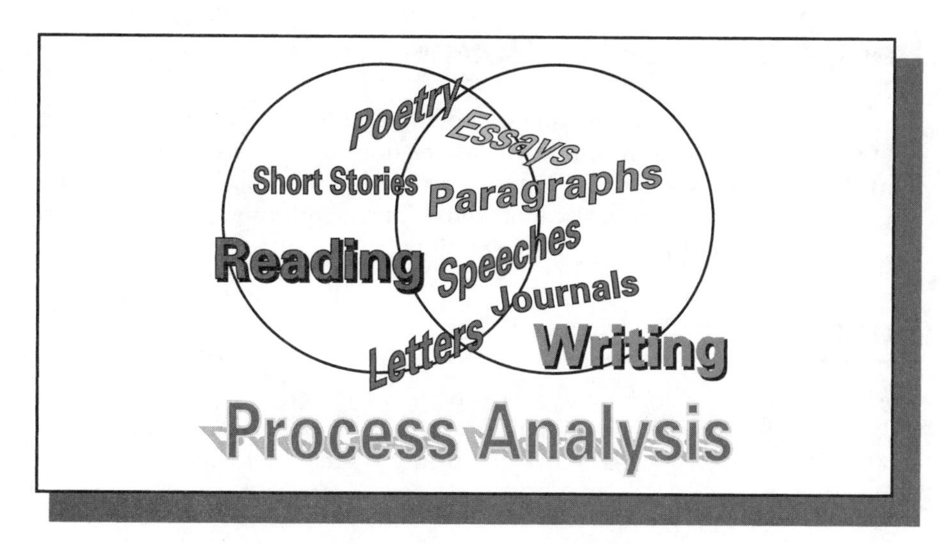

Purpose of Unit:

- *To understand the pattern of process analysis as it relates to reading comprehension and writing*

Idioms for Landmarks

Review the idioms below and discuss their meaning. Apply these idioms to landmarks and travel.

Fifth wheel
On the wagon
Reinvent the wheel
Travel light
Run around
Salt of the earth
The careful foot can walk anywhere.
Along the way there will be thorns. But if you look above them you will discover roses.
Don't rely on others to show you the way, carry your own map.

Earth to ________________
Train of thought
La la Land
Land of milk and honey
Land of the living
A traveler without observation is a bird without wings.
He that travels far knows much.
Seek out all the places where you can be happy—in the city we pine for the country and in the country we long for the city.

Process Analysis: Points to Consider

Business managers, medical workers, students, educators—people of all walks of life are called upon to read and write directions. Directions, either instructions that tell how to do something or how something was done, should be written so that they can be easily followed. When reading and writing process analysis essays, consider the following points.

Purpose

The process, or "how to," mode of writing is used to explain how to perform an action or how to do something or how a process happens or happened. It should be explained so clearly that the reader is either able to perform or to explain the processes.

Types of Process Writing

Process papers that explain or give instructions on how to do something are called **directional.** Topics such as how to make a five-layer cake or how to earn an A in freshman composition follow this developmental style. Process essays and paragraphs that explain an event or a process are called **informational.** Informational process analyses may be used to explain historical, scientific, or educational processes, such as how integration laws were enforced in the 1960s, how cells reproduce, or how children develop critical thinking skills.

Organization

Both process paragraphs and essays must have a clearly stated focus and must be organized in chronological order. A process paragraph should have a topic sentence followed by specific instructions or discussion of stages. Like other essays, a process analysis essay will have an introductory paragraph with a thesis statement, body paragraphs that give the directions or explain stages, and a concluding paragraph.

Transitional Devices

Transitional phrases are extremely important when reading and writing a process analysis. Transitional devices that indicate time must direct the reader easily from one step to another or from one sequence of events to another. Transitional phrases include *first, second, third, next, after, then, at the same time, finally.*

POINT OF VIEW AND TENSE

Directional processes can be written in first, second, or third person and are usually written in present tense.

> ***First person:*** First, when I make a five-layer cake, I gather all of the ingredients and supplies I need.
> ***Second person:*** First, when making a five-layer cake, you should gather all the ingredients and supplies you need.
> ***Second person (you as the understood subject):*** First, when making a five-layer cake, gather all the ingredients and supplies you need.
> ***Third person:*** First, when making a five-layer cake, the cook should gather all the ingredients and supplies he or she needs.

Informational processes will usually be written in third person (he, she, it). For informational processes explaining events of the past, such as an explanation of how civil rights laws were enforced in the 1960s, use past tense. For any process that occurs regularly, such as cell reproduction and critical thinking skills, write in the present tense.

Paragraph and Essay Formats for Writing Processes

Use the following planning guide for process paragraphs.

Subject

Type of Process Analysis ______________________________

Topic sentence ______________________________

List of Steps or Stages

1.

2.

3.

4.

5.

Concluding Sentence ______________________________

Use the following planning guide for process essays.

Subject

Type of Process Analysis

Thesis statement ________________________________

I. Introductory paragraph

II. First body paragraph—Step 1

III. Second body paragraph—Step 2

IV. Third Body paragraph—Step 3

V. Concluding paragraph

Process Analysis Writing Worksheet

1. Survey the assignment and choose your topic. Do one of the prewriting assignments discussed in the introduction of the text.
2. Question the assignment. What is the focus of the assignment? Does the focus ask you to explain how something works, how to do something, or how something occurred? What are steps in the process?
3. Map your essay or paragraph. Number each step.
4. Relate your plan of writing to your writing group. Explain the process you are writing about to your group members. After you have finished, group members should be able to repeat the steps to you. Answer any questions they may have.
5. Record (write) the first draft of your essay or paragraph.
6. Read your paragraph or essay aloud to a student partner. As you read, the partner should listen for each step and ask questions about the details and the sequence of the steps.
7. Revise your essay taking into account the questions that you and your writing group and peer editors asked about your paper.
8. Review your revised paper with your partner and answer the Questions for Review.
9. Reflect upon the comments of your peers and make needed changes.
10. Reread your paper, checking for grammatical errors. Read your paper from top to bottom and from bottom to top. Reading your paper in reverse helps you to read what you wrote, not what you meant to write! As you read your paper, check carefully for consistency in tense and point of view.
11. Read your paper aloud.
12. Write your final draft!

Point of View

When writing, stick to one point of view. Thus you make your writing more unified and less confusing to the reader. Always plan the point of view (person) that you will use in the prewriting stage. Writing down the point of view and corresponding pronouns is an important step for avoiding shifts in person and pronoun reference errors.

Faulty Sentence

> The cook should always measure the ingredients before adding them to their bowl. You do not want to make a mistake when mixing ingredients.

Can you find the two mistakes in the sentence above?

Correct Form

> The cook should always measure the ingredients before adding them to *his or her* bowl. *He or she* does not want to make a mistake when mixing ingredients.

The third person is most preferred for academic writing, but the instructional and directional process analysis lends itself to the second-person point of view—you. Using the third-person plural enables the writer to avoid the "he/she" indefinite gender issue. Using the plural forms of pronouns and nouns—they/them/their/theirs/people/etc.—will make writing clear and sentence casting simpler.

Guide for Point of View:

I/me/my
Your/your/yours
We/us/our/ours
He/she/it/one/someone/the person/the individual
They/them/their/theirs/people/students

Practice with these sentences.

Faulty Form: When a person plans a trip, they should always consult a map.
Correct Form: ______________________________
Faulty Form: My city did their best to make the festival a success.
Correct Form: ______________________________
Faulty Form: When people travel, you never know what experiences will follow them.
Correct Form: ______________________________

Questions for Review

Paragraph Assignment

- What is the topic sentence?
- What process is being explained?

- What order is used to explain the process?
- What transitional words has the author used to take the reader from one step to another?
- What key words has the author used to give the paragraph unity?
- What is the concluding sentence of the paragraph?

Essay Assignment

The Introductory Paragraph

- Does the introduction make you want to read the essay?
- What is the focus of the essay?
- What process is being explained?
- What is the thesis statement?

The Body Paragraphs

- What step is being discussed in each body paragraph?
- Are there any parts of the body paragraphs that are confusing? If so, what can the author do to make the paper clearer?
- What transitional words are used to guide the reader from one paragraph to the next? What transitional words are used within the body paragraphs? Are the transitional words used appropriately?
- What key words are used to give the essay unity?
- List some of the strong verbs the author has used to make the paper more effective.
- What person is the paper written in—first, second, or third? Are there any places where the author makes unnecessary shifts in person? Where are they?

The Conclusion

- How does the author conclude the essay?

Entire Essay

- What is the most effective part of the essay?

READING BEFORE WRITING

Jaunts: Atlanta to Montgomery to Memphis: A Family Trip Through History

Carlton Winfrey

Author Carlton Winfrey reports on the gift of history he bestowed upon his two young sons. For Black History Month, he and his children "spent spring break retracing King's steps by visiting sites throughout the South." Their journey took them from Atlanta, to Montgomery, to Memphis.

Knight Ridder Newspapers 03-12-2005

There's an **infinite** number of material things a father can give his children: some they value, others they don't.

For Black History Month, I wanted to give my kids something that would last a lifetime, something that would entertain and educate. To fill the bill I chose a trip back in time, a history lesson on the Rev. Martin Luther King Jr. We'd spend the kids' spring break retracing King's life by visiting, for the first time for all of us, sites throughout the South.

If it were 40 years ago, I told Reed, 9, and Karli, 7, such a trip would be far different for a black family. They'd pack a lunch of fried chicken wrapped in foil, boiled eggs and pound cake in a shoebox and hit the road in the family **sedan,** driving until they reached a relative's home and praying that they didn't encounter hate-filled **bigots** along the way.

We, on the other hand, packed the camera, a few DVDs (including *Our Friend, Martin,* an animated time-travel adventure about King), a few special stuffed animals and books and started looking for golden arches along Interstate 75. The three of us were making the trip alone. My wife, Carlette, stayed home because of work.

King was born and educated in Atlanta, spent the early part of his ministry as pastor of a Montgomery church and was **felled** by an assassin's bullet during a trip to Memphis, Tenn. So that became our **itinerary,** beginning with a nine-hour drive from Detroit to Nashville, an overnight stay, then four more hours to Atlanta.

Reed and Karli, who looked forward to seeing their grandmother in Nashville, and their uncle in Atlanta, passed most of the time on the road reading, watching DVDs and sleeping.

We began our history lesson Saturday morning at Morehouse College, the all-male private college King entered at age 15 and where he earned a bachelor's degree and obtained many of the skills that would help change a nation.

On this stately campus of **manicured** courtyards and red-brick buildings is the Martin Luther King Jr. International Chapel, home to dozens of **artifacts,** photos and books on King and civil and human rights movements. In the halls surrounding the chapel are dozens of portraits of ministers, **philanthropists,** presidents and **activists,** including Mahatma Gandhi; the Rev. Wyatt Tee Walker, one of the historians of the civil rights movement, and William Jefferson White, the white Baptist minister who in 1867 founded what is now Morehouse.

The chapel is the site of the only statue of King in Georgia, a 20-foot-high monument. It immediately captured Reed and Karli's attention. "There he is, Reed," Karli said.

King was born and raised a few miles away at 501 Auburn Ave. Free tours are given daily of the home, but onsite registration nearby at the King Center is required and slots fill up quickly, as we learned the hard way. Though we didn't get to tour inside, we did stroll by the **Victorian** home and stopped to take pictures.

And the King Center itself offered plenty, from exhibits on human rights struggles globally to displays that helped children understand what life was like during the 1950s and '60s. There is also a theater where short films on the history of civil rights are shown.

The film we watched, *A New Time, A New Voice,* focuses on King's involvement in the **Jim Crow** South and depicts drinking fountains and restrooms marked "colored" or "white only" and restaurants with signs ordering "Negroes" to use the back door. As you exit the King Center, you pass the antique wooden wagon used to carry King's casket in 1968.

After a scenic morning drive from Atlanta along Interstate 85, noting the significance of two other towns—Stone Mountain, Ga., which is referenced by King in his famous "I Have A Dream" speech and where we spent the night at my brother's home, and Tuskegee, which is home to Tuskegee University and the Tuskegee Airmen National Historic Site, where hundreds of black men trained as pilots during World War II—we arrived in Montgomery. It was just in time for services at the church King led spiritually and socially. It was here that Dexter Avenue Baptist Church welcomed its 20th pastor in 1954, replacing another great preacher, the Rev. Vernon Johns.

King, who had been an assistant pastor at Ebenezer Baptist Church in Atlanta, came to Dexter Avenue after graduating from Morehouse, Crozer Theological Seminary in Pennsylvania and completing studies for his Ph.D. at Boston University. He was only 25.

Soon after he arrived, King's nonviolent philosophy was tested.

On Dec. 1, 1955, Rosa Parks, whom many in Montgomery knew as the seamstress at the Montgomery Fair department store, refused to give up her bus seat to a white man, leading to her arrest and prompting church leaders and activists to mobilize. The result was a bus **boycott** that lasted nearly a year and crippled the city's bus service.

A few months later, King's family would be threatened when a bomb was **lobbed** at the church **parsonage** on Jackson Street.

"She was sitting in this room (the dining room) with one of our church members, Mrs. Williams, when they heard something hit the porch," Avis Dunbar, tourism manager of the Dexter Parsonage Museum, said of Coretta Scott King. Dunbar at the time was a child and lived a few houses from the Kings on Jackson Street. "And they ran. Instead of going to the window to look out, they ran down the hall and then the bomb went off."

Reed and Karli had no immediate reaction. But later they got to go out on the porch and see where the bomb left a crater.

King moved back to Atlanta in 1960 to lead the Southern Christian Leadership Conference and became co-pastor at Ebenezer. When he traveled to Memphis to support striking **sanitation** workers in 1968, he and others stayed at the Lorraine Hotel. Today, the hotel is part of the National Civil Rights Museum.

We timed our visit just right, arriving on a Monday afternoon during free admission time.

Like the Dexter parsonage, cameras aren't allowed inside the exhibit areas, which wind along wide halls. Exhibits include a restored bus with a front and rear door that visitors can climb inside and take a seat (anywhere), and a lunch counter that **depicts** the sit-ins of the time with a video on how activists—black and white—prepared for such protests. There are also sections on the role of the church in the movement and *Brown vs. Board of Education*.

Glossary for "Atlanta to Montgomery to Memphis: A Family Trip through History"

in·fi·nite (ĭn'fə-nĭt)

adj.

1. Having no boundaries or limits.
2. Immeasurably great or large; boundless: *infinite patience; a discovery of infinite importance.*
3. Mathematics.
    a. Existing beyond or being greater than any arbitrarily large value.
    b. Unlimited in spatial extent: *a line of infinite length.*
    c. Of or relating to a set capable of being put into one-to-one correspondence with a proper subset of itself.

n.

Something infinite.

[Middle English infinit, from Old French, from Latin īnfīnītus: in-, *not*; see **in-**[1] + fīnītus, *finite* from past participle of fīnīre, *to limit*.]

in'fi·nite·ly *adv.*

in'fi·nite·ness *n.*

Synonyms: *infinite, boundless, eternal, illimitable, sempiternal*

These adjectives mean being without beginning or end: *infinite wisdom; boundless ambition; eternal beauty; illimitable space; sempiternal truth.*

se·dan (sĭ-dăn')

n.

1. A closed automobile having two or four doors and a front and rear seat.
2. A portable enclosed chair for one person, having poles in the front and rear and carried by two other people. Also called **sedan chair.**

[*Origin unknown.*]

big·ot (bĭg'ət)

n.

One who is strongly partial to one's own group, religion, race, or politics and is intolerant of those who differ.

[French, from Old French.]

Word History: Bigots may have more in common with God than one might think. Legend has it that Rollo, the first duke of Normandy, refused to kiss the foot of the French king Charles III, uttering the phrase *bi got,* his borrowing of the assumed Old English equivalent of our expression *by God.* Although this story is almost surely apocryphal, it is true that *bigot* was used by the French as a term of abuse for the Normans, but not in a religious sense. Later, however, the word, or very possibly a homonym, was used abusively in French for the Beguines, members of a Roman Catholic lay sisterhood. From the fifteenth century on Old French *bigot* meant "an excessively devoted or hypocritical person." *Bigot* is first recorded in English in 1598 with the sense "a superstitious hypocrite."

fell (fĕl)

tr.v. **felled, fell·ing, fells**

1. a. To cause to fall by striking; cut or knock down: *fell a tree; fell an opponent in boxing.*
   b. To kill: *was felled by an assassin's bullet.*
2. To sew or finish (a seam) with the raw edges flattened, turned under, and stitched down.

n.

1. The timber cut down in one season.
2. A felled seam.

[Middle English fellen, from Old English fellan, fyllan.]

fell'a·ble *adj.*

i·tin·er·ar·y (ī-tĭn'ə-rĕr'ē, ĭ-tĭn'-)

n. pl. **i·tin·er·ar·ies**

1. A route or proposed route of a journey.
2. An account or record of a journey.
3. A guidebook for travelers.

adj.

1. Of or relating to a journey or route.
2. Traveling from place to place; itinerant.

[Middle English itinerarie, from Late Latin itinerārium, *account of a journey,* from neuter of itinerārius, *of traveling,* from Latin iter, itiner-, *journey.*]

man·i·cure (măn'ĭ-kyo͝or')

n.

A cosmetic treatment of the fingernails, including shaping and polishing.

tr. v. **man·i·cured, man·i·cur·ing, man·i·cures**

1. To trim, clean, and polish (the fingernails).
2. To clip or trim evenly and closely: *manicure a hedge.*

[French : Latin manus, *hand;* see man-[2] in Indo-European Roots + Latin cūra, *care;* see **cure.**]

ar·ti·fact also **ar·te·fact** (är'tə-făkt')

n.

1. An object produced or shaped by human craft, especially a tool, weapon, or ornament of archaeological or historical interest.
2. Something viewed as a product of human conception or agency rather than an inherent element: "The very act of looking at a naked model was an artifact of male supremacy" (Philip Weiss).
3. A structure or feature not normally present but visible as a result of an external agent or action, such as one seen in a microscopic specimen after fixation, or in an image produced by radiology or electrocardiography.
4. An inaccurate observation, effect, or result, especially one resulting from the technology used in scientific investigation or from experimental error: *The apparent pattern in the data was an artifact of the collection method.*

[Latin arte, ablative of ars, *art;* see **art**[1] + factum, *something made* (from neuter past participle of facere, *to make.*)]

ar'ti·fac'tu·al (-făk'cho͝o-əl) *adj.*

philanthropist

n. : someone who makes charitable donations intended to increase human well-being [syn.: altruist]

ac·tiv·ist (ăk'tə-vĭst)

n.

A proponent or practitioner of activism: *political activists.*

adj.

1. Of, relating to, or engaged in activism.
2. Of, relating to, or being an activist.

Vic ·to·ri·an (vĭk-tôr'ē-ən, -tōr'-)

adj.

1. Of, relating to, or belonging to the period of the reign of Queen Victoria: *a Victorian novel.*
2. Relating to or displaying the standards or ideals of morality regarded as characteristic of the time of Queen Victoria: *Victorian manners.*
3. Being in the highly ornamented, massive style of architecture, decor, and furnishings popular in nineteenth-century England.

n.

A person belonging to or exhibiting characteristics typical of the Victorian period.

Jim Crow or **jim crow** (jĭm' krō')

n.

The systematic practice of discriminating against and segregating black people, especially as practiced in the American South from the end of Reconstruction to the mid-twentieth century.

adj.

1. Upholding or practicing discrimination against and segregation of black people: *Jim Crow laws; a Jim Crow town.*
2. Reserved or set aside for a racial or ethnic group that is to be discriminated against: "I told them I wouldn't take a Jim Crow job" (Ralph Bunche).

[From obsolete Jim Crow, *derogatory name for a Black person, ultimately from the title of a nineteenth-century minstrel song.*]

Jim'-Crow'ism (jĭm'krōĭz'əm) *n.*

boy·cott (boi'kŏt')

tr. v. **boy·cott·ed, boy·cott·ing, boy·cotts**

To abstain from or act together in abstaining from using, buying, or dealing with as an expression of protest or disfavor or as a means of coercion.

n.

The act or an instance of boycotting.

[After Charles C. Boycott (1832–1897), English land agent in Ireland.]

boy'cott'er *n.*

lob (lŏb)

v. **lobbed, lob·bing, lobs**

v. tr.

To hit, throw, or propel in a high arc: *lob a beach ball; lob a tennis shot over an opponent's head.*

v. intr.

1. To hit a ball in a high arc.
2. To move heavily or clumsily.

n.

1. A ball hit, thrown, or propelled in a high arc.
2. Slang. A clumsy dull person; a lout.

[From Middle English, *pollack, lout, probably of Low German origin.*]

lob'ber *n.*

par·son·age (pär'sə-nĭj)

n.

The official residence usually provided by a church for its parson; a rectory.

san·i·ta·tion (săn'ĭ-tā'shən)

n.

1. Formulation and application of measures designed to protect public health.
2. Disposal of sewage.

[sanit(ary) + -ation.]

de·pict (dĭ-pĭkt')

tr. v. **de·pict·ed, de·pict·ing, de·picts**

1. To represent in a picture or sculpture.
2. To represent in words; describe.

[Middle English depicten, from Latin dēpingere, dēpict- : dē-, *de-* + pingere, *to picture;* see peig- in Indo-European Roots.]

de·pic'tion *n.*

Reading Comprehension

Answer the following questions about Winfrey's article.

Word Meaning

Using the glossary, select the entry that best completes the sentences below.

1. The huge old hospital building was __________ by the scheduled implosion that was viewed by thousands.
2. The 80-year-old driver still drove her shiny, chrome-covered 1955 Cadillac __________ that she had owned since its arrival from the factory.
3. Despite an __________ that enabled the team extra sleep to overcome jet lag, the American soccer team still lost and was eliminated from World Cup competition.
4. The old man thought that __________ would cure any ailment that he experienced, and he drank a teaspoonful every morning.
5. In an age of multiculturalism, no room for the hatred exhibited by __________ exists in American society.
6. The movie director's newest film __________ the gracious life south of the border at the first vineyard created in Mexico.
7. During a recent archaeological dig in Egypt, the university students discovered some priceless __________—bowls, gold, and jewels—near the tomb of an ancient king.
8. Many political __________ have lobbied Congress for education reform that includes English language courses for recent immigrants.

Literal Meaning

Mark the letter of the option that best answers the statements below.

1. The physical setting of the article is
   a. New York.
   b. Detroit.
   c. a jaunt from city to city.
   d. a border town in Texas.
2. At which college did Martin Luther King NOT study?
   a. Morehouse College
   b. Georgia Tech
   c. Crozer Theological Seminary
   d. Boston University
3. In the article, which city is included among those visited by Winfrey family?
   a. Detroit
   b. Memphis
   c. Chicago
   d. Washington

4. Numbering 1 to 5, place the Winfrey travel itinerary in chronological order.
   a. _____"Reed and Karli looked forward to seeing their grandmother in Nashville . . . "
   b. _____" . . . Stone Mountain, Ga., which is referenced by King in his famous 'I Have a Dream' speech . . . "
   c. _____"We began our history lesson Saturday morning at Morehouse college, . . . "
   d. _____" . . . to Memphis . . . in 1968, he and others stayed at the Lorraine Hotel."
   e. _____" . . . Rosa Parks, whom many in Montgomery knew as the seamstress . . . refused to give up her bus seat to a white man . . . "
5. What was the purpose of the tour made by the Winfrey family?
   a. The children wanted to see their grandmother and uncle.
   b. Winfrey wanted the children to visit the South.
   c. Winfrey needed to take the children on a trip so their mother could complete a work project.
   d. Winfrey wanted to show the children a brief history of Dr. Martin Luther King.

Interpretive Meaning

Complete the questions with the response that best answers the statement.

1. Why does Winfrey believe that the tour is an important part of his children's educational formation?
   a. He thinks children are too spoiled today.
   b. He wants his children to see him at work uncovering material for an article.
   c. He believes that his children should understand the struggle that King endured for freeing African Americans from the legal constraints they experienced.
   d. He thinks that the children need to spend some quality time alone with their father.
2. Why did Rosa Parks refuse to give her seat on the bus to a white man?
   a. She was sick and needed to sit down or faint.
   b. She was tired of being treated like a second-class citizen.
   c. Dr. Martin Luther King asked her to refuse to give up her seat to start a boycott.
   d. She had a ticket that guaranteed a seat on the bus.
3. Why are transitional devices frequently used in this article?
   a. Winfrey wants readers to see that he knows how to write well.
   b. The author knows that the children will read his article.
   c. In articles of sequential order, the transitions enable the reader to follow the points.
   d. Winfrey knows that his editor expects clarity in writing.

4. According to the article, what one word describes the philosophy that King followed?
   a. Rebellion
   b. Warfare
   c. Nonviolence
   d. Religion
5. Why does Winfrey write this article?
   a. He thinks that the itinerary he followed is one that would interest others.
   b. He believes that people should try to relive history as much as possible.
   c. He believes that the hard work that King did should not be forgotten.
   d. All of the above

Score: Number correct _____ out of _____

Writing Assignments

1. Journal Writing

Summary

Summarize the article by explaining not only the places visited but also the reason for the trip. Include steps and details about the visit.

Reaction

Write a one-paragraph reaction to the essay. When reacting to the essay, consider steps that you would like to take to ensure that you and your family are appreciative of your history as well as the history of others.

2. Paragraph

Using the process analysis format, plan a vacation in which you and your family or friends visit landmarks that are important in your personal history, family history, or civic history.

3. Paragraph to Essay

Expand the paragraph written in assignment two to a process analysis essay by writing about each step of the trip in each body paragraph. Remember that you are writing a process paper, so you must have order in your plan. Which landmark would you visit first, second, and last? In your introduction, explain the reasoning for the order.

4. Essay

Write an essay on how to plan a vacation, a party, a reunion, or other event. Follow the organizational format required for orderly development.

A & P

John Updike

Sammy, the main character and narrator of the story, makes a landmark decision when he quits his job at the A & P grocery in protest to the store manager's treatment of three young girls who come into the store in swimsuits.

In walks these three girls in nothing but bathing suits. I'm in the third check-out slot, with my back to the door, so I don't see them until they're over by the bread. The one that caught my eye first was the one in the plaid green two-piece. She was a chunky kid, with a good tan and a sweet broad soft-looking can with those two crescents of white just under it, where the sun never seems to hit, at the top of the backs of her legs. I stood there with my hand on a box of HiHo crackers trying to remember if I rang it up or not. I ring it up again and the customer starts giving me hell. She's one of these cash-register-watchers, a witch about fifty with rouge on her cheekbones and no eyebrows, and I know it made her day to trip me up. She'd been watching cash registers forty years and probably never seen a mistake before.

By the time I got her feathers smoothed and her goodies into a bag—she gives me a little snort in passing, if she'd been born at the right time they would have burned her over in Salem—by the time I get her on her way the girls had circled around the bread and were coming back, without a pushcart, back my way along the counters, in the aisle between the check-outs and the Special bins. They didn't even have shoes on. There was this chunky one, with the two-piece—it was bright green and the seams on the bra were still sharp and her belly was still pretty pale so I guessed she just got it (the suit)—there was this one, with one of those chubby berry-faces, the lips all bunched together under her nose, this one, and a tall one, with black hair that hadn't quite frizzed right, and one of these sunburns right across under the eyes, and a chin that was too long—you know, the kind of girl other girls think is very "striking" and "attractive" but never quite makes it, as they very well know, which is why they like her so much—and then the third one, that wasn't quite so tall. She was the queen. She kind of led them, the other two peeking around and making their shoulders round. She didn't look around, not this queen, she just walked straight on slowly, on these long white **prima donna** legs. She came down a little hard on her heels, as if she didn't walk in her bare feet that much, putting down her heels and then letting the weight move along to her toes as if she was testing the floor with every step, putting a little deliberate extra action into it. You never know for sure how girls' minds work (do you really think it's a mind in there or just a little buzz like a bee in a glass jar?) but you got the idea she had talked the other two into coming in here with her, and now she was showing them how to do it, walk slow and hold yourself straight.

She had on a kind of dirty-pink—beige maybe, I don't know—bathing suit with a little nubble all over it and, what got me, the straps were down. They were off her shoulders looped loose around the cool tops of her arms, and I guess as a result the suit had slipped a little on her, so all around the top of the cloth there was this shining rim. If it hadn't been there you wouldn't have known there could have been anything whiter than those shoulders. With the straps pushed off, there was nothing between the top of the suit and the top of her head except just her, this clean bare plane of the top of her chest down from the shoulder bones like a dented sheet of metal tilted in the light. I mean, it was more than pretty.

She had sort of oaky hair that the sun and salt had bleached, done up in a bun that was unravelling, and a kind of prim face. Walking into the A & P with your straps down, I suppose it's the only kind of face you *can* have. She held her head so high her neck, coming up out of those white shoulders, looked kind of stretched, but I didn't mind. The longer her neck was, the more of her there was.

She must have felt in the corner of her eye me and over my shoulder Stokesie in the second slot watching, but she didn't tip. Not this queen. She kept her eyes moving across the racks, and stopped, and turned so slow it made my stomach rub the inside of my apron, and buzzed to the other two, who kind of huddled against her for relief, and they all three of them went up the cat-and-dog-food-breakfast-cereal-macaroni-rice-raisins-seasonings-spreads-spaghetti-soft drinks-crackers-and-cookies aisle. From the third slot I look straight up this aisle to the meat counter, and I watched them all the way. The fat one with the tan sort of fumbled with the cookies, but on second thought she put the packages back. The sheep pushing their carts down the aisle—the girls were walking against the usual traffic (not that we have one-way signs or anything)—were pretty hilarious. You could see them, when Queenie's white shoulders dawned on them, kind of jerk, or hop, or hiccup, but their eyes snapped back to their own baskets and on they pushed. I bet you could set off dynamite in an A & P and the people would by and large keep reaching and checking oatmeal off their lists and muttering "Let me see, there was a third thing, began with A, asparagus, no, ah, yes, applesauce!" or whatever it is they do mutter. But there was no doubt, this jiggled them. A few house-slaves in pin curlers even looked around after pushing their carts past to make sure what they had seen was correct.

You know, it's one thing to have a girl in a bathing suit down on the beach, where what with the glare nobody can look at each other much anyway, and another thing in the cool of the A & P, under the fluorescent lights, against all those stacked packages, with her feet paddling along naked over our checkerboard green-and-cream rubber-tile floor.

"Oh Daddy," Stokesie said beside me. "I feel so faint."

"Darling," I said. "Hold me tight." Stokesie's married, with two babies chalked up on his fuselage already, but as far as I can tell that's the only difference. He's twenty-two, and I was nineteen this April.

"Is it done?" he asks, the responsible married man finding his voice. I forgot to say he thinks he's going to be manager some sunny day, maybe in 1990 when it's called the Great Alexandrov and Petrooshki Tea Company or something.

What he meant was, our town is five miles from a beach, with a big summer colony out on the Point, but we're right in the middle of town, and the women generally put on a shirt or shorts or something before they get out of the car into the street. And anyway these are usually women with six children and varicose veins mapping their legs and nobody, including them, could care less. As I say, we're right in the middle of town, and if you stand at our front doors you can see two banks and the Congregational church and the newspaper store and three real-estate offices and about twenty-seven old free-loaders tearing up Central Street because the sewer broke again. It's not as if we're on the Cape; we're north of Boston and there's people in this town haven't seen the ocean for twenty years.

The girls had reached the meat counter and were asking McMahon something. He pointed, they pointed, and they shuffled out of sight behind a pyramid of Diet Delight peaches. All that was left for us to see was old McMahon patting his mouth and looking after them sizing up their joints. Poor kids, I began to feel sorry for them, they couldn't help it.

Now here comes the sad part of the story, at least my family says it's sad but I don't think it's sad myself. The store's pretty empty, it being Thursday afternoon, so there was nothing much to do except lean on the register and wait for the girls to show up again. The whole store was like a pinball machine and I didn't know which tunnel they'd come out of. After a while they come around out of the far aisle, around the light bulbs, records at discount of the Caribbean Six or Tony Martin Sings or some such gunk you wonder they waste the wax on, sixpacks of candy bars, and plastic toys done up in cellophane that fall apart when a kid looks at them anyway. Around they come, Queenie still leading the way, and holding a little gray jar in her hand. Slots Three through Seven are unmanned and I could see her wondering between Stokes and me, but Stokesie with his usual luck draws an old party in baggy gray pants who stumbles up with four giant cans of pineapple juice (what do these bums *do* with all that pineapple juice' I've often asked myself) so the girls come to me. Queenie puts down the jar and I take it into my fingers icy cold. Kingfish Fancy Herring Snacks in Pure Sour Cream: 49¢. Now her hands are empty, not a ring or a bracelet, bare as God made them, and I wonder where the money's coming from. Still with that prim look she lifts a folded dollar bill out of the hollow at the center of her nubbled pink top. The jar went heavy in my hand. Really, I thought that was so cute.

Then everybody's luck begins to run out. Lengel comes in from haggling with a truck full of cabbages on the lot and is about to **scuttle** into that door marked MANAGER behind which he hides all day when the girls touch his eye. Lengel's pretty dreary, teaches Sunday school and the rest, but he doesn't miss that much. He comes over and says, "Girls, this isn't the beach."

Queenie blushes, though maybe it's just a brush of sunburn I was noticing for the first time, now that she was so close. "My mother asked me to pick up a jar of herring snacks." Her voice kind of startled me, the way voices do when you see the people first, coming out so flat and dumb yet kind of **tony,** too, the way it ticked over "pick up" and "snacks." All of a sudden I slid right down her voice into her living room. Her father and the other men were standing around in ice-cream coats and bow ties and the women were in sandals picking up herring snacks on toothpicks off a big plate and they were all holding drinks the color of water with olives and sprigs of mint in them. When my parents have somebody over they get lemonade and if it's a real racy affair Schlitz in tall glasses with "They'll Do It Every Time" cartoons stencilled on.

"That's all right," Lengel said. "But this isn't the beach." His repeating this struck me as funny, as if it had just occurred to him, and he had been thinking all these years the A & P was a great big dune and he was the head lifeguard. He didn't like my smiling—as I say he doesn't miss much—but he concentrates on giving the girls that sad Sunday-school-superintendent stare.

Queenie's blush is no sunburn now, and the plump one in plaid, that I liked better from the back—a really sweet can—pipes up, "We weren't doing any shopping. We just came in for the one thing."

"That makes no difference," Lengel tells her, and I could see from the way his eyes went that he hadn't noticed she was wearing a two-piece before. "We want you decently dressed when you come in here."

"We are decent," Queenie says suddenly, her lower lip pushing, getting sore now that she remembers her place, a place from which the crowd that runs the A & P must look pretty crummy. Fancy Herring Snacks flashed in her very blue eyes.

"Girls, I don't want to argue with you. After this come in here with your shoulders covered. It's our policy." He turns his back. That's policy for you. Policy is what the **kingpins** want. What the others want is juvenile delinquency.

All this while, the customers had been showing up with their carts but, you know, sheep, seeing a scene, they had all bunched up on Stokesie, who shook open a paper bag as gently as peeling a peach, not wanting to miss a word. I could feel in the silence everybody getting nervous, most of all Lengel, who asks me, "Sammy, have you rung up this purchase?"

I thought and said "No" but it wasn't about that I was thinking. I go through the punches, 4, 9, GROC, TOT—it's more complicated than you think, and after you do it often enough, it begins to make a little song, that you hear words to, in my case "Hello *(bing)* there, you *(gung)* hap-py pee-pul *(splat)*"—the splat being the drawer flying out. I uncrease the bill, tenderly as you may imagine, it just having come from between the two smoothest scoops of vanilla I had ever known were there, and pass a half and a penny into her narrow pink palm, and nestle the herrings in a bag and twist its neck and hand it over, all the time thinking.

The girls, and who'd blame them, are in a hurry to get out, so I say "I quit" to Lengel quick enough for them to hear, hoping they'll stop and watch me, their unsuspected hero. They keep right on going, into the electric eye; the door flies open and they flicker across the lot to their car, Queenie and Plaid and Big Tall Goony-Goony (not that as raw material she was so bad), leaving me with Lengel and a kink in his eyebrow.

"Did you say something, Sammy?"

"I said I quit."

"I thought you did."

"You didn't have to embarrass them."

"It was they who were embarrassing us."

I started to say something that came out "Fiddle-de-doo." It's a saying of my grandmother's, and I know she would have been pleased.

"I don't think you know what you're saying," Lengel said.

"I know you don't," I said. "But I do." I pull the bow at the back of my apron and start shrugging it off my shoulders. A couple customers that had been heading for my slot begin to knock against each other, like scared pigs in a chute.

Lengel sighs and begins to look very patient and old and gray. He's been a friend of my parents for years. "Sammy, you don't want to do this to your Mom and Dad," he tells me. It's true, I don't. But it seems to me that once you begin a gesture it's fatal not to go through with it. I fold the apron, "Sammy" stitched in red on the pocket, and put it on the counter, and drop the bow tie on top of it. The bow tie is theirs, if you've ever wondered. "You'll feel this for the rest of your life," Lengel says, and I know that's true, too, but remembering how he made that pretty girl blush makes me so scrunchy inside I punch the No Sale tab and the machine whirs "pee-pul" and the drawer splats out. One advantage to this scene taking place in summer, I can follow this up with a clean exit, there's no fumbling around getting your coat and galoshes, I just **saunter** into the electric eye in my white shirt that my mother ironed the night before, and the door heaves itself open, and outside the sunshine is skating around on the asphalt.

I look around for my girls, but they're gone, of course. There wasn't anybody but some young married screaming with her children about some candy they didn't get by the door of a powder-blue Falcon station wagon. Looking back in the big windows, over the bags of peat moss and aluminum lawn furniture stacked on the pavement, I could see Lengel in my place in the slot, checking the sheep through. His face was dark gray and his back stiff, as if he'd just had an injection of iron, and my stomach kind of fell as I felt how hard the world was going to be to me hereafter.

Glossary for "A & P"

pri·ma donna (prē'mə, prĭm'ə)

n.

1. The leading woman soloist in an opera company.
2. A temperamental, conceited person.

[Italian: prima, feminine of primo, *first* + donna, *lady*.]

scut·tle (sk t'l)

n.

1. A small opening or hatch with a movable lid in the deck or hull of a ship or in the roof, wall, or floor of a building.
2. The lid or hatch of such an opening.
3.

tr. v. **scut·tled, scut·tling, scut·tles**

1. *Nautical.*
   a. To cut or open a hole or holes in (a ship's hull).
   b. To sink (a ship) by this means.
2. *Informal.* To scrap; discard: "a program [the] President . . . sought to scuttle" (*Christian Science Monitor*).

[Middle English skottell, from Old French escoutille, possibly from Spanish escotilla.]

ton·y also **ton·ey** (tō'nē)

adj. Informal **ton·i·er, ton·i·est**

Marked by an elegant or exclusive manner or quality: *a tony country club.*

[From tone.]

king·pin (kĭng'pĭn')

n.

Sports.

a. The innermost or central pin in an arrangement of bowling pins.

2. The most important person or element in an enterprise or system.

saun·ter (sôn'tər)

intr. v. **saun·tered, saun·ter·ing, saun·ters**

To walk at a leisurely pace; stroll.

n.

1. A leisurely pace.
2. A leisurely walk or stroll.

[Probably from Middle English santren, *to muse*.]

saun'ter·er *n.*

Reading Comprehension

Answer the following questions about the story by John Updike.

Word Meaning

Using the glossary, select the entry that best completes the sentences below.

1. My uncle assumed the role of __________ after Grandfather died; he made the decisions, organized the holiday celebrations, and determined the housing of Grandma.
2. My spoiled, high-maintenance ex-girlfriend considered herself a __________, and her attitude of superiority and constant pampering ended our relationship.

3. During the 1950s, the prestige of membership in _________ golf or sports clubs was considered an acceptable business expense that rendered big profits to companies.
4. The international tourists were so enthralled with the local sites they were seeing that they slowly _________ down the sidewalks of New York for an entire afternoon.

Literal Meaning

Mark the letter of the option that best answers the statements below.

1. What is the setting of Updike's A & P?
   a. A mini-market in the 1990s
   b. The beach in the 1980s
   c. A butcher shop in the 1930s
   d. A grocery store in a period before 1990
2. Who is the main character in the short story?
   a. Queenie
   b. Sammy
   c. Lengel
   d. McMahon
3. What is the conflict of the story, the event that begins the action of the plot?
   a. Sammy is cashiering at the store.
   b. McMahon licks his lips after the girls pass his meat department.
   c. Three teenaged girls walk into the store in their swimsuits.
   d. Lengel walks to his office after processing a delivery.
4. What do the girls buy?
   a. HiHo Crackers
   b. Chocolate pudding pops
   c. Some steaks
   d. A jar of herring
5. What does Sammy call the shoppers?
   a. Goony-goons
   b. Witches
   c. Sheep
   d. Diet Delights
6. What is the point of view of the short story?
   a. First person
   b. Third person
   c. Third-person omniscient
   d. Third-person limited omniscient
7. What is the event that causes the climax in the story?
   a. Lengel reprimands the girls for entering the store in their swimsuits.
   b. McMahon stares at the girls after talking to them.
   c. Sammy rings up a lady's item twice, thus overcharging her.
   d. The girls steal a $.49 jar of herring in sour cream.

8. Number the following events in sequential order from 1 to 6.
   a. _____ Lengel reprimands the girls for wearing swimsuits in the store.
   b. _____ Sammy quits his job.
   c. _____ Three girls walk into the store in their swimsuits.
   d. _____ The girls talk to McMahon about meats.
   e. _____ The girls walk against the understood but unstated flow of traffic.
   f. _____ Sammy realizes life will be hard.

Interpretive Meaning

Complete the questions with the response that best answers the statement.

1. Why is the short story narrated in the present tense?
   a. The present tense is easier to understand.
   b. The present tense shows that the writer likes action.
   c. The present tense gives a piece a sense of immediacy.
   d. The present tense is easier to write.
2. What is the tone of the short story?
   a. Argumentative
   b. Mildly sarcastic
   c. Informative
   d. Mildly humorous
3. Why does Sammy call the customers sheep?
   a. Sheep are his favorite animals.
   b. The shoppers all wear wool when shopping.
   c. The shoppers follow one another up and down the aisles.
   d. The shoppers wear rollers in their hair.
4. What type of literary device identifies the following line from the story: ". . . as I felt how hard the world was going to be to me hereafter"?
   a. Metaphor
   b. Simile
   c. Irony
   d. Onomatopoeia
5. What is the significance of Sammy's quitting his job at the end of the story?
   a. The action symbolizes Sammy's movement into an adult world.
   b. The action stands for Sammy's love for Queenie.
   c. Sammy is tired of his job anyway.
   d. Since jobs are plentiful, Sammy knows he can find work elsewhere.
6. Much of the story describes the girls and the other customers' movement inside the story. Why does Updike develop this story in this form?
   a. He is enabling Sammy to build up his case for quitting his job.
   b. He dislikes women and uses Sammy as a vehicle to describe the negative aspects of these women in the store.
   c. Updike emphasizes action in his works.
   d. Updike's greatest strength as a writer is description.

7. What is ironic about the quitting scene at the end of the story?
   a. Sammy describes the actions of people whom he does not like and then suddenly quits.
   b. Sammy's reaction is unexpected because of the negative adolescent way in which he describes the girls followed by the girls' lack of awareness of his final action.
   c. Sammy likes his job and plans to manage the store in the future.
   d. Sammy was quite appreciative to Lengel for giving him this job as a cashier.
8. This story first appeared on July 22, 1961, during a period described as the Cold War. What allusion in the story shows Americans' concern with being overtaken by Communists?
   a. Sammy believes in the Communist theory of government ownership of business.
   b. Lengel acts like a Communist dictator.
   c. Sammy renames the A & P with a Russian name.
   d. Sammy knows the government will support him if he quits his job.
9. Why does Updike use colloquial language to represent Sammy as a middle-class adolescent?
   a. He wants young people to identify with the character of Sammy.
   b. As a young man working in a grocery store, Sammy represents that segment of the population.
   c. The dramatic conclusion has much more significance for a young man from the middle-class.
   d. All of the above
10. Write examples of the colloquial language found in the story A & P.

    ____

    ____
11. Using the pyramid design below, fill in the plot steps as they are presented in the short story.

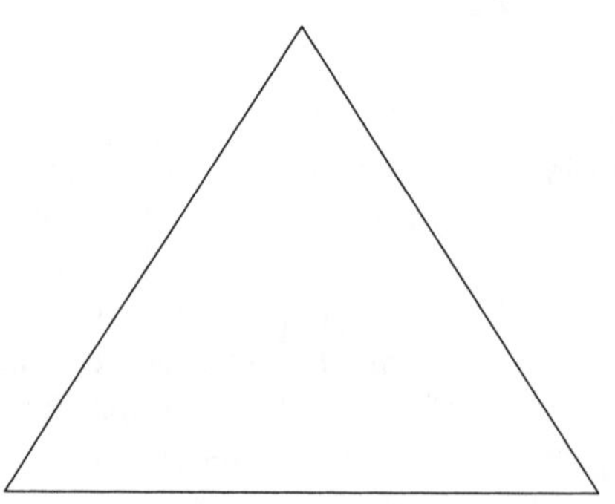

Score: Number correct _____ out of _____

Writing Assignments

1. *Journal Writing*

Summary

Before summarizing the story, analyze the steps of the plot using the pyramid design exercise completed in the Interpretive Meaning reading questions. Then, using the information you gleaned from the activity, write a one-paragraph summary of the story.

Reaction

Write a reaction to the short story. When writing your reaction, consider the following: Do you think Sammy made the right decision? Do you think his decision was a necessary step toward adulthood? What types of decisions must young people make in order to become responsible adults? What decisions have you made in your life that were similar to Sammy's decisions?

2. *Paragraph*

"A & P" is a typical American "coming of age" story. Write a paragraph outlining the steps adolescents must take in order to reach that step of maturity to "come of age."

Alternate Choice: Write a paragraph explaining your own "coming of age" process. Cite examples as evidence of the process that you followed.

3. *Paragraph to Essay*

Expand the paragraph assignment to an essay by focusing on each step in a separate body paragraph. Limit your steps, or body paragraphs, to three or four. Use the planning guide.

4. *Essay*

Write a letter to a friend or relative explaining the steps they should take to become a __________ (responsible adult, conscientious student, sensitive friend, reliable parent).

A Chinese Kitchen

Eileen Yin-Fei Lo

Eileen Yin-Fei Lo is a cooking teacher and cookbook writer. In the reading, she celebrates the cooking traditions of her native China as she remembers her childhood days growing up in her family's kitchen.

Food is not only life-giving but also a source of familial or societal leanings. Our food is **inextricably** linked with manners, with form, with tradition, with history. I grew up with these beliefs. I remember my father, Lo Pak Wan, my first cooking teacher, telling me that we must eat our food first with our eyes, then with our minds, then with our noses, and finally with our mouths. He believed this. He taught this to my brother and me.

He would say, only partly joking, that fine vegetables should be chosen with as much care as one would a son-in-law. He would show me the correct way to prepare rice, telling me that if our rice was old then perhaps more water than customary might be needed to give our **congee** its fine and silky finish. "Keep an open mind," he would say. "Cook the way it has been written, but keep an open mind. If you keep walking only in a straight line, you will go into a wall. You must learn to make a turn if necessary. Do not be narrow." Or he would tell me, *"Tau mei haw yantiu, mo mei haw yan tiu,"* an **aphorism** that translates as "if you don't have a tail, you cannot imitate the monkey; if you do have a tail, then do not imitate the monkey." By this he was telling me to follow the classical manner but not to be a simple, mindless imitator.

My mother, Lo Chan Miu Hau, encouraged me to cook as well. I recall her saying to me, "If you are wealthy and know how to cook, then servants cannot take advantage of you. If you are poor and know how to cook, you will be able to create wonderful meals with few resources." Cooking and its **ramifications** were that important to her, as well as to my father, when I was young and growing up in Sun Tak, a suburb of Canton, now Guangzhou.

They and my Ah Paw, my mother's mother, insisted that I be involved in our family table. Ah Paw, despite her household of servants, despite the presence of a family cook, made certain whenever I visited her, which was every opportunity I had, every school holiday, that I was in her kitchen.

My Ah Paw knew instinctively, without ever having had to personally put a spatula into a wok, how things ought to be cooked, what foods wedded in combination, and what clashed. I am tempted to suggest that she was a brilliant, instinctive kitchen chemist. I will say it. Brilliant she was indeed, her knowledge about foods was **encyclopedic,** and she was never wrong about cooking, then or now, in my memory. I spent much of the Lunar New Year at her house. I liked her home, I liked her kitchen, and she spoiled me. Except when it came to imparting cookery lessons.

When we ate raw fish, *yue sahng,* she taught, one had to prepare the fish in the proper manner. You hit the fish at the front of its head to stun it, then, when it was still **nominally** alive, you scaled it, gutted and cleaned it, then sliced it for eating. This special dish, which we ate on important birthdays, and on the eves of family weddings, had to be prepared this way, only this way, Ah Paw said.

When we steamed a fish, she taught me to softly lay the fish atop a bed of rice at the precise moment that the rice was in the final state of its absorption of water. It would then be perfectly prepared.

Once I steamed a fish, quite well, I thought, and proudly carried it to her at the family table. She sniffed. I had forgotten to pour boiled peanut oil over it just before serving. "Take it back to the kitchen and add the oil," she ordered. My grandmother's kitchen always had a crock of boiled peanut oil near the stove. To pour it over fish was to give the fish fragrance and to dispel any unpleasant odors. It does, even if the oil is not warm.

She would eat no vegetables that were older than two hours out of the ground, which necessitated repeated trips to the markets by her servants, a lesson of the importance of freshness that was not lost on me.

She cautioned me to eat every kernel of rice in my bowl, for if I did not, she warned, the man I married would have a **pockmarked** face, one mark for each uneaten rice kernel. I did as she cautioned, and I must have eaten well, for my husband's face is clear.

Do not shout in the kitchen, Ah Paw would insist. Do not use improper words in the kitchen. Do not show shortness of temper in the kitchen by, for example, banging chopsticks on a wok. All of these would reflect badly on us as a family, she would say, when done in front of Jo Kwan, the Kitchen God, whose image hung on the wall over the oven. For just before the Lunar New Year the image of Jo Kwan, his lips smeared with honey, was always burned so that he would go up to heaven and report only nice things about our family.

Ah Paw would consult her Tung Sing, an astrological book, for **propitious** days on which to begin preparing the special dumplings we made and ate during the New Year festival. She would specify to the second time to make the dough, heat the oven, add the oil, in what we called *"hoi yau wok,"* or, literally translated, "begin the oil in the wok." So admired was she for her knowledge that young married couples, not even of our family, would consult with her. A memory I have is of pumping the pedal of the iron and stone-grinding mill in our town square, at her orders, to get the flour that we would use for our dumplings.

She was an observant Buddhist who declined to eat either fish or meat on the first and the fifteenth of each month and for the first fifteen days of the New Year, and our family ate similarly out of **deference** to her. She was happy that my mother always encouraged me to cook, happy that my father brought kitchen discipline to me as well. She nodded with pleasure, in support of my father, I remember—not in sympathy with me—when I complained how boring it was when my father gave me the task of snapping off the ends of individual mung bean sprouts. "If you wish to learn how to make spring rolls well, learn the beginning of the spring roll. It must be done," Ah Paw said.

We had no grinders. We chopped meats and other seafood with the cleaver on a chopping board. "Clean it," Ah Paw would say when I was finished. "If you do not, the food you chop next will not stick together. It will fall apart. There will be no texture. If it falls apart, I will know that you did not listen."

All of this she **conferred** on me without ever setting foot in the kitchen of her house. As a further example of her vision I should note in passing that my Ah Paw, a most independent woman, as is evident, refused to have bound the feet of my mother, her daughter, much the practice of high born women. This despite the fact that her own feet had been bound since babyhood and were no more than four inches long. This extraordinary woman, never more than seventy-five pounds, who could not **totter** more than one hundred feet and was usually carried by servants, brought my mother and then me into modern times in her own way. I wanted nothing more than to be with her, and I would listen, wide-eyed and receptive, to her talk about food and its meanings. . . .

Glossary for "A Chinese Kitchen"

in·ex·tri·ca·ble (ĭn-ĕk'strĭ-kə-bəl, ĭn'ĭk-strĭk'ə-bəl)

adj.

1. a. So intricate or entangled as to make escape impossible: *an inextricable maze; an inextricable web of deceit.*
   b. Difficult or impossible to disentangle or untie: *an inextricable tangle of threads.*
   c. Too involved or complicated to solve: *an inextricable problem.*
2. Unavoidable; inescapable: *bound together by an inextricable fate.*

in·ex'tri·ca·bil'i·ty or **in·ex'tri·ca·ble·ness** *n.*
in·ex'tri·ca·bly *adv.*

congee

n. : a Chinese rice gruel eaten for breakfast
v. 1: depart after obtaining formal permission; "He has congeed with the King" 2: perform a ceremonious bow

aph·o·rism (ăf'ə-rĭz'əm)

n.

1. A tersely phrased statement of a truth or opinion; an adage.
2. A brief statement of a principle.

[French aphorisme, from Old French, from Late Latin aphorismus, from Greek aphorismos, from aphorizein, *to delimit, define*: apo-, *apo-* + horizein, *to delimit, define*.]
aph'o·rist *n.* **aph'o·ris'tic** (-rĭs'tĭk) *adj.* **aph'o·ris'ti·cal·ly** *adv.*

ram·i·fi·ca·tion (răm'ə-fĭ-kā'shən)
n.

1. A development or consequence growing out of and sometimes complicating a problem, plan, or statement: *the ramifications of a court decision.*
2. a. The act or process of branching out or dividing into branches.
   b. A subordinate part extending from a main body; a branch.
   c. An arrangement of branches or branching parts.

en·cy·clo·pe·dic (ĕn-sī'klə-pē'dĭk)
adj.

1. Of, relating to, or characteristic of an encyclopedia.
2. Embracing many subjects; comprehensive: "an ignorance almost as encyclopedic as his erudition" (William James).

en·cy'clo·pe'di·cal·ly *adv.*

nom·i·nal (nōm'ə-nəl)
adj.

1. a. Of, resembling, relating to, or consisting of a name or names.
   b. Assigned to or bearing a person's name: *nominal shares.*
2. Existing in name only.
3. Philosophy. Of or relating to nominalism.
4. Insignificantly small; trifling: *a nominal sum.*
5. Business.
   a. Of, relating to, or being the amount or face value of a sum of money or a stock certificate, for example, and not the purchasing power or market value.
   b. Of, relating to, or being the rate of interest or return without adjustment for compounding or inflation.
6. Grammar. Of or relating to a noun or word group that functions as a noun.
7. Aerospace & Engineering. According to plan or design: *a nominal flight check.*

n. Grammar
A word or group of words functioning as a noun.
[Middle English nominalle, *of nouns,* from Latin nōminālis, *of names,* from nōmen, nōmin-, *name.*
nom'i·nal·ly *adv.*

pock·mark (pŏk'märk')
n.

1. A pitlike scar left on the skin by smallpox or another eruptive disease.
2. A small pit on a surface: *The gophers left the lawn covered with pockmarks.*

tr. v. **pock·marked, pock·mark·ing, pock·marks**
To cover with pockmarks; pit.
pock'marked' *adj.*

pro·pi·tious (prə-pĭsh'əs)
adj.

1. Presenting favorable circumstances; auspicious.
2. Kindly; gracious.

[Middle English propicius, from Old French propicieux, from Latin propitius.]
pro·pi'tious·ly *adv.* **pro·pi'tious·ness** *n.*

def·er·ence (dĕf'ər-əns, dəf'rəns)

n.

1. Submission or courteous yielding to the opinion, wishes, or judgment of another.
2. Courteous respect.

con·fer (kən-fûr')

v. **con·ferred, con·fer·ring, con·fers**

v. tr.

1. To bestow (an honor, for example): *conferred a medal on the hero; conferred an honorary degree on her.*
2. To invest with (a characteristic, for example): *a carefully worded statement that conferred an aura of credibility.*

v. intr.

To meet in order to deliberate together or compare views; consult: *conferred with her attorney.*

[Latin cōnferre: com-, *com-* + ferre, *to bring;*]

con·fer'ment or **con·fer'ral** *n.* **con·fer'ra·ble** *adj.* **con·fer'rer** *n.*

tot·ter (tŏt'ər)

intr. v. **tot·tered, tot·ter·ing, tot·ters**

1. a. To sway as if about to fall.
   b. To appear about to collapse: *an empire that had begun to totter.*
2. To walk unsteadily or feebly; stagger.

n. The act or condition of tottering.

[Middle English toteren, *perhaps of Scandinavian origin.*]

tot'ter·er *n.* **tot'ter·y** *adj.*

Reading Comprehension

Answer the following questions about Lo's essay.

Word Meaning

Using the glossary, select the entry that best completes the sentences below.

1. When visiting China, Lu Lu's favorite breakfast includes _________ that her aunt makes daily.
2. Many followers of Confucius use his _________ as guidelines for living a healthy life.
3. After working on his book for over ten years, the historian could recite dates and events about his subject because he had become _________ with the facts.
4. Dermatologists have developed many new treatments like laser and acid peels to relieve the problems of a _________ face, often a result of teenage acne.
5. Because he had no college education, Will suffered the _________of his quitting his job for decades.
6. Although the clues to the robbery were quite _________, the experienced detective was able to unearth the evidence and catch the criminal.

7. Many families' holiday celebrations are so _________ entwined with the traditions of their culture that to separate family from culture is often difficult.

Literal Meaning

Mark the letter of the option that best answers the statements below.

1. What is the main idea of Lo's essay?
   a. She tells how she learned to cook.
   b. She explains the system for cooking certain foods.
   c. She gives a biography of her grandmother.
   d. She explains old-world Chinese culture like binding feet.
2. From what socioeconomic group did Lo's Chinese grandmother come?
   a. The lower class
   b. The upper class
   c. The middle class
   d. The upper middle class
3. In the selection, Lo connects food with what other traditions of life?
   a. Religion
   b. Housing
   c. Manners
   d. Shopping
4. What one cooking practice of her grandmother's did Lo dislike doing?
   a. Hitting the fish on its head with a cleaver
   b. Cooking the fish while still alive
   c. Pouring peanut oil on the fish
   d. Chopping duck
5. What picture adorned the wall of Ah Paw's kitchen?
   a. Her granddaughter's picture
   b. Her family portrait
   c. Tung Sing
   d. Jo Kwan, the Kitchen God
6. What religion did Lo's grandmother practice?
   a. Catholicism
   b. Protestantism
   c. Buddhism
   d. Hinduism

Interpretive Meaning

Complete the questions with the response that best answers the statement.

1. Why does Lo end the essay with a statement about her grandmother's bound feet?
   a. She tells her reader that despite Ah Paw's adherence to culture, her grandmother was a very independent woman who refused to bind the feet of her own daughter.
   b. She liked her grandmother's cooking style.

   c. Being a traditional Chinese woman in all forms of life, her grandmother adhered strictly to cooking traditions.
   d. Despite her cooking skills, Lo's grandmother fell often.
2. The reader can conclude from the essay that
   a. Lo attributes her grandmother for her skill in cooking.
   b. Lo learned her cooking skills from both her parents and her grandmother.
   c. Lo is proud of the way she was taught to cook traditional Chinese cuisine.
   d. All of the above
3. Why does Lo say that her family members "never used grinders" when cooking?
   a. She wants the reader to know how hard she worked when learning to cook.
   b. She is expressing how strict her family members were.
   c. Using grinders was against her grandmother's Buddhist practices.
   d. She expresses how food preparation practices make Chinese cuisine outstanding.
4. What does Ah Paw mean by saying to "cook the way it has been written, but keep an open mind"?
   a. She is teaching her granddaughter to avoid the stumbling blocks of cooking.
   b. She means to follow the recipe but also to use common sense.
   c. She wants her granddaughter to follow tradition but also to be creative.
   d. All of the above
5. Why does Lo's father think that eating with the mouth is the last step to eating?
   a. Great cooks know that eating is a sensual activity involving the taste buds.
   b. If people "eat" with their eyes first, then they will not gain weight.
   c. The presentation of food is as important as the taste and smell and thought.
   d. All of the above
6. Cite three examples of Ah Paw's superstitious thinking about successful cooking.

   ____

7. In your own words, summarize the theme of Lo's "The Chinese Kitchen."

   ____

   ____

Score: Number correct _____ out of _____

Writing Assignments

1. Journal Writing

Summary

Utilizing reporter's questions (who, what, where, when, why, how, how much), summarize the essay.

Reaction

Write a two-paragraph reaction to the essay. In the first paragraph, react to the content of the essay. In the second paragraph, analyze the organization of the essay. Which parts of the essay do you consider process analysis? Explain your answer.

2. *Paragraph*

Choice A—Write a paragraph explaining how to appreciate a certain type of food (ethnic or regional).

Choice B—Write a paragraph on one of the following subjects.

a. How to construct a ______________
b. How to repair a ______________
c. How to paint or wallpaper a room
d. How to clean a ______________

3. *Paragraph to Essay*

By dividing the process into three or four parts, expand the paragraph to an essay. Write one body paragraph for each step or process. Add an introductory paragraph that explains the importance or background of the topic and ends with a thesis. Add a concluding paragraph.

4. *Essay*

Write a process analysis essay explaining how to be a loving and responsible grandchild, aunt, uncle, grandparent, or other relative. Before writing, consider the relationship between Eileen Yin-Fei Lo and her grandmother. Organize carefully and supply examples as Lo does.

Telling the Story

Naomi Shihab Nye

Nye, a Palestinian American and national book award finalist, explores her reaction to and the importance of place and time.

In America, what's real
juggles with what isn't:
a woman I know props fabulous tulips
in her flowerbed, in snow.

Streets aren't gold, but they could be.
Once a traveler mailed letters
in a trashcan for a week.
He thought they were going somewhere.
In America everything is going somewhere.

I answered a telephone
on a California street.
Hello? It was possible.
A voice said, "There is no scientific proof
that God is man."
"Thank you." I was standing there.
Was this meant for me?
It was not exactly the question
I had been asking, but it kept me busy awhile,
telling the story.

Some start out
with a big story
that shrinks.

Some stories **accumulate** power
like a sky gathering clouds,
quietly, quietly,
till the story **rains** around you.

Some get tired of the same story
and quit speaking;
a farmer leaning into
his row of potatoes,

a mother walking the same child
to school.
What will we learn today?
There should be an answer,
and it should
change.

in the inner city

Lucille Clifton

Clifton explains why the inhabitants of the inner city are proud to call it home.

in the **inner city**
or
like we call it
home
we think a lot about **uptown**
and the silent nights
and the houses straight as
dead men
and the pastel lights
and we hang on to our no place
happy to be alive
and in the inner city
or
like we call it
home

Glossary for "Telling the Story" and "in the inner city"

ac·cu·mu·late (ə-kyo͞om'yə-lāt')

v. **ac·cu·mu·lat·ed, ac·cu·mu·lat·ing, ac·cu·mu·lates**
v. tr.
To gather or pile up; amass.
v. intr.
To mount up; increase.
[Latin accumulāre, accumulāt-: ad-, *ad-* + cumulāre, *to pile up* (from cumulus, *heap.* See keuə- in Indo-European Roots).]
ac·cu'mu·la·ble (-lə-bəl) *adj.*

rain **(rān)**

n.

1. a. Water condensed from atmospheric vapor and falling in drops.
   b. A fall of such water; a rainstorm.
   c. The descent of such water.
   d. Rainy weather.
   e. A rainy season.
2. A heavy or abundant fall: *a rain of fluffy cottonwood seeds; a rain of insults.*

v. **rained, rain·ing, rains**
v. intr.

1. To fall in drops of water from the clouds.
2. To fall like rain: *Praise rained down on the composer.*
3. To release rain.

v. tr.

1. To send or pour down.
2. To give abundantly; shower: *rain gifts; rain curses upon their heads.*

up·town (ŭp'toun')

n.

The upper part of a town or city.

adv. (ŭp'toun')

To, toward, or in the

inner city

n.

The usually older, central part of a city, especially when characterized by crowded neighborhoods in which low-income, often minority groups predominate. **in'ner-cit'y** (ĭn'ər-sĭ'tē) *adj.* upper part of a town or city.

adj.

Of, relating to, or located uptown.

up'town'er *n.*

Reading Comprehension

Answer the following questions about "Telling the Story" by Nye and "in the inner city" by Clifton.

Word Meaning

Using the glossary, select the entry that best completes the sentences below.

1. The revitalization of many old parts of American cities like Detroit includes the rebuilding of the __________ where many blended neighborhoods now exist.
2. The __________ portion of New Orleans, also known as the "sliver by the river," survived the devastation of Hurricane Katrina.
3. Presents offered by her girlfriends __________ all around the young bride, thus the term bridal shower.

Literal Meaning

Mark the letter of the option that best answers the statements below.

1. Both poems represent what point of view?
   a. Third-person omniscient
   b. Objective
   c. First person
   d. Second person
2. Both poems deal with what sense?
   a. Time
   b. Place
   c. Sound
   d. Sight

3. Who is the narrator in both poems?
   a. A passerby on the street
   b. Someone who knows how to write
   c. Someone who lives in the area
   d. Someone who understands the feeling, or ambience, of the area described
4. What example does Nye use to prove that "what's real/juggles with what isn't"?
   a. Fireworks
   b. Rain
   c. Tulips
   d. Gold

Interpretive Meaning

Select the answer that best completes the statements below.

1. In the Clifton poem, why does the narrator prefer the inner city?
   a. The big city is uncomfortable and stiff without a feeling of home.
   b. The narrator's family lives in the inner city.
   c. The narrator cannot afford the rent in the big city.
   d. The narrator does not like straight houses and pastel lights.
2. The tone of both poems is
   a. sarcastic.
   b. informative.
   c. argumentative.
   e. mildly humorous.
3. In the Nye poem, how does the title represent the meaning of the poem?
   a. The end of the story conveys a lesson.
   b. Nye believes that in America the story told should change just as the view does.
   c. The man in the telephone booth told a story.
   d. Since the author is not from California, she is amazed at the stories she hears on the street.
4. Why does Nye mention a farmer with his potatoes and a mother with her child?
   a. She believes that even the simplest activities reveal a changing story.
   b. She is talking about her family members.
   c. She likes the everyday activities of life.
   d. She says they are going somewhere with their stories.
5. According to Nye, how do stories develop?
   a. Some start out small and grow.
   b. Some start out grand and fizzle.
   c. Some stories seem to lose their energy with repetition.
   d. All of the above
6. How does the narrator develop the theme of home in the Clifton poem?
   a. She builds on what is known to what is unknown.
   b. She builds on what is unknown to what is known.

c. She starts with what is known to what is unknown to what is known.
d. She describes what she does not like.

7. Locate one example of figurative language in each poem and identify the type of language it represents.

   Nye poem: ______________________________

   Clifton poem: ______________________________

Score: Number correct _____ out of _____

Writing Assignments

1. *Journal*

Summary

Write a one-paragraph summary for each of the poems. In the summaries, mention the main idea or the theme in the topic sentence as well as the title of the poem and the author. Then summarize the main ideas of the poem. Use quotations from the poem when necessary to support your ideas.

Reaction

Write a one to two-paragraph reaction to the poems. Compare and contrast the ideas of place and time in the poems. When reacting, consider which poem and which parts of the poem relate to your vision of where you live. Cite specific examples as the authors do.

2. *Paragraph*

Choose one of the topics to write an instructional process analysis. Before you write, decide the tone or attitude you want your assignment to portray.

a. How to survive in the suburbs
b. How to survive in the inner city
c. How to survive in _________ (You choose the time and the place. Be specific.)
d. How to make a house a home
e. How to achieve a feeling of _________ in your home

3. *Paragraph to Essay*

Extend the ideas from the paragraph in assignment two to a five-paragraph essay. Discuss one step of the instruction process in each body paragraph. Add an introduction that grabs the attention of the reader and a concluding paragraph that finalizes and summarizes.

4. *Essay*

Write a four- to five-paragraph essay, depending on the number of steps in your informational process, on how a neighborhood you are familiar with solved a crime problem, created a Neighborhood Watch program, or solved some type of local problem.

REFLECTIVE ASSIGNMENTS

1. Reflect upon the statement "to travel is to live." Write an essay showing how one can incorporate travel into one's life.
2. Write a paragraph or an essay relating one of the idiomatic expressions from the beginning of the unit to your ideas about travel and landmarks.
3. Write a poem about a landmark you cherish.
4. Write an essay explaining how to create a _________ kitchen. You decide the type of kitchen you want to create—regional, ethnic, worry-free. Design the essay according to the directional format. Use specific examples to illustrate your points.

INTERNET FIELD TRIPS—READING AND WRITING ASSIGNMENTS

1. Research famous American landmarks. After doing your research, synthesize the information into a paragraph explaining which landmarks you would like to visit and why.
   To get started try these Web sites:
   - http://library.thinkquest.org/J0113129/landmarks.html
   - http://www.boston.world-guides.com/monuments_landmarks.html
   - http://www.nps.gov/parks.html
2. Surf the Net for information on a destination you have always wanted to visit. Write a paragraph detailing a plan on how to tour the destination in a three-day time period. How should you plan your time? The Web sites you visit, of course, will depend on your ideal location; however, perhaps these Web sites will help you:
   - http://en.wikipedia.org/wiki/Walt_Disney_World
   - http://www.Disneyland.com
   - http://www.familytravelguides.com/articles/southeaststates/Orlando/disstay.html
4. Find out about landmark decisions made by the Supreme Court that have impacted your life. Try the Web site http://www.landmarkcases.org and report your findings. How have these decisions affected you?

FILMS TO VIEW

Cape Fear (directed by Martin Scorsese, 1991)
Cape Fear (directed by J. Lee Thomson, 1962)
Dances with Wolves (directed by Kevin Costner, 1990)
Chinatown (directed by Roman Polanski, 1974)
Fargo (directed by Lewis Collins, 1952)

National Lampoon's Vacation (directed by Harold Ramis, 1983)
King Kong (directed by Peter Jackson, 2005)
Sleepless in Seattle (directed by Nora Ephron, 1993)
North by Northwest (directed by Alfred Hitchcock, 1959)
Speed (directed by Jon de Bont, 1994)
The Wild Bunch (directed by Sam Peckinpah, 1968)

Writing assignments are based on *The Wild Bunch* directed by Sam Peckinpah and written by Walon Green and Roy N. Sickner.

1. The taglines for the movie are "Nine men who came too late and stayed too long" and "Unchanged men in a changing land. Out of step, out of place and desperately out of time."
   Choice A—Write a paragraph explaining the relationship of the taglines to the movie.
   Choice B—Write new taglines for the movie and write a paragraph explaining how the new taglines relate to the movie.
2. Some of the famous landmarks in the movie include the U.S./Mexican border, the bridge on the border, and the Rio Grande. Write a paragraph explaining the significance of these landmarks.
3. As the taglines state, this is a movie about changing times. What steps do the filmmakers take to develop this theme of change? When preparing to write, pay close attention to the setting—the time, place, and atmosphere of the story—as well as the actions of the characters.
4. *The Wild Bunch* has a great deal of violence in it. Do you think the violence is necessary to the development of the plot? Write a paragraph explaining your answer.
5. In early western movies, distinguishing the good guys from the bad guys is often easy. However, in *The Wild Bunch,* distinguishing the antagonists from the protagonists can be difficult. Choose one of the characters from the movie that can be characterized as both a protagonist and an antagonist and analyze the steps the filmmakers take to create the contradictions in the character.

Summary of Unit 5—Landmarks—Process Analysis

Read the student essay entitled "How to Paint Artistically" by Julie Gragg. Analyze it for its content, its organization, and its mechanics. Then, in the Summary of Unit 5 on page 266, complete the column on the right with your responses. Apply the information learned in Unit 5.

How to Paint Artistically

Faux finishing requires more time and different steps than the average painting job, and that is what makes it so unique. This artistic way of painting adds life, color, and texture to a room and it is so pretty that it looks like wallpaper. My Mother is a professional painter and decorator, and I have helped her for many years. By helping my Mother I have learned all the steps in faux finishing. To get your faux finishing started, you must gather all tools needed, choose two to three shades that are from the same color group, then choose which technique would look best for your room.

Before you get into faux finishing, there are a few preparations that are needed. In order to make this project as efficient as possible, there are a few tools that will be needed. The most important tools include masking tape, drop cloths, buckets, stir sticks, measuring cups, ladders, rags or sponges, and a level, pencil, and tape measure. It seems like a lot, but these are just the necessities. Before you can get to the fun part, the faux finishing, you must first paint a base coat. It is best to paint all trim in enamel; I prefer to paint the trim in glossy white enamel to brighten the room. Now you are ready to paint the base coat on the walls. You will want to use satin or semi-gloss wall paint in any color you would like for the base coat. The reason for this is because either one of these wall paints will enable you to wash and remove tape from the wall without leaving a sticky residue. It seems like a lot of work already; however, these preparation steps are very important to the overall look of the project.

After you have finished what my mother and I call "prep work," you are ready to have some fun using your imagination. When faux finishing, you have many different looks to choose from. By choosing different shades of the same color, you will have a monochromatic look, which gives more of a three-dimensional effect. If you would like a bolder look for your walls, choose three contrasting colors. Once you have chosen between the soft monochromatic or the contrasting bold look, you are ready to choose three or more colors that appeal to the style you want. Another way to help your faux finish stand out is to add a glaze to your paint. While there are many supplementary products available for faux finishing, glaze is best for this three-dimensional look. The glaze causes the paint to be semi-transparent to enable each layer and color of paint to stand out. Now it is time to mix things up! Using measuring cups, the paint should be mixed with the glaze in a four-to-one ratio. Each of the three colors should be measured out into separate buckets and then mixed with the right amount of glaze. The colors have been chosen; the paint has been mixed with the glaze. Now you are ready to get your hands dirty.

Although there are many popular faux finishes, striping is one of the most elegant and unique. To start, determine the size and placement of stripes to be painted. The decision must be made whether to have all stripes the same width or to vary the widths. You can make the base coat stripe larger than the faux stripe, or vice versa. After you have chosen your design, use a tape measure or a yardstick to measure and mark the stripes. To draw the vertical lines, use a level to establish a plumb line, and lightly mark with a pencil. Apply tape, that is safe for painted surfaces, on the line you have established, at the ceiling and at the baseboards. Now you are finally ready to start painting the faux. Start with any of the three colors you would like by dipping a rag into the paint and apply it in a blotting motion. Allow the paint to dry before adding the next color. After the paint has dried you may start with the next color by blotting over the paint that was previously applied. Continue this process for as many colors as you desire.

Faux finishing is a very unique improvement you can make to your home, and it will always be a centerpiece for conversation. No two paint finishes are alike. But they all have in common the ability to add color, texture, and attention to your room. So put your imagination to work, roll up your sleeves and get started. First, gather all the tools; second, choose the colors to be used; finally, choose the faux technique that will best fit your personality. Faux finishing requires more skill and time than most painting projects, but the finished result is well worth it in the end.

SUMMARY OF UNIT 5	
1. The thesis of the essay is	1.
2. The main tense in the process analysis is	2.
3. Three transitions used include	3.
4. The tone of this essay is	4.
5. The purpose of this essay is to	5.
6. The writer concludes by	6.
7. The reader can infer that the writer	7.
8. Traits of process analysis present in the essay are	8.
9. Three mechanical errors include	9.

Unit 6

American Music

> *Music . . . can name the unnamable and communicate the unknowable.*
>
> —LEONARD BERNSTEIN

> *If music be the fruit of love, play on.*
>
> —SHAKESPEARE, *TWELFTH NIGHT*

Can you name the performers in this photo? What types of music do they represent?

This middle school music class demonstrates a variety of stringed instruments. In what ways can musical instruments be classified?

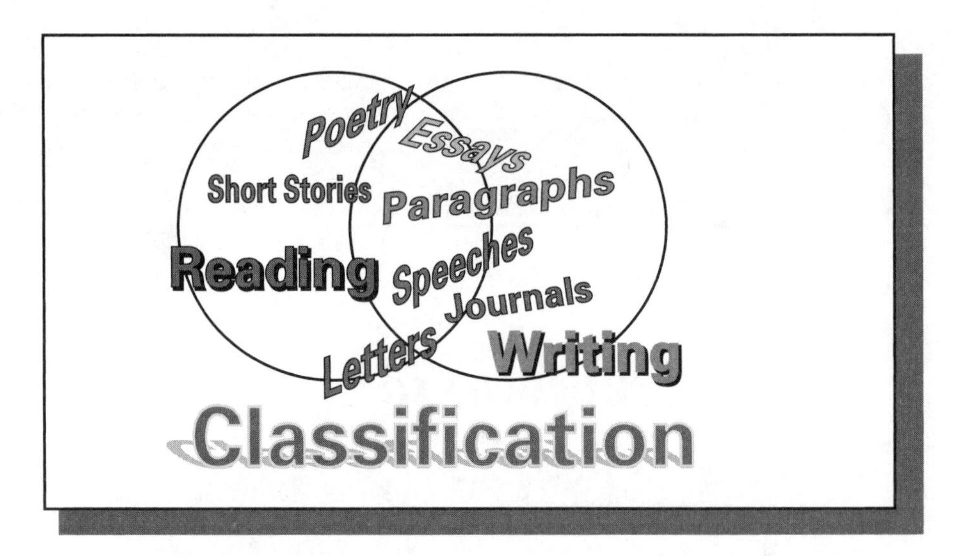

Purpose of Unit:

- *To understand the pattern of classification as it relates to reading comprehension and writing.*

Idioms for American Music

Review the idioms below and discuss their meaning. Apply these idioms to American music.

Face the music.
Tune in.
Tune out.
Out of tune
Tune up
Off-Broadway
Play second fiddle
Play musical chairs.
Sing one's praises
Sing a different tune.
All that jazz
Music to my ears
Rock 'n roll
Elvis has left the building.
Call the tune.
Sing for one's supper
Sing out.
Three dog night
Toot one's horn

Classification: Points to Consider

One way to organize is to divide items or ideas into categories. If you are cleaning out closets, you may put clothing into three stacks: items to be thrown away, items to be given to charitable organizations, and items to keep. If you are deciding where to take a vacation, you may make a list and divide it into three categories: theme park vacations, spa vacations, and adventure vacations. On a business management exam, a professor may ask you to discuss management styles. You may formulate your answer by discussing the delegating, discussing, and directing styles of management. An emergency room doctor must quickly assess her patients as those who are in a life-threatening situation, those who need assistance but whose lives are not in danger, and those whose needs can be met by their doctor during regular office times. This type of organization, whether in personal lives, in the educational arena, or in a professional environment, is called classification. When reading and writing classification essays, consider the following points.

PURPOSE

The purpose of classification is to organize ideas by putting them into categories that share a unifying principle. For example, the clothes in the closet were organized according to what needed to be done with them, and the vacation list was organized according to the activities available on the vacation. The management test called for organizing according to types, most likely based on behavior, and the emergency room physician must organize according to treatment priorities. Words that indicate that the classification method of organization must be used include *types, methods, plans, ways*.

ORGANIZATION AND DEVELOPMENT

When reading and writing material that is organized by categories, notice the relationship among the categories. The categories must have the same unifying principle. For example, the clothes in the messy closet cannot be organized according to those that you will keep, those that will be thrown away, and those that must be laundered. These categories overlap. Clothes that will need to be thrown away may also need to be cleaned. The same material and principles should also be discussed with each category. If, for instance, you are reading or writing a paper on methods of financing a college education, you will need to define any terms in each part of your paragraph or essay, discuss benefits and concerns for each method, and comment on requirements for each method.

TRANSITIONAL DEVICES

The transitional devices used in classification are the same as used when examples and new material are introduced in paragraphs and essays. When progressing from one category to another, try using phrases such as *the first method, the second type, the next category, another method.*

Paragraph and Essay Formats for Classification Writing

For a paragraph, use the following format.

Topic ____________________

Unifying Principle ____________________

Categories ____________________

Topic Sentence ____________________

Category 1

Category 2

Category 3

Concluding Sentence ____________________

For an essay, use the following format.

Topic ____________________

Unifying Principle ____________________

Categories ____________________

Thesis statement ____________________

Introductory paragraph

Category 1—Body Paragraph 1

Details

Category 2—Body Paragraph 2

Details

Category 3—Body Paragraph 3

Details

Concluding paragraph

Classification Worksheet

Before beginning your essay, answer the following questions:

1. What is the subject of the essay?
2. Why are you writing about this subject instead of another one?

3. What necessary, interesting, or new information will you provide for a reader?
4. What classes will you discuss?
    1. ______________________
    2. ______________________
    3. ______________________
5. What information will you include in each of your classes?
6. What is your thesis statement?

PARALLELISM

When classifying, plan the structure of the categories so that a balance exists on all sides of the conjunction or other connecting device. The term for this construction is *parallelism*. Review the correctly constructed sentences below.

Correct Construction

Country music songs can be classified as Rockabilly, Old Time, and Traditional.

Correct Construction

B. B. King is known for singing popular Blues, playing his guitar Lucille, and advertising monitors for diabetics.

Problems for student writers often arise in constructing the topic or thesis statement for a classification paper. To avoid this problem, write categories in the planning stage and then cast a sentence that follows the parallel format.

Faulty Construction

American workers are concerned with wages, benefits and if they get to take a vacation.

Correct Form

American workers are concerned with wages, benefits, and vacation time.

Faulty Construction

Followers of hip hop music can be classified as dancers, singers, and those who want to voice their dissent.

Correct Construction

Followers of hip hop music can be classified as dancers, singers, and dissenters.

Write sentences using the following categories. Include three *parallel* subjects for each category.

Types of rap music ____

Types of folk art ____

READING BEFORE WRITING

Types of Folk Music

Sarah Wilfong

What do you think of when you hear the term folk music? *Do you visualize Scouts singing* I've Been Working on the Railroad *and* Blowing in the Wind *around a campfire? Songs like this demonstrate the communal heritage of folk music—songs everyone can enjoy singing. After all, folk music, present in all cultures, is an art form created and performed by many people; some are classically trained musicians, but many are not.*

In Chicago, The Old Town School of Folk Music uses a thick, spiralbound book called *Rise Up Singing* (edited by **folk** music junkie Peter Blood-Patterson). This songbook is often regarded as the folk song bible. Within the book's covers you'll find a variety of folk songs—everything from the Scottish **ballad** *Barbara Allen,* a ballad that goes back further than the 17th century and whose authorship is unknown, to *Do Re Mi* from *The Sound of Music,* written by Rodgers and Hammerstein in 1959.

Now why, you may ask, is *Do Re Mi* considered a folk song, when it was written for a theatrical production, has direct authorship, and is really quite modern? Good question. Think of all the five-year-olds you know. Now imagine them singing *Do Re Mi.* Chances are they know all the words. Now think of your next door neighbor. Chances are he knows the words, too. The Rodgers and Hammerstein song *Do Re Mi* didn't intend to become a folk song, but almost by **osmosis,** everyone knows it. Even your Scout troop would include it when singing around the campfire. Folk music is not limited to old songs; folk music can also include popular songs that are easily sung by many people.

Another type of folk music is folk-rock. When Mick Jagger recorded *House of the Rising Sun,* an American folk song from New Orleans, and when Metallica recorded *Whiskey in the Jar,* a traditional Irish song, traditional folk music was fused with rock. The result? Folk-rock—music that definitely is not pure folk, nor really rock, either.

Oftentimes, musical traditions influence each other by simply existing in the same geographical area. *Sixteen Tons* is a classic example of this type of blending. Many other examples can be heard in country music and blues.

By the same token, a particular music style will not be influenced if it is kept isolated. When Scottish immigrants came to North America in the

1800's, they and their music were concentrated in two regions, Canada's Cape Breton and the Appalachian Mountains. The Cape Breton style of music continued to evolve through exposure to other peoples and other music. But when the Appalachian music was rediscovered at the beginning of the 20th century, it was found to have remained much closer to its Scottish roots because the people and the music had remained fairly isolated. Strangely enough, this Appalachian-style music is now considered American hillbilly music!

Geography has also played a role in the development of traditional Irish music. Music from one Irish County is separated from the music of another Irish County by its own particular quirk. For example, the fiddle style in southern Clare is different from the fiddle style in northern Donnegal. Even the music of individual towns can be identified by **indigenous quirks.** Why? Because travel between towns was limited, people had little exposure to music from other regions. This led to the development of highly stylized, very clean, musical segmentation.

Storytelling is another vital part of the folk tradition.

Ballads have long been the most popular vehicle for retelling stories about **unrequited** love, war, famine, shipwrecks, and other tragedies. Not all ballads are depressing, but the vast majority of them seem to be! Actually, many ballads have correlating storylines; the phrases used in one ballad are often similar to phrases in another ballad, even when the ballads are from different geographical regions. There are at least thirty-five variations of *Barbara Allen*, some Scottish, some English, and some American, all recorded in the last twenty years!

Many folk songs are very practical. Teaching songs explain things while working songs help laborers work. *The Woodcutter's Song* tells you what type of wood to burn in your fireplace, while *Saltpetre Shanty* helped sailors maintain their rhythm while hauling up sails on a tall ship.

Folk music is unique because it relies heavily on an **aural** tradition to keep it alive. Even today, in spite of the fact that there are hundreds of collections of songs and tunes available, most folk musicians still rely on the tradition of learning songs by ear, from other singers, rather than by reading manuscripts.

In the last thirty years, songwriters have begun writing contemporary folk songs about modern issues and using more modern language. Songs like *The City of New Orleans* and *This Land is Your Land* have none of the **archaic** wording of a ballad like *The Water is Wide*. But just like their older **counterparts,** modern folk songs reflect the emotions of the person writing the song, and are meant to inspire similar emotions in the listener. Modern folk songs still tell stories, just in a more modern fashion.

The struggle to define folk music is ongoing because folk music is always changing. That's what makes folk music interesting, and what helps it to survive. As long as those Scouts keep belting out those campfire tunes, folk music will never die.

I leaned my back against an oak
Thinking it was a trusty tree
But first it bent, and then it broke
And so my false love did to me.

—A verse from "The Water is Wide"

This verse is also found in countless other ballads from the British Isles.

Glossary for "Types of Folk Music"

folk (fōk)

n. pl. **folk** or **folks**

1. a. The common people of a society or region considered as the representatives of a traditional way of life and especially as the originators or carriers of the customs, beliefs, and arts that make up a distinctive culture: *a leader who came from the folk.*
   b. Archaic. A nation; a people.
2. Informal. People in general. Often used in the plural: *Folks around here are very friendly.*
3. People of a specified group or kind. Often used in the plural: *city folks; rich folk.*
4. **folks** Informal.
   a. The members of one's family or childhood household; one's relatives.
   b. One's parents: *My folks are coming for a visit.*

adj.

Of, occurring in, or originating among the common people: *folk culture; a folk hero.*

Idiom:

just folks Informal

Down-to-earth, open-hearted.

[Middle English, from Old English folc.]

bal·lad (băl'əd)

n.

1. a. A narrative poem, often of folk origin and intended to be sung, consisting of simple stanzas and usually having a refrain.
   b. The music for such a poem.
2. A popular song especially of a romantic or sentimental nature.

[Middle English balade, *poem or song in stanza form,* from Old French ballade, from Old Provençal balada, *song sung while dancing,* from balar, *to dance,* from Late Latin ballāre, *to dance.*]

bal·lad'ic (bə-lăd'ĭk, bă-) *adj.*

os·mo·sis (ŏz-mō'sĭs, ŏs-)
n. pl. **os·mo·ses** (-sēz)

1. a. Diffusion of fluid through a semipermeable membrane from a solution with a low solute concentration to a solution with a higher solute concentration until there is an equal concentration of fluid on both sides of the membrane.

   b. The tendency of fluids to diffuse in such a manner.

2. A gradual, often unconscious process of assimilation or absorption: *learned French by osmosis while residing in Paris for 15 years.*

[From obsolete osmose, from earlier endosmose, from French: Greek endo-, *endo-* + Greek ōsmos, *thrust, push* (from ōthein, *to push*).]

os·mot'ic (-mŏt'ĭk) *adj.*

os·mot'i·cal·ly *adv.*

in·dig·e·nous (ĭn-dĭj'ə-nəs)
adj.

1. Originating and living or occurring naturally in an area or environment.
2. Intrinsic; innate.

[From Latin `indigena`, *a native.*]

in·dig'e·nous·ly *adv.*

in·dig'e·nous·ness *n.*

quirk (kwûrk)
n.

1. A peculiarity of behavior; an idiosyncrasy: "Every man had his own quirks and twists" (Harriet Beecher Stowe).
2. An unpredictable or unaccountable act or event; a vagary: *a quirk of fate.*
3. A sudden sharp turn or twist.
4. An equivocation; a quibble.
5. Architecture. A lengthwise groove on a molding between the convex upper part and the soffit.

[*Origin unknown.*]

quirk'i·ly *adv.*

quirk'i·ness *n.*

quirk'y *adj.*

un·re·quit·ed (ŭn'rĭ-kwī'tĭd)
adj.

Not reciprocated or returned in kind: *unrequited love.*

un're·quit'ed·ly *adv.*

au·ral (ôr'əl)
adj.

Of, relating to, or perceived by the ear.

[From Latin auris, *ear.*]

au'ral·ly *adv.*

ar·cha·ic (är-kā'ĭk) also **ar·cha·i·cal** (-ĭ-kəl)
adj.

1. Of, relating to, or characteristic of a much earlier, often more primitive period, especially one that develops into a classical stage of civilization: *an archaic bronze statuette; Archaic Greece.*
2. No longer current or applicable; antiquated: *archaic laws.*
3. Of, relating to, or characteristic of words and language that were once in regular use but are now relatively rare and suggestive of an earlier style or period.

[Greek arkhaikos, *old-fashioned*, from arkhaios, *ancient*, from arkhē, *beginning*, from arkhein, *to begin*.]

ar·cha'i·cal·ly *adv.*

coun·ter·part (koun'tər-pärt')
n.

1. a. One that closely resembles another.
   b. One that has the same functions and characteristics as another; a corresponding person or thing: *Their foreign minister is the counterpart of our secretary of state.*
2. A copy or duplicate of a legal paper.
3. a. One of two parts that fit and complete each other.
   b. One that serves as a complement.

Reading Comprehension

Answer the following questions about the essay by Sarah Wilfong.

Word Meaning

Using the glossary, select the entry that best completes the sentences below.

1. To the surprise of her grandmother, Juliana had learned how to play Rummy through __________ when her grandmother played the card game with her other grandchildren.
2. Early American settlements believed in __________ living and even shared livestock and crops as they worked together to survive the brutal elements.
3. The eccentric athlete had so many __________ that his team members shunned him as he prepared for the games by rubbing old basketball shoes and thumbing a rabbit's foot.
4. The most interesting music of any nation is the unusual sounds of the early __________ groups who settled the lands early in civilization.
5. The ballad singer often wrote tunes about the __________ love from the delightful but snobbish girls of his high school years.
6. Most folk literature and music were passed along to later generations through a/an __________ tradition because most people did not read and write.
7. The use of the word spectacles, for eyeglasses, is an example of a/an __________ word in the English language.
8. The Mexican __________ of American pancakes is the tortilla.

Literal Meaning

Mark the letter of the option that best answers the statements below.

1. From which country did the immigrants NOT originate?
   a. Sierra Leone
   b. Afghanistan
   c. Iraq
   d. Ukraine
2. When did the immigrants arrive in the United States?
   a. 2001
   b. 1999
   c. 2005
   d. 2003
3. What literary transitions does Wilfong use to build unity in her classification of folk music?
   a. *Another*
   b. *Also*
   c. *By the same token*
   d. All of the above
4. What struggle does Wilfong mention in the article?
   a. The struggle to maintain the lyrics of folk music
   b. The need to archive all of the folk song lyrics
   c. The problem of finding folk singers
   d. The problem of defining the term folk music
5. What group does Wilfong say will keep folk music alive?
   a. National Public Radio.
   b. Professional folk singers.
   c. The Scouts.
   d. The churches.

Interpretive Meaning

Complete the questions with the response that best answers the statement.

1. Why does Wilfong say that folk music is difficult to pinpoint as a specific genre?
   a. Folk music is constantly changing.
   b. Folk music is dying.
   c. Many folk singers have turned to other more popular forms of music.
   d. Folk music is rarely performed.
2. What is the tone of the essay? (Mark all that apply.)
   a. Humorous
   b. Informative
   c. Argumentative
   d. Sarcastic
3. According to Wilfong, what is the purpose of folk music?
   a. It makes people want to sing.
   b. It provides a communal identity for people of every culture.
   c. It demonstrates the universal heritage of all people around the world.
   d. It gives song writers a purpose for creating songs.

4. How does Wilfong define folk music?
   a. It is easily sung by many people.
   b. It can be performed by many people.
   c. It can change forms as it blends with other styles.
   d. All of the above
5. Into what categories can American folk music be divided? (Mark all that apply.)
   a. Folk-Rock
   b. Folk Hip-Hop
   c. Folk Heavy Metal
   d. American Hillbilly
6. Why does Appalachian folk music represent the true roots of its Scottish ancestry?
   a. It has evolved over the years.
   b. Everyone enjoys singing it.
   c. It has been exposed to other forms as it is performed.
   d. It has remained isolated from influences of other forms of music.
7. Why do so many forms of folk music exist in America?
   a. Because, according to statistics, Americans move every five years
   b. Because Americans become easily bored with music and create new styles
   c. Because people from all parts of the world settled in America and brought their folk music with them
   d. Because folk music is aural and Americans confuse the lyrics of the songs
8. Why do some of the same lyrics appear in many different ballads?
   a. Because competitions exist for song writers to create a ballad using certain lyrics
   b. Because the storylines are similar, lyrics are also often the same
   c. Because many lyricists steal from other song writers
   d. Because song writers share their lyrics with each other
9. Using Wilfong's essay, write a complete and concise definition for folk music.

   ____

   ____

10. List all of the types of folk music that Wilfong mentions in the essay.

   ____

   ____

Score: Number correct _____ out of _____

Writing Assignments

1. Journal Writing

Summary

Write a summary of the essay. In the topic sentence, state what is being classified, the author, and the title of the essay. Mention the categories in the supporting sentences.

Reaction

In your reaction, consider the organization of the essay as well as to the content.

2. *Paragraph*

Write a paragraph classifying a particular type of music, such as rock, country, jazz, or rap.

Alternate Assignment: Write a classification paragraph on types of dance, types of art, or types of literature.

3. *Paragraph to Essay*

Use the information written in assignment two to organize and write a five-paragraph essay on the same topic. Focus on one category of the subject in each body paragraph. The number of body paragraphs depends on the number of categories.

4. *Essay*

Choose one of the topics below and write a five-paragraph essay supporting the topic.

Careers in music or the entertainment industry
Musicians
Rock stars
Country music stars
Singers
Actors
Fans of musicians and bands
Talk show hosts
News commentators

"I Hear America Singing" *from* Leaves of Grass

Walt Whitman

In this poem, Walt Whitman categorizes the various songs he hears according to the persons singing the song.

I hear America singing, the varied carols I hear,
Those of mechanics, each one singing his as it should be **blithe** and strong,
The carpenter singing his as he measures his plank or beam,
The mason singing his as he makes ready for work, or leaves off work,
The boatman singing what belongs to him in his boat, the deck-hand singing on the steamboat deck,
The shoemaker singing as he sits on his bench, the hatter singing as he stands,
The woodcutter's song, the **ploughboy's** on his way in the morning, or at noon intermission or at sundown,
The delicious singing of the mother, or of the young wife at work, or of the girl sewing or washing,
Each singing what belongs to him or her and to none else,
The day what belongs to the day—at night the party of young fellows, **robust,** friendly,
Singing with open mouths their strong melodious songs.

Glossary for "I Hear America Singing"

blithe (blīth, blīth)

adj. **blith·er, blith·est**

1. Carefree and lighthearted.
2. Lacking or showing a lack of due concern; casual: *spoke with blithe ignorance of the true situation.*

[Middle English, from Old English blīthe.]

blithe'ly *adv.*

blithe'ness *n.*

ploughboy

Plowboy \Plow"boy'\, Ploughboy \Plough"boy'\, *n.* A boy that drives or guides a team in plowing; a young rustic.

ro·bust (rō-bŭst', rō'bŭst')
adj.

1. Full of health and strength; vigorous.
2. Powerfully built; sturdy.
3. Requiring or suited to physical strength or endurance: *robust labor.*
4. Rough or crude; boisterous: *a robust tale.*
5. Marked by richness and fullness; full-bodied: *a robust wine.*

[Latin rōbustus, from rōbur, rōbus, *oak, strength.*]

ro·bust'ly *adv.*

ro·bust'ness *n.*

Reading Comprehension

Answer the following questions about Walt Whitman's "I Hear America Singing."

Word Meaning

Select the word from the glossary that best completes the sentences below.

1. Steady and __________, the workmen building the house played their Spanish music loudly as they worked to finish the job before dusk.
2. Many teenagers learn __________ beer drinking songs in an effort to appear manly.
3. Many old farms in the Northwest depended on __________ for successful farming of the rocky lands near the sea.

Literal Meaning

Mark the letter of the statement that best completes the meaning.

1. The narrator is speaking about what?
   a. The types of songs he hears as he travels around the town
   b. The different types of jobs people perform
   c. The carols people sing during the holidays
   d. The work songs people are writing
2. Whitman is praising the subjects of his poem for what?
   a. For working so blithely
   b. For showing how well they can sing
   c. For opening their mouths when they sing
   d. For doing good work in their trade
3. In this poem, Whitman uses everyday laborers to convey the notion of
   a. the division of labor.
   b. everyday life in early America.
   c. the benefit of singing to do a better job.
   d. the need for more national songs.
4. The poem is organized in the following design.
   a. Examples only
   b. Examples followed by action

c. A lesson only
d. A lecture

5. The narrator states his point, or theme, of the poem in
   a. the first line.
   b. the first and last lines.
   c. throughout the poem.
   d. an implied fashion.

Interpretive Meaning

Complete the questions with the response that best answers the statement.

1. Why does the narrator repeat the word *his* in the first few lines?
   a. He is showing how men do the manual labor.
   b. He is demonstrating the different types of songs associated with work.
   c. He is saying that the choir members all practice while working.
   d. He wants the songs to be heard.
2. Why does Whitman say "singing, with open mouths"?
   a. The singers are well trained.
   b. The singers need air while working.
   c. The singers are proud of the songs they sing and the work they do.
   d. The singers are trying to sing louder than their competitors.
3. What does Whitman mean by "Each singing what belongs to her, and to none else"?
   a. He is creating a songbook of work songs.
   b. He hears that each trade has its own unique chant.
   c. He wants to publish the songs.
   d. He likes the songs of the women best.
4. The poem can be divided into what parts? (Explain the division of the poem.)

   ____

   ____

   ____

   ____

5. What replacements for the workers mentioned in the poem do you think Whitman would see today? What songs would they sing?

   ____

   ____

   ____

6. Why does the narrator say that " . . . laughter/ Is thrown in their faces"?
   a. He likes the way people laugh in the movies.
   b. He thinks that people laugh because they think they are supposed to do so.
   c. He is mildly criticizing canned laughter in film.
   d. He likes to use action verbs.

Score: Number correct _____ out of _____

Writing Assignments

1. *Journal Writing*

Summary

Summarize the literal content of the poem. Pay attention to the organization of the poem and use the same pattern in your summary.

Reaction

In the reaction, interpret the poem. What is Whitman saying about the workers in America? If Whitman were writing this poem today, what workers would he include in the poem? What songs, or praises and concerns, would they sing about America?

2. *Paragraph*

With Whitman's poem in mind, write a paragraph classifying the types of "songs" workers in America today are singing. Begin your paragraph with a clear topic sentence which names the class and the categories.

3. *Paragraph to Essay*

Use the ideas and organizational plan from assignment 2 to write an essay classifying the songs American workers are singing. Remember that the phrase "the songs American workers are singing" refers to figurative language in Walt Whitman's poem.

4. *Essay*

Write a classification essay on one of the topics listed.

a. Job categories in your major or field of study
b. Bosses
c. Employees at your current or past place of employment
d. Problems and concerns at your current or past place of employment
e. Types of skills needed to be a successful ______________

La Música Mexicana

Ellen Jane Rainey

This essay classifies Mexican music into particular categories and mentions the regions from which the music originates.

Do you recognize this song? "Oye Como Va" peaked at number 13 on the Billboard charts in 1971. This version of the song appeared on the album *Abraxas* by the group Santana, led by the young Mexican-American guitarist and composer Carlos Santana. The album was full of acid rock driven by the rhythms of Latin percussion. Another hit on the album, "Black Magic Woman," made it to number 4 on the charts. That an album showing so much Latin influence was so popular in the U.S. is a reflection of the era of multiculturalism that America was entering at the time. This song and others by Santana, however, show many influences that aren't at all typically Mexican. Part of this is the instrumentation, but another part is the origin of the song, as this is the second time it was released to the American public. It was originally written and recorded by the *nuyorican** bandleader and Latin percussionist Tito Puente as a *chachacha* dance tune in the 1950s. Santana's version reflects the multiculturalism of Mexican and American music *and* our societies in general. Let's find out more about that music and multiculturalism.

Los Géneros de la Música Méxicana

El Son Huasteco

The oldest, but still typically Mexican music is a **repertoire** of songs called "*Sones*" whose lyrics derive from old Spanish songs and folk poetry. A way of playing these "Sones", which incorporates a virtuosic fiddle and guitar duet style, is popular in the countryside of many states in Mexico, but most notably in the very warm state of Huasteco, hence the name *Son Huasteco*. The songs run the gamut from comical to romantic to story telling in nature. Though it is an older folkloric music, its best musicians might easily be compared to great American folk musicians like Bill Monroe or Robert Johnson in their rich expressive talent.

Mariachi

Based on this older genre, but with the added instrumentation of more violins and trumpets and guitars, as well as singers with an almost operatic range and power, is a sound that even *norteamericanos* are familiar with: *Mariachi*. Mariachi music is very sophisticated compared to "Son" and incorporates a greater

**Nuyorican*: A New Yorker of Puerto Rican descent.

variety of song and dance styles. Mariachi music also uses a big guitar, called a *guitarron*, to play the bass part. Mariachi music has its roots in the "Son" music of the centrally located state of Jalisco, of which Guadalajara, Mexico's second largest city, is the capital. But all over Mexico many cherish Mariachi music for its purely Mexican sound. Its instrumentation and style are very set, consistent and unique to Mexico.

La Música Norteña

Another type of music that is uniquely Mexican in its sound is *La Música Norteña* and its close relative across the border, Tex-Mex. In Mexico its domain was traditionally the hot desert states along Mexico's northern border, hence the name *norteña*. German immigrants in this region and in Texas introduced the *acordeón* as well as dance tunes like polkas and waltzes whose rhythms are a mainstay of the genre. This music is now popular even with the city dwellers of central Mexico and is probably the most popular music among Mexican-Americans and Mexican immigrants in America. The "Mexican" touch comes in the development of a new style of playing the *acordeón* and the addition of another uniquely Mexican instrument called *the bajo sexto*, a slightly bigger guitar with twelve strings, which provides a great rhythmic punch to drive the music along. . . . Other instruments to be heard in the mix are electric bass and drums and saxophone, though they are not played in a rock style.

La Música Norteña is also known for the singing of *corridos*, songs that pass on the details of recent important events. Many *corridos* were written to tell of events during the Mexican Revolution (1910–1920) to comment on both victories and tragedies. In the 1990s many groups sang *narco-corridos* about the **exploits** and crimes of drug traffickers along the border states, in much the same way "The Ballad of Jesse James" or the "Ballad of Pretty Boy Floyd" are sung to celebrate the audacity of those outlaws. As a recent postscript, many Mexican song writers are composing *corridos* in sympathetic response to the national tragedy of September 11th.

La Música Caribeña

Besides these *géneros típicos* of Mexico, popular music in Mexico also includes music heavily influenced by neighboring cultures such as those of the United States, and Caribbean countries like Cuba, La República Dominicana and Colombia. Each [of] these countries [has] contributed many dance styles to the repertoire of Latin dance. In all three countries the strong cultural influence that set them apart from the many other Latin American nations is their strong African heritage.

The popular[arity] of [the] music of Cuba has had the most far-reaching effects on the music of . . . Latin America. The most commonly known name for the music that Cuba, and to some extent the U.S. territory of Puerto Rico, has created is Salsa, meaning *sauce* in Spanish. Salsa is really a very broad term for a great variety of music with Spanish **tinged** melodies usually played by a hot brass and reed section over the pulse of Afro-Cuban percussion like congas, bongos, timbales and at times ritual African drums called bata. The roots of Salsa lie in the traditional music of the *guajiros* (farm workers of Cuba). This older music, called Son Montuno, is still played by even the younger generation of Salsa musicians and has enjoyed a resurgence of popularity since the release [of] the CD and [the]documentary film *The Buena Vista Social Club.* Salsa bands also use pianos and the *tres*, a smaller Cuban guitar, in their rhythm sections, thus rivaling American Big Bands in their fullness of instrumentation.

Mexican musicians have adopted many rhythms and dance styles from Cuba over the years. *Mambo, chachacha* and *rumba* rhythms have been the basis for a lot of high-energy dance tunes in México. The rhythm of the *bolero* by way of Cuba has been the basis for many slower romantic tunes. Cuba and Mexico also share Cuba's greatest singer of the forties and fifties, Beny Moré, who lived and performed in Mexico for many years before returning to his native land. . . .

From the island of La República Dominicana comes the very danceable rhythm of merengue. A product of the island's African cultural heritage, it has been adopted by the salsa bands in Cuba, Puerto Rico and bands in Latino **enclaves** in the United States. Right now it is enjoying a resurgence in dance clubs in México. Many Mexican musicians are recording in the style of merengue.

The South American country of Colombia on the southern edge of the Caribbean Sea has brought the dance rhythm of cumbia to the world. Cumbia is an indigenous rhythm of Colombia filtered again through an unavoidable African influence. Like merengue it has been taken up by Salsa bands as well as Latin-Jazz bands in the United States. It too is very popular in the dance clubs of Mexico at this time. The moderate tempo of cumbia can be used also in place of a hip-hop beat for adopting *Rap* into Latin music. This has helped to popularize the cumbia again.

La Música Nueva en México

In recent years in Mexico a new music called Banda has emerged based entirely on the sound of percussion, brass and reeds, much like a high school marching band in the United States, but with the use of Latin rhythms. There are typically no guitars or accordions as are heard in La Música Norteña or violins and guitars as are heard in Mariachi orchestras. Though it has come to **fore** only recently, the music is solidly based in many of the same dance styles like waltes, rancheras and cumbias, that can be heard in other types of Mexican music. Banda also sounds very Mexican as opposed to Caribbean.

The other great influence in Mexican music comes of course from its neighbor to the north—you guessed it—the good ole U.S.A., in the form of Rock 'n' Roll and Rap. Rock 'n' Roll in Mexico, as one can hear in the clip of "Oye Como Va", has always incorporated other Latin influences even when using some of the standard electric instrumentation of Rock. And if any musician picks up an electric guitar it's a good bet that the influence of the Blues will come out, too. Rock 'n' Roll in Mexico shows these influences as well as the influence of Reggae, Ska, Punk, Rap, Techno, Pop and Alternative.

Glossary for "La Música Mexicana"

rep·er·toire (rĕp'ər-twär')
n.

1. The stock of songs, plays, operas, readings, or other pieces that a player or company is prepared to perform.
2. The class of compositions in a genre: *has excellent command of the chanteuse repertoire.*
3. The range or number of skills, aptitudes, or special accomplishments of a particular person or group.

[French répertoire, from Old French, from Late Latin repertōrium.]

ex·ploit (ĕk'sploit', ĭk-sploit')
n.

An act or deed, especially a brilliant or heroic one.

tr. v. **ex·ploit·ed, ex·ploit·ing, ex·ploits** (ĭk-sploit', ĕk'sploit')

1. To employ to the greatest possible advantage: *exploit one's talents.*
2. To make use of selfishly or unethically: *a country that exploited peasant labor.*
3. To advertise; promote.

[Middle English, from Old French esploit, from Latin explicitum, neuter past participle of explicāre, *to unfold.*]

ex·ploit'a·bil'i·ty *n.*
ex·ploit'a·ble *adj.*
ex·ploit'a·tive or **ex·ploit'ive** *adj.*
ex·ploit'a·tive·ly or **ex·ploit'ive·ly** *adv.*
ex·ploit'er *n.*

tinge (tĭnj)

tr. v. **tinged,** (tĭnjd) **tinge·ing,** or **ting·ing** (tĭn'jĭng) **ting·es**

1. To apply a trace of color to; tint.
2. To affect slightly, as with a contrasting quality: "The air was blowy and tinged with rain" (Joyce Carol Oates).
   n.

1. A small amount of a color incorporated or added.
2. A slight added element, property, or influence: *a tinge of regret.*

[Middle English tingen, from Latin tingere.]

en·clave (ĕn'klāv',ŏn'-)
n.

1. A country or part of a country lying wholly within the boundaries of another.
2. A distinctly bounded area enclosed within a larger unit: *ethnic enclaves in a large city.*

[French, from Old French `enclaver`, *to enclose*, from Vulgar Latin *`inclāvāre`: Latin `in-`, *in*; see **en-**[1] + Latin `clāvis`, *key*.]

fore (fôr, fōr)
adj.
1. Located at or toward the front; forward.
2. Earlier in order of occurrence; former.

n.
1. Something that is located at or toward the front.
2. The front part.

adv.
1. At, toward, or near the front; forward.
2. At an earlier time.

prep. also **'fore**
Before.

interj. Sports
Used by a golfer to warn those ahead that a ball is headed in their direction.

Idiom:
to the fore
In, into, or toward a position of prominence: *A new virtuoso has come to the fore.*

[Middle English, *beforehand, before, in front of,* from Old English.]

Reading Comprehension

Answer the following questions about the essay by Señora Raney.

Word Meaning

Using the glossary, select the entry that best completes the sentences below.

1. The wedding cake was __________ with raspberry filling and edible gold decorations.
2. The issue of school uniforms came to the __________ when students were attacked for their tennis shoes and athletic jackets.
3. The off-the-field __________ of many professional athletes, both the philanthropic and the questionable ones, are frequently publicized in the national news.
4. Small __________ of settlers still speaking their native language and following their old-world customs exist in the mountains of Tennessee.
5. The vast __________ of the musician made him a popular performer at parties and receptions because he could play all types of music.

Literal Meaning

Mark the letter of the option that best answers the statements below.

1. What topics might be covered in "Sones"?
   a. Romance
   b. Comedy
   c. Nature
   d. All of the above

2. What performer is mentioned in the introduction as a successful cross-over artist?
   a. Carlos Santana
   b. Bill Malone
   c. Robert Johnson
   d. Ricky Martin
3. What instrument distinguishes Mexican music from traditional American sounds?
   a. A trumpet
   b. A big guitar
   c. A violin
   d. A bongo drum
4. What are the songs that convey the stories of important events called?
   a. Sones
   b. Norteña
   c. Corridos
   d. Banda
5. Mexican music contains the sounds of all but which one of the following influences?
   a. Waltzes
   b. Big Band
   c. Rap
   d. Rock 'n' Roll

Interpretive Meaning

Complete the questions with the response that best answers the statement.

1. According to the essay, why was "Black Magic Woman" and other songs with Latin rhythms popular in America a few years ago?
   a. They had excellent record producers known in America.
   b. The promoters worked diligently to get the songs on the radio stations.
   c. The performers traveled in the United States to popularize the songs.
   d. The United States was entering a multicultural period in its history.
2. The essay represents what rhetorical mode/s? (Mark all that apply.)
   a. Argumentation
   b. Classification
   c. Definition
   d. Process analysis
3. What literary transitions unite the divisions of the essay? (Mark all that apply.)
   a. *Besides*
   b. *Also*
   c. *But*
   d. *Moreover*
4. How are *corridos* compared to the American style of ballads?
   a. Both contain lyrics dealing with events that happen along the border.
   b. Both deal with outlaws on either side of the border.

c. Both contain lyrics dealing with events, both comedies and tragedies in life.
d. Both are spread by word of mouth rather than by recordings.

5. Why has Salsa become popular on both sides of the border?
   a. Salsa was popularized in the film *The Buena Vista Social Club*.
   b. Listeners like the sound of Salsa, which is created by a huge array of instruments.
   c. Salsa has roots in many kinds of music that appeals to many different listeners.
   d. All of the above
6. What is the connection between the music of Mexico and Cuba? (Mark all that apply.)
   a. Cuban music is derived from Mexican sounds.
   b. Mexican music is influenced by Cuban sounds.
   c. Mexico and Cuba share a popular singer who lived in both countries.
   d. Both countries' music shares the influence of American music.
7. Why is La Música Norteña the most popular music among Mexican Americans and Mexican immigrants?
   a. Being border music, it is the music most commonly known among immigrants, who often come from border areas.
   b. It is the only Mexican music available to buy in America.
   c. Mexican music in not easily available in the United States, but Mexican immigrants can cross the border to buy this style of music.
   d. This music is taught in the schools, so children learn it early.
8. What is the one universal influence on most of the different sounds of Latin music?
   a. Spanish music
   b. African music
   c. German music
   d. American music
9. Summarize in your own words the main point of this classification essay.

   ____

   ____

Score: Number correct _____ out of _____

Writing Assignments

1. Journal

Summary

Utilizing the reporter's questions (who, what, where, when, why, how, how much), summarize the essay.

Reaction

Write a two-paragraph reaction focusing on the ideas in the essay in the first paragraph and the organization and classification methods used in the second.

2. *Paragraph*
   Write a classification paragraph on Mexican (or other group) influences on culture in the United States. During the planning process of your paper, consider poetry, science, cuisine, dance, and literature, as well as music. When you have narrowed your topic, be able to give examples to support your categories.

3. *Paragraph to Essay*
   Using the paragraph written for assignment two as a body paragraph, write an essay classifying types of cultural influences on American lifestyle.

4. *Essay*
   Write a classification essay on one of the topics listed below.
   Restaurants in your community
   Influences of sports on culture
   Radio programming/programs
   Types of radio stations (according to the music they play) in your community

Nineteen Fifty-Five

Alice Walker

This short story tells the tale of an African-American singer whose songs were used by the leading Caucasian male icon of the era. The story represents the movement from the 1950s into the 1970s through the eyes of the female narrator. The events of the story become a metaphor for the values of the country.

1955

The car is a brandnew red Thunderbird convertible, and it's passed the house more than once. It slows down real slow now, and stops at the curb. An older gentleman dressed like a Baptist deacon gets out on the side near the house, and a young fellow who looks about sixteen gets out on the driver's side. They are white, and I wonder what in the world they doing in this neighborhood.

Well, I say to J.T., put your shirt on, anyway, and let me clean these glasses offa the table.

We had been watching the ballgame on TV. I wasn't actually watching, I was sort of daydreaming, with my foots up in J.T.'s lap.

I seen 'em coming on up the walk, brisk, like they coming to sell something, and then they rung the bell, and J.T. declined to put on a shirt but instead disappeared into the bedroom where the other television is. I turned down the one in the living room; I figured I'd be rid of these two double quick and J.T. could come back out again.

Are you Gracie Mae Still? asked the old guy, when I opened the door and put my hand on the lock inside the screen.

And I don't need to buy a thing, said I.

What makes you think we're sellin'? he asks, in that hearty Southern way that makes my eyeballs ache.

Well, one way or another and they're inside the house and the first thing the young fellow does is raise the TV a couple of **decibels.** He's about five feet nine, sort of womanish looking, with real dark white skin and a red pouting mouth. His hair is black and curly and he looks like a Loosianna **creole.**

About one of your songs, says the deacon. He is maybe sixty, with white hair and beard, white silk shirt, black linen suit, black tie and black shoes. His cold gray eyes look like they're sweating.

One of my songs?

Traynor here just *loves* your songs. Don't you, Traynor? He nudges Traynor with his elbow. Traynor blinks, says something I can't catch in a pitch I don't register.

The boy learned to sing and dance livin' round your people out in the country. Practically cut his teeth on you.

Traynor looks up at me and bites his thumbnail.

I laugh.

Well, one way or another they leave with my agreement that they can record one of my songs. The deacon writes me a check for five hundred dollars, the boy grunts his awareness of the transaction, and I am laughing all over myself by the time I rejoin J.T.

Just as I am snuggling down beside him though I hear the front door bell going off again.

Forgit his hat? asks J.T.

I hope not, I say.

The deacon stands there leaning on the door frame and once again I'm thinking of those sweaty-looking eyeballs of his. I wonder if sweat makes your eyeballs pink because his are sure pink. Pink and gray and it strikes me that nobody I'd care to know is behind them.

I forgot one little thing, he says pleasantly. I forgot to tell you Traynor and I would like to buy up all of those records you made of the song. I tell you we sure do love it.

Well, love it or not, I'm not stupid as to let them do that without making 'em pay. So I says, Well, that's gonna cost you. Because, really, that song never did sell all that good, so I was glad they was going to buy it up. But on the other hand, them two listening to my song by themselves, and nobody else getting to hear me sing it, give me a pause.

Well, one way or another the deacon showed me where I would come out ahead on any deal he had proposed so far. Didn't I give you five hundred dollars? he asked. What white man—and don't even need to mention colored—would give you more? We buy up all your records of that particular song: first, you git **royalties.** Let me ask you, how much you sell that song for in the first place? Fifty dollars? A hundred, I say. And, no royalties from it yet, right? Right. Well, when we buy up all of them records you gonna git royalties. And that's gonna make all them race record shops sit up and take notice of Gracie Mae Still. And they gonna push all them records of yourn they got. And you no doubt will become one of the big name colored recording artists. And then we can offer you another five hundred dollars for letting us do all this for you. And by God you'll be sittin' pretty! You can go out and buy you the kind of outfit a star should have. Plenty sequins and yards of red satin.

I had done unlocked the screen when I saw I could get some more money out of him. Now I held it wide open while he squeezed through the opening between me and the door. He whipped out another piece of paper and I signed it.

He sort of trotted out to the car and slid in beside Traynor, whose head was back against the seat. They swung around in a u-turn in front of the house and then they was gone.

J.T. was putting his shirt on when I got back to the bedroom. Yankees beat the Orioles 10-6, he said. I believe I'll drive out to Paschal's pond and go fishing. Wanta go?

While I was putting on my pants J.T. was holding the two checks.

I'm real proud of a woman that can make cash money without leavin' home, he said. And I said *Umph*. Because we met on the road with me singing in first one little low-life **jook** after another, making ten dollars a night for myself if I was lucky, and sometimes bringin' home nothing but my life. And J.T. just loved them times. The way I was fast and flashy and always on the go from one town to another. He loved the way my singin' made the dirt farmers cry like babies and the womens shout Honey, hush! But that's mens. They loves any style to which you can get 'em accustomed.

1956

My little grandbaby called me one night on the phone: Little Mama, Little Mama, there's a white man on the television singing one of your songs! Turn on channel 5.

Lord, if it wasn't Traynor. Still looking half asleep from the neck up, but kind of awake in a nasty way from the waist down. He wasn't doing too bad with my song either, but it wasn't just the song the people in the audience was screeching and screaming over, it was the nasty little jerk he was doing from the waist down.

Well, Lord have mercy, I said, listening to him. If I'da closed my eyes, it could have been me. He had followed every turning of my voice, side streets, avenues, red lights, train crossings and all. It give me a chill.

Everywhere I went I heard Traynor singing my song, and all the little white girls just eating it up. I never has so many ponytails switched across my line of vision in my life. They was so *proud*. He was a *genius*.

Well, all that year I was trying to lose weight anyway and that and high blood pressure and sugar kept me pretty well occupied. Traynor had made a smash from a song of mine, I still had seven hundred dollars of the original one thousand dollars in the bank, and I felt if I could just bring my weight down, life would be sweet.

1957

I lost ten pounds in 1956. That's what I give myself for Christmas. And J.T. and me and the children and their friends and grandkids of all description had just finished dinner—over which I had put on nine and half of my lost ten—when who should appear at the front door but Traynor. Little Mama, Little Mama! It's that white man who sings ____ ____ ____. The children didn't call it my song anymore. Nobody did. It was funny how that happened.

Traynor and the deacon had bought up all my records, true, but on his record he had put "written by Gracie Mae Still." But that was just another name on the label, like "produced by Apex Records."

On the TV he was inclined to dress like the deacon told him. But now he looked presentable.

Merry Christmas, said he.

And same to you, Son.

I don't know why I called him Son. Well, one way or another they're all our sons. The only requirement is that they be younger than us. But then again, Traynor seemed to be aging by the minute.

You looks tired, I said. Come on in and have a glass of Christmas cheer.

J.T. ain't never in his life been able to act decent to a white man he wasn't working for, but he poured Traynor a glass of bourbon and water, then he took all the children and grandkids and friends and whatnot out to the den. After while I heard Traynor's voice singing the song, coming from the stereo console. It was just the kind of Christmas present my kids would consider cute.

I looked at Traynor, **complicit.** But he looked like it was the last thing in the world he wanted to hear. His head was pitched forward over his lap, his hands holding his glass and his elbows on his knees.

I done sung that song seem like a million times this year, he said. I sung it on the Grand Ole Opry, I sung it on the Ed Sullivan show. I sung it on Mike Douglas, I sung it at the Cotton Bowl, the Orange Bowl. I sung it at Festivals. I sung it at Fairs. I sung it overseas in Rome, Italy, and once in a submarine *underseas.* I've sung it and sung it, and I'm making forty thousand dollars a day offa it, and you know what, I don't have the faintest notion what that song means.

Whatchumean, what do it mean? It mean what it says. All I could think was: These suckers is making forty thousand a *day* offa my song and now they gonna come back and try to **swindle** me out of the original thousand.

It's just a song, I said. Cagey. When you fool around with a lot of no count mens you sing a bunch of 'em. I shrugged.

Oh, he said. Well. He started brightening up. I just come by to tell you that I think you are a great singer.

He didn't blush, saying that. Just said it straight out.

And I brought you a little Christmas present too. Now you take this little box and you hold it until I drive off. Then you take it outside under that first streetlight back up the street aways in front of that green house. Then you open the box and see . . . Well, just *see.*

What had come over this boy, I wondered, holding the box. I looked out the window in time to see another white man come up and get in the car with him and then two more cars full of white mens start out behind him. They was all in long black cars that looked like a funeral procession.

Little Mama, Little Mama, what it is? One of my grandkids come running up and started pulling at the box. It was wrapped in gay Christmas paper—the thick, rich kind that it's hard to picture folks making just to throw away.

J.T. and the rest of the crowd followed me out the house, up the street to the streetlight and in front of the green house. Nothing was there but somebody's gold-grilled white Cadillac. Brandnew and most distracting. We got to looking at it so I till I almost forgot the little box in my hand. While the others were busy making 'miration I carefully took off the paper and ribbon and folded them up and put them in my pants pocket. What should I see but a pair of genuine solid gold caddy keys.

Dangling the keys in front of everybody's nose, I unlocked the caddy, motioned for J.T. to git on the other side, and us didn't come back home for two days.

1960

Well, the boy was sure nuff famous by now. He was still a mite shy of twenty but already they was calling him the Emperor of Rock and Roll.

Then what should happened but the draft.

Well, says J.T. There goes all this Emperor of Rock and Roll business.

But even in the army the womens was on him like white on rice. We watched it on the News.

Dear Gracie Mae (he wrote from Germany),

How are you? Fine I hope as this leaves me doing real well. Before I come in the army I was gaining a lot of weight and gitting jittery from making those dumb movies. But now I exercise and eat right and get plenty of rest. I'm more awake than I been in ten years.

I wonder if you are writing any more songs?

Sincerely,

Traynor

I wrote him back:

Dear Son,

We is all fine in the Lord's good grace and hope this finds you the same. J.T. and me be out all times of the day and night in that car you give me—which you know you didn't have to do. Oh, and I do appreciate the mink and the new self-cleaning oven. But if you send anymore stuff to eat from Germany I'm going to have to open up a store in the neighborhood just to get rid of it. Really, we have more than enough of everything. The Lord is good to us and we don't know Want.

Glad to here you is well and gitting your right rest. There ain't nothing like exercising to help that along. J.T. and me work some part of every day that we don't go fishing in the garden.

Well, so long Soldier.

Sincerely,

Gracie Mae

He wrote:

Dear Gracie Mae,

I hope you and J.T. like that automatic power tiller I had one of the stores back home send you. I went through a mountain of catalogs looking for it—I wanted something that even a woman could use.

I've been thinking about writing some songs of my own but every time I finish one it don't seem to be about nothing I've actually lived myself. My agent keeps sending me other people's songs but they just sound ***mooney.*** *I can hardly git through 'em without gagging.*

Everybody still loves that song of yours. They ask me all the time what do I think it means, really. I mean, they want to know just what I want to know. Where out of your life did it come from?

Sincerely,

Traynor

1968

I didn't see the boy for seven years. No. Eight. Because just about everybody was dead when I saw him again. Malcolm X, King, the president and his brother, and even J.T. J.T. died of a head cold. It just settled in his head like a block of ice, he said, and nothing we did moved it until one day he just leaned out the bed and died.

His good friend Horace helped me put him away, and then about a year later Horace and me started going together. We was sitting out on the front porch swing one summer night, dusk-dark, and I saw this great procession of lights winding to a stop.

Holy Toledo! Said Horace. (He's got a real sexy voice like Ray Charles.) Look *at* it. He meant the long line of flashy cars and the white men in white summer suits jumping out on the drivers' sides and standing at attention. With wings they could pass for angels, with hoods they could be the Klan.

Traynor comes waddling up the walk.

And suddenly I know what it is he could pass for. An Arab like the ones you see in storybooks. Plump and soft and with never a care about weight. Because with so much money, who cares? Traynor is almost dressed like someone from a storybook too. He has on, I swear, about ten necklaces. Two set of bracelets on his arms, at least one ring on every finger, and some kind of shining buckles on his shoes, so when he walks you get quite a few twinkling lights.

Gracie Mae, he says, coming up to give me a hug. J.T.

I explain that J.T. passed. That this is Horace.

Horace, he says, puzzled but polite, sort of rocking back on his heels, Horace.

That's it for Horace. He goes in the house and don't come back.

Looks like you and me is gained a few, I say.

He laughs. The first time I ever heard him laugh. It don't sound much like a laugh and I can't swear that it's better than no laugh a'tall.

He's gitting fat for sure, but he is still slim compared to me. I'll never see three hundred pounds again and I've just about said (excuse me) fuck it. I got to thinking about it one day an' I thought: aside from the fact that they say it is unhealthy, my fat ain't never been no trouble. Mens have always loved me. My kids ain't never complained. Plus, they's fat. And fat like I is I looks distinguished. You see me coming and know somebody's *there.*

Gracie Mae, he says. I've come with a personal invitation to you to my house tomorrow for dinner. He laughed. What did it sound like? I couldn't place it. See them men out there? He asked me. I am sick and tired of eating with them. They don't never have nothing to talk about. That's why I eat so much. But if you come to dinner tomorrow we can talk about the old days. You can tell me about the farm I bought you.

I sold it, I said.

You did?

Yeah, I said, I did. Just cause I said I liked to exercise by working in the garden didn't mean I wanted five hundred acres! Anyhow, I'm a city girl now. Raised in the country it's true. Dirt poor—the whole bit—but that's all behind me now.

Oh well, he said, I didn't mean to offend you.

We sat a few minutes listening to the crickets.

Then he said: You wrote that song while you was still on the farm, didn't you, or was it right after you left?

You had somebody spying on me? I asked.

You and Bessie Smith got into a fight over it once, he said.

You *is* been spying on me!

But I don't know what the fight was about, he said. Just like I don't know what happened to your second husband. Your first one died in the Texas electric chair. Did you know that? Your third one beat you up, stole your touring costumes and your car and retired with a **chorine** to Tuskegee. He laughed. He's still there.

I had been mad, but suddenly I calmed down. Traynor was talking very dreamily. It was dark but seems like I could tell his eyes weren't right. It was like some*thing* was sitting there talking to me but not necessarily with a person behind it.

You gave up on marrying and seem happier for it. He laughed again. I married but it never went like it was supposed to. I never could squeeze any of my own life either into it or out of it. It was like singing somebody else's record. I copied the way it was sposed to be *exactly* but I never knew what marriage meant.

I bought her a diamond ring as big as your fist. I bought her clothes. I built her a mansion. But right away she didn't want the boys to stay there. Said they smoked up the bottom floor. Hell, there were *five* floors.

No need to grieve, I said. No need to. Plenty more where she come from.

He perked up. That's part of what that song means, ain't it? No need to grieve. Whatever it is, there's plenty more down the line.

I never really believed that way back when I wrote that song, I said. It was all bluffing then. The trick is to live long enough to put your young bluffs to use. Now if I was to sing that song today I'd tear it up. 'Cause I done lived long enough to know it's *true.* Them words could hold me up.

I ain't lived that long, he said.

Look like you on your way, I said. I don't know why, but the boy seemed to need some encouraging. And I don't know, seem like one way or another you talk to rich white folks and you end up reassuring *them.* But what the hell, by now I feel something for the boy. I wouldn't be in his bed all alone in the middle of the night for nothing. Couldn't be nothing worse than being famous the world over for something you don't even understand. That's what I tried to tell Bessie. She wanted the same song. Overheard me practicing it one day, said, with her hands on her hips: Gracie Mae, I'ma sing your song tonight. I *likes* it.

Your lips be too swole to sing, I said. She was mean and she was strong, but I trounced her.

Ain't you famous enough with your own stuff? I said. Leave mine alone. Later on, she thanked me. By then she was Miss Bessie Smith to the World, and I was still Miss Grace Mae Nobody from Notasulga.

The next day all three limousines arrived to pick me up. Five cars and twelve bodyguards. Horace picked that morning to start painting the kitchen.

Don't paint the kitchen, fool, I said. The only reason that dumb boy of ours is going to show me his mansion is because he intends to present us with a new house.

What you gonna do with it? He asked me, standing there in his shirtsleeves stirring the paint.

Sell it. Give it to the children. Live in it on weekends. It don't matter what I do. He sure don't care.

Horace just stood there shaking his head. Mama you sure looks *good,* he says. Wake me up when you git back.

Fool, I say, and pat my wig in front of the mirror.

The boy's house is something else. First you come to this mountain, and then you commence to drive and drive up this road that's lined with magnolias.

Do magnolias grow on mountains? I was wondering. And you come to lakes and you come to ponds and you come to deer and you come up on some sheep. And I figured these two is sposed to represent England and Wales. Or something out of Europe. And you just keep on coming to stuff. And it's all pretty. Only the man driving my car don't look at nothing but the road. Fool. And then *finally,* after all this time, you begin to go up the driveway. And there's more magnolias—only they're not in such good shape. It's sort of cool up this high and I don't think they're gonna make it. And then I see this building that looks like if it had a name it would be The Tara Hotel. Columns and steps and outdoor chandeliers and rocking chairs. Rocking chairs? Well, and there's the boy on the steps dressed in a dark green satin jacket like you see folks wearing on TV late at night, and he looks sort of like a fat dracula with all that house rising behind him, and standing beside him there's this little white vision of loveliness that he introduces as his wife.

He's nervous when he introduces us and he says to her: This is Gracie Mae Still, I want you to know me. I mean . . . and she gives him a look that would fry meat.

Won't you come in, Gracie Mae, she says, and that's the last I see of her.

He fishes around for something to say or do and decides to escort me to the kitchen. We go through the entry and the parlor and the breakfast room and the dining room and the servants' passage and finally get there. The first thing I notice is that, altogether, there are five stoves. He looks about to introduce me to one.

Wait a minute, I say. Kitchens don't do nothing for me. Let's go sit on the front porch.

Well, we hike back and we sit in the rocking chairs rocking until dinner.

Gracie Mae, he says down the table, taking a piece of fried chicken from the woman standing over him, I got a little surprise for you.

It's a house, ain't it? I ask, spearing a **chitlin.**

You're getting *spoiled,* he says. And the way he says *spoiled* sounds funny. He slurs it. It sounds like his tongue is too thick for his mouth. Just that quick he's finished the chicken and is now eating chitlins *and* a pork chop. *Me* spoiled, I'm thinking.

I already got a house. Horace is right this minute painting the kitchen. I bought that house. My kids feel comfortable in that house.

But this one I bought you is just like mine. Only a little smaller.

I still don't need no house. And anyway who would clean it?

He looks surprised.

Really, I think, some peoples advance *so* slowly.

I hadn't thought of that. But what the hell, I'll get you somebody to live in.

I don't want other folks living 'round me. Makes me nervous.

You *don't?* It *do?*

What I want to wake up and see folks I don't even know for?

He just sits there downtable staring at me. Some of that feelings is in the song, ain't it? Not the words, the *feeling*. What I want to wake up and see folks I don't even know for? But I see twenty folks a day I don't even know, including my wife.

This food wouldn't be bad to wake up to though, I said. The boy had found the genius of corn bread.

He looked at me real hard. He laughed. Short. They want what you got but they don't want you. They wan't what I got only it ain't mine. That's what makes 'em so hungry for me when I sing. They getting the flavor of something but they ain't getting the thing itself. They like a pack of hound dogs trying to gobble up a scent.

You talking 'bout your fans?

Right. Right. He says.

Don't worry 'bout your fans, I say. They don't know their asses from a hole in the ground. I doubt there's a honest one in the bunch.

That's the point. Dammit, that's the point! He hits the table with his fist. It's so solid it don't even **quiver.** You need a honest audience! You can't have folks that's just gonna lie right back to you.

Yeah, I say, it was small compared to yours, but I had one. It would have been worth my life to try to sing 'em somebody else's stuff that I didn't know nothing about.

He must have passed a buzzer under the table. One of his flunkies zombies up.

Git Johnny Carson, he says.

On the phone? asks the zombie.

On the phone, says Traynor, what you think I mean, git him offa the front porch? Move your ass.

So two weeks later we's on the Johnny Carson show.

Traynor is all corseted down nice and looks a bit fat but mostly good. And all the women that grew up on him and my song squeal and squeal. Traynor says: The lady who wrote my first hit record is here with us tonight, and she's agreed to sing it for all of us, just like she sung it forty-five years ago. Ladies and Gentlemen, the great Gracie Mae Still!

Well, I had tried to lose a couple of pounds my own self, but failing that I had me a very big dress made. So I sort of rolls over next to Traynor, who is dwarfted by me, so that when he puts his arm around back of me to try to hug me it looks funny to the audience and they laugh.

I can see that this pisses him off. But I smile out there at 'em. Imagine squealing for twenty years and not knowing why you're squealing? No more sense of endings and beginnings than hogs.

It don't matter, Son, I say. Don't fret none over me.

I commence to sing. And I sound—wonderful. Being able to sing good ain't all about having a good singing voice a'tall. A good singing voice helps. But when you come up in the Hard Shell Baptist church like I did you understand early that the fellow that sings is the singer. Them that waits for programs and arrangements and letters from home is just good voices occupying body space.

So there I am singing my own song, my own way. And give it all I got and enjoy every minute of it. When I finish Traynor is standing up clapping and clapping and beaming at first me and then the audience like I'm his mama for true.

The audience claps politely for about two seconds.

Traynor looks disgusted.

He comes over and tries to hug me again. The audience laughs.

Johnny Carson looks at us like we both weird.

Traynor is mad as hell. He's supposed to sing something called a love ballad. But instead he takes the mike, turns to me and says: Now see if my imitation still holds up. He goes into the same song, *our* song, I think, looking out at his flaky audience. And he sings it just the way he always did. My voice, my tone, my inflection, everything. But he forgets a couple of lines. Even before he's finished the **matronly** squeals begin.

He sits down next to me looking whipped.

It don't matter, Son, I say patting his hand. You don't even know those people. Try to make the people you know happy.

Is that in the song? he asks.

Maybe, I say.

1977

For a few years I hear from him, then nothing. But trying to lose weight takes all the attention I got to spare. I finally faced up to the fact that my fat is the hurt I don't admit, not even to myself, and that I been trying to bury it from the day I was born. But also when you git real old, to tell the truth, it ain't as pleasant. It gits lumpy and slack. Yuck. So one day I said to Horace, I'ma git this shit offa me.

And he fell in with the program like he always try to do and Lord such a procession of salads and cottage cheese and fruit juice!

One night I dreamed Traynor had split up with his fifteenth wife. He said: *You meet 'em for no reason. You date 'em for no reason. You marry 'em for no reason. I do it all but I swear it's just like somebody else doing it. I feel like I can't remember Life.*

The boy's in trouble, I said to Horace.

You've always said that, he said.

I have?

Yeah. You always said he looked asleep. You can't sleep through life if you wants to live it.

You not such a fool after all, I said, pushing myself up with my cane and hobbling over to where he was. Let me sit down on your lap, I said, while this salad I ate takes effect.

In the morning we heard Traynor was dead. Some said fat, some said heart, some said alcohol, some said drugs. One of the children called from Detroit. Them dumb fans of his is on a crying rampage, she said. You just ought to turn on the t.v.

But I didn't want to see 'em. They was crying and crying and didn't even know what they was crying for. One day this is going to be a pitiful country, I thought.

Glossary for "Nineteen Fifty-Five"

de·ci·bel (dĕs'ə-bəl, -bĕl')

n. Abbr. **dB**

A unit used to express relative difference in power or intensity, usually between two acoustic or electric signals, equal to ten times the common logarithm of the ratio of the two levels.

[deci- + bel.]

Cre·ole (krē'ōl')

n.

1. A person of European descent born in the West Indies or Spanish America.
2. a. A person descended from or culturally related to the original French settlers of the southern United States, especially Louisiana.
   b. The French dialect spoken by these people.
3. A person descended from or culturally related to the Spanish and Portuguese settlers of the Gulf States.
4. often **creole** A person of mixed Black and European ancestry who speaks a creolized language, especially one based on French or Spanish.
5. A Black slave born in the Americas as opposed to one brought from Africa.
6. **creole** A creolized language.
7. Haitian Creole.

adj.

1. Of, relating to, or characteristic of the Creoles.
2. **creole** Cooked with a spicy sauce containing tomatoes, onions, and peppers: *shrimp creole; creole cuisine.*

[French créole, from Spanish criollo, *person native to a locality*, from Portuguese crioulo, diminutive of cria, *person raised in the house, especially a servant*, from criar, *to bring up*, from Latin creāre, *to beget*.]

roy·al·ty (roi'əl-tē)

n. pl. **roy·al·ties**

1. a. A person of royal rank or lineage.
   b. Monarchs and their families considered as a group.
2. The lineage or rank of a monarch.
3. The power, status, or authority of a monarch.
4. Royal quality or bearing.
5. A kingdom or possession ruled by a monarch.
6. A right or prerogative of the crown, as that of receiving a percentage of the proceeds from mines in the royal domain.

7. a. The granting of a right by a monarch to a corporation or an individual to exploit specified natural resources.
   b. The payment for such a right.
8. a. A share paid to a writer or composer out of the proceeds resulting from the sale or performance of his or her work.
   b. A share in the proceeds paid to an inventor or a proprietor for the right to use his or her invention or services.
9. A share of the profit or product reserved by the grantor, especially of an oil or mining lease. Also called **override.**

juke' also **jook** (jo͞ok, jo͝ok) *Southeastern U.S.*

n.

A roadside or rural establishment offering liquor, dancing, and often gambling and prostitution. Also called **juke house, juke joint**.

intr. v. **juked,** also **jooked juk·ing, jook·ing jukes, jooks**

1. To play dance music, especially in a juke.
2. To dance, especially in a juke or to the music of a jukebox.

[Probably from Gullah juke, joog, *disorderly, wicked, of West African origin*; akin to Wolof dzug, *to live wickedly*, and Bambara dzugu, *wicked*.]

Regional Note: Gullah, the English-based Creole language spoken by people of African ancestry off the coast of Georgia and South Carolina, retains a number of words from the West African languages brought over by slaves. One such word is *juke*, "bad, wicked, disorderly," the probable source of the English word *juke*. Used originally in Florida and then chiefly in the Southeastern states, *juke* (also appearing in the compound *juke joint*) was an African-American word meaning a roadside drinking establishment that offers cheap drinks, food, and music for dancing and often doubles as a brothel. "To juke" is to dance, particularly at a juke joint or to the music of a jukebox whose name, no longer regional and having lost the connotation of sleaziness, contains the same word.

com·plic·it (kəm-plĭs'ĭt)

adj.

Associated with or participating in a questionable act or a crime; having complicity: *newspapers complicit with the propaganda arm of a dictatorship.*

[Back-formation from **complicity.**]

swin·dle (swĭn'dl)

v. **swin·dled, swin·dling, swin·dles**

v. tr.

1. To cheat or defraud of money or property.
2. To obtain by fraudulent means: *swindled money from the company.*

v. intr.

To practice fraud as a means of obtaining money or property.

n.

The act or an instance of swindling.

[Back-formation from swindler, *one who swindles*, from German Schwindler, *giddy person, cheat*, from schwindeln, *to be dizzy, swindle*, from Middle High German, from Old High German swintilōn, frequentative of swintan, *to disappear*.]

swin'dler *n.*

moon·y (mooney) (mōō'nē)
adj. **moon·i·er, moon·i·est**

1. Of or suggestive of the moon or moonlight.
2. Moonlit.
3. Dreamy in mood or nature; absent-minded.

cho·rine (kôr'ēn', kōr'-)
n.

A chorus girl.
[chor(us) + -ine[1]]

chide (chīd)
v. **chid·ed,** or **chid** (chĭd) **chid·ed,** or **chid** or **chid·den** (chĭd'n) **chid·ing, chides**
v. tr.

To scold mildly so as to correct or improve; reprimand: *chided the boy for his sloppiness.*

v. intr.

To express disapproval.

[Middle English chiden, from Old English cīdan, from cīd, *strife, contention.*]
chid'er *n.*
chid'ing·ly *adv.*

chit·ter·lings also **chit·lins** or **chit·lings** (chĭt'lĭnz)
pl.n.

The small intestines of pigs, especially when cooked and eaten as food.

[From Middle English chiterling, probably diminutive of Old English *cieter, *intestines.*]

quiv·er' (kwĭv'ər)
intr. v. **quiv·ered, quiv·er·ing, quiv·ers**

To shake with a slight, rapid, tremulous movement.

n.

The act or motion of quivering.

[Middle English quiveren, perhaps from quiver, *nimble* (from Old English cwifer-.)]
quiv'er·ing·ly *adv.*
quiv'er·y *adj.*

ma·tron (mā'trən)
n.

1. A married woman or a widow, especially a mother of dignity, mature age, and established social position.
2. A woman who acts as a supervisor or monitor in a public institution, such as a school, hospital, or prison.

[Middle English matrone, from Old French, from Latin mātrōna, from māter, mātr-, *mother.*]

ma'tron·al *adj.*
ma'tron·li·ness *n.*
ma'tron·ly *adv. & adj.*

Reading Comprehension

Answer the following questions about the short story by Alice Walker.

Word Meaning

Using the glossary, select the entry that best completes the sentences below.

1. As a result of the movement of native dwellers of New Orleans, the cooking style called __________ has entered the American cooking scene in every corner of the country.
2. Hip hop and other recording artists receive their income from the __________ earned from the CDs they make and the presence of their songs in advertising and other media.
3. The elderly grandmother __________ her grandson for his participation in the recent disturbances at his high school.
4. The young lovers were so __________ in their personal behavior toward each other that their peers were sickened by being around them.
5. Many computer scams attempt to __________ Americans of their money by encouraging them to invest dollars in promised wealth from overseas business deals.
6. Many of today's stand-out Broadway singing stars gained their experience as __________ in off-Broadway productions.
7. The constant use of an iPod, a common practice among college students as they walk across campuses, is controversial because the volume of the instrument increases the __________ beyond the acceptable levels for safe hearing.
8. The young man arrested as an accomplice to methamphetamine production testified that he was in no way __________ with the accused drug kingpin who was already sentenced for his crime.

Literal Meaning

Mark the letter of the option that best answers the statements below.

1. When the deacon visits Grace Mae Still for the first time, he is trying to do what?
   a. Buy an old car he sees parked in the driveway
   b. Visit with the couple he knows from years past
   c. Purchase the rights to a song that he wants Traynor to record
   d. Find a friend for Traynor to visit when he is on the road singing
2. Who is the narrator of the short story?
   a. The deacon
   b. The singer Traynor
   c. Grace Mae Still
   d. An unnamed storyteller
3. What is contained in the box that Traynor gives Gracie Mae as a Christmas present?
   a. A record of her song sung by him
   b. A key to a car parked up the street under a streetlight

   c. A new dress made with sequins and satin
   d. A juke box
4. How does Walker achieve coherence and unity in this short story?
   a. By repeating Gracie Mae's attempts to lose weight
   b. By telling about Traynor's generous gift giving
   c. By expressing Traynor's search for the meaning behind the words of Gracie Mae's song, his first hit song
   d. All of the above
5. The story "1955" parallels the life of what singing icon?
   a. Mahalia Jackson
   b. Elvis Presley
   c. Lionel Richie
   d. Bing Crosby

Interpretive Meaning

Complete the questions with the response that best answers the statement.

1. Why does Traynor continue to visit Gracie Mae and bestow gifts upon her?
   a. He is lonely for his roots in the Deep South and the life he knew before his fame.
   b. He feels guilty for recording the song she had written.
   c. He has so much money to spend and no one else with whom to share it.
   d. He wants Gracie Mae to enjoy his success.
2. What is the tone of the essay? (Mark all that apply.)
   a. Humorous
   b. Informative
   c. Argumentative
   d. Sarcastic
3. If a reader were to classify the music represented in the story according to the details implied, it would belong to what category?
   a. Hip hop
   b. Jazz
   c. Rock and Roll
   d. Country
4. How does Walker convey the geographic roots of the singer Traynor and Gracie Mae Still?
   a. She uses specific place names in the story.
   b. She depicts life activities done only in certain parts of the country.
   c. She uses dialectical language in the dialogue.
   d. She states directly the location of the singers.
5. Why does Alice Walker write the story in the present tense?
   a. Present tense is her trademark in the writing world.
   b. Walker believes that stories should be presented in the present tense.
   c. Present tense illustrates the nearness in the timing of the events of the story.
   d. Walker is most comfortable in writing in the present tense.

6. Why does Traynor get angry during his appearance on the *Johnny Carson Show*?
   a. He feels the audience members are disrespectful toward Gracie Mae.
   b. He thinks they are laughing at her weight and his physical decline.
   c. He thinks Johnny Carson does not understand his motives for appearing on the show with Gracie Mae.
   d. All of the above
7. Why does Walker end her story with the statement that "One day this is going to be a pitiful country . . ."?
   a. Walker, in the character of Gracie Mae, thinks the tears shed for a singing icon should be reserved only for national tragedies.
   b. Walker is making a statement about the current overwhelming interest in popular culture icons.
   c. Walker believes that Traynor's death from health problems that could have been controlled is tragic but not so newsworthy.
   d. All of the above
8. Using Walker's short story, write a complete and concise timeline of the events in the story.

   ____

   ____

9. List several dialectical words or phrases used in the story and then explain their meanings in Standard English.

   ____

   ____

Score: Number correct _____ out of _____

Writing Assignments

1. Journal

Summary

Summarize the plot of the short story in one or two paragraphs. Include the setting, the characters, the conflict, and the resolution.

Reaction

Write a reaction to "Nineteen Fifty-Five" in which you address the appeal of the short story and comment on the content.

2. Paragraph

Write a paragraph analyzing the development of the characters in the short story.

3. Paragraph to Essay

Expand the paragraph written in assignment two to an essay by analyzing two other elements of the short story. Analyze one element in each body paragraph so that you will have three body paragraphs. Add an introductory paragraph and a concluding paragraph.

4. *Essay*

Write a classification essay on one of the topics below.

a. Types of _____________ (country music, rock, sports) fans
b. Reactions to fame
c. Types of fame
d. Personality types

REFLECTIVE ASSIGNMENTS

1. Explain the quotation by Bernstein at the beginning of the chapter. Choose a favorite artist and explain how the works of this artist "name the unnamable and communicate the unknowable."
2. Interview several students outside your class and ask them to interpret the meaning of each idiomatic expression. Compare and summarize your findings.
3. Review the short story "1955" and the analysis you did of the main characters. Reflect on the personality type of the main characters Traynor and Gracie Mae Still. What type of characters do Traynor and Gracie Mae Still represent? Write a paragraph explaining your answer.

INTERNET FIELD TRIPS—READING AND WRITING ASSIGNMENTS

1. Find out more about Walt Whitman and his contributions to American literature by exploring the Web sites listed below. After reading the material, write a paragraph classifying the types of subjects Whitman addressed in his poetry.
   - http://www.poets.org
   - whitmanarchive.org
2. Search the Internet for information about Alice Walker. After reading about her life and career, write a paragraph about the types of subjects she addresses in her writing. Begin with these Web sites.
   - http://womenshistory.about.com/library/bio/blbio_walker_alice.htm
   - http://en.wikipedia.org/wiki/Alice_Walker
   - http://www.library.csi.cuny.edu/dept/history/lavender/walker.
3. Read more about genres of music by exploring these Web sites.
   - http://library.music.indiana.edu/music_resources/genres.html
   - http://www.multcolib.org/homework/musichc.html

   From your research, plan a classification essay on types of music with which you are not familiar. Write a sentence outline for the essay, an introductory paragraph, and a concluding paragraph. Your outline should show that you understand the format of a classification essay, and introductory and concluding paragraphs should show your skills for writing introductory and concluding paragraphs.

Films to View

A Hard Day's Night (directed by Richard Lester, 1964)
The Piano Player (directed by Jean-Pierre Roux, 2002)
Selena (directed by Gregory Nelson, 1997)
Hustle and Flow (directed by Craig Brewer, 2005)
Great Balls of Fire (directed by Jim McBride, 1989)
The Blues Brothers (directed by John Landis, 1999)
The Jazz Singer (directed by Alan Crosland, 1927)
Lady Sings the Blues (directed by Sidney J. Furie, 1972)
Ray (directed by Taylor Hackford, 2004)

Writing assignments are based on *Ray* directed by Taylor Hackford and written by Taylor Hackford and James R. White.

1. The tagline for *Ray* is "The extraordinary life story of Ray Charles. A man who fought harder and went farther than anyone thought possible." Write a paragraph explaining the significance of the tagline to the movie.
2. From the information gleaned from the movie, write a character analysis of Ray Charles.
3. Write a paragraph classifying the types of problems Charles faced and overcame. Using your paragraph as a starting point, develop the ideas in the paragraph into an essay.
4. Write a paragraph classifying the types of music Charles performed.
5. Write an outline of a plot for a movie based on the life of one of your favorite performing artists. In the outline, include characters, setting, conflict, resolution, and theme.

Summary of Unit 6—American Music—Classification

Read the student essay entitled "Music of the Heart" by Delanna Sterling. Analyze it for its content, its organization, and its mechanics. Then, in the Summary of Unit 6 on page 311, complete the column on the right with your responses. Apply the information learned in Unit 6.

Music of the Heart

Today the most unlikely of people are linked together by a huge phenomenon. Although it has been around for centuries music still links people's lives together. It links the overworked, the under paid, the rich, the poor, the working class, the upper class and everyone in between. Music has soul and gets to the very heart of every human on the earth, who knows maybe the Martians are rockin' out with all of us on earth. Humans are all linked to music, but there are so many styles, country, rock and roll, punk, rap, hip-hop, etc. to name a few. Different genres of music attract different groups of people and formulate similar ideas; some of the most popular types are rockers of the 60's, 70's, and 80's, the new age of hip-hop, and the all around listeners of country music.

Rockers like the Rolling Stones, AC/DC, Pink Floyd, Areosmith, and Ozzy Osborne are responsible for the classic rock we know today. These four bands and individual brought together a new style of music and a new style of fans. These people were the people that disobeyed their parents, sneaking out at night, and people who just love to rock. They took us were we had never been before, outside of the box, they showed the world that they were going to do what ever they wanted. With that, they brought their fans behind them to think the same thing. The generation that listened to the four and Ozzy carry that same arrogance today. The men and women that once listened to them and many others learned to take charge and do what was good for themselves not just for their parents, but also for their livelihood.

New age hip-hop is one of the most listened to and recorded in 2005. Hip-hop brings together people with dreams, big dreams. Music is not just a blue print. Music is what you feel. Hip-hop proves this true. Why? Hip-hop brings together people of all types, white, black, Hispanic, and people all over the world. This music can give people a new feeling about music. A feeling that anyone can be involved, no color, no stereotype are pulled into play. To many this should spark a nerve to think you can do anything, anywhere, anytime, anyplace, not because you have to but because you can and you can be proud of it.

Like hip-hop and rock and roll country is an expression of self and self-confidence. Although the styles are extremely different, the message is the same. Now if this were just a few years ago I would say I do not know one African-American country artist, but now there is, and his name is Cowboy Troy. Country music brings together the down home farms boys and the Daisy Dukes of the south and all over the United States but now the Cowboy Troy is on the country scene.

Summary of Unit 6

1. The thesis of the essay is	1.
2. The main tense in the classification is	2.
3. Three transitions used include	3.
4. The tone of this essay is	4.
5. The purpose of this essay is to	5.
6. The writer concludes by	6.
7. The reader can infer that the writer	7.
8. Traits of classification present in the essay are	8.
9. Three mechanical errors include	9.
10. This essay is missing	10.

Unit 7

American Lifestyle

If you are lucky enough to find a way of life you love, you have to find the courage to live it.

—John Irving

Many tourists flock to communities such as Chinatown. How do these pockets of diversity affect today's American lifestyle?

The military community is an important part of the American lifestyle. What effects do long deployments have on American families?

Purpose of Unit:

- *To understand the pattern of causal analysis as it relates to reading comprehension and writing*

Idioms for American Lifestyles

Review the American idioms below. Discuss their meaning. Apply these idioms to lifestyles in America and to what you consider to be "an American lifestyle."

Bases loaded	Play havoc
Let's play ball.	It never rains but it pours.
Three strikes you're out.	Upset the apple cart
From Missouri	Walk into a lion's den
New York minute	Drive a hard bargain
Hot potato	Ballpark figure
Leave well enough alone.	Switch gears
Miss the boat	Can of worms

Cause and Effect: Points to Consider

A causal analysis essay is used to explain why an event or problem occurs and what the effects or consequences of the event are. The critical thinking skills needed for reading and writing causal analyses are the same skills used to solve personal, community, national, and even international problems. If a college student fails an exam, he asks why so that he can correct the situation. The **immediate** cause (the cause closest to the situation) may be that he did not study for the test, but a **secondary** cause (the cause further removed from the situation, but important) may be that he is working too many hours and taking an overload of classes. A **remote** cause may be that he is not interested in the subject and is only taking the course because his parents want him to take it. Further, the immediate effects of the situation will be that he must change his study habits or readjust his work schedule. Long term or remote effects may include confronting his parents or rethinking his major. He might also be unprepared for future classes, or he might postpone taking other classes. Businesses, communities, and governments analyze problems and search for solutions in the same way. What are the immediate causes for a lack of customers, crime in neighborhoods, leaks in security, and lack of trust? What are the long-term causes? What are the effects, both long term and short term? Regardless of the topic, you should look for reasons (causes) and results (effects). When reading and writing causal analyses, consider the following points.

PURPOSE

A causal analysis essay or paragraph evaluates reasons (causes) and consequences/results (effects) of a situation or problem. A causal analysis may inform or persuade. Most importantly, a causal analysis should enable the reader and the writer to do the critical thinking needed to solve a problem.

ORGANIZATION AND PLAN

One of the most practical ways of organizing an essay is through causal analysis. When reading or writing a causal analysis, you must first decide if the focus will be on the causes, on the effects, or a combination of the two. A typical causal analysis passage in a textbook or a newspaper often will have a topic sentence that states a problem. The article or information following the statement frequently will focus on either the causes or the effects of the problem. Read the following excerpt from the article "Violent Crime Rate in America Continues Steep Decline," which appeared in *USA Today* on 9/09/2002. Notice how the headlines and the first sentence state the situation, and the following sentences and then the article focus on the reasons for the decline.

> **VIOLENT CRIME RATE IN AMERICA CONTINUES STEEP DECLINE**
>
> The number of people who were victims of all violent crimes except murder fell by 9% in 2001, sending the crime rate to its lowest level since it was first tracked in 1973, the government reported Sunday. The decline was due primarily to a record low number of reported assaults, the most common form of violent crime.

When you write, the same principle applies. You should state a problem or a situation, in this case the decrease in crime rate, and then you should focus on the reasons, the effects, or, occasionally, on both. In this case, the focus is on the low number of reported assaults.

Order of Causes and Effects

One way to list the causes and effects is according to importance, leaving the most important cause or effect last or, as in the newspaper article, beginning with the most important. You may also want to start with secondary causes and end with immediate causes. Another way to organize the causes and effects is by chronological order. Which cause happened first? What was the first effect of the situation? These patterns can be used for both single paragraphs and for body paragraphs within an essay.

Clear Reasoning

Throughout the reading and writing processes, be aware of clear reasoning. Determine the immediate and secondary causes and effects. Make sure that a logical relationship exists between remote, secondary, and immediate causes. Do not make generalizations and false assumptions. For example, do not assume that chronological order signifies cause and effect. Perhaps the student who failed the test walked his dog before going to class. You would, therefore, not make the assumption that walking dogs caused the student to fail a test. Logic plays a significant role in the cause-effect relationship.

Transitional Words

Transitional words and expressions can help the reader and the writer stay focused on the main idea. Expressions such as *the first cause, the second cause, another effect* will guide the reader from one idea to another. Transitional words should also be used within the body of a cause and effect paragraph. Transitional words used to show cause and effect include *accordingly, because, consequently, therefore, to this end, as a result, thus.*

Tone

When reading and writing, pay attention to the tone of the article. When writing, ask yourself what attitude you want to portray. Are you writing to influence the reader, or do you want to present facts in an objective tone so that the reader can come to a conclusion? If the tone of the writing is objective, then the reader's attitude should not be influenced by your opinion. If the object is to persuade the reader, then your language should indicate such. Your goal is to convince the reader of your point of view.

Paragraph Formats for Causal Analysis

Paragraph Focusing on Effects

Topic Sentence: ____________________

A. Effect 1
   Examples
B. Effect 2
   Examples
C. Effect 3
   Examples
D. Effect 4
   Examples

Concluding Sentence ____________________

Essay Focusing on Effects

Thesis statement ____________________

I. Topic Sentence for introductory paragraph
II. Body paragraph 1—Effect 1
III. Body paragraph 2—Effect 2
IV. Body paragraph 3—Effect 3
V. Concluding Paragraph

Essay Focusing on Causes

Thesis statement ____________________

I. Topic Sentence for introductory paragraph
II. Body paragraph 1—Cause 1
III. Body paragraph 2—Cause 2
IV. Body paragraph 3—Cause 3
V. Concluding Paragraph

Alternate Plans

Four-paragraph essay

I. Introduction
II. Body Paragraph on Causes
III. Body Paragraph on Effects
IV. Concluding Paragraph

Essay Focusing on Causes and Effects

I. Introduction
II. Paragraph on Effects
III. Paragraph on Cause 1
IV. Paragraph on Cause 2
V. Concluding Paragraph

Paragraph Focusing on Effects and Causes

I. Introduction
II. Paragraph on Effects
III. Paragraph on Cause 1
IV. Paragraph on Cause 2
V. Concluding Paragraph

Cause and Effect Writing Worksheet

1. Survey the assignment and choose your topic. Do one of the prewriting assignments discussed in the introduction of the text.
2. Question the assignment. What is the focus of the assignment? What problem is being addressed? What are the causes of the problem? What are the results of the problem?
3. Map your essay or paragraph.
4. Relate your plan of writing to your writing group. Discuss the problem you are writing about with your group. Discuss the causes and the effects of the problem. Enlist the opinions of the group about the long- and short-term causes and effects.

5. Record (write) the first draft of your essay or paragraph.
6. Read your paragraph or essay aloud to a student partner. As you read, your partner should listen for connections between the causes and effects. Your partner should question any relationships and conclusions that do not seem logical.
7. Revise your essay, taking into account the questions that your writing group asked about your paper.
8. Review your revised paper with your partner and answer Questions for Review.
9. Reflect upon the comments of your peers and make needed changes.
10. Reread your paper, checking for grammatical errors. Read your paper from top to bottom and from bottom to top. Reading your paper in reverse helps you to read what you wrote, not what you meant to write! As you read your paper, check carefully for punctuation of complex sentences, correct use of subordinate words, and sentence variety.
11. Read your paper aloud.
12. Write your final draft.

Questions for Review

Paragraph Assignment

- What is the topic sentence?
- What problem is being addressed?
- Is the focus of the paragraph on the causes or the effects of the problem?
- What is the pattern of development for the paragraph?
- Are there any parts of the paragraph that are unclear? Is so, what are they, and how can they be corrected?
- What are the transitional words used to guide the reader from one example to another?
- What key words are used to give the paragraph unity?
- What is the concluding sentence of the paragraph?

Essay Assignment

The Introductory Paragraph

- How does the author get the attention of the reader?
- What is the focus of the essay?
- What problem is being addressed?
- Is the focus of the paper on the causes or the effects or a combination?
- What is the thesis statement?

The Body Paragraphs

- What are the topic sentences of each body paragraph?
- What is the focus of each body paragraph?
- What, if any, statements in the body paragraphs are confusing? How can these statements be corrected?
- What transitional words are used to guide the reader from one paragraph to the next?
- What transitional words are used within the body paragraphs?

- Are the transitional words appropriate?
- What key words has the author used to give the essay unity?
- What strong verbs has the author used to make the essay more effective?

The Conclusion

- How does the author conclude the essay?

Entire Essay

- What is the most effective part of the essay?

FRAGMENTS WITH SUBORDINATE CLAUSES

Cause and effect analysis requires paying careful attention to the punctuation and wording of subordinate clauses. When discussing reasons and results, writers must use complete sentences. This is one area in which conversational English can interfere with writing. In informal conversation, the use of fragments is acceptable. Often fragments start with *because*. If a person asks why you are moving across the country, you might respond like this: "Because I got a huge promotion with my company."

In writing, one must compose a full sentence: "I am moving because I got a huge promotion with my company." Or the writer might invert the sentence to say "Because I got a huge promotion with my company, I am moving across the country."

Another problem exists between the use of *therefore* and *because*. *Therefore* is a conjunctive adverb, and *because* is a subordinate conjunction. As such, they require different types of punctuation.

Example

Because the Street Rider program in Philadelphia is in danger of losing its funding, the graduates of the program now sponsor fund-raising programs.

Example

The graduates of the Street Rider program now sponsor fund-raising programs because it is in danger of losing its funding.

Example

The Street Rider program is in danger of losing its funding; therefore, the graduates of the program now sponsor fund-raising programs.

READING BEFORE WRITING

How Things Work

Gary Soto

This poem, written by Latino poet Soto and addressed to the narrator's daughter, deals with the cost of living and the items one can purchase. The main theme expresses the causal chain and ends with the notion of "things just keeping on going."

Today it's going to cost us twenty dollars
To live. Five for a softball. Four for a book,
A handful of ones for coffee and two sweet rolls,
Bus fare, **rosin** for your mother's violin.
We're completing our task. The **tip** I left
For the waitress filters down
Like rain, wetting the new roots of a child
Perhaps, a **belligerent** cat that won't let go
Of a balled sock until there's chicken to eat.
As far as I can tell, daughter, it works like this:
You buy bread from a grocery, a bag of apples
From a fruit stand, and what coins
Are passed on helps others buy pencils, glue,
Tickets to a movie in which laughter
Is thrown into their faces.
If we buy goldfish, someone tries on a hat.
If we buy crayons, someone walks home with a broom.
A tip, a small purchase here and there,
And things just keep going. I guess.

Glossary for "How Things Work"

ros·in (rŏz'ĭn) *n.*

A translucent yellowish to dark brown resin derived from the stumps or sap of various pine trees and used to increase sliding friction, as on the bows of certain stringed instruments, and to manufacture a wide variety of products including varnishes, inks, linoleum, adhesives, and soldering compounds.

tr.v. **ros·ined, ros·in·ing, ros·ins**

To coat or rub with rosin.

ros'in·y *adj.*

[Middle English, variant of resin.]

tip (tĭp) *n.*

1. A small sum of money given to someone for performing a service; a gratuity.
2. a. A piece of confidential, advance, or inside information: *got a tip on the next race.*
   b. A helpful hint: *a column of tips on gardening.*

v. **tipped, tip·ping, tips** *v. tr.*

1. a. To give a tip to: *tipped the waiter generously.*
   b. To give as a tip: *He tipped a dollar and felt that it was enough.*
2. To provide with a piece of confidential, advance, or inside information: *a disgruntled gang member who tipped the police to the planned robbery.*

intr.

To give tips or a tip: *one who tips lavishly.*

[*Origin unknown.*]

tip'per *n.* **tip** (tĭp) *n.*

A small sum of money given to someone for performing a service; a gratuity.

1. a. A piece of confidential, advance, or inside information: *got a tip on the next race.*
   b. A helpful hint: *a column of tips on gardening.*
   tipped, tip·ping, tips
   v. tr.
1. a. To give a tip to: *tipped the waiter generously.*
   b. To give as a tip: *He tipped a dollar and felt that it was enough.*
2. To provide with a piece of confidential, advance, or inside information: *a disgruntled gang member who tipped the police to the planned robbery.*
   v. intr.
   To give tips or a tip: *one who tips lavishly.*

[*Origin unknown.*]

bel·lig·er·ent (bə-lĭj'ər-ənt) *adj.*

1. Inclined or eager to fight; hostile or aggressive.
2. Of, pertaining to, or engaged in warfare.
3. *n.* One that is hostile or aggressive, especially one that is engaged in war.

[Latin belligerāns, belligerant- present participle of belligerāre, *to wage war*, from belliger, *warlike*: bellum, *war* + gerere, *to make*.]

bel·lig'er·ent·ly *adv.*

Reading Comprehension

Answer the following questions about Gary Soto's "How Things Work."

Word Meaning

Select the word from the glossary that best completes the sentences below.

1. The special __________ that the orchestral performers use enables their violins to function smoothly throughout the concert.
2. Many teenagers behave in a __________ manner to their classroom teachers as a means of being accepted by their peers.
3. Many restaurant diners forget that in America servers' main source of income comes from the gratuity, or __________ left for good service.

Literal Meaning

Mark the letter of the statement that best completes the meaning.

1. Soto is speaking to his
   a. class.
   b. children.

   c. friends.
   d. daughter.
2. Soto is teaching an everyday lesson how the system operates in
   a. economics.
   b. baseball.
   c. the restaurant industry.
   d. the world of music.
3. In this poem, Soto uses everyday items to convey the notion of
   a. the difficulty of shopping.
   b. the need for monetary restructuring.
   c. the simplicity of the chain of demand for goods and services.
   d. the need for better tips for restaurant employees.
4. The poem is organized in the following design.
   a. Examples only
   b. Examples and a lesson
   c. A lesson only
   d. A lecture
5. The narrator states his point, or theme, of the poem
   a. in the first line.
   b. in the first and last lines.
   c. throughout the poem.
   d. in an implied fashion.

Interpretive Meaning

Complete the questions with the response that best answers the statement.

1. Why does the narrator say that the cat won't let go of the balled sock until there's a chicken to eat?
   a. He is demonstrating the law of supply and demand.
   b. He is showing how stubbornly the cat is behaving.
   c. He is trying to amuse the reader.
   d. He is using psychology to convey his point.
2. What does Soto mean by the statement "And things just keep going"?
   a. He is summarizing his point.
   b. He wants the reader to expand the message he is giving with more examples.
   c. He says that the world of finance keeps on moving even on a small scale.
   d. He knows the listener will not understand.
3. Why does Soto end his poem with the two words "I guess"?
   a. He himself does not understand the concept.
   b. He is simplifying a really difficult theory that is intangible.
   c. He does not think he has explained the concept well.
   d. He is tired of trying to prove his point.
4. The poem can be divided into three parts that complete the following design:
   a. a topic statement, two sets of examples, and one conclusion.
   b. an introduction, an example, and a conclusion.

c. a topic statement followed by many examples.
d. an implied topic followed by many examples and a conclusion.

5. Why does Soto select the specified examples that one sees in this poem?
   a. They add color to the poem.
   b. The use of everyday elements explains the meaning of the poem.
   c. They represent a variety of items needed in everyday life.
   d. All of the above.
6. Why does the narrator say that ". . . laughter/Is thrown into their faces"?
   a. He likes the way people laugh in the movies.
   b. He thinks that people laugh because they think they are supposed to do so.
   c. He is mildly criticizing canned laughter in film.
   d. He likes to use action verbs.
7. When Soto says the tip he leaves is "wetting the new roots of a child," what does he mean?
   a. The child is getting wet in the rain.
   b. The waitress spilled liquid on the child.
   c. The child is becoming a new consumer of goods.
   d. The child's mother needs to buy some new diapers to contribute to the economy.
8. Soto frequently uses the word *if* to
   a. demonstrate the causal chain.
   b. show how a comma is used after introductory clauses.
   c. prove his point about simplicity.
   d. summarize the poem.
9. Soto's poem is an example of what poetic device?
   a. Rhyming couplets
   b. Iambic pentameter
   c. Free verse
   d. No device present
10. What other title would be most appropriate for this poem?
    a. "An Everyday Lesson"
    b. "Living Is Free"
    c. "Confused"
    d. "Marching On"

Score: Number correct _____ out of _____

Writing Assignments

1. Journal Writing

Summary

Write a one-paragraph summary of the poem. Questions to consider before writing include the following.

- To whom is the narrator writing?
- What is the main point the narrator is trying to make?
- What examples does the narrator give to support the main idea?

Reaction

When reacting to this poem, first consider your initial reaction. What did you like about the poem upon first reading it? Explain anything about the poem that you disliked. What was your overall feeling about the poem? Next, react to the poem after you have analyzed and thought about the poem. Explain any of the lines that are confusing or that you especially agree or disagree with. Why do you think Soto ends the poem with the two words "I guess"? What is the theme of the poem? Does the author state the theme directly or indirectly? When looking closely at the poem, do you see any words or phrases that provide hints to the narrator's feelings or point of view about the subject? What are they? React to the language of the poem. Finally, consider how the poem relates to your world. Have you ever tried to explain "the way of the world" or how things work to anyone? How did you express your thoughts about this subject?

2. ***Paragraph***

Focus on Effects: Write a paragraph explaining how the current economic situation in the United States affects your life as a college student.

Focus on Causes: Write a paragraph explaining the reasons for your current economic situation.

3. ***Paragraph to Essay***

Develop one of the paragraphs from assignment two into a five-paragraph essay by choosing three of the causes or three of the effects discussed in either the cause or the effect paragraph. Devote each body paragraph to one cause or one effect. Add examples and details to explain and support the topic sentences of the body paragraphs. Add an introductory paragraph and a concluding paragraph.

4. ***Essay***

Write a letter to a younger person in your community or family explaining the way of the world or how things work in your community. Focus on a particular problem and explain the causes or the effects to the reader of your letter.

Vietnam to America: An 18-Hour Flight, or an Impossible Journey?

Andrew Lam

Lam discusses the physical, mental, cultural, and emotional distance of the two countries. He explains his family history as a young immigrant and the memories he holds that equal or diverge from those of his family. He ends with, "Tick tock. I was born a Vietnamese. I am reborn an American. I am of one soul."

Pacific News Service, Dec 01, 2004

Editor's Note: As United Airlines prepares to begin direct flights between San Francisco and Vietnam on Dec. 9, PNS editor Andrew Lam, a Vietnamese American who fled his homeland during the Vietnam war, contemplates physical and emotional distance and the modern sense of self in a shrinking world.

In the modern world, the distance between America and Vietnam can be impossibly far or very near.

For my grandmother, who owned a clock in the shape of Vietnam to commemorate her beloved homeland and who died in San Jose, Calif., soon after the Cold War ended, Vietnam was very far. But these days, with United Airlines ready to inaugurate direct flights to Saigon (or Ho Chi Minh City, if you prefer) from San Francisco on Dec. 9, 2004, going home again for me and many others is but a matter of scheduling.

Before the United States lifted the trade **embargo** against Vietnam in 1994 and normalized relations with the country in 1995, a care package or letter sent home took three to six months to reach its intended recipients—if it got there at all.

Up until the late 1980s, my mother would roll $20 bills into a cylindrical shape slimmer than a cigarette and stuff them into a toothpaste tube in hopes that customs officers would fail to catch them. Would Aunty know what we meant when we wrote, "We want to see you smile" in the accompanying letter?

News from Vietnam, too, came slowly to us in America during those Cold War years. It took the form of letters written on recycled, grayish paper—letters that threatened to dissolve with a single tear drop. The letters **unanimously** told of tragic lives: Aunty and her family barely survived; another uncle is indefinitely **incarcerated** in a malaria-infested re-education camp; and there's no news of the cousin and family who disappeared somewhere in the South China Sea.

How far was Vietnam from America then?

For me, who grew up in America reading those grayish letters, Vietnam was my past, **ignoble,** tragic and inaccessible. I assumed it could never again be part my future. For those fleeing on crowded fishing boats out to sea, the distance too was very far. It took one of my cousins 13 times in as many years to escape. But so determined was he that he lived in Vietnam with only one resolve: to reach America at the risk of death and destruction.

Fast-forward two decades or so, and it's a whole new world.

While some native-born Americans blame the forces of **globalization**—communication and transportation technology, mass movements, porous borders, open trade—for breaking down community and family ties, many Asian immigrants will tell you it has often had the reverse effect on their lives. Not long ago the ocean was vast, homesickness was an incurable malady and the immigrant had little more than memories to keep cultural ties alive.

Today, after the Cold War has melted and jumbo jets have shrunk the ocean, the camcorder shows Granduncle back home what life is like in America and the Internet and cell phone connect far-flung relatives across the globe.

The cousin, once a boat person, is now an engineer, wealthy and established, with his own home in the Oakland hills. And I was wrong, as it turned out, regarding my homeland. It became part of my future. As a writer, I've been back to Vietnam half a dozen times. It's as if that old, treacherous ocean has turned into a pond underneath the jet's wings, and the war that was responsible for unspeakable horrors is now only a vague memory.

Vietnam-America. Whatever happened to that bloody embrace?

The ash-blonde woman in her mid-50s at the Cu Chi tunnel, where Viet Cong hid during the war, told me she had to see Vietnam once in her life. "I grew up with Vietnam on my TV set. I grew up protesting that war. I told myself I have to see the country to learn what it's all about." She goes to Vietnam to look for the meaning of the past.

Her young Vietnamese guide has a dream for the future. It's filled with the Golden Gate Bridge and cable cars and two-tiered freeways. "I have many friends over there now," she says, reflecting the collective desire of Vietnamese youth. "They invite me to come. I'm saving money for this amazing trip."

If the encounter between America and Vietnam is remembered as a bloody battle, it has also evolved slowly into a kind of **pas de deux.**

Thus for me, the distance between the two countries remains **enigmatic.** It is both impossible, and an 18-hour flight. The jet plane will and will not take me home again. Or rather, I go home again, but not as the Vietnamese child who left home.

Yesterday my heritage was simple and self-evident. The borders were real. Vietnam and its green, rich rice fields were all there was. Today, my identity is multi-faceted, complex.

I am not alone. The Cold War and its aftermath have given birth to a race of children born elsewhere, of trans-nationals whose memories are layered and whose biographies transgress borders. They are simultaneously aware of two or three different cultures, and they move restlessly from one language to another, from one civilization to the next.

As a result, I think sometimes my real home is portable, something defined by movement, restlessness and a particular yet hybrid sense of self.

If there is a metaphor for it all, the wall in a restaurant in San Francisco's Tenderloin seems to express it. Sometimes I go there and sit and stare at two wooden clocks hanging on opposite corners of that wall. One, like my grandmother's clock, is carved in the shape of Vietnam. The other is hewn in the shape of America.

Tick tock, tick tock. They tick at different intervals. Tick tock. I was born a Vietnamese. Tick tock, tick tock. I am reborn an American. Tick tock. I am of one soul. Tick tock, tick tock. Two hearts.

Glossary for "Vietnam to America: An 18-Hour Flight, or an Impossible Journey?"

em·bar·go (ĕm-bär'gō) *n. pl.* **em·bar·goes**

1. A government order prohibiting the movement of merchant ships into or out of its ports.
2. A prohibition by a government on certain or all trade with a foreign nation.
3. A prohibition; a ban: *an embargo on criticism.*

tr. v. **em·bar·goed, em·bar·go·ing, em·bar·goes**
To impose an embargo on.

[Spanish, from embargar, *to impede*, from Vulgar Latin *imbarricāre, *to barricade*: Latin in-, *in*; (from *barrīca, *barrel, barrier*, from *barra, *bar, barrier*).]

u·nan·i·mous (yo͞o-năn'ə-məs) *adj.*

1. Sharing the same opinions or views; being in complete harmony or accord.
2. Based on or characterized by complete assent or agreement.

[From Latin ūnanimus: ūnus, *one*; see oi-no- in Indo-European Roots + animus, *mind*; see anə- in Indo-European Roots.]
u·nan'i·mous·ly *adv.* **u·nan'i·mous·ness** *n.*

in·car·cer·ate (ĭn-kär'sə-rāt') *tr. v.* **in·car·cer·at·ed, in·car·cer·at·ing, in·car·cer·ates**

1. To put into jail.
2. To shut in; confine.

[Medieval Latin incarcerāre, incarcerāt-: Latin in-, *in*; see **in-**[2] + Latin carcer, *prison*.]
in·car'cer·a'tion *n.* **in·car'cer·a'tor** *n.*

ig·no·ble (ĭg-nō'bəl) *adj.*

1. Not noble in quality, character, or purpose; base or mean.
2. Not of the nobility; common.

[Middle English, *of low birth*, from Old French, from Latin ignōbilis: i-, in-, *not*;]
ig'no·bil'i·ty (-bĭl'ĭ-tē) or **ig·no'ble·ness** *n.* **ig·no'bly** *adv.*

glob·al·ize (glō'bə-līz') *tr. v.* **glob·al·ized, glob·al·iz·ing, glob·al·iz·es**
To make global or worldwide in scope or application.
glob'al·i·za'tion (-lĭ-zā'shən) *n.* **glob'al·iz'er** *n.*

pas de deux (dœ) *n. pl.* **pas de deux**

1. A dance for two, especially a dance in ballet consisting of an entrée and adagio, a variation for each dancer, and a coda.
2. A close relationship between two people or things, as during an activity.

[French: pas, *step* + de, *of, for* + deux, *two*.]

e·nig·ma (ĭ-nĭg'mə) noun

1. One that is puzzling, ambiguous, or inexplicable.
2. A perplexing speech or text; a riddle.

[Latin aenigma, from Greek ainigma, from ainissesthai, ainig-, *to speak in riddles*, from ainos, *fable*.]

Reading Comprehension

Answer the following questions about the article by Andrew Lam.

Word Meaning

Using the glossary, select the entry that best completes the sentences below.

1. The trade __________ between the United States and Cuba, which prevents travel and commerce between the two countries, began over forty-five years ago.
2. The student body __________ voted for the old gray mongrel dog to represent the college as homecoming queen.
3. Since his first days of __________, the man has tried by every means to prove his innocence.
4. Still on the books, the law preventing horses to be tied to hitching posts remains a/an __________ to the city council.
5. The rise in gas prices is caused by the __________ of automobiles and petroleum products into third world countries.
6. Even if their perceptions are inaccurate, many young people who are ashamed of their roots will not divulge the details of their __________ pasts.
7. Having no __________, the student bought every essay submitted in his online course from an Internet site; finally caught, he was dismissed from college.
8. A recent strain of __________ corn has produced enough grain to feed millions of starving humans across the globe.

Literal Meaning

Mark the letter of the option that best answers the statements below.

1. What possession did the author's grandmother own to remind her of her homeland?
   a. A Vietnamese dictionary
   b. Native dress
   c. A clock in the shape of her native country
   d. A photo album of her favorite snapshots

2. What event prompted the author to write this article?
   a. The normalization of relations with Vietnam
   b. The first trip he took back to Vietnam
   c. The arrival of a new group of Vietnamese immigrants
   d. The beginning of a direct flight to Vietnam
3. By using the term *Cold War*, the author refers to what?
   a. The war in Vietnam
   b. The fight against Communism
   c. The immigration of Vietnamese refugees by boat
   d. A period of time when relations between countries are not normalized
4. In what year did the United States and Vietnam normalize relations?
   a. 1975
   b. 2004
   c. 1994
   d. 1980
5. Before the end of the Cold War and the normalization of relations with Vietnam, immigrants
   a. held only memories of their past lives in Vietnam.
   b. thought of the ocean as a vast divide between their current lives and their pasts.
   c. suffered from incurable nostalgia.
   d. All of the above

Interpretive Meaning

Complete the questions with the response that best answers the statement.

1. Why does Lam say that the ocean has shrunk?
   a. Jumbo jet travel has reduced the time to reach another country.
   b. The shores of the ocean are enlarging due to global warming.
   c. Continental Drift has caused Vietnam and America to be geographically closer
   d. Most of Lam's family have moved to America.
2. The tone of the essay is
   a. humorous.
   b. informative.
   c. argumentative.
   d. didactic.
3. Why did Lam's family write the words "We want to see you smile" in their letters accompanying the toothpaste tubes?
   a. The author's family hoped that the new toothpaste would prevent tooth decay.
   b. They wanted to see a photo after the family had used the toothpaste.
   c. They liked to send gifts that would improve the health of the Vietnamese family.
   d. They were giving a clue to look inside the tube for the money that would really make them smile.

4. What does Lam mean by the "bloody embrace" between America and Vietnam?
   a. America and Vietnam fought alongside each other during the war in Vietnam.
   b. Lam is using the British meaning of the word *bloody* to develop sarcasm.
   c. He wants Americans to remember the war.
   d. Many American soldiers fathered children while in Vietnam.
5. Why does the fifty-year-old American woman visit Vietnam?
   a. Her travel agent told her that Vietnam is a great vacation destination.
   b. Vietnam is geographically closer to America now.
   c. She wanted to visit the country she grew up seeing in the news every night.
   d. Her brother fought there during the war.
6. Why does Lam say that the distance between Vietnam and America is enigmatic?
   a. Lam sometimes has passport problems at the border when he arrives in Vietnam.
   b. The food and water in Vietnam make him sick.
   c. Lam travels to Vietnam as a Vietnamese, but he realizes at the same time that he is more American than Vietnamese.
   d. He feels like a child again when he arrives in his native country.
7. Why does Lam stare at the two restaurant clocks shaped in the form of his two countries—Vietnam and America?
   a. He is pondering the meaning of life.
   b. Even though he lives in America, he wonders what nationality he really is.
   c. He is marveling at the wood that the clocks are made of.
   d. His grandfather made the clocks, and he is admiring the craftsmanship.
8. What effect does immigration as a young boy have on Lam?
   a. He feels that he is forgetting his Vietnamese roots.
   b. He has developed a bicultural identity.
   c. He speaks and reads English better than he does the Vietnamese language.
   d. He sees the changes in his country when he returns.
9. Why does Lam use the repetition of the words *tick tock*?
   a. The sound of the clocks relaxes him when he is writing.
   b. The clocks sound musical as they beat at different intervals.
   c. The clocks represent the movement of his career from a novice to a professional writer.
   d. As he listens to the beating of the clock, he realizes that he too is of one soul and two hearts—one Vietnamese and one American.

Score: Number correct _____ out of _____

Writing Assignments

1. Journal Writing

Summary

Summarize the article in one or two short paragraphs.

Reaction

In your reaction, consider the title of the essay and how it relates to the meaning of the essay. What is the connection between the two clocks discussed at the end of the essay and the title of the essay? Consider why this essay is labeled a cause and effect essay. What causes and what effects are being discussed in the essay? What questions do you have about the essay? Choose one or two statements in the essay that you consider to be powerful. Explain why you chose these statements.

2. ***Paragraph***

Focus on Effects: Write a paragraph analyzing the effects of globalization, global reach of communications technology, on immigrants in the United States.

Focus on Causes: Write a paragraph discussing the reasons why many Asian Americans feel that globalization has had a positive effect on their lives.

3. ***Paragraph to Essay***

Choose either the cause or the effect paragraph written for assignment two. Using the paragraph as a springboard for your essay, focus on the three most important causes or effects in the paragraph. In a five-paragraph essay, devote one body paragraph to each reason or each effect. Add specific examples and details to support the topic sentences of the body paragraphs. Add an introductory and a concluding paragraph.

4. ***Essay***

Lam discusses the effects of globalization on family ties and communication in Asian-American families. Write an essay analyzing the status of family ties in your own family, your community, or your city.

Hoofbeats on Fletcher Street

Johnny Dwyer

This article describes the continued work with horses—taking care of them, riding them, racing them—that, though dead elsewhere, continues in one Philadelphia neighborhood. The article explains the reasons this tradition has continued and the positive effects it has on the young boys who participate.

As late as the 1960s, horses hauled milk, ice, fruit, vegetables, and junk through the narrow streets of Philadelphia's inner city; later, they were used purely for recreation. But as the years passed, one stable after another was shuttered, some of them victims of urban renewal. In many neighborhoods, riding traditions that had been passed on from generation to generation simply ceased.

But on Fletcher Street, the tradition remains: A kid from the surrounding neighborhoods comes to learn about horses. That first day, he might be sent to the store to fetch a pack of cigarettes. The next day, he'll get to feed or clean a horse. Before long, he'll get to ride. If he shows dedication, tends to the horses early in the morning, exercises them in the afternoon, then he'll "own" one—meaning, even if one of the elders bought the animal, it becomes his responsibility.

No government funds **subsidize** the stables or the expense of feeding, housing, and caring for the 30 or so animals. The cost of keeping the tradition alive falls on the riders who've gone on to succeed as adults.

For those who came up in Strawberry Mansion, like 35-year-old Lee Cannady, the horses provided a vital **antidote** to the lure of the street. "For a lot of young guys it's about self—and you can't be about self when you got a horse," says Cannady. Though he's moved with his wife and four children to Wynnefield, a short drive away, he still brings them here every weekend for race day—the **culmination** of a week's labors caring for the horses. Like many adults involved with Fletcher Street, Cannady considers it his duty to buy, at auction, horses for the younger generation.

"If we can keep these guys here at the stable, gettin' dirty," he says, "then they're not getting involved in drugs, stealin', killin'."

A lifelong friend of Cannady's, James "Hop" White, 40, owns and runs one of the block's three stables. He makes his living in plumbing and contracting, but he's been riding since he was 2. "This is a tradition that went through generations," he says of Fletcher Street. "You want to be a rider."

When his father died two years ago, White inherited the cramped but tidy 14-stall stable. Now he walks through the stalls as young riders prepare their horses for the afternoon's race. On this spring morning, the crowd of several dozen range in age from an infant **teetering** on the shoulders of his father to Roosevelt, a senior citizen and local legend.

Fletcher Street begins to **percolate** at noon. One by one, the six "runners" are loaded into **dilapidated** horse trailers for the journey to a nearby public park. By 1 p.m., about 50 onlookers have assembled there. Joggers and cyclists pass by as the riders and their horses trot out to the edge of the well-worn clearing that serves as the racetrack. Two riders race at a time. The finish line, a quarter-mile away, is marked only by a group of older men smoking plastic-tipped cigars and drinking tall cans of Budweiser.

Donnie lines up against a Fletcher Street veteran named Keith. With his scraggly beard, cornrows, and jeans, Keith doesn't stand out in the crowd. But once he's on horseback, it's clear that he's a star in the saddle.

There is no starting gate or pistol shot; the two riders decide when to start, and then they simply bolt. The thud of hooves **intensifies,** competing with the hooting of the crowd as the horses approach. Donnie holds close to his opponent for almost 20 seconds before Keith pulls ahead by a length, the crowd parting as he finishes.

After several more races, the group returns to Fletcher Street. Someone has spread buckets of Kentucky Fried Chicken on the hood of a car as a celebratory meal.

Donnie trots No Show Jones out into the lot while the others eat. The sun is setting, and the stables on Fletcher Street will soon close for the night.

Clearly, Donnie feels the horses have helped him. He's not sure what his future holds, but he's considering studying engineering or architecture at college in the fall. Of one thing, though, Donnie is certain: "I'm going to be riding the rest of my life."

Glossary for "Hoofbeats on Fletcher Street"

sub·si·dize (sŭb'sĭ-dīz') *tr. v.* **sub·si·dized, sub·si·diz·ing, sub·si·diz·es**

1. To assist or support with a subsidy.
2. To secure the assistance of by granting a subsidy.

sub'si·di·za'tion (-dĭ-zā'shən) *n.* **sub'si·diz'er** *n.*

an·ti·dote (ăn'tĭ-dōt') *n.*

1. A remedy or other agent used to neutralize or counteract the effects of a poison.
2. An agent that relieves or counteracts: *jogging as an antidote to nervous tension.*

tr. v. **an·ti·dot·ed, an·ti·dot·ing, an·ti·dotes**
To relieve or counteract with an antidote: "Hallie's family life is laced with the poison of self-hatred, a poison that Sam has antidoted with love and understanding" (Christopher Swan).

[Middle English, from Latin antidotum, from Greek antidoton, from antididonai, antido-, *to give as a remedy against*: anti-, *anti-* + didonai, *to give;* see dō- in Indo-European Roots.]
an'ti·dot'al (ăn'tĭ-dōt'l) *adj.*
an'ti·dot'al·ly *adv.*
Usage Note: *Antidote* may be followed by *to, for,* or *against: an antidote to boredom; an antidote for snakebite; an antidote against inflation.*

cul·mi·nate (kŭl'mə-nāt') *v. intr.* **cul·mi·nat·ed, cul·mi·nat·ing, cul·mi·nates**

1. a. To reach the highest point or degree; climax: *habitual antagonism that culminated in open hostility.*

   b. To come to completion; end: *Years of waiting culminated in a tearful reunion.*

2. Astronomy. To reach the highest point above an observer's horizon. Used of stars and other celestial bodies.

v. tr.

To bring to the point of greatest intensity or to completion; climax: *The ceremony culminated a long week of preparation.*

[Late Latin culmināre, culmināt-, from Latin culmen, culmin-, *summit.*]
cul'mi·na'tion *n.*

tee·ter (tē'tər) *v.* **tee·tered, tee·ter·ing, tee·ters** *v. intr.*

1. To walk or move unsteadily or unsurely; totter.
2. To alternate, as between opposing attitudes or positions; vacillate.
3. To seesaw.

v. tr. To cause to teeter or seesaw.
n. Northeastern U.S.

1. A teetering motion.

[Middle English titeren, probably from Old Norse titra, *to shake.*]

per·co·late (pûr'kə-lāt') *v.* **per·co·lat·ed, per·co·lat·ing, per·co·lates** *v. tr.*

1. To cause (liquid, for example) to pass through a porous substance or small holes; filter.
2. To pass or ooze through: *Water percolated the sand.*
3. To make (coffee) in a percolator.

v. intr.

1. To drain or seep through a porous material or filter.
2. Informal. To become lively or active.
3. Informal. To spread slowly or gradually.

n. (-lĭt, -lāt')
A liquid that has been percolated.

[Latin percōlāre, percōlāt- : per-, *per-* + cōlāre, *to filter* (from cōlum, *sieve*).]
per'co·la'tion *n.*

di·lap·i·dat·ed (dĭ-lăp'ĭ-dā'tĭd) *adj.*

Having fallen into a state of disrepair or deterioration, as through neglect; broken-down and shabby.

in·ten·si·fy (ĭn-tĕn'sə-fī') *v.* **in·ten·si·fied, in·ten·si·fy·ing, in·ten·si·fies**
v. tr.

1. To make intense or more intense: *The press has intensified its scrutiny of the candidate's background.*
2. To increase the contrast of (a photographic image).

v. intr.

To become intense or more intense: *The search intensified as dusk approached.*
in·ten'si·fi·ca'tion (-fĭ-kā'shən) *n.*

Reading Comprehension

Answer the following questions about the article by Johnny Dwyer.

Word Meaning

Using the glossary, select the entry that best completes the sentences below.

1. Many of the New Orleans homes that survived Hurricane Katrina quickly became __________ from water damage and were torn down.
2. The Federal Government offers special programs to __________ students who want to study abroad and cannot afford the costs.
3. The best __________ for poverty is education and hard work.
4. The state fair began to __________ at 6 in the evening when the swells of people entered the grounds.
5. The baseball player's shoulder pain began to __________ after he threw his ninetieth pitch to the batter's box.

Literal Meaning

Mark the letter of the option that best answers the statements below.

1. Where is the physical setting of the selection?
   a. Philadelphia, Pennsylvania
   b. Philadelphia, Mississippi
   c. Strawberry Mansion, Texas
   d. Rider, California
2. Lee Cannady, one man interviewed in the article,
   a. financially supports the Fletcher Street project.
   b. still visits the boys on Fletcher Street.
   c. spent his youth working with the horses.
   d. All of the above
3. Number from 1 to 4 the steps that a youth might follow when working with the horses.
   a. He will "own" a horse. _____
   b. He might go buy something for the leaders at the store. _____
   c. He will ride a horse. _____
   d. He will clean or feed a horse. _____
4. The funding for the Fletcher Street project comes from where?
   a. A government grant
   b. A marathon race
   c. Graduates of the program
   d. Local taxation
5. What everyday items are mentioned in the selection?
   a. Kentucky Fried Chicken
   b. Budweiser beer
   c. Plastic-tipped cigars
   d. All of the above

Interpretive Meaning

Complete the questions with the response that best answers the statement.

1. Why is the selection named "Street Rider"?
   a. The boys deliver products door-to-door on the neighborhood streets.
   b. The title combines two possibilities for the youth of this area—living on the street or riding horseback.
   c. The boys race the horses on the streets of the neighborhood.
   d. The boys enjoy playing video games, especially the one with the name of the title.
2. What is the author's purpose for writing a story about these boys?
   a. He is explaining the program and how it helps to save boys.
   b. He is trying to raise funds to support Fletcher Street.
   c. He wants the program to expand to other cities.
   d. He is one of the alumni of the program with horses.
3. What effect does the program on Fletcher Street have on the boys who participate?
   a. Some of the boys have become professional jockeys.
   b. The boys mature by learning to focus on something besides themselves.
   c. The boys win scholarships to college.
   d. The boys earn spending money by delivering groceries in the neighborhood.
4. Why do the adult supporters participate even after becoming parents?
   a. They know the program enabled them to succeed as adults.
   b. They enjoy seeing another generation benefit from the program.
   c. They need their families to share in the positive benefits of the program.
   d. All of the above
5. Why does the author include details like cornrows, jeans, and cigarettes in his article?
   a. He wants to persuade other boys to join in the activities of Fletcher Street.
   b. He uses everyday details to show that these boys are typical youths.
   c. He is trying to impress other journalists with his writing ability.
   d. He likes to use details when he writes.

Score: Number correct _____ out of _____

Writing Assignments

1. Journal Writing

Summary

Write a one-paragraph summary of the selection.

Reaction

Write a reaction focusing not only on the events described in the article but also on the need for or existence of similar programs in your community.

2. ***Paragraph***

   Topic: Consider a tradition that exists in your community.

   Focus on Causes: Write a paragraph discussing the reasons the tradition continues to live.

   Focus on Effects: Write a paragraph discussing the effects of this tradition on your community.

3. ***Paragraph to Essay***

   Use the paragraph written for assignment two to write a four-paragraph essay analyzing the causes and effects of a tradition in your community. Use the introductory paragraph to explain the history and importance of the tradition. End the introduction with a clear thesis statement. Write one body paragraph discussing the reasons for the tradition and one paragraph discussing the effects of the tradition. In the concluding paragraph, summarize your ideas and predict the future of this tradition.

4. ***Essay***

   Write a causal analysis on volunteerism in your community. Focus on either the reasons people volunteer or the effects of the volunteer work.

Ringtail

Rudolph Fisher

This story revolves around two characters and the culture clashes that arise based on their origins even though they both reside in Harlem. Of course, a woman is also at the heart of the problem.

I

The pavement flashed like a river in the sun. Over it slowly moved the churches' **disgorged** multitudes, brilliant, deliberate, proud as a pageant, a tumult of reds and blues and greens, oranges, yellows, and browns; from a window above, outrageous, intriguing, like music full of exotic disharmonies; but closer, grating, repellent, like an orchestra tuning up: this big, broad-faced, fawn-colored woman in her wide, floppy **leghorn** hat with a long **cerise** ribbon streaming down over its side, and a dress of **maize** georgette; or that poor scrawny black girl, bareheaded, her patches of hair captured in squares, her beaded cobalt frock girdled with a sash of scarlet satin. But whether you saw with pleasure or pity, you could have no doubt of the display. Harlem's Seventh Avenue was dressed in its Sunday clothes.

And so was Cyril Sebastian Best. To him this promenade was the crest of the week's wave of pleasure. Here was show and swagger and strut, and in these he knew none could out vie him. Find if you could a suit of tan gabardine that curved in at the waist and flared at the hips so gracefully as his own; try to equal his wide wing-collar, with its polka-dot bow-tie matching the border of the kerchief in his breast pocket, or his heavy straw hat with its terraced crown and thick saucer-shaped brim, or his white buckskin shoes with their pea-green trimmings, or his silver-topped ebony cane. He challenged the Avenue and found no rival to answer.

Cyril Sebastian Best was a British West Indian. From one of the unheard-of islands he had come to Trinidad. From Trinidad, growing weary of coin-diving, he had sailed to Southampton as kitchen boy on a freighter, acquiring en route great skill in dodging the Irish cook's missiles and returning his compliments. From Southampton he had shipped in another freighter for New York under a cook from Barbados, a man who **compunctionlessly** regarded all flesh as fit for carving; and Cyril had found the blade of his own **innate** craftiness, though honed to a hair-splitting edge, no match for an unerringly aimed cleaver. The trip's termination had undoubtedly saved his life; its last twenty-four hours he had spent hiding from the cook, and when the ship had cast anchor he had jumped overboard at night, swimming two miles to shore. From those who picked him up exhausted and restored him to bodily comfort he had stolen what he could get and made his way into New York.

There were British West Indians in Harlem who would have told Cyril Sebastian Best flatly to his face that they despised him—that he would not have dared even address them in the islands; who frequently reproved their American friends for judging all West Indians by the Cyril Sebastian Best standard. There were others who, simply because he was a British West Indian, gathered to their bosoms in that regardless warmth that which the outsider ever welcomes his like.

Among these latter, the more numerous, Cyril accordingly expanded. His self-esteem, his craftiness, his contentiousness, his acquisitiveness, all became virtues. To him self-improvement meant nothing but increasing these virtues, certainly not eliminating or modifying any of them. He became fond of denying that he was "colored," insisting that he was "a British subject," hence by implication unquestionably superior to any merely American Negro. And when two years of contact convinced him that the American Negro was characteristically neither self-esteemed nor crafty nor **contentious** nor **acquisitive,** in short was quite virtueless, his conscious superiority became downright contempt.

It was with no effort to conceal his personal excellence that Cyril Sebastian Best proceeded up Seventh Avenue. All this turnout was but his fitting background, his proper setting; it pleased him for no other reason than that it rendered him the more conscious of himself—a diamond surrounded with rhinestones. It did not occur to him as he swung along, flourishing his bright black cane, that any of the frequent frank stares or **surreptitious** second glances that fell upon him could have any origin other than admiration—envy, of course, as its companion in the cases of the men. That his cocky air could be comic, that the extremeness of his outfit could be ridiculous, that the contrast between his clothes and his complexion could cause a lip to curl—none of these far winds rippled the **complacency** of his ego. He had studied the fashion books carefully. Like them, he was **incontrovertibly** correct. Like them, again, he was incontrovertibly British; while these Harlemites were just American Negroes. And then, beyond and above all this, he was Cyril Sebastian Best.

The group of loud-laughing young men near the corner he was approaching had not regard for the Sabbath, appreciation for the splendor of Seventh Avenue, or respect for any particular person who might pass within earshot. Indeed they derived as great a degree of pleasure out of the weekly display as did Cyril Sebastian Best, but of a quite different sort. Instead of joining the procession, they preferred assembling at some point in its course and "giving the crowd the once-over." They enjoyed exchanging loud comments upon the passers-by, the slightest quip provoking shouts of laughter; and they possessed certain stock **subtleties** which were always sure to **elicit** merriment, such as the whistled tune of "There she goes, there she goes, all dressed up in her Sunday clothes!" A really pretty girl usually won a surprised "Well, hush my mouth!" while a really pretty ankle always occasioned wild embraces of mock excitement.

An especially favored and carefully reserved trick was for one member of the group to push another into a stroller, the latter accomplice apologizing with elaborate **deference,** while the victim stood helpless between uncertainty and rage. In Harlem, however, an act of this kind required a **modicum** of selectivity. The group would never have attempted it on the heavy-set, walnut-visaged gentleman just passing, for all of his suede spats and crimson cravat; but when Cyril Sebastian Best lilted into view the temptation was beyond resistance.

"Push me!" Punch Anderson pleaded of his neighbor. "Not yet, Meg. Wait a minute. Now!"

The impact sent Cyril's cane capering toward the gutter; his hat described progressively narrower circles on the sidewalk; and before Punch could remove his own hat and frame his polite excuse Cyril's **fulminant** temper flashed. Some would have at least considered the possibility of innocent sincerity; others, wiser, would have said nothing, picked up their things, and passed on; but Cyril Sebastian Best reacted only to outraged vanity, and the resultant cloud-burst of **vituperation** staggered even the well-informed Punch Anderson.

"Soft pedal, friend," he protested, grinning. "I'm apologizing, ain't I?"

More damnation. Epithets conceived over kitchen filth; curses born of the sea; worded **fetor.**

Punch's round-faced grin faded. He deliberately secured the West Indian's hat and cane and without a word handed them to him. Cyril snatched them out of Punch's hand as if from a leper and flung out a parting **invective**—a gem of obscenity. Punch's sense of humor died.

"Say that again, you black son of a simian, and somebody'll be holding an inquest over you!"

In the act of raising his hat to his head Cyril said it again. Punch's fist went through the crown of the hat to reach the West Indian's face.

A minute later Cyril, tears streaming, polka-dot kerchief growing rapidly crimson with repeated application, was hurrying through the unbearable stares of gaping promenaders, while in his ears seethed the insult: "Now get the hell out o' here, you ringtail monkey-chaser!"

II

The entrance of the Rosina wears an expression of unmistakable hauteur and you know it immediately to be one of the most arrogant of apartment houses. You need not stand on the opposite side of the Avenue and observe the disdain with which the Rosina looks down upon her neighbors. You have only to pass between her distinguishing gray-granite pillars with their protective, flanking grille-work and pause for a hesitant moment in the spacious hall beyond: the overimmaculate tiled floors, the stiff, paneled mahogany walls, the frigid lights in their crystalline fixtures, the **supercilious** palms, all ask you at once who you are and what you want here. To reach the elevator you must make between two lordly, contemptuous wall-mirrors, which silently deride you and show you how out of place you are. If you are sufficiently courageous or **obtuse,** you gain the elevator and with growing **discomfiture** await the pleasure of the operator, who is just now occupied at the switchboard, listening in on some conversation that does not concern him. If you are sufficiently unimpressed or imprudent, you grumble or call aloud, and in that case you always eventually take to the stairs. Puff, blow, rage, and be damned. This is the Rosina. Who are you?

What more pleasurable occupation for Cyril Sebastian Best, then, than elevator- and switchboard-operator in the Rosina? If ever there was self-expression, this was it. He was the master of her halls, he was the incarnation of her spirit; in him her attitude became articulate—articulate with a Trinidadian accent, but distinctly intelligible, none the less. There were countless residents and their callers to be laughed at; there were endless silly phone-talks to be tapped at the switchboard; there were great mirrors before which he could be sure of the perfect trimness of his dapper gray-and-black uniform; there were relatively few passengers who absolutely required the use of the elevator, and most of those tipped well and frequently. It was a wonderful job.

Cyril's very conformity with his situation kept him ordinarily in the best of humor, the rendering of good service yielding him a certain satisfaction of his own. It was therefore with a considerable shock that one resident, flatteringly desirous, as she thought, of Cyril's aid in facilitating a connection, heard herself curtly answered, "Ah, tell de outside operator. Whaht you t'ink I keer?"—and that a familiar caller in the Rosina, upon being asked, "Whaht floor?" and answering pleasantly, "Third, as usual," heard himself rebuked with "'As usual'! You t'ink I am a mind-reader, 'ey?"

Clearly Cyril Sebastian Best was in no obliging mood to-day.

Nothing amused, nothing even interested him: neither the complexion of the very dark girl who persisted in using too much rouge with an alarmingly cyanotic result, nor the leprously overpowdered nose of the young lady who lived in fifty-nine and "passed" for white in her downtown position. He did not even grin at the pomposity of the big yellow preacher who, instead of purchasing ecclesiastic collars, simply put his lay ones on backward.

Cyril sat before the switchboard brooding, his memory raw with "monkey-chaser" and "ringtail." Now and then a transient spasm of passion contorted his features. In the intervals he was sullen and glum and absorbed in contemplated revenge.

"Cyril! Aren't you ever going to take me up? I'm starving to death!"

He looked up. Hilda Vogel's voice was too sweet, even in dissatisfaction, not to be heeded; and she was too pretty—fair, rougelessly rosy, with dimpled cheeks and elbows. How different from the picture just now in his mind!

Cyril had secret ambitions about Hilda. Like himself, she was foreign—from Bermuda; a far cry, to be sure, from Trinidad, but British just the same. And she was sympathetic. She laughed at his jests, she frankly complimented his neatness, she never froze his pleasantries with silence, nor sneered, nor put on airs. One day, after a week of casual cordialities during their frequent ascents, she had paused for as long as five minutes at her landing to listen to his description of the restaurant he was going to own some day soon. It couldn't be meaningless. She saw something in him. Why shouldn't he have ambitions about her?

"Cyril! How'd you hurt your lip?" she asked in the surprise of discovery as the car mounted.

Merely that she noticed elated him; but he would have bitten the lip off rather than tell her. "I bump' into de door doonsteers."

"Shame on you, Cyril. That's an old one. Do I look as dumb as that?"

He was silent for three floors.

"Goodness! It must have been something terrible. Oh well, if you ignore me—" And she began humming a ditty.

She had never been so personal before. Had his soul not been filled with bitterness, he might have betrayed some of those secret ambitions at once, right there between floors in the elevator. As it was he was content with a saner resolution: he would ask permission to call Wednesday night. He was off Wednesdays.

"You soun' quite happy," he observed, to make an opening, as he slid back the gate at her floor.

"You said it!" she answered gayly, stepping out; and before he could follow his opening her dimples deepened, her eyes twinkled mysteriously, and she added, "I may be in love—you'd never know!" Then she vanished down the hallway with a laugh, while the speechless Cyril wondered what she could mean.

III

In the flat's largest room a half-dozen young men played poker around a dining-table. A spreading gas-dome of maroon-and-orange stained glass hung low over the table, purring softly, confining its whitish halo to the circle of players, and leaving in dimness the several witnesses who peered over their shoulders. One player was startlingly white, with a heavy rash of brown freckles and short kinky red hair. Another was almost black, with the hair of an Indian and the features of a Moor. The rest ranged between.

A phonograph in a corner finished its blatant "If You Don't I Know Who Will," and someone called for the "West Indian Blues."

"That reminds me, Punch," said Meg Minor over his cards. "Remember that monk you hit Sunday?"

"Never hit anybody on Sunday in my life," grinned Punch across the table. "I'm a Christian."

"Punch hit a monk? Good-night! There's gonna be some carvin' done."

"Name your flowers, Punch!"

"'Four Roses' for Punch!"

Meg went on through the comments: "He's an elevator-boy at the Rosina up the Avenue."

"What'd you hit him for, Punch?"

"Deal me threes, Red," requested Punch, oblivious, while Meg told the others what had happened.

"Serves you right for actin' like a bunch of infants," judged Red. "Punch in the Post Office and you supposed to be studyin'—what the hell are you studyin' now, Meg?"

"Serves us right? It was the monk that got hit."

"Hmph! D' you think that's the end of it? Show me a monk that won't try to get even and I'll swallow the Woolworth Building."

"Well, we were just feeling kind o' crazy and happened to meet up with that bunch of don't-give-a-kitty kids. It was fun, only—"

"Bet fifteen cents on these four bullets," said Punch.

"Call!"

"Call!"

"You stole the last pot, bluffin'," calculated Eight-Ball, nicknamed for his complexion's resemblance to the pool ball of that number. He tossed a blue chip into the growing pile.

"Have to protect my ante," decided his neighbor, resignedly.

"I'm a dutiful nephew, too," followed Meg.

Punch threw down three aces and a joker and reached for the pile of chips.

"Four bullets sure 'nough!"

"An' I had a full house!"

"The luck o' the Nigrish. Had a straight myself."

"Luck, hell. Them's the four bullets that monk's gonna put into him."

"Right. Get enough for a decent burial, Punch."

"Deal, friend," grinned the unruffled Punch. "I'm up."

"On the level, Punch," resumed Meg, "keep your eyes open. That little ape looks evil to me."

"Aw, he's harmless."

"There ain't no such thing as a harmless monkey-chaser," objected Red. "If you've done anything to him, he'll get you sooner or later. He can't help it—he's just made that way, like a spring."

"I ain't got a thing for a monk to do, anyhow," interjected a spectator. "Hope Marcus Garvey takes 'em all back to Africa with him. He'll sure have a shipload."

Eight-Ball finished riffling the cards and began to distribute them carefully. "You jigs are worse 'n **ofays,**" he accused. "You raise hell about prejudice, and look at you—doin' just what you're raisin' hell over yourselves."

"Maybe so," Red rejoined, "but that don't make me like monks any better."

"What don't you like about 'em?"

"There ain't nothin' I do like about 'em. They're too damn conceited. They're too aggressive. They talk funny. They look funny—I can tell one the minute I see him. They're always startin' an argument an' they always want the last word. An' there's too many of 'em here."

"Yeah," Eight-Ball dryly rejoined. "An' they stick too close together an' get ahead too fast. They put it all over us in too many ways. We could stand 'em pretty well if it wasn't for that. Same as ofays an' Jews."

"Aw, can the dumb argument," said Meg. "Open for a nickel."

"Raise a nickel."

"Who was the pretty pink you were dancin' with the other night, Punch?" inquired the observer behind him.

The lethargic Punch came to life. "Boy, wasn't she a sheba? And I don't even know her name."

"Sheikin' around some, hey?"

"Nope. My sister Marian introduced me. But I'm so busy looking I don't catch the name, see? When I dance with her she finds out I don't know it and refuses to tell. I ask if I can come to see her and she says nothing doing—wouldn't think of letting a bird call who didn't even know her name."

"Really got you goin', hey?"

"Damn right, she did. I ask Marian her name afterwards and she won't come across either. Says she's promised not to tell and if I really want to locate the lady nothing'll stop me. Can y' beat it?"

"Why don't y' bribe Marian?"

"If you can bribe Marian I can be President."

"All right, heavy lover," interpolated Meg impatiently. "You in this game?"

Punch discovered then that he had discarded the three queens he had intended to keep, and had retained a deuce and a fivespot.

"Well, cut me in my neck!" he ejaculated. "Did you see what I did?"

The man behind him laughed. "Boy, you're just startin'," he said. "Wait till you locate the pink!"

. . .

The gloomy dinginess that dimmed the stuffy little front room of the Rosina's basement flat was offset not so much by the two or three one-bulb lights in surprisingly useless spots as by the glow of the argument, heated to incandescence. Payner, the house-superintendent, whose occupancy of these rooms constituted part of his salary, had not forgotten that he was a naturalized American of twenty years' standing, and no longer fresh from Montserrat; but Barbadian Gradyne had fallen fully into his native word-throttling, and Chester of Jamaica might have been chanting a loud response to prayer in the intervals when the others let his singsong have its say.

"No people become a great people," he now insisted, with his peculiar stressing of unaccented syllables, "except where it dominate. You t'ink de Negro ever dominate America? Pah!"

"Africa," Gradyne lumberingly supported him, "dat de only chance. Teng mo' years, mahn, dis Harl'm be jes' like downg Georgia. Dis a white mahn's country!"

"Back to Africa!" snorted Payner. "Go on back, you b'ys. Me—I doan give a dahm f all de Garveys an' all de Black Star liners in Hell. I stay right here!"

"You t'ink only for you'self," charged Chester. "You t'ink about you' race an' you see I am right. Garvey is de Moses of his people!"

"Maybeso. But I be dahm' if Moses git any my money. Back to Africa! How de hell I'm goin' back where I never been?"

Neither Gradyne's retaliative cudgel nor Chester's answering thrust achieved its mark, for at that moment Cyril Sebastian Best broke unceremoniously in and announced: "De house is pinch'!"

Like a blast furnace's flame, the argument faded as swiftly as it had flared.

"Where you was raised, boy? Don't you got no manners a-tall?"

Cyril banged the door behind him, stuck out his chest, and strutted across the room. "I tell you whaht I hahve got," he grinned.

"A hell of a nerve," grunted Gradyne.

"An' I tell you whaht I'm goin' get," Cyril proceeded. "I'm goin' get rich an' I'm goin' get married."

"How much you pays, 'ey?" asked Chester.

"Pays? For whaht?"

"For you' licker. You's drunk as hell."

"Den I stays drunk all 'e time. I got de sweetes' woman in de worl', boy—make a preacher lay 'is Bible downg!"

"Who it is?"

"Never min' who is it." But he described Hilda Vogel with all the hyperbole of enthusiasm.

Gradyne inspected him quizzically. "Dat gel mus' got two glass eyes," he grinned.

"Or else you have," Payner amended.

"How you know she care anyt'ing about you?" Chester asked.

"I know." Cyril was positive. "She tell me so dis ahfternoon in de elevator. I been makin' time all along, see? So dis ahfternoon when I get to de top floor I jes' staht to pop de question an' she look at me an' roll 'er eyes like dis, an' say, 'I may be in love!' an' run like hell downg de hall laughin'! Boy, I know!"

Payner and Chester and Gradyne all looked at him with pitying sympathy. Then Chester laughed.

"You cahn't tell anything by that, mahn."

"I cahn't, 'ey? Why not?"

"You had de poor girl too far up in de air!"

IV

"Did you see the awful thing Harriet wore?"

"Did I? Who in the world made it?"

"Noah's grandmother." "And that King Tut bob—at her age!"

"Maybe she's had monkey glands—"

Cyril, listening in at the switchboard, found it very uninteresting and, leaving off, deigned to take up three passengers who had been waiting for five minutes in the elevator. When he reached the street floor again, the instrument's familiar rattle was calling him back.

"Apartment sixty-one, please."

Something in the masculine voice made Cyril stiffen, something more than the fact that it sought connection with Hilda Vogel's apartment. He plugged in and rang.

"Can I speak to Miss Vogel, please?"

"This is Miss Vogel."

"Miss Hilda Vogel?"

"Yes."

The masculine voice laughed.

"Thought you'd given me the air, didn't you?"

"Who is it, please?" Cyril noted eagerness in Hilda's voice.

"Give you one guess."

"My, you're conceited."

"Got a right to be. I'm taking the queeniest sheba in Harlem to a show to-night, after which we're going to Happy's and get acquainted."

"Indeed? Why tell me about it?"

"You're the sheba."

Hilda laughed. "You don't lose any time, do you, Mr.—Punch?"

"I don't dare, Miss—Hilda."

Cyril, bristling attention, shivered. Despite its different tone, he knew the voice. A hot wave of memory swept congealingly over him; he felt like a raw egg dropped in boiling water.

"How did you find out I was—me?"

"Oho! Now it's your turn to wonder!"

"Tell me."

"Sure—when I see you."

"I think you're horrid."

"Why?"

"Well, I've got to let you come now or I'll die of curiosity."

"Dark eyes, but a bright mind. When do I save your life?"

"Are you sure you want to?"

"Am I talking to you?"

"You don't know a thing about me."

"More'n you know about me. I looked you up in Who's Who!"

"Now you're being horrid again. What did you find?"

"You work in the Model Shop on the Avenue, you live with your ma and pa, and you're too young and innocent to go around with only girls, sheikless and unprotected."

"How do you know I'm sheikless?" Cyril's heart stumbled.

"You're not—now," said the audacious Punch.

The girl gasped. Then, "You didn't find out the most important thing."

"To wit and namely?"

"Where I am from."

"Nope. I'm more interested in where you're going."

"We're—" she hesitated gravely. "I'm—Do you—object to—foreigners?"

It was Punch's gasp. "What?"

"There! You see, I told you you didn't want to come."

"What are you talking about?"

"We're—I'm a Bermudan, you know."

Punch's ringing laugh stabbed the eavesdropping ears. "I thought you were an Eskimo, the way you froze me that night."

"You're not—prejudiced?"

"Who, me? Say, one of the finest boys down at the P. O. is from Bermuda. Always raving about it. Says it's Heaven. Guess he means it's the place angels come from."

She was reassured. "Not angels. Onions."

"I like onions," said Punch.

"What time are you coming?"

"Right away! Now!"

"No. Eight."

"Seven!"

"Well—seven-thirty."

"Right."

"Good-bye."

"Not on your life. So long, Hilda."

"So long, Punch."

"Seven-thirty."

"Seven-thirty."

The lift was full of impatient people audibly complaining of the delay. The only response from the ordinarily defiant Cyril was a terrific banging open and shut of the gates as he let them out, floor by floor. His lips were inverted and pressed tightly together, so that his whole mouth bulged, and his little eyes were reddened between their narrowed lids.

"I may be in love—you'd never know." He had thought she was encouraging him. He would have made sure the next day had there not been too many people in the car. Fortunately enough, he saw now; for she had been thinking of the ruffian whose blow still rent his spirit, whose words still scalded his pride: "Now get the hell out o' here, you ringtail—"

He had seen Counselor Absalom. Absalom had said he couldn't touch the case—no witnesses, no money, prolonged litigation. Absalom hadn't even been sympathetic. Street brawls were rather beneath Absalom.

Cyril slammed the top gate to and reversed the controlling lever. As the car began to drop, something startled him out of his grim abstraction: the gate was slowly sliding open. It had failed to catch, recoiling under the force with which he had shut it. Yet the car was moving normally. The safety device whereby motion was possible only when all the gates were shut had been rendered useless—perhaps by his own violence just now. He released the lever. The car halted. He pushed the lever down forward. The car ascended. He released it. The car halted again. He pushed the lever down backward. The car descended. Its movements were entirely unaffected.

Cyril paused, undecided. For a long moment he remained motionless. Then with a little grunt he rose again and carefully closed the open gate. His smile as he reached the ground floor was incarnate malevolence, triumphant.

V

Meg Minor was following a frizzly bobbed head and a bright-red sweater up the Avenue. In the twilight he wasn't sure he knew her; but even if he didn't—he might. Introductions were old stuff. If the spark of attraction gleamed, blow on it: you might kindle a blaze.

As he crossed a side street an ambulance suddenly leaped from nowhere and rushed at him with terrifying clangor. He jumped back, the driver swore loudly, and the machine swept around the corner into the direction Meg was going.

"Swore like he was sorry he didn't hit me," he grinned to himself. "Must be out making patients or something. Where's that danger signal I was pacing?"

The red sweater had stopped in the middle of the next block. So had the ambulance. When Meg reached the place, a gathering crowd was already beginning to obstruct passage. Since the sweater had halted, Meg saw no reason for going on himself, and so, edging as close to it as he could, he prayed that the forthcoming sight might make the girl faint into his arms.

He paid no attention to the growing buzz about him. There was a long wait. Then the buzz abruptly hushed and the crowd shifted, opening a lane to the ambulance. In the shift Meg, squirming still nearer to the red sweater, found himself on the edge of the lane.

Two men, one in white, came out of the house, bearing a stretcher covered with a blanket. As they passed, Meg, looking, felt his heart trip and his skin tingle. He started forward.

"Punch! For God's sake—"

"Stand back, please!"

"It's Punch Anderson, Doc! What—what—is he—?" Meg pressed after the white coat.

"Doc—good Lord, Doc—tell me what happened! He's my buddy, Doc!"

"Tried to hop a moving elevator. Both legs—compound fractures."

Doors slammed. The ambulance made off with a roar and a clamor. Meg stood still. He did not see the bright-red sweater beside him or hear the girl asking if his friend would live. He was staring with mingled bewilderment and horror into the resplendent entrance of the Rosina. And, as he stared, the sound of the ambulance gong came back to his ears, peal upon peal, ever more distant, like receding derisive laughter.

Glossary for "Ringtail"

dis·gorge (dis-'gorj) *tr. v.*
dis·gorged; **dis·gorg·ing**
To give up (as illegally gained profits) on request, under pressure, or by court order esp. to prevent unjust enrichment. "ordered a . . . salesman to *disgorge* about $468,000 he had earned by defrauding Iowa banks" (*National Law Journal)*
dis·gorge·ment *noun*

leg·horn. (lĕg'hôrn', -ərn) *n.*

1. a. The dried and bleached straw of an Italian variety of wheat.
   b. A plaited fabric made from this straw.
   c. A hat made from this fabric.
2. Often **Leghorn**. Any of a breed of small, hardy domestic fowl of Mediterranean origin, noted for prolific production of eggs.
3. of doubt aroused by wrongdoing or the prospect of wrongdoing.

ce·rise (sə-rēs', -rēz') *n.*
A deep to vivid purplish red.
[French, from Old French, *cherry*.]
ce·rise' *adj.*

maize *n.* 1: tall annual cereal grass bearing kernels on large ears: widely cultivated in America in many varieties; the principal cereal in Mexico and Central and South America since pre-Columbian times [syn: corn, Indian corn, Zea mays] 2: a strong yellow color [syn.: gamboge, lemon, lemon yellow]

com·punc·tion (kəm-pŭngk'shən) *n.*

1. A strong uneasiness caused by a sense of guilt.

A sting of conscience or a pang

[Middle English compunccioun, from Old French componction, from Late Latin compūnctiō, compūnctiōn-, *puncture, sting of conscience,* from Latin compūnctus, past participle of compungere, *to sting*: com-, *intensive pref.*; see **com-** + pungere, *to prick*; see peuk- in Indo-European Roots.]
com·punc'tious (-shəs) *adj.* **com·punc'tion**

in·nate (ĭ-nāt', ĭn'āt') *adj.*

Possessed at birth; inborn.

in·nate'ness *n.* **in·nate** (in-'At, 'in-") *adjective*
Existing in, belonging to, or determined by factors present in an individual from birth: NATIVE, INBORN "*innate* behavior"—**in·nate·ly** *adverb* —**in·nate·ness** *noun*

con·ten·tious (kən-tĕn'shəs) *adj.*

1. Given to contention; quarrelsome.
2. Involving or likely to cause contention; controversial: "a central and contentious element of the book" (Tim W. Ferguson).

con·ten'tious·ly *adv.* **con·ten'tious·ness** *n.* **contentiousness**
n. : a disposition to fight [syn: aggressiveness, belligerence, pugnacity, quarrelsomeness]

ac·quis·i·tive (ə-kwĭz'ĭ-tĭv) *adj.*

1. Characterized by a strong desire to gain and possess.
2. Tending to acquire and retain ideas or information: *an acquisitive mind.*

ac·quis'i·tive·ly *adv.* **ac·quis'i·tive·ness** *n.* **ac·quis'i·tor** (-tər) *n.*
acquisitiveness n : strong desire to acquire and possess

sur·rep·ti·tious (sûr'əp-tĭsh'əs) *adj.*

1. Obtained, done, or made by clandestine or stealthy means.
2. Acting with or marked by stealth.

[Middle English, from Latin surreptīcius, from surreptus, past participle of surripere, *to take away secretly*: sub-, *secretly*; see **sub-** + rapere, *to seize*; see rep- in Indo-European Roots.]
sur'rep·ti'tious·ly *adv.* **sur'rep·ti'tious·ness** *n.*

com·pla·cen·cy (kəm-plā'sən-sə) *n.*

1. A feeling of contentment or self-satisfaction, especially when coupled with an unawareness of danger, trouble, or controversy.
2. An instance of contented self-satisfaction.

in·con·tro·vert·i·ble (ĭn-kŏn'trə-vûr'tə-bəl, ĭn'kŏn-) *adj.*

Impossible to dispute; unquestionable: *incontrovertible proof of the defendant's innocence.*

in·con'tro·vert'i·bil'i·ty or **in·con'tro·vert'i·ble·ness** *n.* **in·con'tro·vert'i·bly** *adv.*
incontrovertibly *adv.*: in an obvious and provable manner; "his documentary sources are demonstrably wrong" [syn: demonstrably, provably]

sub·tle·ty (sŭt'l-tē) *n.pl.* **sub·tle·ties**

1. The quality or state of being subtle.
2. Something subtle, especially a nicety of thought or a fine distinction.

e·lic·it (ĭ-lĭs'ĭt) *tr.v.* **e·lic·it·ed, e·lic·it·ing, e·lic·its**

1. To bring or draw out (something latent); educe.
2. To arrive at (a truth, for example) by logic.

To call forth, draw out, or provoke (a reaction, for example)
[Latin ēlicere, ēlicit-: ē-, ex-, *ex-* + lacere, *to entice.*]
e·lic'i·ta'tion *n.* **e·lic'i·tor** *n.*

def·er·ence (dĕf'ər-əns, dĕf'rəns) *n.*

1. Submission or courteous yielding to the opinion, wishes, or judgment of another.
2. Courteous respect.

mod·i·cum (mŏd'ĭ-kəm) *n.pl.* **mod·i·cums** or **mod·i·ca** (-kə)

A small, moderate, or token amount: "England still expects a modicum of eccentricity in its artists" (Ian Jack).

[Middle English, from Latin, from neuter of modicus, *moderate*, from modus, *measure*.]

ful·mi·nant (fo͝ol'mə-nənt, fŭl'-) *adj.*

1. Exploding or detonating.
2. Pathology. Occurring suddenly, rapidly, and with great severity or intensity.

[Latin fulminãns, fulminant- present participle of fulminãre, *to strike with lightning*.]

vi·tu·per·a·tion (vī-to͞o'pə-rā'shən, -tyo͞o'-, vĭ-) *n.*

1. The act or an instance of vituperating; abusive censure.
2. Sustained, harshly abusive language; invective.
3. **ep·i·thet** (ĕp'ə-thĕt')*n.*
   1. a. A term used to characterize a person or thing, such as rosy-fingered in *rosy-fingered dawn* or *the Great* in *Catherine the Great.*
      b. A term used as a descriptive substitute for the name or title of a person, such as *The Great Emancipator* for Abraham Lincoln.
   2. An abusive or contemptuous word or phrase.
   3. Biology. A word in the scientific name of an animal or plant following the name of the genus and denoting a species, variety, or other division of the genus, as *sativa* in *Lactuca sativa.*

   [Latin epitheton, from Greek, neuter of epithetos, *added, attributed*, from epitithenai, epithe-, *to add*]

fe·tor (fē'tər, -tôr') also **foe·tor** (fē'tər) *n.* An offensive odor; a stench.

[Middle English fetoure, from Latin fētor, from fētēre, *to stink*.] *to* : epi-, *epi-* + tithenai, *to place*; see dhē- in Indo-European Roots.] **ep'i·thet'ic** or **ep'i·thet'i·cal** *adj.*
sīmus, *snub-nosed*, from Greek sīmos.]

in·vec·tive (ĭn-vĕk'tĭv) *n.*

1. Denunciatory or abusive language; vituperation.
2. Denunciatory or abusive expression or discourse.

adj.

Of, relating to, or characterized by denunciatory or abusive language.

[From Middle English invectif, *denunciatory*, from Old French, from Late Latin invectīvus, *reproachful, abusive*, from Latin invectus, past participle of invehī, *to inveigh against*.]
in·vec'tive·ly *adv.* **in·vec'tive·ness** *n.*

su·per·cil·i·ous (so͞o'pər-sĭl'ē-əs) *adj.*

Feeling or showing haughty disdain.

[Latin superciliōsus, from supercilium, *eyebrow, pride*: super-, *super-* + cilium, *lower eyelid*.]
su'per·cil'i·ous·ly *adv.* **su'per·cil'i·ous·ness** *n.*

ob·tuse (ŏb-to͞os', -tyo͞os', əb-) *adj.* **ob·tus·er, ob·tus·est**

1. a. Lacking quickness of perception or intellect.
   b. Characterized by a lack of intelligence or sensitivity: *an obtuse remark.*
   c. Not distinctly felt: *an obtuse pain.*

2. a. Not sharp, pointed, or acute in form; blunt.
   b. Having an obtuse angle: *an obtuse triangle.*
   c. Botany. Having a blunt or rounded tip: *an obtuse leaf.*

[Middle English, from Old French, from Latin obtūsus, past participle of obtundere, *to blunt.*]

ob·tuse'ly *adv.* **ob·tuse'ness** *n.*

dis·com·fi·ture (dĭs-kŭm'fĭ-chŏŏr', -chər) *n.*

1. Frustration or disappointment.
2. Lack of ease; perplexity and embarrassment.
3. *Archaic.* Defeat.

o·fay (ō'fā') *n.* *Offensive Slang*

Used as a disparaging term for a white person.

[*Possibly of West African origin.*]

Word History: The commonly seen etymology of *ofay*—Pig Latin for *foe*—is of less interest than the more likely story of this word's origins. The word, which is first recorded in the first quarter of the 20th century, must have been in use much longer if it is, as some scholars think, borrowed from an African source. Although this source has not been pinned down, the suggested possibilities are in themselves interesting. One would trace it to the Ibibio word *afia,* "white or light-colored." Another would have it come from Yoruba *ofe,* a word that was said in order to protect oneself from danger. The term was then transferred to white people, regarded as a danger to Black people throughout the wretched days of slavery and beyond.

Reading Comprehension

Answer the following questions about the short story by Rudolph Fisher.

Word Meaning

Using the glossary, select the entry that best completes the sentences below.

1. The wedding party wore matching clothing in the color of __________, a lively shade of red.
2. Many current autumn celebrations include a walk through fields of __________ that are designed in a particular shape from the dried stalks of corn.
3. Since her first days on the field, the star soccer goalie possessed a/an __________ talent for predicting the direction of the kicked ball into the net.
4. To acquire the everyday __________ of a foreign language, a person should reside in the country where the target language is spoken, one advantage of study abroad.
5. Despite the many positive __________ publicized about the criminal, the jury still found him guilty of fraud.
6. The judge ordered the embezzler to __________ one million dollars wrongfully stolen from the company.
7. Having no __________, the student bought every essay submitted in his online course from an Internet site; finally caught, he was dismissed from college.

8. Without a __________ of doubt about their future relationship, the couple, who had met two weeks earlier, flew to Las Vegas to marry in an Elvis impersonator's chapel.
9. Hollywood films are so full of __________ that viewers in other countries believe all Americans use profanity in their everyday lives.
10. Without hesitation, the teenager told his parents his strong opinions about many debatable topics; he knew he was __________ right about his thoughts.

Literal Meaning

Mark the letter of the option that best answers the statements below.

1. What is the setting of Fisher's short story?
   a. Trinidad in the early part of the century
   b. British West Indies in fall 1900
   c. Harlem in the 1920s
   d. Harlem in 2002
2. Who is the main character in the short story?
   a. Punch Anderson
   b. Cyril Sebastian Best
   c. Rosina
   d. Meg
3. What is the conflict of the story, the event that begins the action of the plot?
   a. The parade of the church members on Seventh Avenue
   b. The work as the elevator operator
   c. Arrival from Trinidad by boat
   d. The meeting of Punch, Meg, and Cyril on the street
4. What character trait does *not* describe Cyril Sebastian Best?
   a. Superiority
   b. Pride
   c. Cockiness
   d. Gentleness
5. Which one of Cyril's character traits leads to the injury of Punch in this selection?
   a. Vengeance
   b. Cockiness
   c. Vanity
   d. Jealousy
6. What is the point of view of the short story?
   a. First person
   b. Third person
   c. Third-person omniscient
   d. Third-person limited

Interpretive Meaning

Complete the questions with the response that best answers the statement.

1. What is the theme of "Ringtail"?
   a. Being of the same race but from different backgrounds may create cultural conflicts.
   b. One person's self-image can lead to another person's demise.
   c. Conflict is a regular part of life in small sections of a big city.
   d. Love can cause people to do unthinkable actions toward others.
2. What is the tone of the short story?
   a. Argumentative
   b. Mildly sarcastic
   c. Informative
   d. Outrageously humorous
3. Why did Cyril like Hilda?
   a. Because she flirted with him
   b. Because she was sympathetic and foreign-born like himself
   c. Because she spoke a foreign language that interested him
   d. Because she played word games with him
4. What type of figurative language identifies the following line from the story: "You need not stand on the opposite side of the Avenue and observe the disdain with which the Rosina looks down upon her neighbors"?
   a. Metaphor
   b. Simile
   c. Symbolism
   d. Personification
5. What is the significance of the following line spoken by Meg: "Show me a monk that won't try to get even and I'll swallow the Woolworth Building"?
   a. Meg is boasting about his ability to eat big quantities of food.
   b. Meg's statement shows his comical side.
   c. The statement foreshadows upcoming events in the story.
   d. Meg is answering a question asked by Punch.
6. How does Cyril interpret Hilda's statement about being in love?
   a. Cyril thinks she might be in love with him.
   b. Cyril is happy she has found someone to love.
   c. Cyril plots to find out with whom she is in love.
   d. Cyril thinks she is just making elevator conversation.
7. What is ironic about the statement that Meg "prayed that the forthcoming sight might make the girl faint into his arms"?
   a. He is thinking about the girl's safety.
   b. Even though he wants to impress the girl, he hopes she will also love him.
   c. He is trying to make a move on the girl at that particular moment.
   d. He is thinking about the girl's reaction when suddenly he is the one shocked.
8. What effect does the final event in the story have on the Meg?
   a. He forgets about impressing the girl he was following.
   b. He remains in shock as the ambulance takes off.

   c. He feels helpless in helping his friend Punch.
   d. All of the above
9. Why does Fisher use the slang terms of the time period of the story?
   a. His language choice conveys the era about which he is writing.
   b. He is trying to impress the reader with his knowledge of slang.
   c. He wants the reader to learn slang.
   d. Both a and b
10. What does Fisher mean by " . . . ever more distant, like receding derisive laughter," the final words of the story?
   a. The sound of the ambulance provides a strong sensory image for ending the story.
   b. The sound of the ambulance upsets Meg as he watches the scene unfold.
   c. The words reflect back to Cyril Sebastian Best's personality.
   d. The words represent the final step in the story, the success of Cyril's vengeance.

Score: Number correct _____ out of _____

Writing Assignments

1. Journal Writing

Summary

Write a one-paragraph summary of the plot of the short story.

Reaction

Discuss your initial feelings about the story. Why did you like or dislike the story? What do you consider to be the strongest element of the short story? Explain your answer.

2. Paragraph

Focus on Causes: Write a paragraph explaining the reasons "there were British West Indians in Harlem who would have told Cyril Sebastian flatly to his face that they despised him." Cite examples from the short story to support your reasons.

Focus on Effects: Write a paragraph explaining the effects of Sebastian's vanity upon the plot of the short story.

3. Paragraph to Essay

Write an essay analyzing the problems Sebastian faced and how he reacted to the problems. Use the paragraph (or paragraphs) from assignment two as the basis of your ideas. When writing this, reflect upon Sebastian's attitude and demeanor in the first body paragraph. In the remaining body paragraph, focus on the effects of his demeanor.

4. Essay

Write an essay analyzing the effects of revenge in one's life.

Reflective Assignments

1. Reflect on the quotation by John Irvin at the beginning of the unit: "If you are lucky enough to find a way of life you love, you have to find the courage to live it." Write an essay explaining either the consequences of living a life that you love (or do not love). Reflect upon education, career, and/or your personal life.
2. Write a poem in which you explain "how things work" in your community. Model your poem after Soto's.
3. Choose an idiom from the list at the beginning of the chapter that reflects your attitude toward your life. Write a paragraph explaining how this idiom is reflective of your lifestyle. To develop substance, cite personal examples from your life. How does your lifestyle reflect the meaning of the idiom?
4. Choose idioms from the list at the beginning of the chapter that best reflect the attitude of Cyril Sebastian Best and Punch Anderson in the short story "Ringtail." Use the idioms as a foundation of a character analysis of the two characters.
5. Write a paragraph comparing the character traits of Cyril Sebastian Best to the personified traits of the entrance of the hotel Rosina in the short story "Ringtail." The entrance is given human qualities. How do these traits compare to the traits of the main character Cyril Sebastian Best?

Internet Field Trips—Reading and Writing Assignments

1. To read about Harlem and the Harlem Renaissance, explore the Web sites listed below.
   - http://www. iniva. org/harlem/hren.htm
   - http://nfo. net/usa/harlem.htm
   - http://www.fatherryan.org/harlemrenaissance/
   - http://www.poets.org/
   - http://www.pbs.org/newshour/forum/february98/harlem_2-20.html
   - http://www.bcc.ctc.edu/thejibsheet/

   A. After reading the information, write an essay explaining the reasons for the Harlem Renaissance or the effects of the movement on literature.

   B. Write a paragraph explaining what characteristics of the Harlem Renaissance are displayed in the short story "Ringtail."
2. Use the Internet to find out more about Gary Soto. Read several of his poems and become familiar with his background. Write a paragraph explaining how Soto's heritage is reflected in his work. The following Web sites should be helpful.
   - http://www.garysoto.com
   - http://project1.caryacademy.org/echoes/poet_Gary_Soto/DefaultSoto.htm
   - http://www. georgetown. edu/faculty/bassr/heath/syllabuild/iguide/soto.html

3. Search the Internet to find information about the work volunteers do in America. After reading the information, write a causal analysis on volunteering in America. The following Web sites should help:
   - http://www.npr.org/templates/story/story.php?storyId=1142996;
   - usafreedomcorps.gov; http://usinfo.state. gov/scv/life_and_culture/volunteerism.htm
4. For more information about urban cowboys, explore these Web sites:
   - http://www.philadelphiaweekly.com/view.php?id=7827
   - http://www.jrn.columbia.edu/studentwork/cns/2002-03-13/285.asp
   - http://www. harlemlive.org/arts-culture/sports/rodeo

   Write a paragraph explaining the effects that the programs described in the Web sites have had on youth and the community.

Films to View

Becoming American: The Chinese Experience (directed by Thomas Lennon, 2003)
How Stella Got Her Groove Back (directed by Kevin Rodney Sullivan, 1998)
Somebodies (directed by Hadjii, 2006)
Grapes of Wrath (directed by John Ford, 1940)
American Graffiti (directed by George Lucas, 1973)
Philadelphia (directed by Jonathan Demme, 1993)
On Golden Pond (directed by Mark Rydell, 1981)
Ferris Bueller's Day Off (directed by John Hughes, 1986)
Brokeback Mountain (directed by Ang Lee, 2005)

Writing assignments are based on *Philadelphia* directed by Jonathan Demme and written by Ron Nyswane

1. Write a summary of the film and a reaction to it. In your reaction, remember that the film was produced in 1993 when an AIDS diagnosis was considered a death sentence. With this information in mind, what do you think the effect of the movie was upon moviegoers at the time? What effect does the movie have on you?
2. If you were going to write an updated version of this film, what changes would you make? Write two paragraphs, one explaining the changes and one explaining the reasons for the changes.
3. Write a causal analysis of the reactions of the character Andrew Beckett's employer and fellow employees to his illness and sexual orientation.
4. Write a causal analysis explaining how representing Andrew Becker affects attorney Joe Miller.
5. The tagline for *Philadelphia* is "No one would take on his case . . . until one man was willing to take on the system." Write a paragraph explaining how this tagline relates to the story.

SUMMARY OF UNIT 7—AMERICAN LIFESTYLE—CAUSE AND EFFECT ANALYSIS

Read the student essay entitled "Divorce" by Natalie Edwards. Analyze it for its content, its organization, and its mechanics. Then, in the Summary of Unit 7 on page 362, complete the column on the right with your responses. Apply the information learned in Unit 7. Notice that in this essay the author has used MLA documentation to cite the sources she has used.

Divorce

As most people know, today, not only in the United States, but also throughout the whole world, the number of couples seeking a divorce is rising. Between 1960 and 1980, the divorce rate spiked by 250 percent (Galston 14). It is said that marriages in the United States are currently characterized as instable and more than half of all marriages will end in divorce (Bodenmann 178). That huge increase and statement gives proof to the problem that most people today do not know what it takes to create and maintain a strong marriage, therefore causing most marriages today to end in divorce. Although there are many underlying problems to this one large problem of divorce, I am just going to focus on a few of them and give solutions for each of the underlying problems focused on. Hopefully, by giving solutions to the small underlying problems will help the large problem at hand. Reasons for divorce include not knowing the other person well enough, marrying too soon or waiting too long, bad premarital counseling, problems in communication, and it being too easy to obtain a divorce.

Why does it really matter to other people whether or not our growing divorce rate increases, decreases, or stays the same? Besides the fact that divorce brings great pain to people inside and outside the marriage that is broken down, it also affects the children in a number or ways. Although it affects them at the immediate time that the divorce occurs, the main problem that we should be concerned with is when it affects them subconsciously down the road in their future relationships that could possibly turn into a life-long, or in 50 percent of cases, a short marriage. Those effects will be felt long down the road, possibly affecting people who have never before been involved in a divorce. About one and one-half million children in today's society will experience their parent's divorce per year. These children that have been through a divorce are more likely to experience intimacy and communication problems, and ultimately end up experiencing their own divorce (Mullett 40). This is a very large number of people that will eventually end up in serious relationships with other people that have never been through any type of divorce, or that could have dealt with divorce, that will most likely bring some emotional "baggage" to the relationship causing future problems. The statistics from studies say that if only the man in the marriage has experienced a parental divorce, his marriage will be no more likely to end in divorce than if he had not experienced the divorce. If only the woman has experienced a parental divorce, the chance of her marriage ending in divorce is eighty seven percent more likely to end in divorce then if she had not experienced it. If both the man and the woman have experienced parental divorce, their marriage is 620 percent more likely to end in divorce then a couple whom neither had experienced it (Mullett 40–1). Hopefully, now it is shown why it is so important to prevent divorce, especially when there are children involved. It is not only a private affair of the couple involved since it is obviously passed from generation to generation; it affects everyone in our society (Bodenmann 178). Preventing divorce now will ultimately prevent divorce in the future generations to come, saving a lot of pain and suffering. If it cannot be prevented now, will there ever be hope to prevent it in the future?

Many of today's couples think that they know each other really well, but sometimes their assumptions are wrong. This can be a huge problem in a marriage. Without knowing the other person in a marriage, how can someone think that the marriage could ever be life-long? Some things that we think are small differences or that we do not even see can ultimately end up making or breaking our marriages. It is found that not having similar tastes and preferences, and not having similar ways in dealing with social matters affects the risk factors for divorce. The lack of similarity in tastes and preferences create two times more of a risk for divorce than the lack in social matters (Lowenstein 160). Is it not interesting that the small differences in someone's tastes and preferences cause more divorces than differences dealing with social matters? Does that not show why it is so important to truly know the other person in the relationship before committing your life to them? Those small tastes and preferences could be something so small such as which side of the bed to sleep on, or it could be something as large as whether or not to have children or not, or whether or not to have a Christian home or not. It goes to show that not knowing the other person in the relationship and not working out the differences ahead of time increases the risk for the marriage ending in divorce.

The second problem causing divorces is that people are either marrying too early or too late into the relationship. Sometimes it is said that when people marry too early into the relationship, their marriage will end in divorce because they do not know each other well enough, and when people are together for a very long time before marriage, their marriage will be the life-long marriage that everyone tries for. There are people out there that disagree with that statement. They say that there is a "happy medium" for the time to date for a marriage to be successful. They say that marrying too early means that the partners cannot know each other well enough, but marrying after a very long time of dating implies commitment problems. In the study done, the ones that married after the longest courtship were the first to divorce, even before the ones who married very soon (Lombardi 1–3). What does this show? It shows that there is a "happy medium" for marriage and that waiting and being cautious is not necessarily the best thing to do.

The next problem I am going to talk about is premarital counseling. Even though people can think they know each other, it always helps for an outsider that is specialized to help point out the differences that maybe other people overlook that could possibly hurt a marriage. That is one of the main reasons people receive premarital counseling. A very large portion of people who receive premarital counseling are Christians because most Christian churches require that it be done before they can be married in the church. It was seen that in 1999, more Christians than average people were getting divorced. This was caused because the Christian church's premarital counseling programs were not even making the minimum requirements that they were supposed to (Lowenstein 162). The reason that the Christian divorce rate was higher at that time was because most of them were not receiving the good counseling that they had been receiving and now are receiving. This shows just how important premarital counseling is. It shows that a large cause of divorce is that people are either not receiving premarital counseling or they are not receiving adequate premarital counseling.

The fourth cause of divorce that I would like to address is that there is a lack in communication when dealing with stress, and there is not enough time spent together between spouses. Many studies show that the reason marriages are not withstanding is because there is a lack of ability to communicate and solve problems among both partners (Bodenmann 177–8). Lowenstein tells us that, "other factors important in relationships and frequently neglected were positive time spent by the spouses with one another" (160). The key words in that quote are "positive time spent." These two problems are interrelated because if two people cannot communicate and solve problems efficiently, how are they going to spend positive time together? These facts show that people today lack the ability to communicate and spend positive time together, causing an increase in divorce.

The fifth, and final, cause of divorce that I would like to talk about is that it is too easy to get a divorce and get it fast. In the United States, there is a no-fault divorce, which means that either partner can file for divorce without having to report why the other partner is at fault. With this law, it is easier to obtain a divorce very fast. From a 50 state survey, it is shown that when switching from fault to no-fault divorce, the rate increased (Galston 17). Another set of research says that states with a waiting period and counseling laws that mandate counseling before a divorce will be granted have slightly lower divorce rates (Beaulieu 2). Those waiting periods may give couples a chance to work out their differences, and the counseling laws that force the couples into counseling may make the couple see what can be fixed, preventing divorce. From this data, we can see that having easy access divorces cause people to get divorces more often.

Now that I have told about the main problems that I see causing divorce, I am going to propose a solution to this big problem of rising divorce rates. This solution is made up of many smaller solutions to the smaller problems that, when put together, will in turn, solve the large problem at hand. The main part of my solution is preventing people from getting married that should not be getting married.

If we can prevent bad marriages, we can ultimately prevent divorce. If someone is already married, there are other measures that can be taken to make the bad marriages better and in turn prevent divorce. The essence of my solution is to make sure that each partner knows the other the best that they can before they decide to get married. This does not just apply to what they like to do or not like to do, but it also applies to the big things like having children and religion. Another aspect that will help the partners to know each other better is the best premarital counseling possible. In a Christian aspect, many churches need to make a new concrete premarital counseling program that will focus on preventing bad marriages, rather than having to fix bad ones in the future (Lowenstein 162). When it comes to the best amount of time to date before getting married, that is open to the "user's discretion." It is known that dating too long means that there are most likely commitment problems that will never go away, and dating for to short of a time means that the people could not possible know each other well enough (Lombardi 2–3). There is a happy medium to the time to date, but it has to do with the people involved and the circumstances, so do not hang on too long, but do not let it be too short. When it comes to the communication skills, the main thing is to make sure that the skills are present and working before the marriage begins. There needs to be efforts among both partners when one of them is undergoing stress or when there is stress within the couple. The two partners can work together or one partner can support the other (Bodenmann 179–80). The main thing is that the two people involved are always communicating efficiently with each other. If they can communicate, they will be able to spend positive time together to strengthen their relationship, which is said to help build a positive relationship. The final aspect of my solution deals with marriages that are already in existence and the divorce laws in place. The laws should be in place so that divorce does not have easy access. There should not be a no-fault divorce, and there should be a specified waiting time before a divorce is granted. In that waiting time, the people involved should be required by law to seek counseling. These things will hopefully make the people in struggling marriages seek help, keeping them a marriage and not turning into a divorce. So in conclusion, my solution for lowering the divorce rate is to make sure that partners know each other, to make sure they go through premarital counseling, to make sure they analyze their dating time table, to make sure they can communicate effectively, and to make sure that there are more strict divorce laws in place. All of these things should, when combined, lower the divorce rate.

Works Cited

Bodenmann, Guy. "Can Divorce Be Prevented by Enhancing the Coping Skills of Couples?" Journal of Divorce and Remarriage. Ed. Craig A. Everett. Vol. 27 (3/4) 1997. The Haworth Press, Inc: 1997. 177–180.

Beulieu, Richard, John Crouch, Scott Dukat . . . Divorce Rate and Laws: USA & Europe. April 22, 2006.

Galston, William A. "Divorce American Style." Public Interest. Issue 124. Summer 1996. 12–21.

Lombardi, Lisa. "Your Courtship Clock—Decoded." April 22, 2006. http://lifestyle.msn.com/Relationships/CouplesandMarriage/ArticleIV2

Lowenstein, Ludwig F. "Causes and Associated Features of Divorce as Seen by Recent Research." Journal of Divorce and Remarriage. Vol. 42 (3/4) 2005. The Haworth Press, Inc: 2005. 156–162.

Mullett, Elizabeth and Arnold L. Stolberg. "Divorce and Its Impact on the Intimate Relationships of Young Adults." Journal of Divorce and Remarriage. Vol. 38 (1/2) 2002. The Haworth Press, Inc: 2002. 40–43.

SUMMARY OF UNIT 7

1. The thesis of the essay is	1.
2. The main tense in the causal analysis is	2.
3. Three transitions used include	3.
4. The tone of this essay is	4.
5. The purpose of this essay is to	5.
6. The writer concludes by	6.
7. The reader can infer that the writer	7.
8. Traits of causal analysis present are	8.
9. Three mechanical errors include	9.
10. Comments on wording include	10.

Unit 8

New Frontiers

Small opportunities are often the beginning of great enterprises.

—DEMOSTHENES, GREEK PHILOSOPHER

Exploration is really the essence of the human spirit.

—FRANK BORMAN, U.S. ASTRONAUT

Often scientists like Gertrude B. Elion receive rewards like the Nobel Prize for inventions and discoveries. Why did she receive the Nobel Prize? How should scientists combine medicine with physiology to find cures for diseases?

Today's scientists explore many American medical frontiers. What emerging realms of discovery should these scientists explore? What rules, if any, should govern their exploration?

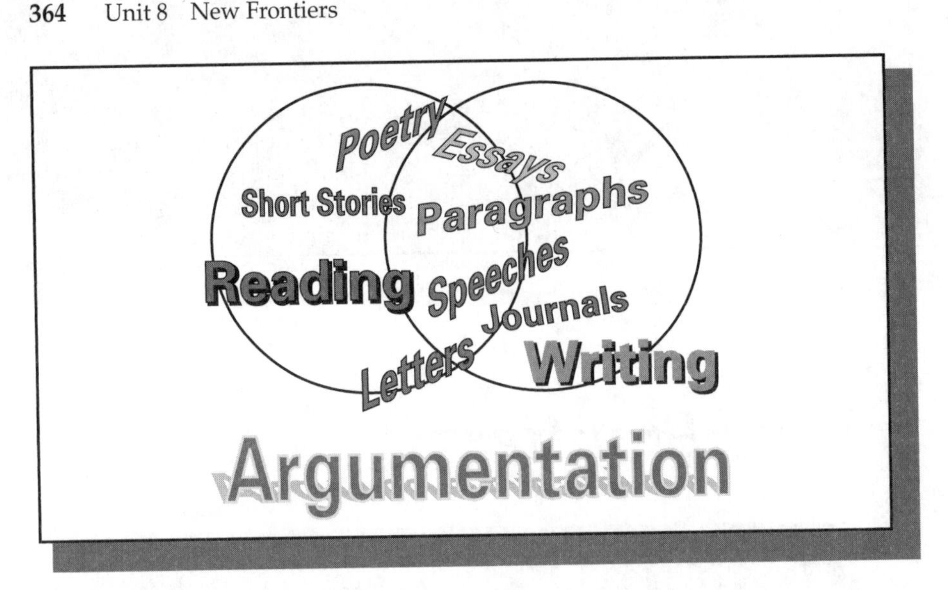

Purpose of Unit:

- *To understand the pattern of argumentation as it relates to reading comprehension and writing.*

Idioms for New Frontiers

Review the idioms below. Discuss their meaning. Apply these idioms to the idea of exploring new frontiers.

A shot in the dark
Lend me your ear.
A toss-up
About face
Actions speak louder than words.
All that glitters is not gold.
The ends justify the means.
The sky is the limit.
Back to the drawing board
Finding your feet
Out on a limb
Without a doubt
It's a small world.
The jury is out.
Turn over a new leaf.
Up for grabs

ARGUMENTATION: POINTS TO CONSIDER

People in all ages and times have debated issues and argued over solutions to problems. With each generation and the exploration of new frontiers come problems that must be solved, rules that must be made, and ideas that must be analyzed. While the ideas and concepts learned in all of the chapters in this text can be used to present and analyze a logical argument, argumentative writing does differ from informative writing. In a persuasive essay, the author is arguing for one side, not just presenting information. The purpose of an argument is to convince the reader to think as the author does or to call the reader to action. The principles of writing, reading, and analyzing arguments not only can be used in reading and English classes, but also in other college classes, at work, and in the community. When reading and writing arguments, you should consider the following points. These ideas will guide you into more logical thinking and clearer persuasive writing.

Purpose

The purpose of an argumentative essay is to convince the reader to think as the writer does or to call the reader to action about a particular issue.

Organization and Plan

Argumentative writing must have a strong thesis which is supported with evidence—examples, statistics, testimonials, and facts. To be effective, the evidence should be presented in an organized manner. When reading the assignments in the text or arguments made in other academic essays or editorials, identify the argument and mark the verbal support the author gives for the argument. When planning the writing of an argument, decide the focus of your paper and write it in a strong thesis statement. Plan how you are going to support the thesis and evaluate your support.

Argumentative Paragraphs

The topic sentence in an argumentative paragraph should clearly state the point of the argument. The supporting sentences should convince the reader that you are right about the issue. The concluding sentence can call for action, remind the reader of how important the argument is, or predict the future if the argument is or is not accepted.

Argumentative Essays

The essays assigned in this unit call for introductory paragraphs that include a thesis statement and body paragraphs that support the thesis. Concluding paragraphs in argumentative essays generally remind the reader of the importance of the topic and contain a call for action. Often, the writer will predict the wonderful consequences that will occur if the writer's argument is heeded and the dire consequences if the argument is rejected. Some formal arguments will have a paragraph that refutes the strongest argument of the opposition and/or one that concedes one of the points of the opposition. To concede a point does not mean that the writer is conceding the argument, just one of the points.

Transitional Expressions

The transitional expressions used in argumentation depend on the need of the paragraph. To introduce examples for support, use expressions such as *for example, another reason, such as, to illustrate*. To show intensity and emotion, use expressions such as *truly, of course, certainly*. To show contrast, use expressions such as *in contrast, unlike, in spite of, nevertheless, however.*

Language and Tone

The language used in writing will reflect the tone or the attitude of the writer. When writing an argument, use strong verbs such as *ought to, shall, should, must, can*. You are taking a stand in an argument, so the reader needs to know your viewpoint. However, avoid name-calling and making generalizations, as both are unprofessional and weaken your argument. Likewise, you should be skeptical when you read arguments that insult the opposition and make broad generalizations.

Emotion and Reason

Although you can appeal to the reader's sense of justice and righteousness, by definition, argumentative writing is based on facts and evidence rather than on emotion. As a critical reader, become aware of arguments that only appeal to emotion by using words that connote certain feelings or by making generalizations and assumptions.

Paragraph Format for Writing Argumentative Analysis

Use the following format for writing an argumentative paragraph.

Topic Sentence

Example or Reason 1

Example or Reason 2

Example or Reason 3

Concluding Sentence

Essay Format for Writing Argumentative Analysis

Use the following format to write an essay with 3 body paragraphs. Each body paragraph should argue a reason why your argument is valid. In your outline and essay, include several examples to support your topic sentence or one extended example.

Subject ______________________________

Narrowed Subject ______________________________

Thesis Statement ______________________________

I. Topic Sentence for introductory paragraph

II. Body Paragraph 1—Topic Sentence

  a. Supporting example

  b. Supporting example

  c. Supporting example

III. Body Paragraph 2—Topic Sentence

  a. Supporting example

  b. Supporting example

  c. Supporting example

IV. Body Paragraph 3—Topic Sentence

  a. Supporting example

  b. Supporting example

  c. Supporting example

V. Conclusion

Use the outline below to plan an essay with three body paragraphs, plus a paragraph of concession and a paragraph of refutation. The concession paragraph demonstrates that the opposition demonstrates a valid point that you concede, or give to the writer. The refutation paragraph is one that takes an opponent's argument and demonstrates the fallacy in thinking based on your evidence. Each of the body paragraphs should focus on one reason your argument is valid.

Subject ______________________________

Narrowed Subject ______________________________

Thesis Statement ______________________________

I. Topic Sentence for introductory paragraph

II. Concede

III. Body Paragraph 1—Topic Sentence
   a. Supporting example
   b. Supporting example
   c. Supporting example

IV. Body Paragraph 2—Topic Sentence
   a. Supporting example
   b. Supporting example
   c. Supporting example

V. Body Paragraph 3—Topic Sentence
   a. Supporting example
   b. Supporting example
   c. Supporting Example

VI. Refute

VII. Topic Sentence for concluding paragraph

Argumentative Analysis Writing Worksheet

1. Survey the assignment and choose your topic. Do one of the prewriting assignments discussed in the introduction of the text.
2. Question the assignment. What is the argument? What are the two sides to the argument?
3. Map your essay or paragraph.
4. Relate your plan of writing to your writing group. Present your argument to the group. Discuss the points you want to make. Discuss what you consider to be the strongest and weakest points of the opposition.
5. Record (write) the first draft of your essay or paragraph.
6. Read your paragraph or essay aloud to a student partner. As you read, your partner should listen for logical arguments.
7. Revise your essay, taking into account the questions your peer editors asked about your paper.
8. Review your revised paper with your partner and answer Questions for Review.
9. Reflect upon the comments of your peers and make needed changes.
10. Reread your paper, checking for grammatical errors. Read your paper from top to bottom and from bottom to top. Reading your paper in reverse helps you to read what you wrote, not what you meant to write! As you read your paper, check carefully for strong decisive language.

11. Revise your argument with corrections made to the logic and the content. Also, make corrections to any mechanical errors found in the essay.
12. Write your final draft.

Plagiarism

Argumentation often requires research. Writers should know as much or more about the opposing view as they know about their side of the issue. Therefore, plagiarism can become a problem with this mode of writing.

Whenever writers summarize an idea, paraphrase an author's words, or quote directly from the source, they must give credit to the author. A parenthetical citation or the mention of the author in the sentence is required. Most handbooks outline the format.

Strong Verbs

With the mode of argumentation, writers must take a position about a controversial issue. The readers must understand from the beginning what stand the writers are taking. Verbs such as *should, should not, must, must not, ought, ought not* express strong opinion and are recommended. When proofreading the paper, non-native English speakers should pay special attention to the verb forms used with these modal auxiliary verbs. The present tense stem, or base form, is always used with the auxiliaries above.

Using strong verbs to express opinions, write a sentence below with the correct verb forms.

1. Space exploration of Mars

____

2. Stem cell use for curing disease

____

Questions for Review

Paragraph Assignment

- What is the topic sentence?
- What argument is being made?
- What is the pattern of development for the paragraph?
- Are there any parts of the paragraph that are unclear? What are they? How can they be corrected?
- Has the author used transitional words to take the reader from one example to another? What are they?
- What key words has the author used to give the paragraph unity?
- What is the concluding sentence? Does it call for action?

- What questions do you have for the author?
- What is the best part of the paragraph?
- On what points do you agree with the author? On what points do you disagree?

Essay Assignment

The Introductory Paragraph

- Does the introduction make you want to read the essay?
- What is the focus of the essay? What subject is being argued?
- What is the thesis statement?
- Does the author take a stand on the subject? What is it? How can you tell?

The Body Paragraphs

- Does each body paragraph have a clear topic sentence that directly relates to the thesis statement?
- What is the focus of each body paragraph?
- Are there any parts of the paragraphs that are confusing? If so, what are they and how can they be corrected?
- What transitional words does the author use to guide the reader from one paragraph to the next? What transitional words has the author used within the body paragraphs? Are all the transitional words used correctly? If not, which ones need to be corrected?
- What key words has the author used to give the essay unity?
- Has the author used more active voice verbs than passive voice verbs?
- What are the strong verbs that the author has used?
- List examples of persuasive language.

The Conclusion

- Does the author come to a conclusion in the essay or does the author summarize his or her ideas? Does the author both conclude and summarize?
- What predictions does the author make in the concluding paragraph?

Overall Paper

- What questions do you have for the author?
- On which points do you agree with the author?
- On which points do you disagree with the author?
- What is the best part of the essay?

READING BEFORE WRITING

Act II

Diane Brady

This article explains the bold step that Ann Fudge, a high-powered African-American CEO, took when she surprised corporate America by taking a two-year sabbatical from the industry. It argues the question of whether one, especially a woman who was simply burned out, can quit and still be highly sought after.

In February, 2001, Ann Fudge did something that has become achingly common among high-powered career women. She quit. After a quarter-century as a rising star in Corporate America and just one year after she had been promoted to run a $5 billion division of Kraft Foods Inc. (KFT), Fudge walked away. She didn't do it for her two sons, who were already grown and embarked on careers of their own. She didn't do it to accept another turnaround challenge, building on her reputation for reviving brands from Minute Rice to Maxwell House. Like a number of her peers, she simply wanted to define herself by more than her professional status, considerable as it was, and financial rewards, sizable as they were. "It was definitely not dissatisfaction," says Fudge, now 52. "It was more about life."

For Fudge, that meant cycling around Sardinia and going to movies on Sunday nights. It meant finally enjoying her Westport (Conn.) home, where she had done little more than grab a few hours sleep amid the grind of corporate life—"things like going out on the deck and writing in my journal." It meant rising to do yoga instead of racing to work, reading books about moving the soul instead of moving products, and sitting down to dinner with her husband, Rich, instead of grabbing a slice of pizza at the office. And, perhaps most refreshing for a woman cast as a role model for much of her career, it meant **anonymity.** "I loved it. You drop off the map, and nobody cares about you anymore."

Well, not quite. About two years into her **sojourn,** Fudge got a call from Martin Sorrell, chief executive of Britain's advertising **conglomerate,** WPP Group PLC (WPPGY). He wasn't interested in seeking her reflections on retirement. If anything, he says, "I thought, what a waste." If everybody followed Fudge's lead, he argues, "look at the damage to the economy to have all these talented 50-year-olds out." No, Sorrell called to tempt Fudge back in with an offer to run Young & Rubicam Inc., the distressed advertising and communications giant that he had bought for $4.7 billion in 2000. He thought that Fudge, with her marketing expertise and renowned people skills, could rescue a company that two CEOs in three years couldn't. And he certainly wasn't **oblivious** to the buzz that hiring a prominent black woman would create. Besides, the notoriously hands-on boss contends, "women are better managers than men."

What an offer, though: Fudge would take over a company with about 40% of the revenues of the unit she ran at Kraft, a company that a former Y&R client calls "distracted and uninspired" in an industry worried about becoming **irrelevant.** All at a time when Fudge was dreaming of starting her own children's media venture. But here was a chance to make a difference in a hurry. As CEO, she could alter the way that business was done—turning the company from an insular idea factory **stymied** by its own turf battles to a truly client-focused and efficient operation. Her ideal: a collaborative family in which independent businesses work together to diagnose and solve customers' problems. This was a company where she could put her marketing **savvy** and management ideas into practice, a company that needed her, a company of her own. And so in May, 2003, she became chairman and chief executive of what is now called Young & Rubicam Brands, as well as Y&R, its **flagship** ad agency.

In this way, Fudge stands out among top-tier executive women who choose to leave the corporate world because of its **unrelenting** demands: Most who walk away seem not to return, unless it's to found and run their own businesses. In a culture that exalts loyalty to the job, if not the company, and **disparages,** however quietly, those who try to limit its hold on their lives, leaving is often seen as a sign of weakness, a sometimes unforgivable lack of ambition. Most Americans are even reluctant to take all of their annual vacation; Fudge herself measured her maternity leaves in weeks, not months. While PepsiCo Inc. (PEP) CEO Steven S. Reinemund, who has watched several high-level female colleagues quit for personal reasons, says he has thought about taking a long break "a number of times" over his career, he hasn't. Few have. It shouldn't be a **stigma,** but it is.

No wonder that what really **intrigues** Fudge's female peers isn't that she left but that she went back. Or, just as important, that she could go back. Few high-level women dropouts have the opportunity to rejoin the corporate elite with their credibility intact. And even for Fudge, that is anything but certain: At Young & Rubicam, she has been welcomed with as much **skepticism** as enthusiasm. Fudge was an **unconventional** choice as chief executive, and she is taking an unconventional approach—importing a management rigor and an inclusive style rarely associated with advertising. Fudge's leadership could result in dramatic improvements or end in very public failure.

Awkward Match

Fudge traded her enlightened early retirement and entrepreneurial plans for a daunting challenge. She has thrust her newly centered self smack in the middle of a company that has endured neglect, executive greed, and a messy merger. Some big clients have left in frustration: Burger King Corp. pulled Y&R as its lead ad agency on its estimated $350 million account less than a year after awarding it; executives there declined to say why. According to *AdWeek*, which tracks the industry, billings at Y&R'S New York headquarters have shrunk from $3.4 billion at the end of 1998 to about $1 billion today—a downward trend that company insiders acknowledge but say is exaggerated by several spinoffs. The various divisions of the group, from direct marketer Wunderman to brand consultancy Landor, rarely work together. Some employees are bitter. And now many are peeved to have a consumer-products executive who espouses management principles like "Lean Six Sigma" at the helm of an ad agency, where a **modicum** of chaos is thought to be necessary for creativity. To them, it's an awkward match.

The new CEO acknowledges that it'll take time to create goodwill among a group of people who have been so **disillusioned** for the past few years. A slew of senior executives, including CEO Peter A. Georgescu, cashed out after the 75-year-old company went public in May, 1998—the largest initial public offering in advertising history and one that ate up two years of attention within the company. In 2000, Sorrell acquired the group after a stormy five-month takeover that had all the hallmarks of a high school romance—tantrums, tears, intrigue, and shifting infatuations. Insiders say a second CEO took the money and left; his successor barely showed his face outside the office.

While it's too soon to judge the success of Ann Fudge's second act, an intriguing drama is starting to unfold. Some colleagues speak glowingly of her vision, intelligence, and warmth, saying she has brought a healthy **disdain** for outdated practices to the offices of Young & Rubicam worldwide. Others dismiss her as a celebrity CEO who lacks a feel for the industry and a rousing competitive instinct. Not only is she an outsider, she is someone who opted out.

A surprising number doubt—quietly for now, anyway—that a woman who openly hugs fellow execs and values her life beyond the workplace can raise Y&R to new creative and financial heights. As one senior executive puts it: "I just don't know if someone who can spend months on a bicycle has the 24/7 drive we need." Even outsiders wonder about the fire in her belly. "Does Y&R need a General Patton or a well-rounded, solid business leader?" ponders veteran consultant Richard Roth, whose firm helps clients find the right ad agency. "Ann certainly represents the latter." Fudge laughs off the **innuendo.** "I really love doing things differently from the norm," she says.

The notion that she is somehow not up to the job because she took time off **rankles** her peers. "What's two years in a career that trumps most careers that are twice as long?" says Mary Lou Quinlan, a consultant and former ad exec who was handling marketing for Folgers coffee when Fudge was working wonders at Maxwell House. "The thought that you can't take two years off and come back to work intensely is ridiculous," adds Ellen R. Marram, a partner in private-equity firm North Castle Partners LLC, who took a year off after stepping down as CEO of Tropicana Beverage Group when it was sold to PepsiCo. Especially since Fudge regularly puts in 15-hour days and has already crisscrossed the world to visit Y&R offices, reorganized top staff to make them directly responsible for all their clients' needs, moved to cut costs, and is pushing to garner more business in areas like technology, health care, and direct-to-consumer marketing.

But it is Fudge's vision for how Y&R should operate that really puts her at odds with some of her new colleagues. She brings a client's perspective to the job in a way that is fundamentally different from the usual ad agency **ethos.** In Fudge's world, creativity is only worthwhile if the client appreciates it. That's practically **heresy** to some. As an experienced marketing executive, she knows all too well the limits of the traditional 30-second commercial. When clients approach her agency for help selling a product, she believes the response should be to find the best possible combination of services, drawing on all the far-flung units in the empire. To underscore this, she launched the Young & Rubicam Brands name for the group's family of companies. That's a difficult mind shift for a confederation of businesses used to working independently and even competing against one another. Meanwhile, many insiders complain that despite the change in **nomenclature,** Fudge has failed to give Y&R the dynamic, fresh identity it needs to draw customers and talent back into the fold. Instead, from her open cubicle at Madison Avenue, she has focused on meeting with customers and encouraging her employees to unite in giving them better service. Her goal: more revenue from existing clients, rather than the buzz of new business. Y&R Vice-Chairman Stephanie Kugelman calls the griping "old world ad-speak," arguing that marshaling resources for clients trumps fresh slogans. "This is what you have to do these days," says Kugelman. "The whole business has changed."

Fudge may not have won the hearts and minds of all her staffers, but at least some clients are in sync with the kinds of changes she's trying to make. "Too many people add a lot of cost and not a lot of value," says M. Carl Johnson III, chief strategy officer at client Campbell Soup Co. (CPB). "They have to stop doing stuff that's stupid." Fudge's first big success was Microsoft Corp.'s (MSFT) recent decision to give roughly $250 million of its customer-relationship management business to Y&R. "If it wasn't for her leadership, we wouldn't have been able to close the deal," says John B. Kahan, Microsoft's general manager of corporate customer-relationship management. "Most agencies come to the table with: 'Here's what I did for other customers.' She says: 'What does it take to delight your customer?' "

Bruising Egos

But even that deal has sparked internal grumbling. The bulk of the business will be done by Wunderman, the direct-marketing unit that arguably has a more potent brand name at the moment than Y&R. Few of the company's divisions want to be grouped under a single brand, and they certainly don't want to work more closely with what they regard as the high-handed and **dysfunctional** Y&R ad agency. As one unit exec puts it: "Who wants to dull down a **pitch** by bringing someone you wouldn't choose to the table?" Fudge says she "absolutely totally respects the individual entities," arguing that more collaboration does not necessarily mean the end of their independence. "The concern is more at the senior level," she sighs. "The middle guys get it."

Fudge's message of discipline is also bruising egos. Many openly snicker at her attempts to introduce Six Sigma, the rigid and almost religious quality-control program long associated with General Electric Co. (GE) (where Fudge sits on the board). They call it Sick Sigma. She calls the initiative FIT—for focus, innovation, and teamwork—and says it's tailored to simplifying processes in the ad industry. She now has staffers trained as Six Sigma "green belts," who tackle everything from sourcing supplies to **honing** the process for developing creative strategies. Despite resistance, several converts are already excited about the results, with Y&R account manager Kathryn Burke arguing: "This really needed to be done." Fudge saw how the program boosted productivity at Kraft, and she believes it'll actually free up time for more creativity at Young & Rubicam. As she says: "Do we really need six meetings to get an idea?"

One of Fudge's most critical—and allegedly most strained—relationships is with Michael Patti, the brilliant, often **bellicose** worldwide creative director of Y&R ad agency and head of its New York office. Terms like "client-centric" don't seem to figure in his vocabulary. While some insiders say the duo barely talk, both deny a rift. "We read each other's minds!" says Fudge. But Patti, who was hired in a multimillion-dollar deal mere weeks before Fudge joined with a **lucrative** multiyear contract of her own, clearly has a different view of what will it take to turn around Y&R. His dream definition of the agency: "Young and Restless. Hungry." He calls his boss a "touchy-feely . . . gatherer" of ideas who has brought a "calming effect" to the office. In his view, Fudge helps to nurture clients, while he pushes the "wow!" creative work. "She can hold their hands as we go there, and I can go out and get it done, hopefully," says Patti, adding that "it's a pleasant change to be partnering with a woman." This from a man who spent the past 18 years in what he calls the "testosterone culture" of BBDO Worldwide ad agency.

Such observations underline two obvious characteristics that set Fudge apart: She is female, and she is black. That may account for the **preponderance** of adjectives like "lovely," "nurturing," and "nice" that get thrown at her. It may also explain why Fudge says she is used to being underestimated. On a recent business trip, someone mixed up Fudge and a junior associate, who is white. "I almost think it's funny," says Fudge, noting that she has experienced racism every day of her life. When her sons were teenagers, she used to tell them not to put their hands in their pockets, in case people thought they were carrying guns. "It's not different for any person who grows up black in this country. You understand who you are. You deal with it." The bigger issue, she says, is "the challenge of being questioned all the time."

Always So Adult

Growing up with a brother 11 years her junior in a middle-class neighborhood of Washington, Fudge says the racism she felt was outweighed by a close-knit community and strong role models. Her mother worked as a manager at the National Security Agency; her father had a job with the U.S. Postal Service. After 12 years of Catholic school education, she headed off to Simmons College in Boston, where she earned a degree in management in 1973. More important to Fudge, she left Simmons at age 22 with a husband—she married Harvard Graduate School of Education student Rich Fudge in her sophomore year—and a child, Rich Jr. A friend and former classmate, Lynne White, recalls that Fudge was "always so adult, so ahead of the rest of us." As black women in a predominantly white women's college, they were active in student politics and civil rights. All the while, Fudge seemed to balance her studies, motherhood, marriage, and extracurricular activities as if "it wasn't a juggle or a struggle for her."

Fudge says it was tough but claims she simply didn't consider doing it differently. She worked two years in human resources at GE and had a second son, Kevin, by the time she arrived at Harvard, where she received her MBA in 1977. After graduating, she avoided applying to companies such as McKinsey & Co. because the long hours and travel would be hard on her family. Her situation was so unusual in those days that her first boss at General Mills Inc. (GIS) asked how she could do her job as a marketing assistant with two children at home and a husband who worked full-time in the training department of 3M Corp. She swallowed her fury and outdid her colleagues. After work, she would pick up her sons from day care and, once they were in bed, settle down to review pages of data. Her boss later gave her a book, *Games Mother Never Taught You: Corporate Gamesmanship for Women*, as an apology.

Although she seemed to have found a delicate balance as a working mother, Fudge had also begun planning for an early exit from the workforce during her 23-year ascent at General Mills and General Foods, which later became part of Kraft. In her late thirties, she asked a financial adviser about retiring at 50—not because she was unhappy at work but because events such as her sister-in-law's diagnosis of multiple sclerosis made her realize that there was more she wanted to do than climb the corporate ladder.

Former colleagues say that sense of personal priorities was always evident, despite her obvious drive and **intuitive** marketing savvy. At Kraft, where she rejuvenated such brands as Kool-Aid, Log Cabin syrup, and Stove Top Stuffing, she never inflated the importance of the work. Jeri Finard, senior vice-president and general manager of Kraft's coffee division, sums it up as the "perspective that we're not in the business of saving lives, we're in the business of selling coffee." And sell coffee she did: Fudge obsessed over product quality while keeping costs under control—and significantly increased profits at Maxwell House during her eight-year stint managing the brand.

Still, many were shocked when Fudge resigned barely a year after she became head of Kraft's Beverages, Desserts & Post Division, which made up about 15% of the company's total revenues. Retired GE Chief Executive Jack Welch, who brought Fudge onto his board, gave her one piece of advice when she was considering her departure: "Don't leave without another job to go to." Welch, who has never taken more than a few weeks off at a time, jokes: "It's the only piece of advice I ever gave her, and she didn't take it." Fudge explains that she didn't feel right talking to investors ahead of the company's IPO if she wasn't planning to stick around. And she wasn't. Her mother had recently died and two friends also had passed away within a few months of each other. She was ready to explore life outside the corporate world.

A Deep Breath

While Fudge remained active on several boards after leaving Kraft, she devoted most of her time to work that was closer to her heart. She completed *The Artist's Way at Work*—a best-selling book of exercises aimed at unleashing creativity and innovation on the job that she still follows. Cathleen P. Black, president of Hearst Magazines and a friend, says "she took a deep breath for a couple of months" before delving into her other passions. She traveled to Morocco, Thailand, and Bali, played with her three grandchildren, and even helped organize Kevin's wedding. "It was stepping back and asking: 'What are you really here for? What do you really want to accomplish?' " Fudge explains.

Going into advertising wasn't exactly at the top of her list. But when Sorrell called, she couldn't resist the offer to run a company where she could apply her new ideas and one that was in an industry she was already familiar with. The children's media venture could wait. Her sons were enthusiastic but warned: "Don't lose what you gained over the past two years." To this day, they call frequently to check on her stress level. So far, she laughs, they tell her "you haven't lost it yet."

Quite the opposite. Fudge seems distinctly uninterested in the **clandestine** infighting and overt sniping that has characterized Y&R in recent years. In fact, pals like Ann Moore, chairman and CEO of Time Inc., observe that she seems "amazingly energized" by the new challenge. And what a challenge it is. At a recent town hall meeting in Chicago's Hard Rock Hotel, the CEO gave her signature upbeat talk to a somewhat stony-faced group of staffers from several of the group's brands. Few asked questions and, despite the spread of wine, beer, and nibbles, many returned to their offices mere minutes after she delivered her speech. That followed a lunch meeting with key executives such as Kary McIlwain, the president and CEO of Y&R's Chicago office, who told Fudge that "here in the prairie, people are still looking for the momentum of change." Although nodding and taking notes, Fudge said: "If you're looking for a big nuclear bomb revolution, it's not going to happen."

What Fudge has done is to try to reassure staff that she is paying attention to them. Before she came in, Jed Beitler, chairman and CEO of Sudler & Hennessey, a Young & Rubicam unit that specializes in health-care communications, recalls long periods of feeling, well, ignored: "There were predecessors to Ann who couldn't even pronounce the name of our company." Fudge, in contrast, knows the names and faces of people in offices around the world. William Eccleshare, who heads up Y&R/Wunderman in Europe, the Middle East, and Africa, believes she brings much-needed enthusiasm and a "huge intuitive understanding of the business." Beitler says he's "relieved and pleased" to see a leader who is meeting his people and clients for a change. "There are a lot more of these *Kumbaya* get-togethers where we actually talk to each other," he says, adding that "there are a helluva lot of people who are prepared to fall on their sword for Ann."

Then there are those who would stick it in her back. After calling her an incredibly nice person, such critics launch into a volley of concerns over her priorities. They question whether she is creating an environment that fosters creativity and attracts the best talent. They want to see some new lieutenants at the helm—and more new clients. One executive says he's in "show-me mode" while another complains that "we're just supposed to get more efficient and cozy with clients." And, once again, there is that **sabbatical:** "A few years is a long time to be away."

Does Fudge see some resistance ahead? Sure. Does she care what people are whispering behind her back? Not really. "At this juncture in my life, it's so much not about me," says Fudge. Sorrell figures it could take at least three years to revitalize the group and, given her outsider status, "with Ann, it might take longer than that." He shrugs off the grumbling as an inevitable consequence "whenever people try to change things" and says he simply wants to see results. Of course, Fudge is well-acquainted with the **imperatives** of the corporate world. But she wants be remembered as someone who "made a difference in how people view themselves individually and how they view themselves collectively." Guess Sorrell knew that when he hired her.

Glossary for "Act II"

an·o·nym·i·ty (ăn'ə-nĭm'ĭ-tē) *n. pl.* **an·o·nym·i·ties**

1. The quality or state of being unknown or unacknowledged.
2. One that is unknown or unacknowledged.

so·journ (sō'jûrn', sō-jûrn') *intr.v.* **so·journed, so·journ·ing, so·journs**

To reside temporarily.

n.

A temporary stay; a brief period of residence.

[Middle English sojournen, from Old French sojorner, from Vulgar Latin *subdiurnāre: Latin sub-, *sub-* + Late Latin diurnum, *day* (from Latin, *daily ration*, from neuter of diurnus, *daily*, from diēs, *day*.)]

so'journ'er *n.*

con·glom·er·ate (kən-glŏm'ə-rāt') *v.* **con·glom·er·at·ed, con·glom·er·at·ing, con·glom·er·ates**

v. intr.

1. To form or gather into a mass or whole.
2. To form into or merge with a corporate conglomerate.

v. tr.

To cause to form into a mass or whole.

n. (-ər-ĭt)

1. A corporation made up of a number of different companies that operate in diversified fields.
2. A collected heterogeneous mass; a cluster: *a city-suburban conglomerate; a conglomerate of color, passion, and artistry.*
3. Geology. A rock consisting of pebbles and gravel embedded in cement.

adj. (-ər-ĭt)

1. Gathered into a mass; clustered.
2. Geology. Made up of loosely cemented heterogeneous material.

[Latin conglomerāre, conglomerāt-: com-, *com-* + glomerāre, *to wind into a ball* (from glomus, glomer-, *ball*).]

con·glom'er·at'ic (-ə-răt'ĭk) or **con·glom'er·it'ic** (-ə-rĭt'ĭk) *adj.* **con·glom'er·a'tor** *n.*

o·bliv·i·ous (ə-blĭv'ē-əs) *adj.*

1. Lacking all memory; forgetful.
2. Lacking conscious awareness; unmindful.

o·bliv'i·ous·ly *adv.* **o·bliv'i·ous·ness** *n.*

Usage Note: Either *of* or *to* can be used with *oblivious*: *The party appeared oblivious to* (or *of*) *the mounting pressures for political reform.*

ir·rel·e·vant (ĭ-rĕl'ə-vənt) *adj.*

Unrelated to the matter being considered.

ir·rel'e·vant·ly *adv.* ***Synonyms:*** *irrelevant, extraneous, immaterial, impertinent*

These adjectives mean not pertinent to the subject under consideration: *an irrelevant comment; a question extraneous to the discussion; an objection that is immaterial; mentioned several impertinent facts.*

sty·mie also **sty·my** (stī'mē) *tr.v.* **sty·mied,** (-mēd) **sty·mie·ing,** also **sty·my·ing** (-mē-ĭng) **sty·mies** (-mēz)

To thwart; stump: *a problem in thermodynamics that stymied half the class.*

n.

1. An obstacle or obstruction.
2. <u>Sports.</u> A situation in golf in which an opponent's ball obstructs the line of play of one's own ball on the putting green.

[*Origin unknown.*]

sav·vy (săv'ē) <u>Informal</u> *adj.* **sav·vi·er, sav·vi·est**

Well informed and perceptive; shrewd: *savvy Washington insiders.*

n.

Practical understanding or shrewdness: *a banker known for financial savvy.*

tr. & intr.v. **sav·vied,** (săv'ēd) **sav·vy·ing, sav·vies** (săv'ēz)

To understand; comprehend.

[From Spanish sabe (usted), *(you) know*, from saber, *to know*, from Old Spanish, from Vulgar Latin *sapēre, from Latin sapere, *to be wise*.]

sav'vi·ly *adv.*

flag·ship (flăg'shĭp') *n.*

1. A ship that carries a fleet or squadron commander and bears the commander's flag.
2. The chief one of a related group: *the flagship of a newspaper chain; the flagship of a line of reference books.*

un·re·lent·ing (ŭn'rĭ-lĕn'tĭng) *adj.*

1. Having or exhibiting uncompromising determination; unyielding: *an unrelenting human rights worker.*
2. Not diminishing in intensity, pace, or effort: *an unrelenting ice storm.*

un're·lent'ing·ly *adv*

dis·par·age (dĭ-spăr'ĭj) *tr.v.* **dis·par·aged, dis·par·ag·ing, dis·par·ag·es**

1. To speak of in a slighting or disrespectful way; belittle.
2. To reduce in esteem or rank.

[Middle English disparagen, *to degrade*, from Old French desparager : des-, *dis-* + parage, *high birth* (from per, *peer*.)]

dis·par'age·ment *n.* **dis·par'ag·er** *n.* **dis·par'ag·ing·ly** *adv.*

stig·ma (stĭg'mə) *n. pl.* **stig·ma·ta** (stĭg-mä'tə, -măt'ə, stĭg'mə-) or **stig·mas**

1. A mark or token of infamy, disgrace, or reproach: "Party affiliation has never been more casual. . . . The stigmata of decay are everywhere" (Arthur M. Schlesinger, Jr.).
2. A small mark; a scar or birthmark.
3. <u>Medicine.</u> A mark or characteristic indicative of a history of a disease or abnormality.
4. <u>Psychology.</u> A mark or spot on the skin that bleeds as a symptom of hysteria.
5. **stigmata** Bodily marks, sores, or sensations of pain corresponding in location to the crucifixion wounds of Jesus, usually occurring during states of religious ecstasy or hysteria.
6. <u>Biology.</u> A small mark, spot, or pore, such as the respiratory spiracle of an insect or an eyespot in certain algae.
7. <u>Botany.</u> The receptive apex of the pistil of a flower, on which pollen is deposited at pollination.
8. <u>Archaic.</u> A mark burned into the skin of a criminal or slave; a brand.

[Middle English stigme, *brand*, from Latin stigma, stigmat-, *tattoo indicating slave or criminal status*, from Greek, *tattoo mark*, from stizein, stig-, *to prick*.]

stig'mal *adj.*

in·trigue (ĭn'trēg', ĭn-trēg') *n.*

1. a. A secret or underhand scheme; a plot.
   b. The practice of or involvement in such schemes.
2. A clandestine love affair.

v. **in·trigued, in·trigu·ing, in·trigues** (ĭn-trēg')
v. intr.

To engage in secret or underhand schemes; plot.

v. tr.

1. To effect by secret scheming or plotting.
2. To arouse the interest or curiosity of: *Hibernation has long intrigued biologists.*

[From French intriguer, *to plot,* from Italian intrigare, *to plot,* from Latin intrīcāre, *to entangle.*]

in·trigu'er *n.* **in'trigu'ing·ly** *adv.*

Usage Note: The introduction of the verb *intrigue* to mean "to arouse the interest or curiosity of" was initially resisted by writers on usage as an unneeded French substitute for available English words such as *interest, fascinate,* or *puzzle,* but it now appears to be well established. Seventy-eight percent of the Usage Panel accepts it in the sentence *The special-quota idea intrigues some legislators, who have asked a Washington think tank to evaluate it,* whereas only 52 percent accepted it in a 1968 survey.

skep·ti·cism also **scep·ti·cism** (skĕp'tĭ-sĭz'əm) *n.*

1. A doubting or questioning attitude or state of mind; dubiety.
2. *Philosophy.*
   a. The ancient school of Pyrrho of Elis that stressed the uncertainty of our beliefs in order to oppose dogmatism.
   b. The doctrine that absolute knowledge is impossible, either in a particular domain or in general.
   c. A methodology based on an assumption of doubt with the aim of acquiring approximate or relative certainty.

Doubt or disbelief of religious tenets.

un·con·ven·tion·al (ŭn'kən-vĕn'shə-nəl) *adj.*

Not adhering to convention; out of the ordinary.

un'con·ven'tion·al'i·ty (-shə-năl'ĭ-tē) *n.* **un'con·ven'tion·al·ly** *adv.*

mod·i·cum (mŏd'ĭ-kəm) *n. pl.* **mod·i·cums** or **mod·i·ca** (-kə)

A small, moderate, or token amount: "England still expects a modicum of eccentricity in its artists" (Ian Jack).

[Middle English, from Latin, from neuter of modicus, *moderate*, from modus, *measure.*]

dis·il·lu·sion (dĭs'ĭ-lo͞o'zhən) *tr.v.* **dis·il·lu·sioned, dis·il·lu·sion·ing, dis·il·lu·sions**

To free or deprive of illusion.

n.

1. The act of disenchanting.
2. The condition or fact of being disenchanted.

dis·dain (dĭs-dān') *tr.v.* **dis·dained, dis·dain·ing, dis·dains**

1. To regard or treat with haughty contempt; despise.
2. To consider or reject as beneath oneself.

n.

A feeling or show of contempt and aloofness; scorn.

[Middle English disdeinen, from Old French desdeignier, from Vulgar Latin *disdignāre, from Latin dēdignārī: dē-, *de-* + dignārī, *to deem worthy* (from dignus, *worthy*.]

in·nu·en·do (ĭn'yo͞o-ĕn'dō) *n. pl.* **in·nu·en·does**

1. An indirect or subtle, usually derogatory implication in expression; an insinuation.
2. Law.
   a. A plaintiff's interpretation in a libel suit of allegedly libelous or slanderous material.
   b. A parenthetic explanation of a word or charge in a legal document.

[From Latin innuendō, *by hinting*, ablative of innuendum gerund of innuere, *to nod to*: in-, *to, toward*; see **in-**[2] + -nuere, *to nod*.]

ran·kle (răng'kəl) *v.* **ran·kled, ran·kling, ran·kles**

v. intr.

1. To cause persistent irritation or resentment.
2. To become sore or inflamed; fester.

v. tr.

To embitter; irritate.

[Middle English ranclen, from Old French rancler, alteration of draoncler, from draoncle, *festering sore*, from Latin dracunculus, diminutive of dracō, dracōn-, *serpent*.]

Word History: A persistent resentment, a festering sore, and a little snake are all coiled together in the history of the word *rankle.* "A little snake" is the sense of the Latin word *dracunculus* to which *rankle* can be traced, *dracunculus* being a diminutive of *dracō,* "snake." The Latin word passed into Old French, as *draoncle,* having probably already developed the sense "festering sore," because some of these sores resembled little snakes in their shape or bite. The verb *draoncler,* "to fester," was then formed in Old French. The noun and verb developed alternate forms without the *d-*, and both were borrowed into Middle English, the noun *rancle* being recorded in a work written around 1190, the verb *ranclen,* in a work probably composed about 1300. Both words had literal senses having to do with festering sores. The noun is not recorded after the sixteenth century, but the verb went on to develop the figurative senses having to do with resentment and bitterness with which we are all too familiar.

e·thos (ē'thŏs') *n.*

The disposition, character, or fundamental values peculiar to a specific person, people, culture, or movement: "They cultivated a subversive alternative ethos" (Anthony Burgess).

[Greek ēthos, *character*.]

her·e·sy (hĕr'ĭ-sē) *n. pl.* **her·e·sies**

1. a. An opinion or a doctrine at variance with established religious beliefs, especially dissension from or denial of Roman Catholic dogma by a professed believer or baptized church member.
   b. Adherence to such dissenting opinion or doctrine.

2. a. A controversial or unorthodox opinion or doctrine, as in politics, philosophy, or science.
   b. Adherence to such controversial or unorthodox opinion.

[Middle English heresie, from Old French, from Late Latin haeresis, from Late Greek hairesis, from Greek, *a choosing, faction*, from haireisthai, *to choose*, middle voice of hairein, *to take*.]

no·men·cla·ture (nō'mən-klā'chər, nō-mĕn'klə-) *n.*

1. A system of names used in an art or science: *the nomenclature of mineralogy.*
2. The procedure of assigning names to the kinds and groups of organisms listed in a taxonomic classification: *the rules of nomenclature in botany.*

[Latin nōmenclātūra, from nōmenclātor, *nomenclator*.]

no'men·cla'tur·al *adj.*

dys·func·tion also **dis·func·tion** (dĭs-fŭngk'shən) *n.*

Abnormal or impaired functioning, especially of a bodily system or social group.

dys·func'tion·al *adj.*

pitch (pĭch) *v.* **pitched, pitch·ing, pitch·es**
v. tr.

1. a. To throw, usually with careful aim.
   b. To discard by throwing: *pitched the can out the window.*
2. *Baseball.*
   a. To throw (the ball) from the mound to the batter.
   b. To play (a game) as pitcher.
   c. To assign as pitcher.
3. To erect or establish; set up: *pitched a tent; pitch camp.*
4. To set firmly; implant; embed: *pitched stakes in the ground.*
5. To set at a specified downward slant: *pitched the roof at a steep angle.*
6. a. To set at a particular level, degree, or quality: *pitched her expectations too high.*
   b. *Music.* To set the pitch or key of.
   c. To adapt so as to be applicable; direct: *pitched his speech to the teenagers in the audience.*
7. *Informal.* To attempt to promote or sell, often in a high-pressure manner: "showed up on local TV to pitch their views" (Business Week).
8. *Sports.* To hit (a golf ball) in a high arc with backspin so that it does not roll very far after striking the ground.
9. *Games.*
   a. To lead (a card), thus establishing the trump suit.
   b. To discard (a card other than a trump and different in suit from the card led).
   v. intr.

1. To throw or toss something, such as a ball, horseshoe, or bale.
2. *Baseball.* To play in the position of pitcher.
3. To plunge headlong: *He pitched over the railing.*
4. a. To stumble around; lurch.
   b. To buck, as a horse.

5. a. Nautical. To dip bow and stern alternately.
   b. To oscillate about a lateral axis so that the nose lifts or descends in relation to the tail. Used of an aircraft.
   c. To oscillate about a lateral axis that is both perpendicular to the longitudinal axis and horizontal to the earth. Used of a missile or spacecraft.
6. To slope downward: *The hill pitches steeply.*
7. To set up living quarters; encamp; settle.
8. Sports. To hit a golf ball in a high arc with backspin so that it does not roll very far after striking the ground.

   n.

1. The act or an instance of pitching.
2. Baseball.
   a. A throw of the ball by the pitcher to the batter.
   b. A ball so thrown.
3. Sports. The rectangular area between the wickets in cricket, 22 yards (20.1 meters) by 10 feet (3.1 meters). Also called **wicket.**
4. a. Nautical. The alternate dip and rise of the bow and stern of a ship.
   b. The alternate lift and descent of the nose and tail of an airplane.
5. A steep downward slope.

hone (hōn) *n.*

1. A fine-grained whetstone for giving a keen edge to a cutting tool.
2. A tool with a rotating abrasive tip for enlarging holes to precise dimensions. *tr.v.* **honed, hon·ing, hones**

1. To sharpen on a fine-grained whetstone.
2. To perfect or make more intense or effective: *a speaker who honed her delivery by long practice.*

Phrasal Verb: hone in

1. To move or advance toward a target or goal: *The missiles honed in on the military installation.*
2. To direct one's attention; focus: *The lawyer honed in on the gist of the plaintiff's testimony.*
   a. [Middle English, from Old English hān, *stone*; Hone in alteration of home in.]

bel·li·cose (bĕl'ĭ-kōs') *adj.*

Warlike in manner or temperament; pugnacious.

[Middle English, from Latin bellicōsus, from bellicus, *of war*, from bellum, *war.*]
bel'li·cose'ly *adv.* **bel'li·cos'i·ty** (-kŏs'ĭ-tē) or **bel'li·cose'ness** *n.*

lu·cra·tive (lo͞o'krə-tĭv) *adj.*

Producing wealth; profitable: *a lucrative income; a lucrative marketing strategy.*

[Middle English lucratif, from Old French, from Latin lucrātīvus, from lucrātus, past participle of lucrārī, *to profit*, from lucrum, *profit.*]

pre·pon·der·ance (prĭ-pŏn'dər-əns) also **pre·pon·der·an·cy** (-ən-sē) *n.*

Superiority in weight, force, importance, or influence.

in·tu·i·tive (ĭn-to͞o'ĭ-tĭv, -tyo͞o'-) *adj.*

1. Of, relating to, or arising from intuition.
2. Known or perceived through intuition.
3. Possessing or demonstrating intuition.

in·tu'i·tive·ly *adv.* **in·tu'i·tive·ness** *n.*

clan·des·tine (klăn-dĕs'tĭn) *adj.*

Kept or done in secret, often in order to conceal an illicit or improper purpose.

[Latin clandestīnus, probably blend of *clam-de, *secretly* (from clam.]

clan·des'tine·ly *adv.* **clan·des'tine·ness** or **clan'des·tin'i·ty** *n.*

sab·bat·i·cal (sə-băt'ĭ-kəl) also **sab·bat·ic** (-ĭk) *adj.*

1. Relating to a sabbatical year.
2. **Sabbatical** also **Sabbatic** Relating or appropriate to the Sabbath as the day of rest.
   n. A sabbatical year.

[From Late Latin sabbaticus, from Greek sabbatikos, from sabbaton, *Sabbath.*]

adj. 1: of or relating to the Sabbath; "Friday is a sabbatical day for Muslims" 2: of or relating to sabbatical leave; "sabbatical research project" *n.*: a leave usually taken every seventh year.

im·per·a·tive (ĭm-pĕr'ə-tĭv) *adj.*

1. Expressing a command or plea; peremptory: *requests that grew more and more imperative.*
2. Having the power or authority to command or control.
3. Grammar. Of, relating to, or constituting the mood that expresses a command or request.
4. Impossible to deter or evade; pressing: *imperative needs.*

n.

1. a. A command; an order.
   b. An obligation; a duty: *social imperatives.*
2. A rule, principle, or instinct that compels a certain behavior: *a people driven to aggression by territorial imperatives.*
3. *Grammar.*
   a. The imperative mood.
   b. A verb form of the imperative mood.

[Middle English imperatif, *relating to the imperative mood,* from Old French, from Late Latin imperātīvus, from Latin imperātus, past participle of imperāre, *to command.*]

im·per'a·tive·ly *adv.* **im·per'a·tive·ness** *n.*

Reading Comprehension

Answer the following questions about the article written by Diane Brady.

Word Meaning

Using the glossary, select the entry that best completes the sentences below.

1. The huge computer __________ covered every need a person might have, including financing, parts, and shipping.

2. Such a __________ was attached to the practice of carrying weapons that the school expelled anyone carrying any sort of illegal deadly devices.
3. Despite their growing popularity, automobiles using unusual types of fuels are still considered __________ in the United States.
4. Many children whose families never overcome the obstacles of divorce or separation become quite __________ and require counseling to rebuild family relationships.
5. Road rage is such a problem that government agencies have created anger management programs to teach drivers how to deal with their __________.
6. Even a student with a two-year degree can enter into a job with __________ pay if the degree is marketable in a competitive business environment.
7. After thirty years as a small business owner, the proprietor returned to school and began __________ his management skills to meet the current business demands.
8. The president visited the country under disguise and __________ so as not to be attacked by the militants.

Literal Meaning

Mark the letter of the option that best answers the statements below.

1. Ann Fudge left the chairmanship position with what company to take a sabbatical?
   a. Young & Rubicam
   b. Maxwell House
   c. A Kraft Foods Division
   d. Disney
2. What event/s prompted Fudge to take her sabbatical?
   a. The completion of her book
   b. She had another job to go to
   c. The arrival of her grandchild
   d. The deaths of her mother and two friends
3. During her sabbatical, Fudge did what activities?
   a. She traveled to Morocco and Thailand.
   b. She wrote a book.
   c. She took a yoga class.
   d. All of the above
4. Fudge returned to the corporate world in what position?
   a. The CEO of the Hard Rock Corporation
   b. The CEO of the Burger King Corporation
   c. The CEO of Young & Rubicam Brands
   d. The CEO of General Electric Corporation.
5. Who hired Ann Fudge for her new position?
   a. Jack Welch
   b. Martin Sorrel
   c. Cathleen P. Black
   d. Ellen R. Marram

Interpretive Meaning

Complete the questions with the response that best answers the statement.

1. Why did Ann Fudge return to work two years after taking a sabbatical?
   a. She was bored.
   b. She needed the income that comes with the new executive position.
   c. She wanted to test the concepts in the book *The Artist's Way at Work.*
   d. She was tempted by the challenge to revive a sluggish company.
2. The tone of the article is
   a. humorous.
   b. informative.
   c. argumentative.
   d. didactic.
4. Why have certain employees in her new company received Fudge coolly?
   a. Because she is from a minority group
   b. Because they do not believe she can perform well in this particular type of competitive environment
   c. Because Ann Fudge represents a threat to the employees
   d. Because Ann Fudge plans to lay off many employees
5. Why is this article called "Act II"?
   a. Fudge is working in the theatrical world.
   b. Since she works in New York City, the title is appropriate for Broadway.
   c. Fudge wrote a play that is performed in a theater.
   d. Fudge has launched into a second career.
6. Why does the Brady use theatrical terms in this article about corporate America?
   a. She is using clever English.
   b. She makes an analogy between the theater and Fudge's return to work.
   c. Brady knows that he will receive an award for outstanding writing.
   d. She is trying to impress the reader with is style.
7. Why does Fudge think her style of management will work universally?
   a. People like to be respected as humans even in the world of management.
   b. Advertising is the perfect venue for trying new techniques.
   c. She has succeeded before in another market environment.
   d. Fudge was hired to try new ideas with her new employees.
8. Why is she deemed a "celebrity CEO" by some of her employees?
   a. She has performed a play on Broadway.
   b. She has many famous friends who invite her to parties with celebrities.
   c. She is known and respected among the people in her high position.
   d. She is well known for her successful leadership in other companies.
9. Why does Fudge accept the grumbling in her company?
   a. She knows that people resist change and will let them vent their frustration.
   b. She likes to keep people stirred up psychologically.
   c. She measures success by the amount of grumbling done.
   d. She does not listen to the complaints.

10. Why does Fudge represent the unconventional CEO?
    a. She is a woman.
    b. She has a novel management style.
    c. She is from a minority group.
    d. She allows employees to take their children to work.

Score: Number correct _____ out of _____

Writing Assignments

1. *Journal Writing*

Summary

Summarize the article. Include the topic and points that support that topic.

Reaction

In your reaction, consider the title of the essay and how it relates to the meaning of the essay. What questions do you have about the essay? In what ways do you consider Ann Fudge to be a role model?

2. *Paragraph*

Write a paragraph arguing for changes that need to be made in your workplace, your home, or your community.

3. *Paragraph to Essay*

Expand the ideas from assignment two to an argumentative essay.

4. *Essay*

Argue this question: Should the work ethic in America be re-examined? In your prewriting, examine what you consider to be the American work ethic and the values associated with work. You may also want to explore ideas concerning retirement, maternity leave, maternity benefits, and sabbaticals from work.

There'll Be No Place to Hide in Our Brave New Biometric World

Paul Saffo

This article argues that soon humans will be unable to hide anywhere due to DNA tests, eye scans, and other biometric identity systems. The author argues that "it is time to fix the problems in our current systems" to prevent crooks from "stealing [our] fingers and face. . . ."

If you're worried about privacy and identity theft, imagine this:

The scene: Somewhere in Washington. The date: April 3, 2020.

You sit steaming while the officer hops off his electric cycle and walks up to the car window. "You realize that you ran that red light again, don't you, Mr. Witherspoon?" It's no surprise that he knows your name; the intersection camera scanned your license plate and your guilty face, and matched both in the DMV database. The cop had the full scoop before you rolled to a stop.

"I know, I know, but the sun was in my eyes," you plead as you fumble for your driver's license.

"Oh, don't bother with that," the officer replies, waving off the license while squinting at his hand-held scanner. Of course. Even though the old state licensing system had been revamped back in 2014 into a "secure" national program, the new licenses had been so compromised that the street price of a phony card in Tijuana had **plummeted** to five euros. In frustration, law enforcement was turning to pure **biometrics.**

"Could you lick this please?" the officer asks, passing you a **nanofiber** blotter. You comply and then slide the blotter into the palm-sized gizmo he is holding, which reads your DNA and runs a match against a national **genomic** database maintained by a consortium of drug companies and credit agencies. It also checks half a dozen metabolic fractions looking for everything from drugs and alcohol to lack of sleep.

The officer looks at the screen, and frowns, "Okay, I'll let you off with a warning, but you really need more sleep. I also see that your retinal implants are past warranty, and your car tells me that you are six months overdue on its navigation firmware upgrade. You really need to take care of both or next time it's a ticket."

This creepy scenario is all too **plausible.** The technologies described are already being developed for industrial and medical applications, and the steadily dropping cost and size of such systems will make them affordable and practical police tools well before 2020. The resulting intrusiveness would make today's system of search warrants and wiretaps quaint **anachronisms.**

Some people find this future alluring and believe that it holds out the promise of using sophisticated ID techniques to catch everyone from careless drivers to bomb-toting terrorists in a biometric dragnet. We have already seen places such as Truro, Mass., Baton Rouge, La., and Miami ask hundreds or thousands of citizens to submit to DNA mass-testing to catch killers. Biometric devices sensing for SARS symptoms are omnipresent in Asian airports. And the first **prototypes** of systems that test in real time for SARS, HIV and bird flu have been deployed abroad.

The ubiquitous collection and use of biometric information may be inevitable, but the notion that it can deliver reliable, theft-proof evidence of identity is pure science fiction. Consider that oldest of biometric identifiers—fingerprints. Long the exclusive domain of government databases and FBI agents who dust for prints at crime scenes, fingerprints are now being used by electronic print readers on everything from ATMs to laptops. Sticking your finger on a sensor beats having to remember a password or toting an easily lost smart card.

But be careful what you touch, because you are leaving your identity behind every time you take a drink. A Japanese **cryptographer** has demonstrated how, with a bit of gummi bear gelatin, some **cyanoacrylic** glue, a digital camera and a bit of digital fiddling, he can easily capture a print off a glass and confect an artificial finger that foils fingerprint readers with an 80 percent success rate. Frightening as this is, at least the stunt is far less grisly than the tale, perhaps **apocryphal,** of some South African crooks who snipped the finger off an elderly retiree, rushed her still-warm digit down to a government ATM, stuck it on the print reader and collected the victim's pension payment. (Scanners there now gauge a finger's temperature, too.)

Today's biometric advances are the stuff of tomorrow's hackers and clever crooks, and anything that can be detected eventually will be counterfeited. Iris scanners are gaining in popularity in the corporate world, exploiting the fact that human iris patterns are apparently as unique as fingerprints. And unlike prints, iris images aren't left behind every time someone gets a latte at Starbucks. But hide something valuable enough behind a door protected by an iris scanner, and I guarantee that someone will figure out how to capture an iris image and transfer it to a contact lens good enough to fool the readers. And capturing your iris may not even require sticking a digital camera in your face—after all, verification requires that the representation of your iris exist as a cloud of binary bits of data somewhere in cyberspace, open to being hacked, copied, stolen and downloaded. The more complex the system, the greater the likelihood that there are flaws that crooks can exploit.

DNA is the gold standard of biometrics, but even DNA starts to look like fool's gold under close inspection. With a bit of discipline, one can keep a card safe or a PIN secret, but if your DNA becomes your identity, you are sharing your secret with the world every time you sneeze or touch something. The novelist Scott Turow has already written about a hapless sap framed for a murder by an angry spouse who spreads his DNA at the scene of a killing.

The potential for DNA identity theft is enough to make us all wear a gauze mask and keep our hands in our pockets. DNA can of course be easily copied—after all, its architecture is designed for duplication—but that is the least of its problems. Unlike a credit card number, DNA can't be retired and swapped for a new sequence if it falls into the hands of crooks or snoops. Once your DNA identity is stolen, you live with the consequences forever.

This hasn't stopped innovators from using DNA as an indicator of authenticity. The artist Thomas Kinkade signs his most valuable paintings with an ink containing a bit of his DNA. (He calls it a "forgery-proof DNA Matrix signature.") We don't know how much of Tom is really in his paintings, but perhaps it's enough for forgers to duplicate the ink, as well as the distinctive brush strokes.

The biggest problem with DNA is that it says so much more about us than an arbitrary serial number does. Give up your Social Security number and a stranger can inspect your credit rating. But surrender your DNA and a snoop can discover your innermost genetic secrets—your ancestry, genetic defects and predispositions to certain diseases. Of course we will have strong genetic privacy laws, but those laws will allow consumers to "voluntarily" surrender their information in the course of applying for work or pleading for health care. A genetic marketplace not unlike today's consumer information business will emerge, swarming with health insurers attempting to prune out risky individuals, drug companies seeking customers and employers managing potential worker injury liability.

Faced with this prospect, any sensible privacy **maven** would conclude that DNA is too dangerous to collect, much less use for a task as unimportant as turning on a laptop or working a cash machine. But society will not be able to resist its use. The pharmaceutical industry will need our DNA to concoct customized wonder drugs that will fix everything from high cholesterol to **halitosis.** And crime fighters will make giving DNA information part of our civic duty and national security. Once they start collecting, the temptation to use it for other purposes will be too great.

Moreover, snoops won't even need a bit of actual DNA to invade our privacy because it will be so much easier to access its digital representation on any number of databanks off in cyberspace. Our Mr. Witherspoon will get junk mail about obscure medical conditions that he's never heard of because some direct marketing firm **"bot"** will inspect his digital DNA and discover that he has a **latent** disease or condition that his doctor didn't notice at his annual checkup.

It is tempting to conclude that Americans will rise up in revolt, but experience suggests otherwise. Americans profess a concern for privacy, but they happily reveal their deepest financial and personal secrets for a free magazine subscription or cheesy electronic trinket. So they probably will eagerly surrender their biometric identities as well, trading fingerprint IDs for frequent shopper privileges at the local supermarket and genetic data to find out how to have the cholesterol count of a teenager.

Biometric identity systems are inevitable, but they are no silver bullet when it comes to identity protection. The solution to identity protection lies in the hard work of implementing system-wide and nationwide technical and policy changes. Without those changes, the deployment of biometric sensors will merely increase the opportunities for snoops and thieves—and escalate the cost to ordinary citizens.

It's time to fix the problems in our current systems and try to anticipate the unique challenges that will accompany the expanded use of biometrics. It's the only way to keep tomorrow's crooks from stealing your fingers and face and, with them, your entire identity.

Glossary for "There'll Be No Place to Hide in Our Brave New Biometric World"

plum·met (plŭm'ĭt) *n.*

1. Something that weighs down or oppresses; a burden.
   intr. v. **plum·met·ed, plum·met·ing, plum·mets**

1. To fall straight down; plunge.
2. To decline suddenly and steeply: *Stock prices plummeted.*

[Middle English plomet, from Old French, *ball of lead*, diminutive of plom, plomb, *sounding lead*, from Latin plumbum.]

bi·o·met·rics (bī'ō-mĕt'rĭks) *n. (used with a sing. verb)*
The statistical study of biological phenomena.

bi'o·met'ric or **bi'o·met'ri·cal** *adj.* **bi'o·met'ri·cal·ly** *adv.*

nano- (nanofiber) *pref.*

1. often **nanno-** Extremely small: *nannoplankton.*
2. One-billionth (10^{-9}): *nanosecond.*

[Greek nānos, nannos, *little old man, dwarf*, from nannās, *uncle*.]

ge·nome (jē'nōm') **also ge·nom** (-nŏm) *n.*

1. The total genetic content contained in a haploid set of chromosomes in eukaryotes, in a single chromosome in bacteria, or in the DNA or RNA of viruses.
2. An organism's genetic material.

[gen(e) + -ome.]

ge·nom'ic (-nŏm'ĭk) *adj.*

plau·si·ble (plô'zə-bəl) *adj.*

1. Seemingly or apparently valid, likely, or acceptable; credible: *a plausible excuse.*
2. Giving a deceptive impression of truth or reliability.
3. Disingenuously smooth; fast-talking: "Ambitious, unscrupulous, energetic, . . . and plausible—a political gladiator, ready for a 'set-to' in any crowd" (Frederick Douglass).

[Latin plausibilis, *deserving applause*, from plausus, past participle of plaudere, *to applaud*.]

plau'si·bil'i·ty or **plau'si·ble·ness** *n.* **plau'si·bly** *adv.*

Synonyms: *plausible, believable, colorable, credible*

These adjectives mean appearing to merit belief or acceptance: *a plausible pretext; a believable excuse; a colorable explanation; a credible assertion.*

a·nach·ro·nism (ə-năk'rə-nĭz'əm) *n.*

1. The representation of someone as existing or something as happening in other than chronological, proper, or historical order.
2. One that is out of its proper or chronological order, especially a person or practice that belongs to an earlier time: "A new age had plainly dawned, an age that made the institution of a segregated picnic seem an anachronism" (Henry Louis Gates, Jr.).

[French anachronisme, from New Latin anachronismus, from Late Greek anakhronismos, from anakhronizesthai, *to be an anachronism*: Greek ana-, *ana-* + Greek khronizein, *to take time* (from khronos, *time*).]

a·nach'ro·nis'tic or **a·nach'ro·nous** (-nəs) *adj.* **a·nach'ro·nis'ti·cal·ly** or **a·nach'ro·nous·ly** *adv.*

pro·to·type (prō'tə-tīp') *n.*

1. An original type, form, or instance serving as a basis or standard for later stages.
2. An original, full-scale, and usually working model of a new product or new version of an existing product.
3. An early, typical example.
4. *Biology.* A form or species that serves as an original type or example.

[French, from Greek prōtotupon, from neuter of prōtotupos, *original*: prōto-, *proto-* + tupos, *model*.]

pro'to·typ'al (-tī'pəl) or **pro'to·typ'ic** (-tĭp'ĭk) or **pro'to·typ'i·cal** (-ĭ-kəl) *adj.*

cryp·tog·ra·pher (krĭp-tŏg'rə-fər) *n.*

One who uses, studies, or develops cryptographic systems and writings.

cy·a·no·ac·ry·late (sī'ə-nō-ăk'rə-lāt', sī-ăn'ō-) *n.*

An adhesive substance with an acrylate base that is used in industry and medicine.

a·poc·ry·phal (ə-pŏk'rə-fəl) *adj.*

1. Of questionable authorship or authenticity.
2. Erroneous; fictitious: "Wildly apocryphal rumors about starvation in Petrograd . . . raced through Russia's trenches" (W. Bruce Lincoln).
3. **Apocryphal** *Bible.* Of or having to do with the Apocrypha.

a·poc'ry·phal·ly *adv.*

ma·ven also **ma·vin** (mā'vən) *n.*

A person who has special knowledge or experience; an expert.

[Yiddish meyvn, from Hebrew mēbîn, active participle of hēbîn, *to understand* derived stem of bîn, *to discern*.]

hal·i·to·sis (hăl'ĭ-tō'sĭs) *n.*

The condition of having stale or foul-smelling breath.

[Latin hālitus, *breath* (akin to hālāre, *to breathe*) + **-osis.**]

bot (bŏt) *n.*

A software program that imitates the behavior of a human, as by querying search engines or participating in chatroom or IRC discussions.

[Short for `robot`.]

la·tent (lāt′nt) *adj.*

1. Present or potential but not evident or active: *latent talent.*
2. Pathology. In a dormant or hidden stage: *a latent infection.*
3. Biology. Undeveloped but capable of normal growth under the proper conditions: *a latent bud.*
4. Psychology. Present and accessible in the unconscious mind but not consciously expressed.

n.

A fingerprint that is not apparent to the eye but can be made sufficiently visible, as by dusting or fuming, for use in identification.

[Middle English, from Old French, from Latin latēns, latent—present participle of latēre, *to lie hidden.*]

la'tent·ly *adv.* ***Synonyms:*** *latent, dormant, quiescent*
These adjectives mean present or in existence but not active or manifest. What is *latent* is present but not evident: *latent ability. Dormant* evokes the idea of sleep: *a dormant volcano. Quiescent* sometimes—but not always—suggests temporary inactivity: "For a time, he [the whale] lay quiescent" (Herman Melville).

Reading Comprehension

Answer the following questions about the article by Paul Saffo.

Word Meaning

Using the glossary, select the entry that best completes the sentences below.

1. Lili, the fire department's Dalmatian, has such horrible __________ that the captain of the fire company put some mint-scented breath drops in her water bowl.
2. To entertain the audience, Shakespeare used many __________ in his plays; one example was the use of the word bedlam that comes from the name of a psychiatric hospital not present during the time that the play was set.
3. After many years of working as a dentist, Dr. Rodriguez discovered his __________ musical talent and became a professional drummer at the age of 50.
4. As a result of the increase of fuel prices, manufacturers are now creating __________ of vehicles that will operate on fossil fuels.
5. The plot of a famous novel in which the hero must decode a message was created around the science of __________.
6. Whenever a date whose numbers have some __________ occurs, someone always forecasts doomsday, or the end of the world.
7. Many energy __________ have joined the fight against using imported fuels and are recommending more travel in the South by light rail.
8. As a result of the attack in New York City on September 11, 2001, the stock market __________ to a record low point for the decade.

Literal Meaning

Mark the letter of the option that best answers the statements below.

1. What setting does the author of the article use?
   a. 2020
   b. A computer lab in 2002
   c. Somewhere in Washington in 2020
   d. The FBI office in 2014
2. What topic(s) prompted the author to write this article?
   a. The need for privacy
   b. The first theft of identity
   c. His identity's being stolen
   d. The worry over privacy and identity theft
3. What is the oldest biometric identifier?
   a. A footprint
   b. An eye scan
   c. A strand of hair
   d. A fingerprint
4. The author fears a "genetic marketplace" where what will happen?
   a. Health insurers will try to avoid risky clients.
   b. Drug companies will market to the clients needing medication.
   c. Employers will not hire a person with the potential of being injured on the job.
   d. All of the above
5. The character created by the author is named what?
   a. Mr. Witherspoon
   b. Scott Turow
   c. Tijuana Menendez
   d. Paul Saffo

Interpretive Meaning

Complete the questions with the response that best answers the statement.

1. Why does the author place his scenario in the future?
   a. He does not want to be sued.
   b. All things are possible in the future.
   c. He fears his identity will be stolen again.
   d. He feels less guilty for having written such an article.
2. Why does Saffo address the reader as "you"?
   a. He is trying to become familiar with his audience.
   b. He is trying to improve his readership ratings with the newspaper.
   c. He wants to carry on a sort of conversation with the reader.
   d. He is speaking to a college physics class.
3. Why does Saffo use the words "Brave New Biometric World" in his title?
   a. He is trying to stir his reader to action.
   b. He is creating a word play with the Aldous Huxley book of a similar title.

   c. Being a professional writer, he uses alliteration to draw attention to the article.
   d. He is attempting to frighten his readers.
4. Why does Saffo say that DNA looks like fool's gold?
   a. He believes the gold reserves will be depleted by 2020.
   b. DNA answers the questions that investigators ask when solving a crime.
   c. DNA can be used fraudulently and maliciously to trap unsuspecting victims.
   d. DNA does not guarantee results when invading someone's privacy.
5. Why does Saffo say that "today's biometric advances are the stuff of tomorrow's hackers and clever crooks"?
   a. Criminals always prove how savvy they are when plotting their bank robberies.
   b. The technological advances of today will become the source of crimes tomorrow.
   c. Criminals study technology carefully and are crafty computer hackers.
   d. Americans will revolt against these technological advances.
6. What effect does DNA proof have on Saffo's futuristic world?
   a. DNA can be used recklessly to outsmart investigators.
   b. DNA will be able to be used to frame innocent people for a crime.
   c. DNA will be stolen and used as another way of stealing identity.
   d. All of the above.
7. Why does Saffo end his article with a call for action?
   a. He fears life in the future.
   b. He wants the reader to consider the power of DNA.
   c. He says that criminals work faster and more cleverly than the regular population and challenges the reader to outsmart them.
   d. He is trying to protect his fingers and irises for transplantation in the future.
8. What words or phrases does Saffo use in his article to call his readers to action?

   ____

   ____

Score: Number correct _____ out of _____

Writing Assignments

1. Journal Writing

Summary

Write a one-paragraph summary of the article.

Reaction

Write a three-paragraph reaction to the article. In the first paragraph, react to the ideas presented in the essay. In the second paragraph, comment on the organization and types of arguments used in the article. In the third paragraph, discuss the effectiveness of the arguments.

2. *Paragraph*

   Write a paragraph arguing for or against specific rules governing technology, such as surveillance equipment in public places, televisions in automobiles, and laptops in classrooms.

3. *Paragraph to Essay*

   Expand the ideas developed in assignment two to an argumentative essay. In the essay, have one paragraph that either concedes or refutes the strongest or weakest point of the opposition.

4. *Essay*

   Write an essay arguing for or against policies governing ethical responsibility for a specific technical advancement such as biometric identity systems, cloning, stem cell research, or gene modifications and alterations.

Technology and Medicine from The Other Man Was Me: A Voyage to the New World

Rafael Campo

The poem depicts the trend to consider the human as a mere subject of a battery of tests without regard to human qualities like beauty and feelings.

The transformation is complete. My eyes
Are microscopes and **cathode** X-ray tubes
In one, so I can see bacteria,
Your underwear, and even through to bones.
My hands are **hypodermic** needles, touch
Turned into blood: I need to know your salts
And chemistries, a kind of **intimacy**
That won't bear pondering. It's more than love,
More weird than **ESP**—my mouth, for instance,
So small and sharp, a dry computer chip
That never gets to kiss or taste or tell
A brief truth like "You're beautiful," or worse,
"You're crying just like me; you are alive."

Glossary for "Technology and Medicine"

cath·ode (kăth'ōd') *n. Abbr.* **ka**

A negatively charged electrode, as of an electrolytic cell, a storage battery, or an electron tube.

The positively charged terminal of a primary cell or a storage battery that is supplying current.

[Greek kathodos, *descent*: kat-, kata-, *cata-* + hodos, *way, path.*]

ca·thod'ic (kă-thŏd'ĭk) *adj.* **ca·thod'i·cal·ly** *adv.*

hy·po·der·mic (hī'pə-dûr'mĭk) *adj.*

1. Of or relating to the layer just beneath the epidermis.
2. Relating to the hypodermis.
3. Injected beneath the skin.

n.

1. A hypodermic injection.
2. A hypodermic needle.
3. A hypodermic syringe.

hy'po·der'mi·cal·ly *adv.*

in·ti·ma·cy (ĭn'tə-mə-sē) *n. pl.* **in·ti·ma·cies**

1. The condition of being intimate.
2. An instance of being intimate.

ESP (ē'ĕs-pē') *n.*

Communication or perception by means other than the physical senses. [e(xtra)s(ensory) p(erception).]

Reading Comprehension

Answer the following questions about Rafael Campo's "Technology and Medicine."

Word Meaning

Select the word from the glossary in your textbook that best completes the sentences below.

1. The special problems education course taught the student teachers how to work in programs for students who have been labeled as having __________.
2. The __________ rays coursing through the patient's body enabled the surgeon to pinpoint the exact location of the tumor.
3. The act of self-disclosing both the positive and negative side of one's personality is one of the best ways of achieving __________ with another human being.

Literal Meaning

Mark the letter of the statement that best completes the meaning.

1. In his narrative argumentative poem, Campo is speaking in what point of view?
   a. First person
   b. Third-person omniscient
   c. Third-person limited omniscient
   d. Objective
2. Campo expresses dismay at what practice?
   a. Having too many tubes inserted into his body
   b. The random and frequent use of x-rays
   c. The dehumanizing aspect of the medical system
   d. Receiving too many shots
3. In this poem, the narrator speaks in the voice of
   a. the doctor.
   b. the nurse.
   c. the counselor.
   d. the patient.
4. The poem is organized in the following design.
   a. Examples only
   b. Examples followed by a concluding statement

c. A summary statement followed by examples
d. A statement with a response

5. The narrator states his point, or theme, of the poem in
   a. the first line.
   b. the first and last lines.
   c. throughout the poem.
   d. an implied fashion.

Interpretive Meaning

Complete the questions with the response that best answers the statement.

1. Why does the narrator say that the "the transformation is complete"?
   a. He is summarizing his feeling after putting on his hospital clothes.
   b. He is showing how he looks after he dresses in his lab clothes.
   c. He is preparing the reader for what follows the statement.
   d. He is using psychology to confuse the reader.
2. What does Campo mean by "a dry computer chip/that never gets to kiss or tell / a brief truth . . . "?
   a. He feels distanced from his wife.
   b. He feels sorry for his laboratory robot.
   c. He explains how important remaining human is to medicine.
   d. He is outraged by the use of technology.
3. Why does Campo end his poem with the words "You're crying just like me; you are alive"?
   a. He parallels his feelings with those of the person being addressed.
   b. He is trying to build a friendship.
   c. He wants the medical profession to stop using so much technology.
   d. He is appealing to the insurance companies to pay for more tests.
4. What type of figurative language is represented by the following lines: "My hands are hypodermic needles, touch / turned into blood"?
   a. Metaphor
   b. Hyperbole
   c. Simile
   d. Onomatopoeia
5. Why does Campo use many details like hypodermic needles, x-rays, and computer chips in this poem?
   a. They are medical objects with which everyone is familiar.
   b. They represent new medical technology.
   c. They cause fear in patients.
   d. They are easy to use in a laboratory.
6. Why does the narrator NOT say that " . . . You're beautiful"?
   a. He is afraid of being sued.
   b. He thinks people will laugh at him.
   c. He is not allowed the freedom and flexibility to get that close to another person.
   d. The medical community does not allow him to get that involved with a person in the hospital.

7. When Campo calls the body's salts and chemistries "a kind of intimacy / That won't bear pondering," what does he mean?
   a. The body is a wonderful machine.
   b. He means that medicine invades the personal private space of people.
   c. The lab results tell all of the truths about the body.
   d. Running tests can save lives.
8. What kind of verse does Campo use in this poem?
   a. Free verse
   b. Couplets
   c. Rhyming metric verse
   d. Metric stanzas
9. Summarize Campo's message in one statement.

   ____

   ____

10. What is Campo arguing for in his poem?
    a. More humanity should be infused in the practice of medicine.
    b. More advancements should be made in medicine.
    c. More people should go into the medical field.
    d. More technology should be used in the treatment of diseases.

Score: Number correct _____ out of _____

Writing Assignments

1. Journal Writing

Summary

Write a summary of the ideas in the poem. Consider the title, the narrator, and the message.

Reaction

In your reaction, consider any personal experiences you have had with medicine and technology.

2. Paragraph

Most medical schools today do not offer courses in patient relations. Write a paragraph for or against making such courses mandatory in medical schools.

3. Paragraph to Essay

Expand your paragraph in assignment two to an essay. Devote each body paragraph to a reason to support your argument.

4. Essay

Write an essay arguing that hospitals should take steps to ensure that all personnel treat patients as individuals and with dignity.

The End of the Beginning

Ray Bradbury

This science fiction story expresses the beginning of life on a space station and the earthlings' anticipation for such life; their excitement is followed by the ordinary activity of mowing the lawn at night once they realize that the spaceship did not blow up upon launch.

He stopped the lawn mower in the middle of the yard, because he felt that the sun at just that moment had gone down and the stars come out. The fresh-cut grass that had showered his face and body died softly away. Yes, the stars were there, faint at first, but brightening in the clear desert sky. He heard the porch screen door tap shut and felt his wife watching him as he watched the night.

"Almost time," she said.

He nodded; he did not have to check his watch. In the passing moments he felt very old, then very young, very cold, then very warm, now this, now that. Suddenly he was miles away. He was his own son talking steadily, moving briskly to cover his pounding heart and the **resurgent** panics as he felt himself slip into fresh uniform, check food supplies, oxygen flasks, pressure helmet, space-suiting, and turn as every man on earth tonight turned, to gaze at the swiftly filling sky.

Then, quickly, he was back, once more the father of the son, hands gripped to the lawn-mower handle. His wife called, "Come sit on the porch."

"I've got to keep busy!"

She came down the steps and across the lawn. "Don't worry about Robert; he'll be all right."

"But it's all so new," he heard himself say. "It's never been done before. Think of it—a manned rocket going up tonight to build the first space station. Good lord, it can't be done, it doesn't exist, there's no rocket, no proving ground, no take-off time, no technicians. For that matter, I don't even have a son named Bob.

The whole thing's too much for me!"

"Then what are you doing out here, staring?"

He shook his head. "Well, late this morning, walking to the office, I heard someone laugh out loud. It shocked me, so I froze in the middle of the street. It was me, laughing! Why? Because finally I really knew what Bob was going to do tonight; at last I believed it. Holy is a word I never use, but that's how I felt stranded in all that traffic. Then, middle of the afternoon I caught myself humming. You know the song. 'A wheel in a wheel. Way in the middle of the air.' I laughed again. The space station, of course, I thought. The big wheel with hollow spokes where Bob'll live six or eight months, then get along to the moon. Walking home, I remembered more of the song. 'Little wheel run by faith, Big wheel run by the grace of God.' I wanted to jump, yell, and flame-out myself!"

His wife touched his arm. "If we stay out here, let's at least be comfortable." They placed two wicker rockers in the center of the lawn and sat quietly as the stars dissolved out of darkness in pale crushings of rock salt strewn from horizon to horizon. "Why," said his wife, at last, "it's like waiting for the fireworks at Sisley Field every year."

Bigger crowd tonight . . ."

"I keep thinking—a billion people watching the sky right now, their mouths all open at the same time."

They waited, feeling the earth move under their chairs.

"What time is it now?"

"Eleven minutes to eight."

"You're always right; there must be a clock in your head."

"I can't be wrong tonight. I'll be able to tell you one second before they blast off.

Look! The ten-minute warning!"

On the western sky they saw four crimson flares open out, float shimmering down the wind above the desert, then sink silently to the extinguishing earth.

In the new darkness the husband and wife did not rock in their chairs.

After a while he said, "Eight minutes." A pause. "Seven minutes." What seemed a much longer pause. "Six . . ."

His wife, her head back, studied the stars immediately above her and murmured, "Why?" She closed her eyes. "Why the rockets, why tonight? Why all this? I'd like to know."

He examined her face, pale in the vast powdering light of the Milky Way. He felt the stirring of an answer, but let his wife continue.

"I mean it's not that old thing again, is it, when people asked why men climbed Mt. Everest and they said, 'Because it's there'? I never understood. That was no answer to me."

Five minutes, he thought. Time ticking . . . his wrist watch . . . a wheel in a wheel . . . little wheel run by . . . big wheel run by . . . way in the middle of . . . four minutes! . . . The men snug in the rocket by now, the **hive,** the control board flickering with light.

His lips moved.

"All I know is it's really the end of the beginning. The Stone Age, Bronze Age, Iron Age; from now on we'll lump all those together under one big name for when we walked on Earth and heard the birds at morning and cried with envy. Maybe we'll call it the Earth Age, or maybe the Age of Gravity. Millions of years we fought gravity. When we were **amoebas** and fish we struggled to get out of the sea without gravity crushing us. Once safe on the shore we fought to stand upright without gravity breaking our new invention, the spine, tried to walk without stumbling, run without falling. A billion years Gravity kept us home, mocked us with wind and clouds, cabbage moths and locusts. That's what's so god-awful big about tonight . . . it's the end of old man Gravity and the age we'll remember him by, for once and all. I don't know where they'll divide the ages, at the Persians, who dreamt of flying carpets, or the Chinese, who all unknowing celebrated birthdays and New Years with strung ladyfingers and high skyrockets, or some minute, some incredible second the next hour. But we're in at the end of a billion years trying, the end of something long and to us humans, anyway, honorable."

Three minutes . . . two minutes fifty-nine seconds . . . two minutes fifty-eight seconds . . .

"But," said his wife, "I still don't know why."

Two minutes, he thought. Ready? Ready? Ready? The far radio voice calling. Ready!

Ready! Ready! The quick, faint replies from the humming rocket. Check! Check! Check!

Tonight, he thought, even if we fail with this first, we'll send a second and a third ship and move on out to all the planets and later, all the stars. We'll just keep going until the big words like immortal and forever take on meaning. Big words, yes, that's what we want. Continuity. Since our tongues first moved in our mouths we've asked, What does it all mean? No other question made sense, with death breathing down our necks. But just let us settle in on ten thousand worlds spinning around ten thousand alien suns and the question will fade away. Man will be endless and infinite, even as space is endless and infinite. Man will go on, as space goes on, forever. Individuals will die as always, but our history will reach as far as we'll ever need to see into the future, and with the knowledge of our survival for all time to come, we'll know security and thus the answer we've always searched for.

Gifted with life, the least we can do is preserve and pass on the gift to infinity.

That's a goal worth shooting for.

The wicker chairs whispered ever so softly on the grass.

One minute.

"One minute," he said aloud.

"Oh!" His wife moved suddenly to seize his hands. "I hope that Bob . . ."

"He'll be all right!"

"Oh, God, take care . . ."

Thirty seconds.

"Watch now."

Fifteen, ten, five . . .

"Watch!"

Four, three, two, one.

"There! There! Oh, there, there!"

They both cried out. They both stood. The chairs toppled back, fell flat on the lawn. The man and his wife swayed, their hands struggled to find each other, grip, hold. They saw the brightening color in the sky and, ten seconds later, the great uprising comet burn the air, put out the stars, and rush away in fire flight to become another star in the returning **profusion** of the Milky Way. The man and wife held each other as if they had stumbled on the rim of an incredible cliff that faced an **abyss** so deep and dark there seemed no end to it. Staring up, they heard themselves sobbing and crying. Only after a long time were they able to speak.

"It got away, it did, didn't it?"

"Yes . . ."

"It's all right, isn't it?"

"Yes . . . yes . . ."

"It didn't fall back . . . ?"

"No, no, it's all right, Bob's all right, it's all right."

They stood away from each other at last.

He touched his face with his hand and looked at his wet fingers. "I'll be damned," he said, "I'll be damned."

They waited another five and then ten minutes until the darkness in their heads, the retina, ached with a million specks of fiery salt. Then they had to close their eyes.

"Well," she said, "now let's go in."

He could not move. Only his hand reached a long way out by itself to find the lawn-mower handle. He saw what his hand had done and said, "There's just a little more to do . . ."

"But you can't see."

"Well enough," he said. "I must finish this. Then we'll sit on the porch awhile before we turn in."

He helped her put the chairs on the porch and sat her down and then walked back out to put his hands on the guide bar of the lawn mower. The lawn mower. A wheel in a wheel. A simple machine which you held in your hands, which you sent on ahead with a rush and a clatter while you walked behind with your quiet philosophy. Racket, followed by warm silence. Whirling wheel, then soft footfall of thought.

I'm a billion years old, he told himself; I'm one minute old. I'm one inch, no, ten thousand miles, tall. I look down and can't see my feet they're so far off and gone away below.

He moved the lawnmower. The grass showering up fell softly around him; he relished and savored it and felt that he was all mankind bathing at last in the fresh waters of the fountain of youth.

Thus bathed, he remembered the song again about the wheels and the faith and the grace of God being way up there in the middle of the sky where that single star, among a million motionless stars, dared to move and keep on moving.

Then he finished cutting the grass.

Astronauts, Teachers Converse at Ames

Julie O'Shea

NASA astronaut Ed Lu and Russian cosmonaut Yuri Malenchenko, wearing red-flowered Hawaiian shirts, conduct a televised interview from aboard the International Space Station 220 miles above Earth.

Friday, August 08, 2003

Educators participating in the NASA Explorer Schools program had a couple of guest lecturers last week who were literally out of this world.

The chill 220 miles above Earth didn't stop NASA astronaut Ed Lu and Russian cosmonaut Yuri Malenchenko from donning red-flowered Hawaiian shirts as they conducted a televised interview from aboard the International Space Station on July 31.

"You are loud and clear there in sunny California," Lu greeted his audience seated inside the conference center at Moffett Field.

Lu and Malenchenko, a metal bar bolting them to the station, spent about 30 minutes answering questions from middle-school teachers from around the nation who had come to NASA/Ames for a five-day workshop.

Besides talking about the spectacular view—the men said they can see lava flow from the Hawaiian volcanoes and explained how they witness a sunrise and sunset every hour and a half—Lu and Malenchenko also modeled exercise techniques they use to stay in shape and demonstrated the peculiar nature of water in microgravity. (Water, pumped out of a container by Malenchenko, floated out of a straw in a solid mass and directly toward the camera. "It's headed right for my sleeping compartment," said Lu with a laugh.)

They were asked about their work day. On most days, Lu said, the crew begins working on experiments shortly after its 8 a.m. conference call with Mission Control and wraps up its work day around 7 p.m.

No, connection to the World Wide Web is pretty much non-existent, but "we get messages from the ground all the time," said Malenchenko through the aid of a translator.

Yes, when something breaks, there are power tools on board to fix the problems, Lu said, adding that what's currently broken is the kitchen can opener.

"We are actually having a pretty good time up here," Lu said. "On the whole, this is the place I'd like to be right now."

Both men, on their current mission since the beginning of summer, are seasoned space explorers. For Malenchenko, a former military pilot, this is his third trip to space.

"When you get to space for the first time, it takes awhile to get used to it," Malenchenko said. "The body adjusts differently. I like being weightless."

Another adjustment astronauts undergo, said John Entwistle, a specialist with the NASA Explorer Schools program, is the shedding of skin from the soles of their feet. Because they aren't walking around in space, Entwistle said, the bottoms of their feet lose that coarse, hard skin and become soft. When they land back on Earth, many complain about how painful it is to walk around on firm ground again, Entwistle added.

This is the pilot year for NASA's explorer program, a three year partnership between the federal space agency and participating schools from around the U.S. Currently, there are no schools from Mountain View enrolled in the program, said Jonas Dino, a NASA spokesperson.

The goal of the program is to put a focus on math, science and technology learning in grades four through nine.

Setting up a televised conversation between astronauts aboard the space station and grade-school students in their classrooms is just one perk NASA extends to participating schools, though Entwistle cautions that the waiting list to arrange such an event is long.

Explorer schools also have access to additional professional development, grants, and, of course, NASA researchers and scientists.

Recruitment for next year's program will begin Sept. 1. For more information, visit http://www.explorerschools.nasa.gov/.

E-mail Julie O'Shea at **joshea@mv-voice.com**

From Space Station, NASA Astronaut Ed Lu '84 Speaks with CU Students

Blaine P. Friedlander Jr.

Astronaut Ed Lu, an alumnus of Cornell, speaks with students from the Space Station via NASA's Amateur Radio Onboard the International Space Station (ARISS) program.

Cornell Chronicle, September 11, 2003

Far above Cayuga's waters—hundreds of miles, in fact—NASA astronaut and Cornell alumnus Ed Lu reached out Sept. 4 and spoke directly, via shortwave radio, to fellow Cornellians for 11 minutes. Lu was aboard the International Space Station some 240 miles above Earth as it passed over North America. It was the first time Cornell students have spoken to an astronaut in space.

"This is really exciting; this is great and it all worked," said Chase Million, a Cornell junior from Hagerstown, Ind., who is president of the Cornell Amateur Radio Club. A physics major, Million plans on a career in the space industry after he graduates. "Today was more than just a hands-on experience; we actually got to talk to a guy who is on the space station," Million said following the shortwave conversation. The hookup was part of NASA's Amateur Radio Onboard the International Space Station (ARISS) program.

Lu, who graduated from Cornell in 1984 with a degree in electrical engineering, has been aboard the space station since April and is expected to return to Earth in late October. He is joined on the mission by the Russian cosmonaut Yuri Malenchenko. Both men have been conducting scientific experiments in the low-gravity environment.

Mike Hammer, director of data management at Cornell's College of Engineering and the radio club's faculty adviser, had been arranging this call since May. Because time was valuable, the students had rehearsed their questions over the previous weekend. Hammer called the space station via a Kenwood shortwave radio with a home-built antenna.

At 9:39 a.m. EDT, the space station was above Manitoba, Canada, rising just slightly above Ithaca's northwestern horizon. The room high atop the Barton Hall tower on campus was hushed, and students closed windows to reduce the noise. "N A 1 S S, W 2 C X M," Hammer called out on the microphone, exchanging call signs. "Good morning, Ed."

Lu replied, "I read you loud and clear." Then Kent Fuchs, dean of Cornell's engineering college, expressed greetings from the university, and he was followed by the lineup of questioners.

Leading off for the students, Million asked Lu about the space station experiments being conducted in microgravity. Lu explained that he conducted experiments from basic physics to applied-medical tests. Lu said that he was working on ways to eliminate the bone loss that astronauts experience. "In fact, we've almost eliminated it," he said.

A few minutes later, before the space station passed over Ithaca, Curry Taylor, a graduate student in physics, wanted to know if Lu would accept an invitation for a Mars expedition. "Absolutely," replied Lu. "I hope that before my career is over I get a chance to do that."

As the space station was directly over Ithaca, Phani Ramachandran, a graduate student in physics, asked: "We saw Mars, the tiny red planet, from Earth. Is the view any better from up there?"

With noticeable excitement in his voice, Lu said, "Mars is quite beautiful from here." And he described seeing the red planet just minutes earlier from the dark side of the Earth. "It's a very neat sight."

By 9:46 a.m., there were four minutes to go before the Earth's curvature would end the rare long-distance call. Carl Franck, Cornell professor of physics, asked Lu what was the "coolest tool" he used on the space station. Lu said it was a screwdriver, two-and-a-half feet long, used to service the toilet aboard the craft. That answer drew laughs from club members.

Finally at 9:50 a.m., as the space station sped across the Atlantic Ocean toward Bermuda, Kevin Feeney, a network engineer with Cornell Information Technologies, wanted to know how computer equipment was maintained in space. Unfortunately, due to the space station's trajectory and the Earth's curvature, contact was lost before Lu could answer. At the crackling sound of static from cosmic ether indicating the end of the session, the Cornell audience burst into applause.

Before his current mission, Lu had flown into space twice, both times on the shuttle Atlantis. He was a mission specialist in 1997 and a mission specialist and payload commander in 2000. As a space shuttle astronaut, he logged about 8.5 million miles and 504 hours, including a walk in space for 6 hours and 14 minutes. Lu graduated from R.L. Thomas High School in Webster, N.Y., in 1980, and at Cornell, he was a Merrill Presidential Scholar and a member of the Big Red wrestling team. He earned his doctoral degree in applied physics from Stanford University in 1989.

The Cornell Amateur Radio Club dates back to 1915. The modern-day club has had the call sign W2CXM since 1951, and it is affiliated with the American Radio Relay League. The club participates in amateur radio competitions for sport and emergency preparedness. These competitions test operating skills and equipment performance. The club also uses its equipment to provide a number of public services. During natural disasters, members have aided in moving messages to and from afflicted areas. The club has also provided "phone patches" for international Cornell students to call their families.

Glossary for "The End of the Beginning"

re·sur·gent (rĭ-sûr'jənt) *adj.*

1. Experiencing or tending to bring about renewal or revival.
2. Sweeping or surging back again.

hive (hīv) *n.*

1. a. A structure for housing bees, especially honeybees.
   b. A colony of bees living in such a structure.
2. A place swarming with activity.

v. **hived, hiv·ing, hives**

v. tr.

1. To collect into a hive.
2. To store (honey) in a hive.
3. To store up; accumulate.

v. intr.

1. To enter and occupy a beehive.
2. To live with many others in close association.

Phrasal Verb: hive off

To set apart from a group: *hived off the department into another division.*

[Middle English, from Old English hȳf.]

a·moe·ba also **a·me·ba** (ə-mē'bə) *n. pl.* **a·moe·bas** or **a·moe·bae** (-bē)

Any of various one-celled aquatic or parasitic protozoans of the genus *Amoeba* or related genera, having no definite form and consisting of a mass of protoplasm containing one or more nuclei surrounded by a flexible outer membrane. It moves by means of pseudopods.

[New Latin, *genus name,* from Greek amoibē, *change,* from ameibein, *to change.*]

a·moe'bic (-bĭk) *adj.*

pro·fu·sion (prə-fyo͞o'zhən, prō-) *n.*

1. The state of being profuse; abundance.
2. Lavish or unrestrained expense; extravagance.
3. A profuse outpouring or quantity: "A profusion of chiles—mild Anaheim to hot jalapeño—perks up everything" (Gene Bourg).

a·byss (ə-bĭs') *n.*

1. An immeasurably deep chasm, depth, or void: "lost in the vast abysses of space and time" (Loren Eiseley).

2. a. The primeval chaos out of which it was believed that the earth and sky were formed.
   b. The abode of evil spirits; hell.

[Middle English abissus, from Late Latin abyssus, from Greek abussos, *bottomless*: a-, *without*; see **a-**[1] + bussos, *bottom*.]

Reading Comprehension

Answer the following questions about the story by Ray Bradbury.

Word Meaning

Using the glossary, select the entry that best completes the sentences below.

1. My co-worker picked up a polluted salad filled with many _________ that made him so sick that they nearly caused his death.
2. The sailors felt so cozy in their _________ that they forgot they were sleeping in a submarine bunk.
3. Due to his lack of productivity, the college student had sunk so low in his studies that he felt himself fall into a deep _________ where he became lost for the entire semester.
4. Guadalupe's parents and family members hosted a reception for her *quinceanera* that had such a _________ of food that people ate until midnight.
5. After two weeks of water aerobic exercise, the weary senior citizens felt such _________ energy that they began to enjoy life again.

Literal Meaning

Mark the letter of the option that best answers the statements below.

1. What is the setting of Bradbury's short story?
   a. New York City in 2020
   b. New York City in 2006
   c. Cape Canaveral in 1956
   d. A front yard near the desert at nightfall
2. Who is the main character in the short story?
   a. The wife
   b. The son
   c. The father
   d. The narrator
3. What is the conflict of the story, the event that begins the action of the plot?
   a. The rocket is about to take off.
   b. The lawn mower stops working.
   c. The wife taps her husband on the shoulder.
   d. The stars appear in the sky.
4. Who is in the rocket?
   a. The couple's son
   b. NASA's best astronaut

c. The first female astronaut
d. The first amateur astronaut

5. Where is the rocket heading?
   a. To Mars
   b. To the moon
   c. To the Milky Way
   d. To outer space.
6. What is the point of view of the short story?
   a. First person
   b. Third person
   c. Third-person omniscient
   d. Third-person limited omniscient
7. What is the mission of the space team?
   a. To add another level to the existing space station
   b. To complete a space walk
   c. To build a space station
   d. To find life on the moon

Interpretive Meaning

Complete the questions with the response that best answers the statement.

1. What is the theme of "The End of the Beginning"?
   a. The casualness of the launch means nothing to humankind.
   b. Space exploration has become a commercial flight endeavor.
   c. The event is so mind boggling that the father seems in an existential confusion.
   d. The father is thrilled that his son is on the spacecraft.
2. What is the tone of the short story?
   a. Argumentative
   b. Mildly sarcastic
   c. Informative
   d. Outrageously humorous
3. Why did the father say " . . . I don't even have a son named Bob"?
   a. Because he is so confused about the technology of the spacecraft
   b. Because he feels so out of touch with the advances in modern technology
   c. Because he cannot believe that space endeavors are possible
   d. Because he is so doubtful about the possibility of the mission that it is as if he does not have a son
4. What type of figurative language identifies the following line from the story: ". . . where that single star, among a million motionless stars, dared to move and keep on moving"?
   a. Metaphor
   b. Simile
   c. Symbolism
   d. Personification

5. What is the significance of the restarting the lawn mower after the launch?
   a. The man is completing an activity that he understands.
   b. The father is trying to understand the enormity of what he is witnessing.
   c. The simplicity of the lawn mower contrasts with the complexity of the rocket.
   d. All of the above
6. Why does the wife return to the front porch?
   a. The couple is a traditional American couple where the husband does the lawn.
   b. She is too worried and upset to remain with her husband.
   c. She has to sweep the porch while he works in the yard.
   d. The wife cannot see in the dark.
7. What is ironic about the scene in the front yard?
   a. The simplicity of the couple's activity contrasts with the high tech space mission.
   b. The yard is well manicured like space.
   c. The couple does not have a strong relationship with their son.
   d. The mission is easy to believe given the modern life of the times.
8. Summarize in one sentence the climax of the short story.

   ____

   ____

Score: Number correct _____ out of _____

Writing Assignments

1. *Journal Writing*

Summary

Write a summary of the plot of the story. Consider the rising action, the conflict, the resolution, and the role of the characters.

Reaction

In your reaction, reflect on the following: This story was written in 1956. Which elements of the story can still be considered science fiction? Which parts of the story appeal to human emotions? How do you think this combination affects the appeal of the story?

2. *Paragraph*

Write a paragraph arguing for or against funding for space exploration.

3. *Paragraph to Essay*

Using your paragraph from assignment two as a basis for your essay, write an editorial based on logical arguments and reasoning arguing for increased funding or elimination of governmental funding for NASA's space exploration program.

4. *Essay*

Reflect on the statement made by the father in the short story: "All I know is it's really the end of the beginning. The Stone Age, Bronze Age, Iron Age; from now on we'll lump all those together under one big name for when we walked on Earth and heard the birds at morning and cried with envy."

Choice 1 Write an essay arguing the importance of this statement to the short story.

Choice 2 What name would you give to the current age, the age that includes the twenty-first century? Write an essay defending your answer. (Prove that the name you have selected is appropriate.)

Reflective Assignments

1. Reflect upon the quotation by the Greek philosopher Demosthenes: "Small opportunities are often the beginning of great enterprises." Using this quotation as a thesis, write a letter to your great-grandchildren or to future generations in the form of an argument in which you encourage them to take advantage of opportunities.
2. Reflect on the quotation "Exploration is really the essence of the human spirit," by Frank Borman, U.S. astronaut. Using this as a topic sentence, write a paragraph defending or refuting this statement.
3. Choose several idioms from the list of the Idioms for a New Frontier. Write a journal entry that reflects how these idioms apply to the frontiers in your life.
4. Write a poem with a theme of the importance of exploring new frontiers.
5. Write an essay arguing for the exploration of new frontiers in personal lives. Be specific about the frontiers to be explored. You may consider such topics as living and studying in another country, learning a new language, changing careers, etc.

Internet Field Trips—Reading and Writing Assignments

1. Read about problems women (and men) face when re-entering the workplace. After researching the topic, write an essay arguing for steps that employees and employers can take to make this adjustment easier. Try these Web sites.
   - http://hbswk.hbs.edu/item.jhtml?id=5331&t=career_effectiveness
   - http://www.womenandequalityunit.gov.uk/women_work_commission
   - http://www.womenwork.org/
2. Read more about Ann Fudge and her achievements. Summarize your results. These Web sites may help with the research.
   - http://www.time.com/time/2004/obesity/speakers/fudge.html

- http://www.ucg.net/SPECIALS/2002/black.history/stories/04.fudge/index.html
- http://hbswk.hbs.edu/item.jhtml?id=5214&t=leadership
- http://www.africanpubs.com

3. Cell phones in classrooms have become part of a heated debate in many communities and school districts. Read what educators, students, and community leaders have to say about this topic. Write an argumentative essay supporting your solution to the problem. Try these Web sites.
   - http://news.com.com/2061-10800_3-5978556.html
   - http://www.pbs.org/teachersource/learning.now/2006/05/shouldstudents_be_allowed_to. html
   - http://www. schoolmate.com/news/Issues/Winter01

FILMS TO VIEW

An Inconvenient Truth (directed by Davis Guggenheim, 2006)
Apollo 13 (directed by Ron Howard, 1995)
The Day the Earth Stood Still (directed by Robert Wise, 1951)
Jurassic Park (directed by Steven Spielberg, 1993)
2001: A Space Odyssey (directed by Stanley Kubrick, 1968)
Star Wars (directed by George Lucas, 1977)
The Chronicles of Narnia: The Lion, the Witch and the Wardrobe (directed by Andrew Adamson, 2005)
Good Night and Good Luck (directed by George Clooney, 2005)
Brokeback Mountain (directed by Ang Lee, 2005)
The Devil Wears Prada (directed by Wendy Fineman, 2006)

Writing assignments are based on *Good Night and Good Luck* directed by George Clooney and written by Grant Heslov and George Clooney.

1. Review the speech that Edward R. Murrow gives at the end of the movie. Using the speech as the base for your ideas, write an essay arguing that Murrow's principles withstand or do not withstand the test of time.
2. Write an argumentative essay using the following statement as your thesis: Today's electronic journalists uphold or do not uphold Murrow's belief that journalists must tell people what they need to know, not just what they want to know.
3. Write a paragraph comparing the lifestyles and culture portrayed in the movie to lifestyles and culture of today.
4. One tagline of the movie is "We will not walk in fear of one another." Write two paragraphs based on this tagline. In the first paragraph, explain the relevance of this statement to the movie. In the second, argue that this statement does or does not relate to journalistic principles today.
5. Research the following names and terms: *McCarthyism and Senate hearings, Cold War, The Red Scare, Edward R. Murrow*. Another tagline of the movie is "In a nation terrorized by its own government, one man dared to tell the

truth." Using this tagline as a topic sentence and the information gleaned from your research of the terms, write an essay explaining the background information needed to understand the film.

6. Television was a new frontier for the 1950s. Write a speech similar to the one that Murrow gives at the end of the movie [October 15, 1958 at the Radio-Television News Directors Association (RTNDA) Convention] in which you give advice to those involved with new frontiers of today. In the speech, argue for steps that must be taken so that the new technology is beneficial to society.
7. A Greek chorus is a company of actors who comment by speaking or singing in unison on the action in a classical Greek play. Write an essay explaining how the background music by jazz singer Dianne Reeves can be compared to a Greek chorus.

Summary of Unit 8—New Frontiers—Argumentation

Read student Penny Collins' analysis of the poem "The Planned Child." Analyze it for its content, its organization, and its mechanics. Then, in Summary of Unit 8 on page 418, complete the column on the right with your responses. Apply the information learned from Unit 8.

The Planned Child

Sharon Olds

I hated the fact that they had planned me, she had taken
a cardboard out of his shirt from the laundry
as if sliding the backbone up out of his body,
and made a chart of the month and put
her temperature on it, rising and falling,
to know the day to make me—I would have
liked to have been conceived in heat,
in haste, by mistake, in love, in sex,
not on cardboard, the little x on the
rising line that did not fall again.

But when a friend was pouring wine
and said that I seem to have been a child who had been wanted,
I took the wine against my lips
as if my mouth were moving along
that valved wall in my mother's body, she was
bearing down, and then breathing from the mask, and then
bearing down, pressing me out into
the world that was not enough for her without me in it,
not the moon, the sun, Orion
cartwheeling across the dark, not
the earth, the sea—none of it
was enough, for her, without me.

"The Planned Child" by Penny Collins

In the poem "The Planned Child," Sharon Olds writes about the understanding gained by a young woman who questions the circumstances under which she was conceived. As the poem progresses, there is a distinct change in tone from anger to acceptance. "The Planned Child" offers to the reader the defining moment in a young woman's life when she is able to see past her own selfish desires in order to appreciate her mother's desperate struggle to have a baby.

The first stanza of the poem enriches the reader with the poet's anger as she compares her romantic ideals to the cold meticulous planning involved in her own conception. In order to express her disgust surrounding the calculated methods her mother used to become pregnant, the speaker states "I hated the fact that they had planned me" (line 1). In the statement "she had taken / the cardboard out of his shirt from the laundry / as if sliding the backbone up out of his body" (lines 1–3), her mother takes charge of the conception and removes any objection the poet's narrator's father may have had. The poet obviously resents these proactive decisions as her mother "made a chart of the month and put/ her temperature on it, rising and falling / to know the day to make me" (lines 4–6). She sees her mother as selfish and calculating. With little to say about her father, it is safe to presume that the author resents his submissiveness to her mother.

Olds continues and describes the perfect conception. Using anaphora to add emphasis, she dreams that she should "have been conceived in heat, / in haste, by mistake, in love, in sex, / not on cardboard" (lines 7–8). The romantic vision of a child conceived by a man and woman overwhelmed by spontaneous lust inundates the poet into a state of mind that all men and women are fertile and that all children offer to their parents memories of a moment of unprecedented lovemaking. She is unable to grasp that a child conceived in the heat of the moment is often an object of regret. Ultimately, the poet refuses to consider that the joy for some parents may result from the actual conception, but for others, the joy is in the child.

There is a distinct change of attitude in the last stanza as the author gains an acceptance and admiration of her mother's valiant efforts to have a child. An observation from a friend forces the poet to ponder her mother's motives. "But when a friend was pouring wine / and said that I seem to have been a child who had been wanted" (lines 11–12) defines the moment of realization for the poet. No longer clinging to her ideals, the poet finally understands her mother's motivation and fierce determination.

As the poet imagines her mother's physical effort in giving birth, she envisions her journey through the birth canal as her mother "was / bearing down, and then breathing from the mask, and then / bearing down, pressing me out" (lines 15–17). By repeating words to emphasize her mother's palpable efforts, the poet embraces her mother's struggle.

The poem ends as the author summarizes the journey and acknowledges the void in a mother's life with no children. In the line "the world that was not enough for her without me in it" (line 18), the poet realizes that she was the pot of gold at the end of her mother's rainbow. She was the only thing that her mother desired. By mentioning celestial bodies, "not the moon, the sun, Orion / cartwheeling across the dark, not / the earth, the sea" (lines 19–21), the poet emphasizes that there is no worldly possession other than a baby that would satisfy her mother.

The author is now able to understand that it was she who was selfish, not her mother. She finds peace in the fact that sometimes it matters not how you win the battle; it only matters that the battle is won.

Works Cited

Olds, Sharon. "The Planned Child." Literature: An Introduction to Reading and Writing. Ed. Edgar V. Roberts and Henry E. Jacobs. 7th ed. Upper Saddle River: Pearson, 2004. 776–777.

Summary of Unit 8	
1. The thesis of the essay is	1.
2. The tense in the poetry analysis is	2.
3. Three transitions used include	3.
4. The tone of this essay is	4.
5. The purpose of this essay is to	5.
6. The writer concludes by	6.
7. The reader can infer that the writer	7.
8. Traits of argumentation include	8.
9. Mechanical errors include	9.

Credits

Text

pp. 3–4: "I Wanted to Share My Father's World," copyright © 1995 by Jimmy Carter. Illustrations copyright © 1997 by Sarah Elizabeth Chuldenko, from *Always a Reckoning and Other Poems* by Jimmy Carter. Used by permission of Time Books, a division of Random House, Inc.

pp. 10–11: Reprinted with permission of Andy Ling.

pp. 52–53: "Chapter 1," from *The Secret Life of Bees* by Sue Monk Kidd, copyright © 2002 by Sue Monk Kidd. Used by permission of Viking Penguin, a division of the Penguin Group (USA) Inc.

pp. 94–95: Reprinted by permission of Peter Blue Cloud.

pp. 106–107: Reprinted with permission from AAA Going Places Magazines.

pp. 113–117: Reprinted with permission of the Susan Bergholz Literary Agency on behalf of Sandra Cisneros.

pp. 126–128: Reprinted by permission of the Friedrich Agency on behalf of Frank McCourt.

pp. 133–134: "St. Patrick's: The Critters," Charles Cochran, *Savannah Morning News,* March 18, 2003. Copyright © 2003 The Savannah Morning News. Reprinted with permission.

pp. 140–141: Alberto Rios, "Day of the Refugios" from *The Smallest Muscle in the Human Body.* Copyright © 2002 by Alberto Rios. Reprinted with permission of Copper Canyon Press, www.coppercanyon.org.

pp. 158–164: Reprinted with permission of Mary Hufford, Director of the Center for Folklore & Ethnography.

pp. 184–186: Paula Geise, © 1995, 1996, 1997.

pp. 187–189: "Cinderella" from *Transformations* by Anne Sexton. Copyright © 1971 by Anne Sexton, renewed 1999 by Linda G. Sexton. Reprinted by permission of Houghton Mifflin Company. All rights reserved.

pp. 197–198: Reprinted with permission of NPR.

p. 199: "John Henry," pp. 56–57 from *Mules and Men* by Zora Neale Hurston. Copyright 1935 by Zora Neale Hurston; renewed © 1963 by John C. Hurston and Joel Hurston. Reprinted by permission of Harper Collins Publishers.

pp. 200–201: From the *Journal of American Folklore, Long Steel Rail: The Railroad in American Folksong.* Copyright 2000 by Board of Trustees. Used with permission of the University of Illinois Press.

pp. 210–213: From *Dress Your Family in Corduroy and Denim* by David Sedaris. Copyright © 2004 by David Sedaris. By permission of Little Brown & Company.

pp. 231–233: Carlton Winfrey, *Detroit Free Press,* March 12, 2005. Reprinted with permission.

pp. 240–244: "A&P," from *The Early Stories, 1953–1975* by John Updike, copyright © 2003 by John Updike. Used by permission of Alfred A. Knopf, a division of Random House, Inc.

pp. 250–252: Text as submitted (approximately five pages) from *The Chinese Kitchen* by Eileen Yin-Fei Lo. Copyright © 1999 by Eileen Yin-Fei Lo. Reprinted by permission of HarperCollins Publishers, Inc.

p. 258: Reprinted by permission of Naomi Shahib Nye.

p. 259: Lucille Clifton, "in the inner city" from *Good Woman: Poems and a Memoir 1969–1980*. Copyright © 1987 by Lucille Clifton. Reprinted with permission of BOA Editions, Ltd., www.boaeditions.org

pp. 272–274: "Types of Folk Music" by Sarah Wolfgong, fiddler for *Mustang Sally*. Copyright © 2001 by Sarah Wilfong. Reprinted by permission of the author. The article is available at www.aw-wrdsmth.com/scuttlebutt/types_of_folk_music.html

pp. 284–287: Courtesy of Peter Howard.

pp. 292–303: "Nineteen Fifty-Five" from *You Can't Keep a Good Woman Down*, © 1981 by Alice Walker, reprinted by permission of Harcourt, Inc.

p. 320: "How Things Work" from *A Fire in My Hands*, Revised and Expanded Edition, © 2006, 1990 by Gary Soto, reprinted with permission of Harcourt, Inc.

pp. 332–333: Reprinted with permission of *Life* Magazine.

pp. 338–349: Reprinted with permission of Natalie Edwards.

pp. 371–378: Copyright © 2004 Business Week.

pp. 389–392: Reprinted by permission of Paul Saffo.

p. 398: "Technology and Medicine" is reprinted from the publisher of *The Other Man Was Me* by Rafael Campo © 1994 Arte Publico Press-University of Texas.

pp. 402–405: Reprinted by permission of Don Congdon Associates, Inc. Copyright © Ray Bradbury 1956, renewed 1984.

pp. 406–407: Reprinted by permission of the Mountain View Voice.

pp. 408–410: Reprinted by permission of the Cornell Chronicle.

p. 416: "The Planned Child," from *The Wellspring* by Sharon Olds, copyright © 1996 by Sharon Olds. Used with permission of Alfred A. Knopf, a division of Random House, Inc.

pp. 417–418: Reprinted with permission of Penny Collins.

Photos

p. 1 (top): Steve Gorton © Dorling Kindersley.

p. 1 (bottom): Library of Congress.

p. 48 (left): Private Collection/The Bridgeman Art Library.

p. 48 (right): AFP/Agence France Presse/Getty Images.

p. 103 (left): Arvind Garg/Ambient Images.

p. 103 (right): Joan Slatkin/Omni-Photo Communications, Inc.

p. 150 (top): ©Lake County Museum/CORBIS.

p. 150 (bottom): John Henry on the Right, Steam Drill on the Left, 1944–47, Palmer Hayden, oil on canvas, 30 x 40 in., Collection of The Museum of African American Art, Los Angeles, CA. Palmer C. Hayden Collection, Gift of Miriam A. Hayden.

p. 224 (top): Robert Fried/robertfriedphotography.com.

p. 224 (bottom): Deborah Hunt.

p. 267 (top): Michael Ochs Archives Ltd./Getty Images Inc—Los Angeles.

p. 267 (bottom): Pearson Education Corporate Digital Archive.

p. 312 (left): Richard Carroll/Ambient Images.

p. 312 (right): Peter Bennett/Ambient Images.

p. 363 (left): Deni McIntyre/Photo Researchers, Inc.

p. 363 (right): Jimmy W. Crawford/Research Triangle Foundation of North Carolina.